Transforming the Theological Turn

Reframing Continental Philosophy of Religion

Series Editors
Steven Shakespeare, Senior Lecturer in Philosophy, Liverpool Hope University
Duane Williams, Senior Lecturer, Liverpool Hope University

Reframing Continental Philosophy of Religion aims to revitalize continental philosophy of religion. It challenges the standard Western Christian framework which has dominated philosophy of religion in the academy. It provides a platform for voices, theories, and traditions which have been suppressed or marginalized by that framework, and offers genuinely new and constructive openings in the field. It is motivated by an imperative to liberate original thinking about religion from the legacy of Empire.

The series is experimental, creative, subversive, and risky. It promotes work which brings continental philosophy of religion into fruitful dialogue with postcolonial theory; Islamic studies; heretical, esoteric, or mystical, or otherwise marginalized Western traditions; non-Western philosophical traditions; and critical studies of power, race, gender, and sexuality. Taking seriously the fertility of European philosophy, it does not, however, merely subject "other" discourses to a European gaze, but allows different discourses to interact and mutate one another on a mutual basis.

Reframing Continental Philosophy of Religion will not leave continental philosophy of religion as it finds it.

The series is published in partnership with the Association for Continental Philosophy of Religion at Liverpool Hope University.

Titles in the Series

Speculation, Heresy, and Gnosis in Contemporary Philosophy of Religion: The Enigmatic Absolute, edited by Joshua Ramey and Matthew S. Haar Farris

Simone Weil and Continental Philosophy, edited by A. Rebecca Rozelle-Stone

The Art of Anatheism, edited by Matthew Clemente and Richard Kearney

Theology and Contemporary Continental Philosophy: The Centrality of a Negative Dialectic, by Colby Dickinson

Esoteric Lacan, edited by Philipp Valentini and Mahdi Tourage

Transforming the Theological Turn: Phenomenology with Emmanuel Falque, edited by Martin Koci and Jason W. Alvis

Transforming the Theological Turn

Phenomenology with Emmanuel Falque

Edited by Martin Koci and Jason W. Alvis

ROWMAN & LITTLEFIELD
Lanham • Boulder • New York • London

Published by Rowman & Littlefield
An imprint of The Rowman & Littlefield Publishing Group, Inc.
4501 Forbes Boulevard, Suite 200, Lanham, Maryland 20706
www.rowman.com

6 Tinworth Street, London SE11 5AL, United Kingdom

Selection and editorial matter © 2020 by Martin Koci and Jason W. Alvis
Copyright in individual chapters is held by the respective chapter authors.

All rights reserved. No part of this book may be reproduced in any form or by any electronic or mechanical means, including information storage and retrieval systems, without written permission from the publisher, except by a reviewer who may quote passages in a review.

British Library Cataloguing in Publication Information Available

ISBN: HB 978-1-78661-622-7

Library of Congress Cataloging-in-Publication Data
Library of Congress Control Number: 2020943720

ISBN: 978-1-78661-622-7 (cloth)
ISBN: 978-1-5381-4834-1 (pbk)
ISBN: 978-1-78661-623-4 (electronic)

Contents

Acknowledgments	vii
Foreword *Richard Kearney*	ix
Introduction: Transgressing the Boundaries: Introducing Emmanuel Falque *Martin Koci and Jason W. Alvis*	xiii
Part I: Interpreting Emmanuel Falque	**1**
1 Philosophy and Theology: New Boundaries *Emmanuel Falque*	3
2 Where Is the Philosophical/Theological Rubicon?: Toward a Radical Rethinking of "Religion" *Bruce Ellis Benson*	25
3 Philosophy and Theology: What Happens When We Cross the Boundary? *Jakub Čapek*	41
4 Foreign Exchange or Hostile Incursion? *William C. Woody*	51
5 The Geography of the Rubicon: Philosophy, Theology, and Religious Studies in the American Context *Tamsin Jones*	63

Part II: Emmanuel Falque in Comparison — 73

6 At the Confluence of Phenomenology and Non-Phenomenology: Maurice Blondel and Emmanuel Falque — 75
William L. Connelly

7 A Friendly Tussle between Hermeneutics and Phenomenology: From Ricœur to Falque and Beyond — 93
Katerina Koci

8 *Hoc est corpus meum*: Kenosis, Responsibility, and the Ethics of the Spread Body between Levinas and Falque — 107
Lorenza Bottacin Cantoni

9 God's Word and the Human Word: Philosophy and Theology in Emmanuel Falque's Phenomenology — 121
Francesca Peruzzotti

Part III: Constructive-Critical Engagements — 133

10 *Oportet transire*: How "Crossing" Becomes a *quaestio de homine* — 135
Carla Canullo

11 Phenomenology and the Metaphysics of Conversion — 149
Andrew Sackin-Poll

12 Transforming Heideggerian Finitude?: Following Pathways Opened by Emmanuel Falque — 163
Barnabas Aspray

13 The Sense of Finitude in Emmanuel Falque: A Blondelian Engagement — 175
Victor Emma-Adamah

14 The Power at Work within Us — 187
Steven DeLay

Conclusion: To Die of Not Writing — 203
Emmanuel Falque

Bibliography — 207

Falque's Books — 217

Index — 219

About the Contributors — 223

Acknowledgments

A collection of essays is always the result of teamwork. Without academic collegiality, commitment, and discipline, this book would have not come into existence. At the beginning, there was a modest idea to compile and publish a few essays on Emmanuel Falque's *Crossing the Rubicon*—the book discussed at numerous colloquia. Yet things developed unexpectedly. From out of a book-focused roundtable, a more comprehensive project to assess Falque's thought in a broader context emerged. The result is the first critical volume on Falque's work in the English language. We would like to thank the following people who contributed to the work on this project and to the institutions who made this book possible. Thanks must go to a wonderful team of people at Rowman & Littlefield: Frankie Mace, Sarah Campbell, Rebecca Anastasi, and Scarlet Furness for their support, helpfulness, and genuine interest in our project. We are grateful to Sarah Horton and Megan Megaher for translating Emmanuel Falque's texts, Magdalena Sedmak for her assistance in preparing the manuscript, and to the Institute for Philosophy at the University of Vienna for offering us excellent working conditions. Last but not least, the Austrian Science Fund (FWF) has granted us generous financial support for the project "Revenge of the Sacred: Phenomenology and the Ends of Christianity in Europe" [P 31919], of which this book is the result.

Foreword

Richard Kearney

Emmanuel Falque crossed the Rubicon and came back to tell the tale. James Joyce once wrote that Dublin was a city where Caesar and Christ walked hand in glove. I would not align Falque with either Caesar or Christ but describe him rather as a philosopher who thinks *between*, riding mid-river, one foot in the stirrup of classic metaphysics, the other in the stirrup of Christian tradition. Falque does not hesitate to straddle the divide, to cross Latin horses with Hebrew donkeys. His *esprit* is mulish at best, and while happy to render to Caesar what is Caesar's, he never forgets the hosannas of Palm Sunday. In other words, Falque does not fear to trespass where his phenomenogical mentors—Husserl and Heidegger—dared not tread. He defies the Freiburg embargo on the God question, a prohibition based on the requirement that all religious beliefs be bracketed when engaging in genuine philosophical questioning, that faith and phenomenology never meet. By contrast, in his scouting out the frontiers between the *Seinsfrage* and *Gottesfrage*, Falque throws down the gauntlet to Heidegger's claim in the *Introduction to Metaphysics* that "Christian philosophy is a round square and a misunderstanding." For Falque nothing is *verboten*. Giving his hermeneutic mule his head, he rides the waves of the Rubicon to the other side.

    Falque's work displays the audacity of a thinker who carves his own path rather than ape his Masters. He reads Husserl without becoming Husserlian, Aquinas without becoming Thomist, Scotus without becoming Scotist, and more recently Freud and Marx without becoming Freudian or Marxist. His thinking is constantly morphing and metamorphosing from one disciplinary discourse to the next—from ontology to eschatology, from epistemology to ethics, from psychoanalysis to palliative care. Thinking, for Falque, is a process of creation rather than repetition, invitation rather than imitation, while never ceasing to dialogue with numerous interlocutors. There is always give and take in what Falque likes to call, after Jaspers, *un combat amoureux*. Each successive book offers new recipes for cross-fertilization, resulting in a rare intellectual crossbreed: a brilliant metaphysical mutt.

One might also see the crossing of the Rubicon as a summons to a new way of being. A passage from text to action. But in waving us back to the life-world, Falque always remains "reflective." He never lets his metaphysics—his "army of mobile metaphors" (Nietzsche)—be swept away in the cross-currents of topicality. While his philosophy is deeply *engagé*, his commitments are less short term than long, preferring the *longue durée* to *des faits divers*. Falque engages with his contemporaries (Ricœur, Breton, Chrétien, Marion) as vigorously as with the ancients and medievals he loves to revisit and rethink. And with each *Auseindersetzung* he gives as much as he receives. His exchanges are two-way journeys: between past and present philosophies as much as between his own philosophical perspective and that of his conversation partners, ever ready to be transformed in a process of mutual enhancement. So when Falque, the self-avowed philosopher, takes on theology, psychoanalysis, or medicine, he is prepared to have his mind altered and amplified by each hermeneutic detour. Thus for Falque, as for Ricœur before him, the hermeneutic circle becomes a hermeneutic spiral. After the odyssey one returns to oneself "othered," transfigured by each successive turn of the of the gyre. Oneself as another, again and again.

What we have in Falque's work is a call to a new rapport between philosophy and theology—*une invitation au voyage* (Baudelaire)—where one is ready to lose oneself in order to find oneself anew. Borderlands are there to be traversed without denying that borders exist or that different countries have a right to co-exist in fruitful commerce rather than be invaded or annexed. As with EU passports, Falque's intellectual landscapes share the same color cover with distinct images for each member. Or to pursue the analogy, Falque's interdisciplinary thinking calls for a pooling of multiple sovereignties rather than their dissolution into one. He displays an *esprit frontalière* from first to last. Hovering over thresholds, invigilating crossings, keeping philosophical doors open without ever ignoring the different spaces they delimit, Falque offers conceptual hospitality to many different guests. He knows what dialogue means—*dia-legein*: welcoming a plurality of voices. Not reducing them to one.

As the chapters in this volume attest, Falque is a philosopher of continuity rather than of rupture. A practitioner of open conversation rather than an apologist of sectarian separation or conversion. His writings returns to the "things themselves," as they are found in the great texts of classical, medieval, and modern thought, but also in the existential phenomena of everyday life: eros, death, finitude, anxiety, flesh, birth, malady, animality, chaos. Nothing human is alien to Falque's phenomenology, and nothing animal or divine either. And it is this radical hospitality to all comers that makes Emmanuel Falque a thinker in perpetual (at times exhausting) motion. In sum, he might be described as a Parisian Hermes, mercurial and mobile, guardian of thresholds and promoter of migrant thoughts that never come to rest.

What is true of Falque is also true of his commentators in this volume. The editors have enlisted here an impressive array of young scholars eager to think "with Falque" rather than "according to Falque." Creatively rather than mimetically. Sometimes agreeing, other times disagreeing, the contributors do not subscribe to some Falquesque mission or doctrine. As if there was one. While his interpreters know that Falque's first name is Emmanuel, they confuse him neither with Christ nor Caesar. They respond in their different ways to his invitation to think for themselves—in critical dialogue. Always celebrating the metaphysical mongrel he is.

Dog bless Emmanuel!
  —Richard Kearney

Introduction

*Transgressing the Boundaries:
Introducing Emmanuel Falque*

Martin Koci and Jason W. Alvis

Today, new borders are being set up faster than old ones are being torn down. In what seems to be a societal backlash against globalization and its original naiveté regarding borders, perspectives on topics such as migration, climate change, and political allegiance are becoming less diverse and more polarized, establishing more borders between us. Such polarization has made the possibility of or even interest in crossing borders much more challenging.

To claim that research from within the enclaves of "continental" philosophy of religion or theological phenomenology somehow could help alleviate these problems of borders at first would seem rather naïve. On the contrary, both academic and public opinion regarding philosophy of religion today would be justified in thinking that its practitioners have done precisely the opposite. We indeed have tendencies toward specialization and a division of labor that both (1) isolates us and closes our work off from others of different opinion and specialization, and (2) builds a border between our research and the often disorderly realities of everyday life. Thus, recent decades of philosophy of religion may even be partly to blame for our contemporary problems of borders, given our tendencies toward establishing echo chambers and orders of enlightenment against those we deem "unreasonable," even within the interior of our own academic sub-disciplines.

It is in these regards that the work of Emmanuel Falque really becomes intriguing, for it seems both of the aforementioned critiques do not directly apply to his research. He is a leading figure who has fought to establish both "loving struggles" between philosophers, theologians, and scholars of religion, and everyday lived experience of the human body at the center of his philosophical work. Both efforts have served to breathe new life into thinking about *passage* over porous, yet still necessary, borders between our bodies and minds, between our sacred and secular souls, between ourselves and others, between our academic disciplines.

Of course, Falque does not always address borders in a direct way. He engages more so in describing the theoretical beliefs that make our interests in erecting borders so prominent and pronounced. His theological anthropology points to how our finitude is on a *pendulum* that does not gravitate toward openness, but rather to a closure that leads to an encrusted solipsism under which we unfortunately submit ourselves to suffering and dying alone. His approach is centered upon the *human body* (which is the "first" site of border-traversing), and the conviction that the passage between borders involves a fundamental *suffering* that does not end simply in the *cul-de-sac* of theodicy, but rather in the clarion to a radical alterity or heteronomy.

The call of suffering demands a response. And this call is not an overly romanticized or optimistic one. Borders certainly are not benign, but rather places of potential suffering and, as a result, can birth both negative and positive *transformation*. The details are not to be lost on *how* we are to cross the various aforementioned borders, and what models of thought best allow for accurate depictions of the passage or crossing of their limitations. Yet further, philosophers of religion and phenomenologists of all types might find in Falque's work a model for shifting their own methodological reflections toward much higher stakes. Within the still growing group of researchers associated with the once pejoratively named "Theological Turn in Phenomenology," Falque's voice is a steady reminder that the stakes of its internal debates are much higher than any mere discussion about divisions of disciplines. These stakes concern an introspective struggle *with ourselves* to become externalized, or to think and to rely upon others, and in a way that implements our very bodies (which we do not *have*, but *are*). And this gives us reason to believe that Emmanuel Falque does not simply seek a transformation of the theological turn in French phenomenology. He instead actively chooses to develop the very *idea* of transformation (especially, as border passage) in a way that previous thinkers associated with this group are yet to do in any substantive way.

Such an idea has served to give greater explanation to the kind of cavalier bellicosity of crossing between phenomenology and theology initiated by the thinkers associated with the aforementioned "turn." Falque alludes to Caesar's aggressive crossing of the Rubicon as a more realistic analogy for what takes place when such thinkers have crossed from theology to philosophy, or from philosophy to theology. But must we, today, cross the Rubicon in the same ways? And what are the consequences of Falque's thought-provoking project? Critical readings of Falque included on the following pages accept his invitation to think about the multiple meanings of transformative passing and, at the same time, to expose themselves to the risk that this intellectual leap might result in their own, unexpected transformation. In other words, this collection should not be read as an authoritative guide to yet another French master thinker; rather, the goal is to unfold the potential of debates opened by Falque, which thus far have proven to be quite fruitful and passionate. Our primary aim is not simply to describe or critique his work, for each of our contributors demonstrates their own task of thinking, for which they find a reservoir of inspiration in the work of the philosopher *and* theologian Emmanuel Falque.

This book, the first of its kind in English,[1] therefore scrupulously adheres to constructive-critical explorations of whether philosophers, theologians, and scholars of religion must not—to retain the metaphor—set their feet into the rivulet whose waters turn out to be turbulent and wild. One thing is clear: For Falque, the borders between these disciplines are ever in flux, and this should leave no one calm and quiet.

THE SPACE BETWEEN THEOLOGY AND PHILOSOPHY

Falque's work comprises four main areas: (1) historical-philosophical as well as theological studies in Patristics and medieval philosophy; (2) phenomenology; (3) philosophy of religion with a special regard to the category of experience; and, last but not least, (4) the methodological inquiry into the relationship between the disciplines of philosophy and theology. Paradigmatic examples demonstrating how it is difficult for our author to keep these research fields separate are two trilogies in Falque's bibliography. *Triduum philosophique* (*The Guide to Gethsemane*, *The Metamorphosis of Finitude*, and *The Wedding Feast of the Lamb*) is written in the style of philosophical-theological essays, having the effect of challenging the traditional employment of both disciplines. Then Falque reflects explicitly upon his methodological approach in the *Trilogié méthodologique*, a more spontaneous result of Falque's effort to explain what he is doing when writing, and for whom he is writing. There, we find *Parcours d'embûches* (which currently remains untranslated into English), *The Loving Struggle*, and (in)famous *Crossing the Rubicon*.

It will not be an exaggeration to say that the English translation of *Crossing the Rubicon*, one of the most provocative works on relations between theology and philosophy published in recent years, has triggered vivid discussions leading many theologians, philosophers, and scholars of religion to describe their own position—often in a critical way—in regard to Falque's in general. Although the legacy of debating the sustainability and/or impropriety of *passing* between philosophical and theological perspectives is mirrored on nearly every page of this collection, we also intend to examine Falque's project in its broader context.

Falque's thesis concerning new frontiers and their transformation throws down the gauntlet to both philosophers and theologians. Over the course of recent years, a number of workshops dedicated to Falque's thought took place (e.g., Society for Continental Philosophy and Theology in Memphis, conferences in Prague and Cambridge). These events bear witness that, when responding to Falque's provoking propositions (such as *the more we theologize, the better we philosophize*, or the imperative to *liberate theology by philosophy*), both camps of philosophers and theologians involved in these discussions tend to express unease and ostentatiously defend the separation of disciplines.

Philosophers object that the act of *crossing* the Rubicon is comparable to a declaration of war. Setting aside the possible hostility of such a movement, philosophers insist that there are plenty of phenomena, questions, and problems that serve to gain nothing from theological reflection. The examples vary from the crisis of democracy to the philosophical engagement with the logic of technological systems.[2] From the other bank, theologians are inclined to keep a radical asymmetry between philosophy and their discipline. They often juxtapose the horizontality of philosophical explorations with the verticality of theology. From this perspective, it is not possible to traverse from one to another, as they both are on two entirely different planes. For theology, some claim necessary is the leap (of faith).[3] In one way or another, philosophers' response to Falque is that they do not need the theological in order to explain philosophical concepts; theologians assert their discipline remains the "Queen of the sciences," situating theology hierarchically above philosophy. Philosophy and theology make two.

These critical concerns (rightly) bear witness to a reasonable worry over the confusion of genres and the merging of discourses. However, as Falque's extensive chapter included in this volume shows clearly, he shares this worry. The point in the making is neither confusion nor the supremacy of one over the other. Falque is interested in the double trajectory: (1) the phenomenological inspiration for theology (and thus the transformation of theology), and (2) the backlash of theology onto phenomenology (transforming phenomenology itself). The movement of *crossing* runs in both directions.

Historically speaking, we all know that theology was never without philosophy and that philosophy always moved within an orbit not alien to theology. It is not only the case that theology and philosophy have shared the majority of their history together, for they also often share the same libraries even today. It would be pretentious to interpret Falque's project as calling for a paradigm shift for the entirety of philosophy, or the totality of theology. Instead, it is necessary to note that Falque comes from a specific tradition; philosophically speaking, he is a phenomenologist. According to his own classification, he belongs to the third generation of the French phenomenologists. The first generation among which Falque counts Emmanuel Levinas, Michel Henry, and Paul Ricœur, all of whom were occupied with the Husserlian legacy. The second generation found its inspiration in Heidegger, and its principal proponents are Jean-Luc Marion, Jean-Yves Lacoste, and Jean-Louis Chrétien. Finally, Falque (together with Claude Romano and Renaud Barbaras, although they do not claim religion to be a primary sphere of interest) marks the third generation, highly influenced by Merleau-Ponty. This has resulted in an emancipation from the scope of the previous debates (e.g., the obsession concerning the overcoming of onto-theology) and an opening up of the question of the limit of phenomenological explorations, ultimately enlarging their field of interest. As Falque confesses: "Whether their focus is Christianity, art, literature, politics, psychiatry, or film, contemporary phenomenologists are aware that they can no longer content themselves with philosophy alone."[4]

At the same time, Falque is steeped in the Catholic theological tradition and indeed explicitly identifies himself with his extensive theological training. This also established a crucial point of difference from his fellow countrymen who are claimed to have committed the theological turn in French phenomenology. Levinas, Marion, Henry, Chrétien, and Ricœur certainly are not theologically naïve. Nevertheless, Falque stands out for not only conducting his research as a philosopher at the Institut Catholique de Paris—a specific place on the French academic scene—but also graduating in theology from an ecclesial institution.[5] Nevertheless, this should not mislead anyone to read Falque as attempting to turn phenomenology into theology, or to *baptize* it as a new *ancilla theologiae* (even though phenomenology might indeed be the most productive tool for enriching theological discussions).[6] The philosopher is not asked to convert to become a theologian, and the theologian is not required to give up theology. Both are called to transform themselves.

Falque's discourse on method thus seems to not *assist* theology (the sections written by the *équipe theologique* in this volume will demonstrate how phenomenology poses challenges to theologians). It also does not simply command philosophy to include theology into its reflections (the chapters written by philosophers in this collection frequently challenge Falque in this respect). Asking the questions whether to cross the Rubicon, whether to let our respective perspectives be transformed, and whether to challenge the well-established disciplinary borders concerns nothing less than the very care for the fecundity of thought; that is, the recovering of the *logos* and the meaning of thinking.

Falque is convinced that to perform this task appropriately, one must not exclude the theological from the sphere of thought (as one does not exclude literature, culture, psychoanalysis, gender, or perspectives from other aspects always influencing the *conditio humana*). Just as the theologian has no other experience of God but the human experience, and is expected to begin their exploration from the position of being-in-the-world while acknowledging the burden of finitude, so is the philosopher, focused on manifestations from within the world, expected to take into consideration the religious sphere of human life.

SOURCES OF THE RUBICON: THE GENEALOGY OF THE DEBATE

Crossing the Rubicon is the turning point on a long journey. Falque has always been interested in the relationship between theology and philosophy. Although he always defines himself first as a professional philosopher and only then, sometimes, as a theologian, the personal motivation behind venturing into the waters of the Rubicon is undeniable. In *Parcours d'embûches*, Falque explains that the act of passage is not primarily about the geography of academic disciplines, or the challenging of frontiers between philosophy and theology. Instead the center of gravity is the internal struggle within ourselves.[7] This of course echoes the sentiments of the tradition of Ignatian introspection and inner examination of the self: faithful to the imperative *primum vivere*—first live then think—as it is confessed in the epilogue of *Crossing the Rubicon*, Falque writes first for himself and then for others.

Yet let us be clear here. Falque's position is by no means the result of subjectivism. Falque's thought is based on a careful *Dasein* analysis as described by the phenomenological tradition. The explorations of being-in-the-world and the structures of human experience lead Falque to the thought trajectory that sometimes turns out to be a loving struggle with his own philosophical tradition and his sources, because he also recognizes certain limits of phenomenology and philosophy in general.

The first substantial formulation of Falque's position concerning the relationship between these two disciplines is in the 2006 essay aptly titled "Philosophy and Theology: New Frontiers." From this text we learn more about the context and academic motivation behind Falque's project. Regarding the context of the debate on theology and philosophy, Falque points out the following paradox. Despite the prevailing *laïcité* in the French educational system, philosophy seems to be very busy with theological matters: "God is philosophized in France. Paradoxically, the more secular French universities are, the more they are occupied by theological questions."[8] This is not an abrupt intrusion, but rather a natural inclination of philosophy to the theological. Just as thinkers such as Kierkegaard, Pascal, Aquinas, Augustine, or St. Paul recognized the enduring relevance of topics essential to the religious life-world, so should we, even in our so-called secular context. Hence, regarding the motivation of Falque's project, he aims at a double renewal. The first renewal concerns overcoming the lacuna within philosophical thought after theology is marginalized. This is not an attempt at a renewal of ancient theological customs or classical dogma according to which philosophy is required to conduct itself, but rather one of the *possibility* for the philosopher to *become* a theologian—to cross the border for a moment—and to draw from theology general conclusions that can be applied to their own work. The second renewal concerns the field of theology and its need to confront itself with the interests and insights of philosophy. If the philosophers are scandalized by Falque's recourse to theology, even more so should the theologians be shaken by the intrusion of phenomenological perspectives into their work.

At first, these renewals seem rather simplistic and perhaps even overly optimistic. However, Falque is well aware of field-shaping debates such as, for example, Heidegger's treatment of the subject in "Phenomenology and Theology,"[9] where the distinction is made between the ontic science of faith (theology) and the ontological science of being (philosophy). Falque's strong preference for a phenomenological mode of thinking does not seem to dispute Heidegger's delineation of the borders. Rather, he takes seriously the oft-overlooked imperative within this essay that theology, as the positive science of faith, needs philosophy as "the ontological corrective of the ontic."[10] In other words, Falque does not take an issue with a phenomenological critique of theology. Instead, he criticizes his own theological tradition for falling prey to the idolatrous practice of presuming that an objective science and positive—pragmatic—inquiry truly can yield its projected results of specifically propositional content, all on the basis of the exploration of divine revelation. With this in mind, Falque's conception of theology cannot be confused with a ready-made box of simply functioning answers, and thus as a divine reservoir of inspiration for philosophy. Perhaps the first lesson to be drawn from Falque is that within the realm of philosophy, a great liberation from reductively simplistic conceptions of theology (as a still-surviving mythology) is essential. At the same time, theology must accept the challenge to present itself in a new, not only understandable, but also credible manner that can shatter the old impressions that theology is a unitary, monolithic discourse on received ahistorical truth void of human interpretation. According to Falque, philosophy's input plays a crucial role in this transformative renewal of theology.

It is difficult to resist invoking again the critical voice of Dominique Janicaud at this point. Although he does not discuss Falque's work, Janicaud's words seem to address the issue directly:

> The dice are loaded and choices made, faith rises majestically in the background. The reader, confronted by the blade of the absolute, finds him- or herself in the position of a catechumen who has no other choice than to penetrate the holy words and lofty dogmas.[11]

Alea iacta est—Falque has made an irreversible decision despite Janicaud's warning. Nevertheless, Falque is much more explicit and radical than the rest of his colleagues in the theological turn (as Janicaud labeled them) would be ready to admit. Yet unsurprisingly, for this Falque earns plenty of criticism. For example, Joseph O'Leary expresses his surprise over Falque's foundation of philosophical reasoning within the theological.[12] Crina Gschwandtner does not hesitate to critique that Falque renders the boundaries between theology and philosophy, despite his proclamations, inoperative and even superficial.[13] More recently, the contributors to a special issue of the journal *Philosophy Today* on "Futures of the Theological Turn" unanimously reject Falque's project as a flawed "movement on the part of philosophy [toward theology that] shall give it occasion to realize its full potential as a grammar or discourse about ultimacy."[14]

Yet again, *alea iacta est*. These are the words Ceasar pronounced before *crossing the Rubicon*. The intentional link between Falque's work considered as the response to Janicaud's critique is clear. However, if we look more closely at the genealogy of Falque's discourse on method, we might be surprised to detect a close proximity between his and Janicaud's respective points.

Janicaud's declaration of war is not against theological interests, but the endorsement of honesty on the part of philosophers, namely phenomenologists, who disrespect the method in assertions of specific theological claims. Janicaud insists that phenomenology must be focused solely upon an exploration of the field of immanence. Heidegger's introduction of the inapparent or inconspicuous,[15] Levinas's revelation of the other, Marion's third reduction and the givenness of saturated phenomena, Henry and Chrétien's respective confusions of the methods of procedure are all, according to Janicaud, irregular developments in the field of phenomenology and, as a result, mark a violent intrusion of the invisible into the visible. These "New Theologians,"[16] as Janicaud pejoratively called them—among whom he certainly would have included Falque—masquerade as philosophers and disrespect the unbridgeable gap between phenomenology and theology.[17]

The starting point, however, is the same for both Falque and Janicaud's respective critiques. When Falque claims "the more we theologize, the better we philosophize," one immediately must add that "the only experience of God we have—the experience theology dares to explore—is the human experience."

This though-provoking claim concerning the human experience appears at various points throughout Falque's oeuvre.[18] What kind of experience does Falque have in mind? The foundational experience of all thought, including theological reflection, is the experience of finitude. The opening volume of Falque's *Triduum philosophique—The Guide to Gethsemane*—is a book-length argument for finitude as the ontological condition of the human being before any reference to God ever comes into discussion. The *preemption of the infinite* is a bad practice Falque associates with much of what is done in the name of theology today. In other words, there is no way to escape or to leap over immanence. Or as Falque suggests, *Being and Time* constitutes the first chapter of any theology. However, Falque also charges his fellow phenomenologists with unjustly crossing the border from "the horizon of man as such,"[19] and thus criticizes any over-decentering of the modern subject, which is current in recent phenomenologies attuned to theological interests.

In short, by situating Falque's project within the debate on the theological turn we come to the conclusion that Falque's challenge of *Crossing the Rubicon* is a double critique: first, it unfolds Janicaud's critique, that is, the critique of those whom Janicaud criticizes; and second, it is the critique of Janicaud's own criticism of a so-called pure phenomenological discourse. Falque's proposal of intertwining between philosophy and theology must be read in this specific context.

TRANSFORMING BOUNDARIES, OR CONFUSION

Falque's challenge to interrupt the self-referential discourses of philosophy and theology, respectively, is the kernel of criticisms formulated against his work. Of course, the claim that "the more one theologizes, the better one philosophizes" is really the principle instigation. Joseph O'Leary, one of Falque's most vocal critics, charges the French author with claiming that "philosophy can only flourish under theological tutelage."[20] Such interpretations often lead to the misunderstanding that Falque is the direct successor of the theological turn, and a cursory reading of Falque's work can lend to the impression that he seeks an even deeper radicalization and abrupt intrusion of the theological into the philosophical. Even worse, one might think he intends to exact theological imperialism over philosophy, ultimately reducing any phenomenologically gained insights to ready-made theological truths. It is no wonder, then, that some claim he confuses genres, methods, and disciplines; a confusion that does damage to both theology and philosophy. Interestingly, Falque's critics often even submit what seem to be contradictory statements in order to make sense of his work. For example, O'Leary also claims that Falque's approach amounts to a kind of Hegelianism that instead *displaces* theology from its proper modes of procedure (that is, the realm of revealed faith), ultimately converting theology into a speculative philosophical system.[21] Which, in fact, would critics claim to be Falque's "queen of the sciences"?

One intention of this book is to illustrate that Falque's project is much more complex than critics may give it credit. And although there certainly are critical points, which will become obvious on many pages of this volume, it is indisputable that Falque takes great pains to present his work as a careful differentiation between theological inspiration and philosophical inquiry. In this respect, an instructive passage is found in the introduction to *The Metamorphosis of Finitude*, where Falque explicitly differentiates between the two sections of the book: one is explicitly theological, the other philosophical. Furthermore, part two of *Crossing the Rubicon*, entitled "Deciding," is devoted to the struggle with philosophical faith (or "trust in the world"), which he claims to indeed precede any religious faith or particular "theological" confession.[22]

Falque builds his case upon a classical phenomenological imperative of the analysis of the life-world (Husserl), the analytics of being-in-the-world (Heidegger), and an irreducible, embodied existence inextricably intertwined with the world (Merleau-Ponty). These help him defend his conception of philosophical faith (which resembles both Ricœur's and Jaspers' treatments of the concept). Here we run into problems with how to read and interpret Falque's position on this concept, which seems crucial for a proper understanding of his demand for passing between the two riverbanks of theology and philosophy. One level of understanding such problems is existential; every single person operates in the realm of philosophical faith before giving a thought to religion or particular theological confessions. For example, the barista at *Café de Flore* operates with a philosophical faith both before and during attending the church service in the Abbey of Saint-Germain-des-Prés. This is more of an involuntary act that precedes reflection, and thus philosophy as a discipline. However, another level is reflective; the ambitions of Falque's *Crossing the Rubicon* are to describe not only this universally human, existential faith, but also the methodological relationship between the disciplines of philosophy and theology.

In this respect, Falque's adherence to the Catholic tradition plays an eminent role, and understanding the continuum between philosophical positions—on both existential and reflective levels—and theological positions is crucial for a correct understanding of it. Broadly conceived, the traditional Catholic position deems it impossible to interpret the Bible as revelation without simultaneously dealing with the question of the historical tradition, for example, with how we have interpreted the origination of the Bible. Thus, it likewise is impossible to begin with the theological without first going through the philosophical—the human experience. This seems entirely in continuity with the early Christians, who did not pit theology in opposition to a philosophy that would extract them from the world. In contrast, Christianity once was conceived as a philosophical way of engaging in the exploration of the human experience in the world—*coram et cum Deo*.

Falque, knowledgeable of the tradition of Christian thought, is a strong Catholic in this respect. When saying that we need to start with a philosophical position, he does not expect his barista in the famous Parisian café to engage with him in a profound philosophical discussion (the reflective level) even though, Falque believes, on the existential level they both share a certain philosophical faith. Rather, the point in the making is that in fidelity to the tradition of *fides quaerens intellectum*, contemporary (Catholic) theology is urged to start from the best philosophical position available. And that is, in Falque's opinion, phenomenology. With that said, one must immediately add that Falque does not propose to canonize phenomenology as the only philosophical propaedeutic to theological reasoning.

We propose, and this book at many instances ventures in this direction, that the correct interpretation is exactly the opposite. Falque demonstrates the limit of phenomenology, however not to provide us with a theological phenomenology, but a phenomenological theology, or a theology conducted in a phenomenological fashion. Such an effort is discernible in certain parts of his *Triduum philosophique*. Nevertheless, in the context of the discourse on method, it must be stated clearly that the joint practice of theology and philosophy *does not result* in their fusion, which necessarily would result (and indeed already has) in confusion. The point in the making is that in crossing the Rubicon one is allowed to pass onto the other bank, look around, and then come back home before getting lost in its waters. In this sense, the boundaries are not abolished (Lacoste) or confused (as Falque's critics interpret his work) but are transformed. The same movement of existential metamorphosis also applies to the very understanding of the meaning of theology and philosophy.

The one-way passage—from theology to philosophy—often is the point of criticism. If this were the case, the critics would be right that Falque radicalizes the attack of theology on philosophy. The problem with these criticisms and the kernel of their misreading is their presupposed notion of theology, which is deemed a quasi-objective knowledge. Arguably, the fear of interaction between philosophy and theology is caused by a—still present—qualification of theology as a science of faith; perhaps even worse, theology often is seen by philosophers as attempting to assert its objective science of revelation as an ahistorical discourse that pushes the human experience into the margins.

And here lies a major point of misunderstanding. Falque indeed draws inspiration from the Heideggerian analytics of being-in-the-world, of human finitude, of the critique of theology as positive ontic science of revelation. However, Falque's point in the making is not strictly Heideggerian. Theology, in Falque's conception, is a task of thinking based on the philosophical exploration of the human condition in the midst of the world. Falque rather uses this concept to depict the state of our existence—the unavoidable starting point for further reflection both in philosophy and theology. To summarize, in *God, the Flesh, and the Other* Falque attempts to read theology phenomenologically. This order of wording is very important: reading theology phenomenologically. Then, his *Triduum Philosophique* concerns the possibility of doing theology in a phenomenological fashion. Finally, Falque provides us with a discourse on method—*Crossing the Rubicon*—that reflects on the transformative encounters between these disciplines. In other words, Falque's thought trajectory follows this pattern: first, a phenomenological analysis of being-in-the-world; second, a theological reading beginning with that worldly situation (we have no other experience of God but the human experience); and then finally, the reflection on the backlash of theology on philosophy, which entails the opening of new horizons. Falque does not start from a clear and distinct theological—confessional—position but from the lived facticity, which is not void of religious strands.

In this particular sense Falque indeed goes against Janicaud's criticisms (adopted and updated by many) that the theological turn is an abrupt intrusion of some ready-made, that is, positive contents from theology into philosophy. Nevertheless, Falque is absolutely clear about his parting ways with theological positivism and imperialism in relation to philosophy when he clearly rejects, for example, the maxim of Hans Urs von Bathasar concerning regaining philosophy's beginning from theology.[23] The point where both theology and philosophy start is the "texture of existence," and this has consequences for both disciplines: Janicaud's perspective of *font deux* is correct, yet, as Falque reminds us, their borders are porous and allow for mutual transformation.

Regarding the transformation of philosophy, it need not be so radical as it at first might seem. The point is not so much to integrate the invisible into philosophy, but rather to open philosophy to gaining insights from the specifically bodily experience of the theological (especially the fleshly condition of a religious being-in-the-world). This does not entail leaving the sphere of immanence. In the famous §58 of Husserl's *Logical Investigations*, the founder of phenomenology brackets God's transcendence; however, does it mean that any discourse on the question of God is prohibited as such? Are we—as phenomenological thinkers—deprived of any possibility of transcendence? There are other ways of reading this peculiar passage of Husserl's, however. For example, as Jan Patočka suggests:

> If we reduce all conscious reality to absolute, pure phenomena, then, after the reduction, transcendence does not disappear, it is not crossed off and destroyed, but rather continues to belong to immanence, though no longer as *real transcendence* but as the *phenomenon of transcendence*, as the objective correlate of what is purely *reell*ly immanent lived experience with its components and moments he [Husserl] calls *noesis*.[24]

There is no other experience of God but the human experience, says Falque. And if phenomenology deals strictly with appearances in the world made available for human experience, then it seems difficult to justify any a priori exclusion of human *religious* experience or experience with God, which indeed has gone by different names in philosophy such as the absolute, the unconditional, or the infinite.

The debates included in this book further explore these thought-provoking movements to which Falque's work gives rise. Although there are a number of critical perspectives on his work, the intention is not so much to add to the already existing debate on whether Falque is doing something just or unjust. On the contrary, the aim is to move further with Falque by offering new readings of his work (part I), comparing him with eminent figures in philosophy of religion (part II), and applying his ideas to more constructive and original contexts (part III).

INTERPRETING EMMANUEL FALQUE

The first part is devoted to detailed commentaries that provide numerous clarifications that shed light on Falque's work. However, we open this section with an original chapter written by Falque himself, in which he presents a condensed version of his argument concerning the porosity of the borders between philosophy and theology. This key text raises essential questions to which subsequent chapters in this book react. In the first step, Falque argues for the unity of phenomenology and hermeneutics, stressing the shared interests of both approaches in the factual experience of the life-world. In the second step, his position is presented concerning the "always believing" character of the philosophical enterprise. Building upon this classical phenomenological presupposition, he claims that before religious or confessional belief, everyone has trust in the world. This philosophical faith does not contradict the methodological atheism applied in philosophical reasoning. Instead, it functions as a common space whereby philosophy and theology can discover a new grammar for mutual and unavoidable dialogue. In the third and last step is an elaboration on the actual moment of passing—crossing—between philosophy and theology. In fact, Falque argues for two things here. First, he critically examines phenomenology to demonstrate its limits, and, second, he turns to theology to overcome them. Both philosophers and theologians are invited to temporarily visit the other camp in order to transform their understanding of their own basic disciplinary questions and presumptions, before returning to their own domain. Both camps are called upon to overcome the somewhat self-referential debates on whether the theological turn in French phenomenology ever happened, and, if it happened, whether it was a legitimate or illegitimate turn. This chapter ultimately points to a transformation of the theological turn in French phenomenology, opening up questions that can lead such research beyond itself, and provoke and prolong productive discussion within the field.

Bruce Benson's chapter raises the question "where is the philosophical/ theological Rubicon?" However, Benson's reading is much more than a mere geography of the disciplines: its main concern is the problem of power. Put differently, the crucial issue of Falque's project and its consequences could be encapsulated as follows: who has the upper hand over the discourse that, as Falque endorses and Benson confirms, deals with similar concepts (e.g., God, the absolute, transcendence, religious experience) but from differing and often competing perspectives? Benson opens his chapter with the attempt to localize the Rubicon, yet comes to the recognition that it is something that is not fixed, is never simply there, and is always ahead of us. The Rubicon is a kind of no-place waiting for adventurous explorers and their steps of crossing. It thus poses a constant hermeneutical challenge that leads Benson to an original interpretation of the so-called theological turn in phenomenology, or, more generally conceived, the return to the religious in philosophy. After the long reign of the *hermeneutics of suspicion* toward all things non-empirical, transcendent, and explicitly religious, Falque's project challenges the suppression of the religious field in recent philosophical discussions. According to Benson, Falque reorients the presupposed philosophical default position of neutrality to *philosophical faith*—the trust in the world—which is common to all humans and the prerequisite for any meaningful discussion. Benson finds Falque's project genuinely helpful in order to move beyond the somewhat stuck discussion between philosophers and theologians. However, he notices that Falque seems to overlook one crucial element essential for such an attempt. For Benson, any discussion on religion has profound political consequences. Hence, the passage from the theological to the philosophical and vice versa cannot be reduced to the transformation between academic disciplines. The point here is that the division at stake involves the relationship between the Church and the State. The question of crossing the Rubicon, as Benson sees it, is therefore not so much about the borders of disciplines, but about the power, authority, and enforceability over who controls the discourse: the Church and/or the State. And this "political Rubicon" will be much more difficult to overcome in terms of Falque's thesis: "the more we theologize, the better we philosophize."

Jakub Čapek asks his question straightforwardly: What happens when we cross the boundary? In his modestly critical account, formulated from an explicitly philosophical perspective, Čapek charges Falque with the failure to keep the promise of holding the two disciplines autonomous. In contrast to Paul Ricœur, who serves as an example worth following when it comes to the proper relations between philosophy and theology, Falque ultimately synthesizes both. Instead of reading the situation as the challenge to cross from one riverbank to another, Čapek's chapter proposes that philosophy and theology are two different, mutually exclusive perspectives. Adopting one perspective entails leaving or bracketing the other. Transitioning from one perspective to another is possible; however, one must be dedicated and explicit about this switch of discourse. In this sense, Čapek follows the critique of Janicaud, even endorsing the point that phenomenology gains nothing from engagement with the theological. Reflections on faith should be left to the theologians, whereas the reflection on the given phenomena belongs to the philosophers. This claim is illustrated by pointing to how the two fields have entirely incommensurable ways of interpreting the concept of *free will*. The philosopher is not permitted to first accept the idea of the re-creating action of God upon the will, whereas the theologian cannot accept, at least not without further qualification, the idea of the self-determination of the will. Čapek concludes that Falque indeed changes his perspective, and from his starting position of being a philosopher, he becomes a theologian. This indeed is what Falque has taught us. However, Čapek adds that Falque has crossed the boundary but never came back, and thus we should not follow Falque's advice to cross from one riverbank to another. This does not necessarily denigrate Falque's work, but rather simply reframes it: Falque's challenge should be read as the contemporary plea for the natural theology. Interestingly, this particular diagnosis, formulated by a professional philosopher, runs contrary to observations in this volume formulated by professional theologians (e.g., Barnabas Aspray), who argue that Falque's project *excludes* any possibility of natural theology. It is as if, for the philosopher, Falque is not philosophical enough; and for the theologian, not theological enough.

William Woody continues on a similar note. This time from a theological perspective, Woody ventures further to the meaning of the passage between two disciplines at stake in *Crossing the Rubicon*. Woody argues that—despite Falque's stated intention—the relationship between theology and philosophy recedes into the background of *Crossing the Rubicon* as a secondary concern. Rather, he contends that the text functions primarily as an apologetical justification for Falque's larger philosophical project. As such, Woody seeks to contextualize *Crossing the Rubicon* within Falque's existing philosophical oeuvre, as well as the cultural milieu of the contemporary French academy. Woody points to Falque's repeated emphasis on the primacy of the incarnate, finite body and his insistence on a phenomenological perspective grounded in immanence as two pervasive (and characteristically Falquean) themes grounding the text. He further highlights the many critiques Falque levies against the previous generation of "theological turn" phenomenologists (e.g., Marion, Levinas, Ricœur) in an attempt to distinguish himself from his philosophical forerunners and to justify further his more "porous" model of traversing the boundaries between philosophy and theology. Despite this, Woody designates Falque's project as *theological phenomenology*, yet his chapter provides us with more than a simple repetition of Janicaud's critique. In fact, after reading the descriptive part of Woody's chapter, one understands that Falque, perhaps surprisingly, agrees with Janicaud's criticism in many instances, mainly on the need to not wear masks when conducting ourselves phenomenologically or theologically. Apart from being clear about, first, the primacy of immanent phenomenology for any intellectual endeavor, and, second, crossing the threshold of theological reasoning, Woody's chapter appreciates Falque's contribution to overcoming unnecessary divisions between disciplines by relying upon the commonly shared "trust in the world," the philosophical faith preceding religious or confessional faith. Woody then considers and critiques Falque's proposed model for understanding the relationship between the two disciplines, noting that Falque preserves their distinction solely to "traverse and continually recross" their boundary, putatively allowing each to be transformed by the other. Yet Woody does not share in Falque's enthusiasm entirely. In the end he raises concerns for the supposed potential benefits (or even outright necessity) of a strict division and mutual suspicion between philosophy and theology.

The claim for the strict division between disciplines applies not only to theology and philosophy but also, and perhaps even more so, to theology and religious studies. The last chapter of the first section of this volume moves in this direction. Tamsin Jones' chapter puts Falque's understanding of the philosophy/theology relationship to the test, pointing to its strengths and weaknesses beyond the French Catholic context. Jones considers specifically American institutions (namely, the two divinity schools at Harvard and the University of Chicago) that for decades have sought interdisciplinary engagements between scholars in religious studies, theology, and philosophy of religion. Jones wonders if the erasure of the borders between philosophy and theology (an erasure she rightly observes to not be total for Falque) can be helpful in raising the discourse in the American context to a higher level. One detects a suspicion here that some of Falque's claims in *Crossing the Rubicon*, if translated into other cultures, would not bear the hoped-for results Falque aims to achieve. Jones observes that in some cases the diminishment of methodological distinctions between philosophy and theology has in the United States born its various discontents, one of which today can be observed in the explicit suspicion of "philosophy of religion" as a trojan horse for dogmatic theology (a suspicion that has contributed to the replacement of these positions in religious studies departments with other, more practically "relevant" approaches to religion, such as historical, material, and gender/race). A crux of the matter comes down to Falque's depictions of theology as discourses "beginning with God," based in descriptions of *reality*, and of philosophy as discourses beginning with the human experience of "the God-phenomenon" based in *possibility*.[25] Here, suspicions of Falque's approach are not shrouded: this particular depiction would be a very tough sell to American scholars, especially in religious studies. But Jones also points out that for decades two of the most influential divinity schools (Harvard and Chicago) have been operating according to a model that coalesces with Falque's vision, specifically of mutual crossing, respect, and influence between philosophy and theology. Yet again, the approaches of these institutions have not been without their discontents, namely a kind of "theologology" (as Sarah Coakley has referred to it), which at points strips theology of its explanatory power by reducing it to a second-order discipline, a merely historical process, and an ever-disputable human phenomenon (what Falque likely would refer to as a vulgarization of theology). Jones realizes that there is no easy solution out of the problems all of this raises, yet insists that the discipline of theology should be at the vanguard of methodological humility, never forgetting that it also cannot escape its finitude.

EMMANUEL FALQUE IN COMPARISON

The second part of this volume moves both Falque as well as our debate to a broader intellectual context. In particular, specialists in various schools of phenomenology and hermeneutics will put Falque's work under investigation. The golden thread running throughout this section is a re-reading and re-interpreting of Falque's sources of inspiration, as well as those against which he critically positions himself.

William L. Connelly, a current student of Falque, opens this section with a detailed analysis of the relationship between Maurice Blondel and Falque, between phenomenology and non-phenomenology. Connelly's chapter rightly stands directly after the more interpretative first part of this book, because he complements the picture of the intellectual background of Falque's thought by concretizing its development in the French phenomenological tradition. More specifically, he demonstrates Falque's taking leave of the program of Husserlian intentionality through Levinasian counter-intentionality, and to Merleau-Pontian embodied intentionality of the flesh. After these initial analyses, Connelly furnishes a close reading of Blondel and presents his works as a challenge to phenomenology; a challenge taken up by Falque. For Blondel, the most pressing question is how religion and religious experience are to be understood in immanently human terms, even going so far as to declare that no genuine philosophy of religion is yet to be truly established. Falque's conscientious reception of Blondel demonstrates a substantial response to Blondel's call for establishing a genuine philosophy of religion. Falque is able to help lay some groundwork for renewing the basis of philosophy of religion by bringing together Blondel's phenomenological sensitivities in questions of religion, history, and dogma, with Husserl's and Heidegger's phenomenological developments in philosophy, all the while simultaneously negating both Blondel's strict boundaries between theology and philosophy, and the often atheistic tendencies in the broader phenomenological tradition. It is concluded that Falque serves to establish a link between two distinct yet parallel philosophical traditions, thereby illuminating the way for a more fruitful philosophical engagement with theology, helping to provide critical advancements in philosophy of religion.

Katerina Koci's chapter is a critical encounter with Falque's discourse on hermeneutics presented in his book *Crossing the Rubicon: The Borderlands of Philosophy and Theology*. Falque does not cross the symbolic Rubicon only between philosophy and theology, even though this endeavor is the most popular subject of his followers as well as critics. More subtle and often overlooked is Falque's ambiguous use of categories as well as methods of hermeneutics and phenomenology. Drawing from the already existing discussion on hermeneutics between Falque and Jean Greisch, Koci draws from her perspective of biblical hermeneutics to address one of the most relevant issues yet to be discussed: the complex dialectic between the text and its readers, which is something Falque renders, in Koci's opinion, somewhat superficially. The point of departure is Falque's review and evaluation of Ricœur's Protestant hermeneutics. Koci points out that review of Falque's juxtaposition of Ricœur's position in comparison to his own "hermeneutics of the body and voice" draws a different conclusion regarding the role of the reader/addressee/interpreter in the hermeneutical process than Falque actually presents in his own methodological book. Falque starts with a hermeneutical interpretation and then proceeds to phenomenology, yet Koci calls the merits of this approach into question, both in general and in the context of Falque's specific project. Instead, the claim is made that Falque will make a stronger, more consistent case if he changes the order (i.e., if he first starts with phenomenology, then afterward applies his hermeneutical perspective). Falque, who indeed privileges phenomenology over hermeneutics, should begin with the phenomenology of believing, and from there proceed to the hermeneutics of understanding. In other words, experiencing does not come *after* we have interpreted (as Falque presents in the first part of *Crossing the Rubicon*, and in the opening chapter of this volume) but *before* any interpretation can occur. This observation helps Koci qualify that Falque's work concerns a "friendly tussle between hermeneutics and phenomenology"; despite Falque's own preference for the winner, the tussle ends up in tie.

Lorenza Bottacin Cantoni offers an in-depth comparison between Falque and Levinas on the body, taking inspiration from Falque's juxtaposition between Catholic and Jewish perspectives. A representative of the Jewish view, Levinas depicts a rebellious body that exceeds the boundaries of the will, testifying to an otherness within ourselves. Suffering is the glue that holds *Körper* and *Leib* together, and sends out signals to our attachment to the other. This acts as a reminder that a simple hermeneutic of the body without an embodied ethics is insufficient. Incarnation is a fundamental hospitality, and the other's pain requires me to understand *without words of explanation*. For Falque, suffering concerns a "suffering body," and, like Levinas, entails a fundamental transformation of the self that is not reducible to being merely an experience within consciousness. As opposed to the way we typically understand the body as a kind of vessel, the body is a "spread body" that lives *in* me. Yet differently from Levinas, the body affirms this power in both *pathos* and *logos*: not only through suffering (which cannot mentally be bracketed out) but also through creative expression. Palliative care becomes an important point for Falque, for it can force us into action and creative expression despite the chaos of pain. Theologically speaking, the task is to recognize ourselves as a spread body, and to overcome the self, following Christ's incarnation of taking on the finite, human frame. Bottacin Cantoni successfully demonstrates that for both thinkers we receive a fundamental responsibility in relation to the body and its transcendence, especially when it comes to caring for the other's [suffering] body. Yet for Falque there is a fundamental meaning of the body as it speaks and says something new as a result of both my suffering and the other's.

Falque's reliance upon the primacy of the body is achieved both to the detriment of the text and to his hopes for crossing the Rubicon, claims Francesca Peruzzotti. For Falque hermeneutics should refer itself more so to the body than to the text; more so to Christ as the original *logos* at the beginning of creation in Genesis than to written texts of interpretation: "Should not the hermeneutical *relief*, as understood in its Catholicity, move in the direction of *corporality* rather than *textuality*?" asks Falque.[26] Although God speaks first through nature, then through scripture, our traditions privilege the text over the body, which has amounted to our forgetting the body as a "book of experience." Instead, the body has priority over the text; the "speaking" of nature first concerns experience. Falque ultimately draws some distinctions between the differences of confessions (Catholic: body; Protestant: text), although he seeks an inter-confessional approach that takes our theoretical reliance seriously. Peruzzotti arrives at a few important concerns for his approach. First, there is a dichotomy set up in *Crossing the Rubicon* between philosophy and theology, in part due to the reliance upon a specific qualification of *faith*. This faith amounts to a certain *extrincisism* of reason, projecting the self outward, thus raising questions about Falque's call for neutral territory of shared "philosophical faith." Second, this disciplinary dichotomy ultimately follows from an even more primordial separation between speech and body. This "binary structure," which runs throughout his entire work, keeps these concepts (and subsequently, these two disciplines) far from a harmonious synthetization, as Falque hopes. And third, although Peruzzotti is sympathetic to the forgetting of the body, there also is concern about overly characterizing the reading of texts as merely a cognitive exercise (for example, the Bible rests upon a living, intersubjective dimension, which resonates in our theological experience). As a corrective to Falque's proposal, theology can only offer something to philosophy if it retains its synthetic unity of *logos* as *both* nature/experience *and* text, which informs history, reason, and human social development beyond the individual's private theater of consciousness.

CONSTRUCTIVE-CRITICAL ENGAGEMENTS

In the third and final part, we shift the debate once more: the authors of the final chapters take Falque's thought as the point of departure for further philosophical and theological discussions.

Carla Canullo takes Falque's oft-repeated claim seriously, that "we have no other experience of God but human experience," and offers a densely fruitful hermeneutic account of Falque's depiction of how *thought* must begin with the humanity of finitude, and how this, as a foundation or beginning, is one that insists upon transformation. The first transformation that a turn to finitude is intended to produce is one of *experience itself*. Canullo provides an in-depth analysis of *God, the Flesh, and the Other: From Irenaeus to Duns Scotus*, focusing especially on his reading of Meister Eckhart's depiction in the *Sermons* of the differences between the figures of Martha and Mary in the Gospels (Luke 10:39 esp.). Mary, far too attached to the world and the "thingliness" of the Lord in their midst, lives according to "the Natural Attitude." While Martha (1) is detached from the world in order to experience it aright; (2) expresses an intentionality in her engaging in *Gewerk* as opposed to *Werk (interior* activity as opposed to exterior work) in order to undergo a transformation or conversion within herself through the God who is present; and (3) thus performs the *phenomenological epochē*, a kind of passage. The passage here is not one that is entirely easy, however. Even in Christ's passage through Gethsemane a metamorphosis of his existential condition took place. Indeed, Christ is the perennial Exemplar of transformation for Falque: Christ's substitutionary atonement is both a passing and a passage that teaches us about human finitude as a model of openness at risk of closure or an "unbreakable solipsism of suffering and dying flesh."[27] The Substition (*Stell-vertretung*, "taking place") of the human that Christ enacts in the suffering passage also is one whereby the burden of finitude is passed from the Son to the Father, and this again makes Christ a model for human finitude. The human also can offer her suffering to God, can extend it to an interior alterity. With Christ's resurrection (which Falque claims "changes everything") comes the advent of human transfiguration that demonstrates *possibilities* for all humans. Thus, as Canullo is especially strong in pointing out, there is the necessary correlation in Falque's work between finitude as a "suffering finitude," and the *crossing* or *passage* that we must undertake from philosophy to theology and vice versa. This methodological suffering-as-passage makes one infinitely open, giving also the philosopher *reason* for crossing over into theology. Necessary is a means to hold open Augustine's depiction of the human as *mihi quaestio factus sum* indicating how a struggle of thinking is likewise a struggle of passage, and of relying upon others. Struggle, suffering, and passage are what can help ensure that one becomes a "never-ending passing and living openly." Yet Canullo does not hide the fact that theology makes *necessary* leaps into the possible of the impossible, while philosophy must develop itself according to the impossibility of the impossible. In the end, one contribution of theology is that it can help remind philosophy that every human has the opportunity to have their experience of finitude transfigured and metamorphosed.

Thinking with Falque, while also developing the possibility of thought beyond Falque's project, is clearly visible in Andrew Sackin-Poll's chapter, which offers a close reading of one particular idea from *Crossing the Rubicon*: "The crossing of the Rubicon not only joins the two banks (philosophy and theology) by a single thread but also 'casts the rope' (in the nautical sense of the phrase) to metaphysics itself. Phenomenology and metaphysics can thus discover, if not a place for *conciliation*, at least terms for the *discussion*."[28] This chapter argues that if Falque's crossing joins philosophy and theology by a "single thread," and, further, if this casts the rope toward metaphysics itself, then this suggests that the rope is cast out toward another site for discussion. Drawing inspiration from Étienne Gilson's *metaphysics of conversion* and in dialogue with Michel Henry's phenomenology of the body, Sackin-Poll proposes that this discussion can take place at an additional place, not between phenomenology and theology (which the crossing outlines and draws together very well) but this time between phenomenology and metaphysics. The goal is not the recovery of metaphysics for theology, as the final pages of *Crossing the Rubicon* on the overcoming of metaphysics might seem to indicate, but rather to outline a secular grammar of metamorphosis and conversion. This will help develop a metaphysics entirely consistent with the crossing, yet this time starting from an *henryenne* phenomenology of the body (and therefore, on the one hand, using Falque's ideas constructively and, on the other, challenging Falque's own critique of Henry).

Barnabas Aspray challenges Falque's project, striking its very nerve: the ontological category of finitude, viewed by Falque, as the new common grammar for both theologians and philosophers. Aspray's chapter comments upon and tests Falque's reverse interpretation of *sin* as disrespecting human finitude, and thus takes issue with Falque's insistence that any theology worthy of the name necessarily would begin (although Falque would add, certainly not end) with a Heideggerian perspective. Aspray identifies in Falque a strong adherence to Heidegger. The normativity of the phenomenology of finitude is perhaps too strong from a theologian's perspective (Aspray's preferred side of the Rubicon). In Aspray's reading, the choice of phenomenology for the foundational basis of a future engagement with the theological outplays the tradition of natural theology (here contradicting Čapek's claim in this volume that Falque's project is an attempt to reconstitute natural theology). For Aspray, Falque seems to focus only on a one-directional approach; that is, from phenomenology to theology. As pointed out in many chapters of this volume, this tendency certainly is present in Falque's project of a joint practice of theology and philosophy; however, Aspray's critical reading presents a challenge to Falque to clarify the issue of natural theology in his project.

Victor Emma-Adamah's contribution engages more deeply Falque's choice to develop his conception of finitude in a decidedly Heideggerian way, which began with the anguish of death in the *Guide to Gethsemane* and led to the resurrection of the body within *The Metamorphosis of Finitude*. Along the way are careful readings of Falque's interlocutors, primarily Blondel, from whom Falque distinguishes his work on finitude. The concern and question with which Emma-Adamah busies himself is modest: could the beginning with the limits of finitude inadvertently set a transcendental limit upon the outside? Borrowing from Maleuvre's insights, the worry would be that Falque's insistence upon finitude as an immanent "closed horizon" entails that the boundaries have simply been turned outward as opposed to being focused inward. This also would give reason for suspicion of Falque's hopes for neutral ground between the disciplines of philosophy and theology. Emma-Adamah develops a defense of Blondel's approach to finitude, which productively harkens to the German Romanticists' openness toward a "native infinite orientation" that does not fall prey to a kind of onto-theological critique. Falque rejects a Blondelian "immanentistism" that presumes infinitude to be lodged immanently within the finite. Overall, however, Falque knows that he cannot remain with a conception of finitude that is unsurpassable, for this would disregard the metamorphosis we tend to interpret in Christianity and the theological question of the infinite. Emma-Adamah does not shroud concerns for the Heideggerian (and Deleuzian) approach, which, despite attempts to the contrary, may be more dogmatic than we realize. Thus, in the end are we in possession of any models that allow us to conceive commensurability between the infinite and finite?

Concluding, through an original employment and application of Falque's work, Steven DeLay's contribution provokes, tests, and prods not only the boundaries between philosophy and theology, but also the limits of possibility Falque's work affords us. DeLay turns specifically to Falque's phenomenology of embodiment, then applies it to a pre-modern understanding of philosophy, not as a merely cognitive enterprise, but as a "way of life." This is in order to continue the "explosion" of the borders between philosophy and theology so as to demonstrate that the stakes of our life are much higher than any such disciplinary division might offer. This approach bears both promise and peril for Falque's work. Promise, for it presumes that the transformation of the *conditio humana* in everyday life is the *point du capitaine* of philosophy, thus making the body an incarnate form of our will, or "I can." As DeLay rightly interprets Falque, the body should not be understood only according to its expression of power *or* weakness, yet also according to where weakness is equated with power, for such limitations are transcendental reservoirs of power. Embodiment, for example, is empowered by its constraints and limitations. His claim that "we are so weak that we have no say even over the extent to which we are weak" also is a claim of our dynamism. Yet in DeLay's depiction, implicit perils for Falque's insistence on the body as an originary site of border-traversing arise. Under DeLay's application, one arrives at a practical or moral theology that also comes in tow if the border indeed is exploded (the specific explosion of which Falque himself likely might challenge). This threatens to reduce the theoretical to the practical. Yet for DeLay this is not a weakness of Falque's approach to the body and finitude, but rather a strength; that is, at least for the Christian, the transformation—which one might dare call a reduction—of the natural body to the spiritual body, is not a peril, but an opportunity built upon the resurrected Christ (who "alone has the means to open immanence to . . . eternity," claims Falque).[29] The paradox remains that the weakness of the body is its greatest strength in the sense that infinite power can work through it, taking that Kantian "I can" where it never would have thought possible to go, within the limits of reason alone.

PHILOSOPHIA ANCILLA THEOLOGIAE?

The purpose of this book is not to argue that Falque has given the final, definitive word on the disciplinary relationship between theology and philosophy, but rather that his work has shifted the fulcrums of debate from some of the shop-worn critiques initially proposed by Janicaud that have seized and stalemated the dialogues surrounding the relationship specifically between phenomenology and theology; namely, by also developing an *embodied* understanding of transformation and passage. Not only has the methodological paradigm changed since the original critiques of the theological turn were launched on the basis of phenomenology's establishment as a neutral methodological atheism. The general culture in which we are thinking, and the problems we are facing, also have changed: philosophers of religion now also need to engage with interlocutors who do not necessarily aggressively challenge religion, but rather seem to dismiss its relevance all together. The work of Emmanuel Falque gives reason to believe that the relevance of religion, and the philosophical and theoretical engagements with it, can indeed be reestablished.

The double identity of Falque being a philosopher *and* theologian is reflected on the following pages with scrupulous attention. After all, many in the field of philosophy of religion as well as theology are undergoing inner struggle with how to take into consideration thought-provoking challenges of other fields. Perhaps because Falque claims to be, first, a philosopher, and, second, sometimes also a theologian, it seems that theology in particular finds a reservoir of challenges and inspiration in his thought. First and foremost, the idea of crossing calls into question the very idea of *philosophia ancilla theologiae*. The accomplishment of the liberation of theology by means of philosophy can happen under the condition that both disciplines retain their autonomy. Hence, the service of philosophy to theology has to be conceived differently. From the perspective of theology, philosophy does not provide simply the argumentative tools for apologetics; rather, it offers the analytics of being in the world. This means that philosophical reflection can nourish theological thought and can give it a starting point according to the principle "we have no other experience of God but the human experience." Last but not least, instead of proposing God's coming to phenomenology, theology is called to come to the world. In other words, what is at stake is the credibility of Christianity and not simply its rationality. If we could associate Falque with a certain theology in a phenomenological fashion, it would refer to a theology that is not apologetic, but rather reflective. In particular, this theology starts with the reflection on its position in the world.

From the perspective of phenomenology in particular, and philosophy of religion in general, Falque's thought points to the conclusion that theology also is a part of the discourse. However, the meaning of the statement that "the more one theologizes, the better one philosophizes" does not suggest the theologization of phenomenology, or turning phenomenology into a crypto-theology. Rather, the more one theologizes, the better one is equipped to see the blind spots and limits of phenomenology and thereby to do the proper philosophical job of description. On the one hand, the theological contextualization of certain debates in the history of philosophy helps us understand the hermeneutical framework that (at least for exemplary philosophical giants of the tradition, such as Augustine, Kierkegaard, Pascal, and Descartes) is inherently religious, and to a degree, theological. On the other hand, the portrait of theology Falque offers to philosophers is not a positive science (as was rightly rejected by Husserl and criticized by Heidegger).[30] It is in this ambivalent space and productive tension between the two that Falque invites his readers to consider a theological-existential mode of being.

NOTES

1. A comprehensive volume, *Une Analytique du passage: Rencontres et confrontations avec Emmanuel Falque*, edited by Claude Brunier-Coulin (Paris: Éditions Franciscaines, 2016),

summons the debates with Falque that took place in France after the publication of his *Triduum philosohique*.

2. See, for example, Christian Godin, "Entre philosophie et théologie, des frontières ou des limites? À propos de *Passer le Rubicon*," in *Une Analytique du passage*, 341–50; here 345.

3. Philippe Nouzille, "D'une gué à l'autre: Le Rubicon et le Yabbock," in *Une Analytique du passage*, 351–64.

4. Emmanuel Falque, "The Collision of Phenomenology and Theology," in *Quiet Powers of the Possible: Interviews in Contemporary French Phenomenology*, edited by Tarek R. Dika and W. Chris Hackett (New York: Fordham University Press, 2016), 211–27; here 213.

5. Emmanuel Falque and Jean-Yves Lacoste are exceptions among the group of internationally famous French phenomenologists interested in religion and theological issues, because they both hold academic degrees in both philosophy and theology.

6. Jeffrey Bloechl, "Eschatology, Liturgy, and the Task of Thinking," in Jean-Yves Lacoste, *From Theology to Theological Thinking* (Charlottesville: University of Virginia Press, 2014).

7. Emmanuel Falque, *Parcours d'embûches: S'expliquer* (Paris: Editions Franciscaines, 2016), 134.

8. Emmanuel Falque, "Théologie et philosophie: nouvelles frontières," *Études* 404:2 (2006): 201–10; here 202.

9. Martin Heidegger, "Phenomenology and Theology," in *Pathmarks*, edited and translated by William McNeil (Cambridge: Cambridge University Press, 1998), 39–62.

10. Heidegger, "Phenomenology and Theology," 53.

11. Dominique Janicaud, *Phenomenology and the "Theological Turn": The French Debate*, translated by Bernard G. Prusak (New York: Fordham University Press, 2000), 27.

12. See Joseph O'Leary, "Review of *Passer le Rubicon: Philosophie et théologie. Essai sur les frontières*," *Theological Studies* 64:2 (2013): 841–45.

13. Christina M. Gschwandtner, *Postmodern Apologetics? Arguments for God in Contemporary Philosophy* (New York: Fordham University Press, 2013), 184.

14. Joseph Rivera, "Introduction: Futures of the Theological Turn," *Philosophy Today* 62:1 (2018), 89–97; here 90.

15. See Jason W. Alvis, *The Inconspicuous God* (Bloomington: Indiana University Press, 2018).

16. Janicaud, *Phenomenology and the "Theological Turn*,*"* 98.

17. Janicaud, *Phenomenology and the "Theological Turn*,*"* 103.

18. Falque's claim that we have no other experience of God but the human experience is found, for example, in his *Crossing the Rubicon: The Borderlands of Philosophy and Theology*, translated by Reuben Shank (New York: Fordham University Press, 2016), chapter 5; *God, the Flesh, and the Other: From Irenaeus to Duns Scotus*, translated by William C. Hackett (Evanston, IL: Northwestern University Press, 2015), 1–16; *The Metamorphosis of Finitude: An Essay on Birth and Resurrection*, translated by George Hughes (New York: Fordham University Press, 2012), 6 and then §5; "Théologie et philosophie," 205.

19. Falque, "The Collision of Phenomenology and Theology," 218.

20. Joseph O'Leary, "Phenomenology and Theology: Respecting the Boundaries," *Philosophy Today* 62:1 (2018), 99–117; here 99.

21. O'Leary, "Phenomenology and Theology," 100–01.

22. "We adhere to the world in philosophy as we adhere to God in theology in an originary posture—always given in advance—such that the philosophical faith in the world heuristically precedes the theological faith in God." Falque, *Crossing the Rubicon*, 84.

23. Falque, *Crossing the Rubicon*, 187n20.

24. Jan Patočka, *An Introduction to Husserl's Phenomenology* (Chicago: Open Court, 1999), 102.

25. Falque, *Crossing the Rubicon*, 127.

26. Falque, *Crossing the Rubicon*, 40.

27. Falque, *God, the Flesh, and the Other*, 102.

28. Falque, *Crossing the Rubicon*, 157.

29. Falque, *Crossing the Rubicon*, 22.

30. See Martin Koci, *Thinking Faith after Christianity: A Theological Reading of Jan Patočka's Phenomenological Philosophy* (Albany: SUNY Press, 2020), 19–45.

Part I

Interpreting Emmanuel Falque

Chapter One

Philosophy and Theology

New Boundaries

Emmanuel Falque[1]

With Leibniz's question, the era of monadology certainly opens, but so does a new way of conceiving of adventure and even of crossing boundaries: "why he [Caesar] crossed the Rubicon rather than stopped at it and why he won rather than lost at Pharsalus."[2] Crossing the waterway, or rather the small river (*flumen*), that separates Emilia-Romagna from Cisalpine Gaul, Caesar has no less changed the face of the earth, for all the risk was great when he thus committed himself. *Alea iacta est*—"the die has been cast"—the future emperor allegedly exclaimed; this is a way not of imitating him or following in his footsteps, but of hereby admitting that no advance can be made without exposing oneself, in that "thinking is deciding" (Heidegger).

We should therefore recognize this, at least with regard to the field (of battle?) that separates philosophy and theology in France. Under the repeated blows of hermeneutics and phenomenology, the boundaries between the disciplines have already moved, and we must, at a minimum, take note of this if we are to not continue to deceive ourselves. Hans-Georg Gadamer and Paul Ricœur on the one hand (hermeneutics), and Emmanuel Levinas, Michel Henry, Jean-Louis Chrétien, Jean-Luc Marion, or Jean-Yves Lacoste on the other (phenomenology), mark so many respective, even also progressive, stages through which boundaries are no longer set up as barriers, nor disputes as oratorical jousts. Whether or not there has been a "theological turn in French phenomenology" (D. Janicaud), this fact cannot be contested: phenomenology has made a real, abundant contribution *to* theology since the publication of *Totality and Infinity* (1961), such that today theologians themselves gain by referring to it. Moreover, what was said *ad intra* in the questioning of Judaism (Levinas) or of Christianity (Marion, Lacoste, Henry,

Chrétien, etc.) is now also formulated *ad extra* outside of any confessional sphere, as if the "religious," and even theological content, as such, could not leave indifferent even those who profess to not adhere to it—Nietzsche and resurrection (D. Franck), denegation and negative theology (J. Derrida), contemporary art and the Crucifixion (G. Deleuze), deconstruction and Christianity (J.-L. Nancy), universalism and Saint Paul (A. Badiou), etc.

A question nevertheless remains, and not one of the least. If phenomenology's contribution to theology has certainly borne fruit, such that the Saying of God (Levinas), the relation to writing (Ricœur), the Incarnation (Henry), the Eucharist (Marion), prayer (Chrétien), or liturgy (Lacoste) have found in the vein of the "descriptive" the wherewithal for renewing a previously expositive interpretation, phenomenology itself, for its part, has not, or has scarcely, questioned itself about the transformations that theology would this time impose on it. Everything has indeed happened as if the "phenomenologization of theology" were not at the same time accompanied by a "theologization of phenomenology." Let me be clear here. It is not at all a question of calling for a crypto-theology within philosophy, and even less of confounding the disciplines by wanting too much to gather them together. A "counter-blow" should rather be thought from the one to the other, but following a two-way street this time: certainly from phenomenology *to* theology, but also from theology *to* phenomenology. Tertullian's taking into account of the "carnal" and "corporeal" Christ, for example, could well compel a return to the hypertrophy of the flesh or of the "lived experience of the body" in phenomenology (*The Wedding Feast of the Lamb*), the consideration of the Resurrection could well release the true stake of the horizontality of our existence (*The Metamorphosis of Finitude*), or also the hypothesis of a divine inter-Trinitarian pathos could well transform the unilateral sense of suffering (*The Guide of Gethsemane*).[3] If phenomenology has therefore practiced for some time a "one-way trip"—certainly from phenomenology *to* theology—we will therefore take, just for once, a "return ticket": from theology *to* phenomenology this time. By thinking "in one direction," be it out of interest for what it discovers, philosophy risks not letting itself be transformed by what it precisely has just encountered. One will agree, therefore, to here practice the double trajectory, at the risk, inversely, of either losing oneself or of never having traveled.

Pathei mathos, or "self-apprenticeship by suffering," such is the great lesson of Aeschylus, and the sense of the *great crossing* or the "passage," here in the double sense of "*pâtir*," that is, "suffering," as also of "*passer*," that is, "crossing." In the act of interpreting (hermeneutics), as also of deciding (belief and faith) and of crossing (philosophy and theology), the "round trip" will therefore constantly play out, or this Iliad that is never without an Odyssey, such that one will never be satisfied to cross without returning changed by that which one visited.

THE HERMENEUTICAL QUESTION

"Scripture grows with its readings" (*Scriptura cum legentibus crescit*).[4] The memorable formula of Gregory the Great does not indicate first or only that *I* grow with Scripture or that *I* am its principle destinary. On the contrary, and according to an inversion that is, to say the least, surprising, it is Scripture that grows through my own reading, the text living from my life rather than me nourishing myself from its life: "[the Bible] is a living being that grows and develops before our eyes," as we must say, following Paul Claudel.[5] If there is thus a hermeneutical relief, certainly in theology (by the senses of Scripture) but also in philosophy (by interpretation), this relief will, I contend, play out less in the text than in the body, in the self than in the world. "Is hermeneutics fundamental?" The interrogation will here take the baton from the famous question of Emmanuel Levinas: "Is ontology fundamental?"[6] On the one hand, phenomenology (Husserl and Heidegger in particular) will play the game of the "short route," that is to say, that of the "ontology of understanding," or of the lived experience of the intentional subject, in that it is projected and transformed in the text itself. On the other hand, hermeneutics (Hans-Georg Gadamer, certainly, but Paul Ricœur even more) will explicitly refer to the "long route," that is to say to analyses of language, to history, and to the detour by various mediations, such that the human subject is never directly apprehended but is always mediated by "cultural works." Such is the debate that we must question again today, and the decision of Paul Ricœur, followed by the whole of hermeneutical theology, which we must think again: "substituting for the short route of the Analytic of Dasein, the long route that begins by analyses of language."[7]

Let us be clear here. It is not in the least a question—this goes without saying—of not first highlighting the great merit of Ricœurian hermeneutics, and in particular its boundless fecundity for theology. We will question only—but at the same time decisively—its being anchored in textuality alone rather than in corporeality, in the "book of Scripture" (*liber Scripturae*) rather than in the "book of the world" (*liber mundi*). Without reducing an inspiration to a confession, it is necessary to recognize that no existence could be said without an experience, and that nothing in philosophy, particularly when it acknowledges its spiritual debt, could so easily strip off its traditional heritage. Paul Ricœur's Protestantism roots his art of interpreting in *sola Scriptura*, which of course corresponds to his tradition, as also to his confession. Likewise, Emmanuel Levinas' Judaism finds a refuge in the "body of the letter," with the Torah signing the act of "a contraction of the Infinite in Scripture" or "God's precarious dwelling place in the letters."[8] What hermeneutics here has of "confessional" (the Protestant hermeneutic of the meaning of the text and the Jewish hermeneutic of the body of the letter) in no way harms its conceptual character, and still less its universal vocation.

There remains a question, and an aim, that we cannot not interrogate. If Ricœurian hermeneutics takes root in Protestantism (the meaning of the text), and Levinasian hermeneutics in Judaism (the body of the letter)—for which one could not reproach them, according to an ecumenism that is necessary and in good taste—what, then, would a properly "Catholic" hermeneutic be like? In other words, with the "meaning of the text" and the "body of the letter," is it not also suitable to deploy the program of a so-called Catholic hermeneutic of the "body and the voice," such that to the *table of Scripture* the *Eucharistic table* would always be linked: "the faithful are nourished in the word of God at the double table of the Sacred Scripture and the Eucharist."[9]

HERMENEUTICS AND THE SENSE OF SCRIPTURE

Tracking the four senses of Scripture, one indeed follows the deployment of hermeneutics, for today and tomorrow: "the letter teaches 'that which took place,'" emphasizes the Dominican Augustine of Dacia, an heir in this of Origen and a contemporary of Thomas Aquinas, "allegory 'that which you are to believe,' the moral sense (tropological) 'that which you are to do,' the anagogical sense 'that towards which you must tend.'"[10] We know this, many having more or less recognized it. The advent of historical-critical exegesis in France, following the Second Vatican Council and continuing up to the 1970s, permitted a real renewal of the reading of texts, certainly for the reading of the Bible, but also for theology and even philosophy. What the *letter* of the text teaches here, since it is a matter of referring to the first sense of Scripture, amounts less to restricting oneself to its literality (what the text says), but rather to its historicity (that to which the text refers). The historical-critical method, by way of the first sense of Scripture, refers precisely to "what took place" (*littera gesta docet*) by its taking account of the context, the referent, the traditions in which the text was written, the true history to which it refers, etc. So many exegetical proceedings that finally permitted us to make of Genesis a "myth," of the historical accounts a composite of different traditions (Yahwists, Elohists, and priestly), and of Paul's epistles an aggregate sometimes of several authors or of another author (the epistle to the Hebrews, for example). The historical-critical method refers not to the letter of the text as it is written but to its literality in history and the referent where the letter of the text was given.

A sort of exhaustion of the historical-critical method, like that which is probably also occurring in textual hermeneutics today, leads one to wait and hope for a relief, in particular in Catholic theology, and that Protestant hermeneutics paradoxically managed to procure. With "The Hermeneutical Function of Distanciation" (1975), Paul Ricœur finally, or anew this time, proposed a type of interpretation that "may abolish all reference to a given reality."[11] A triple reduction or *epochē* would permit the operation of an "emancipation with respect to the one who wrote the text (the author)," "an emancipation from the one who receives the text (the reader)," and an "emancipation from that to which the text refers (the referent)."[12] One will have understood this. The advance here is considerable. A "world of the text" is born for itself, such that a "meaning of the text" is valid by itself, in its proper unity, regardless of the circumstances in which the message was composed and the intention for which it was destined.[13] The pastoralia, in particular in France, knew how to take full advantage of this, with all the deviations in projecting oneself into the text against which Paul Ricœur himself had always fought. It finally became possible to read, or reread, the Bible for itself, to no longer believe oneself to be or desire to be a *savant* in order to understand it, and to recognize that this message was first addressed to *me* in its unity and was not always derived from a history that, all in all, shatters it. The text is a "world in itself," and no exterior knowledge is required, save my good will for reading it, and even also for understanding it, or understanding (*Verstehen*) *myself* in it.

It is, however, there that the problem lies; not yesterday when hermeneutics had come to renew everything (in the 1980s), but today when we have somewhat exhausted its possibilities (in the 2000s). The "proposed world" that the text opens, as Ricœur emphasizes, aims first and principally at "the *appropriation (Aneignung)* of the text, its *application (Anwendung)* to the present situation of the reader," be it one's capacity to "*understand oneself* in front of the text" or to "*expos[e oneself]* to the text and receiv[e] *from it* an enlarged self."[14] If the text is a "world in itself," I am no less its principal destinary: "the text is the *medium* through which *we understand ourselves*."[15] Here it is indeed a matter, with Paul Ricœur's hermeneutics, of recognizing and seeing in the text "that which you are to do" (*quid agas*), which designates, properly speaking, the moral or tropological sense. All reading aims for the "transformation of the self by the text," such that numerous deviations and pastoral practices are drawn from it, as if one of Paul's letters, the letter to the Ephesians for example, were directly addressed to me. Paradoxically, the mediation of the text in its language and culture that was so important for Paul Ricœur has sometimes been forgotten in favor of the mere appropriation and modification of the self by the text.

We will, then, and for today, call for a "phenomenality of the text" by way of a relief of the "historicity of the text" (literal sense) and the "hermeneutics of the text" (tropological sense). No longer only attentive to "that which took place" (literal sense) or to "that which you are to do" (moral sense), we will aim this time for "that which you are to believe" (*quid credas*, allegorical sense) and "that towards which you must tend" (*quo tendas*, anagogical sense). Rather than finding ourselves in the text, we will lose ourselves in it. And more than "understanding ourselves before it," we will be taken (*pris*) into and understood (*com-pris*) in it; incorporating myself into the body of the Bible in the liturgy of the word as I incorporate myself into the body of the resurrected one and of the Church in the Eucharistic liturgy: "But to say that we question the Scriptures is incorrect," as Paul Claudel wonderfully emphasizes. "It is better to admit that *the Scriptures question us*."[16] "[The Bible] is a drama, I would say, not enacted by us so much as through him, just as the actors of the Old Testament lived through him."[17] The phenomenality of the text will be centered less on my lived experiences as its destinary than on the lived experiences that are *internal to the text itself*, by way of its only proprietor. As with Flaubert's Mme. Bovary or Stendhal's Julien Sorel, an intersubjectivity plays out also and first in the play of the characters among themselves, of which I am not the principal beneficiary—if not losing myself, or at the very least not finding myself. "Have this mind in yourselves, which is yours in Christ Jesus," proclaims the hymn to the Philippians (Phil 2:5),[18] and not the reverse. It is not he who understands himself *in me*, as if my interpretation could contain him, but I who understand myself in him; "allowing [my]self to be read authoritatively by the Holy Scripture," to take up here the formula of Jean-Louis Chrétien.[19]

In short—and one will have understood this—the text contains a "world," as Paul Ricœur has emphasized well while, however, orienting it toward appropriation, but also in that it says something of the world that precedes it and that incorporates itself in it. Hermeneutics understood as the "meaning of the text" (Ricœur) or as the "dwelling of the letter" (Levinas) indeed first honors a text or a writing, but not the world or creation as such. Yet such is probably the originality of the hermeneutical aim that is "Catholic," and no longer "Protestant" or "Jewish." The first to be given, emphasizes Bonaventure commenting on the *Canticle of Creation* and followed in this by Thomas Aquinas with the five cosmological ways, was the "book of the world" (*liber mundi*), and it therefore suffices to decipher it to see God present there. It is only because, by sin, "this book (*iste liber*), that is, the world (*scilicet mundus*), was then as it were dead and defaced, that another book (*alius liber*)—the book of Scripture (*liber Scripurae*) —was necessary, by which humans would be illumined in order to be able to interpret the metaphors of things."[20] The text does not come *before* but *after*, and that is probably the great originality of a so-called Catholic hermeneutic. Ceasing to bring its attention to bear on the mediation of the text and its structures, in the manner of the examination of the finger that indicates the moon without ever aiming for the moon itself, the "phenomenality of the text" causes one to enter into a veritable *intentional intercorporeality* of the reader and the actors of the text itself, such that it is the Christ that I encounter there (allegorical sense) or the union to God himself (anagogical sense) and not, or no longer, a history that has just unfolded for me (literal sense) or an interpretation that is destined for me (moral or tropological sense). Thus one will give oneself the means to encounter it anew, or rather for it to show itself otherwise. The Catholic hermeneutic of "the body and the voice" (our own perspective) will here take over, insofar as that is possible, from the Protestant hermeneutic of the "meaning of the text" (Ricœur) and from the Jewish hermeneutic of the "body of the letter" (Levinas).

OF THE BODY AND THE VOICE

The "voice" has this property: it requires a body, which may be hidden but not absent or suppressed. One can, and sometimes even must, read a text in forgetfulness of its author, and likewise also celebrate a word in commemoration of an actor. The so-called Catholic hermeneutic is not, however, that of reading (the Protestant aim) or of hearing (the Jewish intention). It celebrates and waits for visibility more than invisibility, the body more than the word: "Whoever has seen me has seen the Father," Jesus answers Philip. "How can you say, 'Show us the Father?'" (John 14:9). How, then, to see him whom we no longer see, and hear him whom we no longer hear, at the very least, no longer in the same way as the disciples who were his contemporaries? Here the formula of Hugh of Saint-Victor takes its place, a sort of leitmotif of a so-called Catholic hermeneutic of the body and the voice: *hic intelligenda est vox Verbi quod ibi caro Dei*—"the voice of the Word must be understood at present as the flesh of God was understood then."[21]

Let me be clear here. It is not at all a question of "hearing voices or his voice," nor of hearing the Word with our "ears of flesh," even though Francis of Assisi mentioned this in order to insist on the conversion of our corporeality. The analogy counts here, more than the resonance of the sound: "now, *each day*, this same Word comes himself to us under the cover of a human voice," the Victorine clarifies. "Certainly its manner by which it makes itself known to humans is different according to whether it's *by his flesh* or *by the human voice*."[22] The hermeneutics of the voice compels us to recognize that there exists in the vocal an absence become presence of a rare intensity, and of which the mode of the tele-phoned (or of that which is heard from afar), today allows us to apprehend its originality. At the end of a line that is more than ever virtualized, the voice of my Beloved resonates. *It is he, it is I.* There is no need to speak to each other to recognize each other. The other is always already there in the timbre of his sending, and his breath or his vibration suffices to identify him. There exists a "singularity of the voice" that no other phenomenon could equal, such that God himself makes exemplary use of the voice, including in the Bible, to express himself today: "Everyone who is of the truth *listens to my voice*" (*akouei mou tes phones*), Jesus answers in court before Pilate (John 18:37); and one will name "good shepherd" he who opens the door to the sheep who "listen to his voice" (*tes phones autou akouei*) because they "know his voice" (*oti oidasin ten phonen autou*) (John 10:3–4).

Present in His *body* on the Eucharistic table, God is therefore also present by His *voice* in the Holy Scripture. The word is no longer only "text" (Ricœur) or "trace" (Levinas), but also pro-feration, even voci-feration, of a "this is my body" come in bread to give itself, and in its word to vibrate. No longer seeing his body of flesh, like the disciples formerly, we now *hear his voice*, we recognize him from his manner more than from his matter, from his tonality more than from his visibility. Moreover, he keeps himself by his voice hidden in his flesh; not absent, since there will never be a voice without a body, but present otherwise. There where the body keeps itself hidden "under the veil of nature" in his Incarnation and "under the species of bread and wine" in the Eucharist, according to Pascal's words in his letter to Charlotte Roanez (1656), his voice resonates *for us* in the depths of this body that is totally present and nonetheless concealed, such that we are this time the destinaries not only of an articulated text, but of a mode of being of God expressed by his body: "This *voice (phône)* has come *for your sake (alla di umas), not mine (ou di me)*" (John 12:30).

Far from keeping itself in the snare of writing or of the *gramme* (Derrida, *Voice and Phenomenon*), the voice therefore waits to be proffered. There is a forgetting of the voice, more even than of being. The voiceless thought of philosophy would probably gain, as if by a "counterblow," from learning that there is a "great voice," or a *megalê phôné*, in theology: "And at the ninth hour, Jesus cried with a great voice (*phôné megalê*), 'Eloi, Eloi, lema sabachthani?' which means 'My God, my God, why have you forsaken me?'" (Mk 15:34).[23] The voice here is not only *nue*, that is, "naked," by virtue of a "call" that always covers it or confers signification on it (Heidegger); it is first *crue,* that is, "raw" or "believed," in the double sense of the rawness of what is given without having been prepared and of the apprenticeship by which we give it our faith without, however, ever becoming used to it. The *voix crue,* that is, the "raw voice," the "believed voice" (my perspective) rather than the *voix nue*, that is, the "naked voice" (Chrétien)—that is what makes the vociferation of the voice, by which Christ himself in his great cry on Golgotha gives himself in his passions more than in his articulations, in his *pathemes* more than in his *phonemes*: "spoken sounds are symbols of affections in the soul (*pathemata*)," Aristotle famously emphasizes, "and written marks symbols of spoken sounds."[24] The "Word on the cross" thus gives itself as a "Word in the voice," keeping the voice in the body (Eucharistic) and giving a body to the voice (liturgical): "let us hear *our voice in him (in illo voces nostras)* and *his voice in us (voces eius in nobis)*," we must emphasize following Saint Augustine in his *Enarationes in Psalmos*.[25]

DECIDING TO BELIEVE

Having thus "interpreted," it now remains to "decide." The Catholic hermeneutic of the body and the voice certainly opens onto a new, and other, mode of expressivity, but nothing ensures that it will not make us leave our common humanity. The great crossing, or the crossing of the Rubicon, would risk much, and even too much, by abandoning a bank in forgetfulness of what was left. "Yes, but you must wager. It is not optional; you are embarked," famously proclaims Pascal at the heart of his *Pensées*.[26] Since man is embarked, nothing will be forgotten of what makes him, in particular for navigating. "The human per se," or the horizon of finitude, constitutive of the figure of man in his modernity, could not be forgotten by God. Belief in this sense does not spring from the confessant alone. We still believe "in the world" or "in others" before believing (or not) "in God." An originary belief or confidence (*Urdoxa*) precedes and founds all disbelief or all mistrust. *Nothing is harder to believe than the absence of belief*; not that it is first a question of religion, but of philosophy or of the human as such. Philosophy or the human per se will therefore first endeavor to suspend the abstractions of doubt or of the *epochē*, even if it means leaving to the theologian the charge of "transforming the concept of decision at the moment of decision," in that the Christian is no longer in this case "one," or even "two," but "three" deciding (the Trinity).

THE IRREDUCIBLE BELIEF

At any rate, therefore, one believes. "Perceptual faith," to say it with Maurice Merleau-Ponty and according to a homology of "faith" that shows to what extent philosophical belief precedes "religious faith," testifies to an "irreducible belief in the world." "Notion of faith to be specified," emphasizes a note in *The Visible and the Invisible*: "It is *not faith in the sense of decision*, but in the sense of what is *before any position*, animal faith."[27] Modern philosophy was certainly able to return to consciousness by distrusting the world, and the power of hyperbolic doubt, like the discovery of the cogito, certainly makes Descartes "that French horseman who took off at such a good pace," to say it with Péguy.[28] Moreover, the *epochē* or "bracketing" marks the true birth certificate of phenomenology in Husserl, such that it does not suffice to describe situations to call oneself a phenomenologist (in the frequent manner of the use of the word phenomenology within the framework of theology). It is, rather, proper in phenomenology to return to the "acts of consciousness" that constitute our "lived experiences of things" as the things themselves, rather than to their empiricity or their objectivity. In short, doubting or bracketing indeed constitutes the birth certificate of a reflective philosophy, the soundness of which we cannot here deny.

There remains, however, paradoxically, a "universal ground of belief in the world" that I will never be able to reduce: "Everything, which, as an existing object, is a goal of cognition is an existent *on the ground of the world*, which is *taken* as existing as *a matter of course*," acknowledged Husserl at the end of his life. "*Consciousness of the world*," the philosopher adds, "is consciousness in the mode of *certainty of belief*."[29] One will not find, therefore, any greater prejudice than that of the absence of prejudice. *Sum credendus*—"I am believable (or ought to believe)"—precedes in its certainty, I contend, the *cogito ergo sum* ("I think, therefore I am," Descartes), and even the *sum moribundus* ("I am dying," Heidegger). That I can believe *in* Santa Claus does not require *that* Santa Claus is. "I *believe* with certainty," and that is the highest certainty: "If I wanted to doubt the existence of the earth long before my birth," we must conclude with Ludwig Wittgenstein, "I should have to doubt all sorts of things that stand fast for me"—namely, "belief itself."[30]

An irreducible "there is" therefore remains on the threshold and at the foundation of all belief, and even before all mistrust and all distrust. To Leibniz's question, "Why is there something rather than nothing?" we indeed must first recognize that "there is" something. Not that the thing "is," but that I cannot not "believe" that it is, and that this precisely is indubitable and irreducible, namely my belief itself. It matters little what it is. Only the idea, or the belief, counts, according to which "I cannot believe" that it is not. "Philosophical faith" (in the world and in others) precedes and founds "religious faith" (in a transcendence) and likewise "confessing faith" (in a God acting and present in me). Just for once, belief in God no longer strays from the ensemble and from the rest of humanity; the "small remnant" (Israel) never remaining less than when it ignores the "large remnant" (of humanity). The *Es gibt* or the *Il y a, There is*, no longer say only the givenness of what gives itself, but this *philosophical foundation of our common belief* that we should find again, if we do not want, *qua* confessing believer, to be separated from "our human brothers" (Bernanos), borrowed like us from that unsayableness of chaos that we should acknowledge: "The *brute* or *savage being* that has not yet been converted into an object of vision or choice is what we want to rediscover," as Maurice Merleau-Ponty acknowledges in a quasi-testamentary way.[31] One will no longer wait, following Husserl, for "pure experience and one might say, mute still" to be "brought to express its own meaning."[32] The "prereflective," in its very formulation, still expects "everything" and "too much" from the reflective, as it is entirely and uniquely oriented toward it; in the manner of the "unconscious" in Freud's first topography (unconscious, preconscious, conscious), for this reason replaced by the "Id" in the second topography (Id, Ego, Superego): "Rather than to a God," as Emmanuel Levinas acknowledged at the end of the war, "the notion of the *there is* leads us to the *absence of God, the absence of any being*. Primitive men live *before* all revelation, *before* the light comes."[33]

PHILOSOPHY OF RELIGIOUS EXPERIENCE

There is, therefore, a philosophy before theology, and a foundation of "common belief" (at least in the world and in others) that structures them both. By carrying out the *Great Crossing*, or by *crossing the Rubicon*, we will thus first sound the depths of the river, and we will acknowledge that it is evident that a "common water," murky though it be, constitutes us—*all* of us—first and primarily. We are "woven from the same flesh" (Merleau-Ponty), and admitting this avoids ruptures and leaps from which phenomenology and theology, as I will show, do not remain exempt. If there is indeed a "philosophy of religion," at least in the sense of a disengagement of the philosophical concept at the very heart of the theological representation (the dialectic at the heart of the Trinity in Hegel, for example), there is yet a "philosophy of religious experience" in which the decision of faith is also important, no longer uniquely in the community of an originary belief (*Urdoxa*), but in the specificity of a confessing and experiential adhesion: "We cannot but recognize the benefit of *the personal practice of religious experience*," admits Henry Duméry. "*Without being eligible*, it is often *a great help* in the critique of the religious object."[34]

"Philosophy of religious experience," rather than "religious philosophy" (with its overly psychological tones), will thus designate a discipline that is to be found again today and of which Pascal, Kierkegaard, and Nietzsche were, for us, the pioneers. Such a philosophy will take its root in the "life" that Heidegger, moreover, names "facticial"—not simply the "fact of living as such" but enduring its ordeal and fully engaging oneself in this dimension of existing. We will call "facticial life," precisely in the framework of a "phenomenology of religious life" rather than of a "philosophy of religion," "the fact that the *experiencing self* and *what is experienced* are not torn apart like [two] things," to follow anew here the young Heidegger.[35]

One can certainly wonder if one must have had, or shared, the "religious experience" to be able to speak about religious matters. In other words, if the crossing of the Rubicon demands not only that one accept abandoning, be it only for a time, the bank of philosophy to reach that of theology, but if the "lived experience" of which it is a question in theology itself (Christ) must possess its own content that is sensible for everyone, then one would risk, conversely, understanding nothing of what the philosopher or the theologian could indeed enunciate: "only a *religious man* can understand *religious life*," adds Heidegger, "because, if it were not so, he would not dispose of an authentic givenness."[36]

Let me be clear here. It is not at all a question, either for myself or for the philosopher from Freiburg, of proclaiming an exclusivism of experience whereby the lived experience of the thing itself would be the only way to honor it. There is a sort of *terrorism of experience* in religious matters (the effusive encounter with God) and likewise in psychoanalysis (being put on the couch) that causes us to wrongly forbid one who has not shared it from being able to speak about it. We will rather maintain, and entirely to the contrary, that the "non-experience of the experience" can just as well orient it otherwise, or at the very least cause it to be seen in a light that one would not have suspected. Moreover, the experience of the experience itself is not necessarily required for one who wants to apprehend it all the same—and this is what makes the particularity of the "philosophy of religious experience"—we recognize that the author or the artist to whom we refer could not say it independently of a "(facticial) life" on the basis of which his discourse was fertilized. The adherence to the Christ of the Gospel is not the condition *sine qua non* of the reading of a Pascal or a Kierkegaard, for example, any more than of the contemplation of a Rouault or a Caravaggio. It remains, however, that these thinkers and artists themselves have never thought, written, or painted *outside* of such an adherence to the object of belief, marking at least *for them* their first (but not their only) aim. The "philosophy of religious experience" does not defer to the idols of "lived experience alone" or of "every experiential," in the manner of many sentimentalist drifts today. It refers, uniquely but fully, to the *coefficient of experience* at the source of all discourse, sure that what is "for oneself" is also "for others," in a singularity that we should recognize instead of rejecting.

DECIDING IN COMMON

At the moment of decision, one will therefore not be *all alone*; be it a matter of philosophical, religious, or confessing experience, at least in that the "phenomenology of experience" is also an "experience of phenomenology," and that it belongs to the one as to the other—to experience as to phenomenology—to be unable to give itself independently of a certain alterity. It remains that the confessing believer, saying, "I believe" by way of a *credo*, opens onto a dimension of existing that only the Christian is capable of sharing. There where "philosophical faith" or "perceptive faith" would serve as a common pedestal for an "originary belief" (*Urdoxa*) in others or in oneself, belief in God, by his Resurrection in the framework of Christianity, attests to an alterity living in oneself that modifies through and through the art and the manner of deciding: "It is no longer I who live, but Christ who lives in me"

(Gal 2:20). *Qua* confessing believer, one is no longer "one" or "two" but "three" deciding, supposing that the Christian considers himself as included in the second person of the Trinity and that it is in him (in the Son) that he makes the choice to love communally.

One will therefore certainly have the choice, but certainly not any choice about having the choice. And it was, paradoxically, the task of the "philosophy of religious experience" more than of the "philosophy of religion" to have shown the necessity of this. Far from choosing between "this or that" according to the imperative of free will (Descartes) or assuming "what has been chosen" according to the rule of responsibility (Kant), the believer who decides will first understand that he is not choosing *something* but that he himself first *chooses himself choosing*. There is no choice about having the choice, for refusing to choose is already choosing. Thus embarked, we are in a horizon of choice that we cannot refuse, the true choice first amounting to keeping oneself in that dimension of existing rather than deciding for or against a motive at the very heart of that horizon: "What takes precedence in my Either/Or is, then, the ethical," Kierkegaard emphasizes. "Therefore, the point is still not that of *choosing something*; the point is not the reality of *what is chosen* but *the reality of choosing.*"[37] A choice of the choice that will thus become, for Heidegger, the place of *making up for not choosing*, that is, the possibility for the authentic *Dasein* of "deciding for a potentiality-of-being, and making this decision from one's own self."[38]

That the human subject decides, and even decides *himself alone* to decide: this is, however, the quasi-Nietzschean proposition of the *authentic Dasein* that the *believing* or *confessing* subject could not accept for himself. The debate on demythologization has, for its part, largely shown this. If the "kerygma is not first of all the interpretation of a text; it is the announcement of a person," to say it with Rudolf Bultmann, taken up and commented on concerning this point by Paul Ricœur, it is not only because it is suitable to demythologize and return to the idea of a pure faith (regarding which, Ricœur's critique fully bears on this point), but thereby because "the word of God is, not the Bible, but Jesus Christ."[39] With the confession of faith, more than anywhere else, the "decision in view of transformation" entails the "transformation of the concept of decision."[40] Believing *in* God indeed is not believing *that* he is but believing that he is *him* by whom it is given to me to believe. "Certainly no one would believe if he maintained that he 'had' faith, so that nothing was lacking to him, and that he 'could' believe," Karl Barth indicates, as a just witticism.[41] God believes *in me* more than (and in order that) I believe *in him*. Such is the paradoxical structure of the decision of faith, which entails that I become with him what I was not, more than I accomplish only what I have always been called to be. Not, or no longer, contenting itself with Pindar's formula duly taken up by Nietzsche or Heidegger—"Become what you are"—theology reverses its enunciation to enter into a history that involves at least two: "Be what you are becoming" or "*I will be with you*" (Ex 3:12). Such is the in-common of the decision that at least allows it to be decided that one does not decide *all alone*, and that on the human pedestal of philosophical faith or of belief in the world and in others is grafted also the Christian specificity of a belief in God that converts, modifies, and metamorphoses the vision of the structure of the world itself.

God is for us the "cause enabling all operating agents to operate" (Thomas Aquinas), as he is, according to our own formulation this time, "the cause of the decision of all that decides."[42] Far from deciding *without us*, God decides *with us* (Emmanuel). But as he decides with us, we do not cease to be *with him*, his decision preceding and covering the ensemble of our decided acts, such that no anonymity of the call, of the caller, or of the called remains for the confessing believer, himself keeping himself clearly, and in a fully identified way, under the shadow of He who leads him to decide: "It *not only demands* that he should make *a decision* in conformity with it," we must conclude anew with Barth, "but *as it does so*, and as man decides in conformity or contradiction to it, it *presses a decision about man*."[43]

IN PASSING[44]

After having "interpreted" (hermeneutical status) and defined the conditions of the act of "deciding" (existential philosophy), there comes the moment of "crossing" (relation of philosophy and theology). We will cross the river, and we will learn from the other camp what we never knew, or had perhaps forgotten. Rather than thinking, as usual, that we will all the better preserve the disciplines the more we separate them, we maintain, to the contrary, and as a leitmotif, that *the more we theologize, the better we philosophize*. This is true here of the relation between philosophy and theology as of the *Summa Theologica* of Thomas Aquinas. There is no *secunda pars* on "human acts" (philosophy) without a *prima pars* on "the Trinity" and a *tertia pars* on "the Christ" (theology). The theological frames and makes possible the philosophical. It is by knowing *when* and *where* we theologize that we know *when* and *where* we philosophize. And it is not by wanting to "cross the Rubicon" or reach the two banks that one believes that one always bathes in the same river.

FOR A RECOVERY

We do not *first* have any experience of God other than that of man. This is the point of departure of all reflection, in this sense firstly philosophical. The paradox is there. Perhaps it could happen that one would be more a philosopher by being more a theologian. We will find no other beginning, at least in a first movement, than that of man "by himself," the experience of finitude as such, or of the overcast horizon of our own existence. The constant illusions of many philosophers and even theologians, in blissful amazement before the supposed smiles of the newborn, still and always cannot found a theology, or even a philosophy, that would not at the same time and immediately appeal to another virtuality; that of death as such. The tragedy of the human cannot confine itself to the end (the cross) without also inheriting the beginning (birth). There is no bringing into the world without the birth of a world, as I have also shown (*The Metamorphosis of Finitude*). But by *mettant bas*, that is, "whelping," according to an expression that is certainly more animal than properly human, one remains no less *en bas*, that is, "below"; that is to say, taken and confined in a contingency that nothing permits or authorizes one to exceed. The disciples of Emmaus certainly recognized Christ when "he vanished from their sight" (Lk 24:31), according to the extraordinariness of his divinity (phenomenology of the unlimited), but without failing at the same time to mention their "hearts burn[ing]" (Lk 24:32) while they walked with him without recognizing him, and *first* meeting precisely his pure and simple humanity (phenomenology of the limit). The "limited phenomenon" here is not opposed to the "saturated phenomenon," nor the ordinary carnal to the excess of the phenomenon. The second way completes and radicalizes the first. *Nihil potest recipere ultra mensuram suam*—"nothing can be received from beyond one's own measure," as we must acknowledge with Thomas Aquinas. Created in *its limit* on the pattern of his status as a creature, man will in reality do nothing to exceed it, at the risk, conversely, of leaving his rank of man that God has conferred on him. Created and wanted as a "limited being," man will respect and love *his limit*, allowing God to live there without, nevertheless, ever exceeding it.[45]

Three movements thus define the genesis, and the process, of the meeting and the transformation of philosophy by theology. (1) We will first find in Duns Scotus the point of departure for a philosophy anchored in *contingency*, at the origin also of the modern act of philosophizing. If the univocity of the being (*étant*) could not act as the last word on the relation between philosophy and theology, it does, however, mark the prelude to it, or at least the initial bank: "it cannot be shown by natural reason that something supernatural exists in the wayfarer, nor that it is required necessarily for his perfection; nor can even he who possesses it know that it is present in him."[46] (2) It remains that such a beginning could not forbid a possible *overlaying* of the disciplines, in the Christological way of theology going out to meet philosophy this time. Sacred doctrine uses the philosophical sciences "as of the lesser and as handmaidens," as we must acknowledge with Thomas Aquinas, not as "serfs" or "slaves," but as "servants (*ancillas suas*) whom *wisdom has called from the highest point of the city*" (Prov 9:3).[47] Such is the moment of the "tiling," of the crossing of the river or of the meeting where Christ himself rejoins the disciples on the road to Emmaus. (3) There finally comes the moment of *conversion*, or of the *transformation* of philosophy by theology. "If this is said with a view to the creation," emphasizes Hans Urs von Balthasar concerning Saint Bonaventure, "nevertheless it is true first of all in the inner life of God."[48] Trinitarian monadology will here serve as the crucible for the metamorphosis of man in God, or of philosophy in theology, explicitly agreeing this time to cross the Rubicon or to cross over to the other bank. The philosopher who is also a theologian will go so far as to think the Resurrection or the "metamorphosis of finitude" of man into God in order to let himself be converted into Him without denying anything of his own weight of humanity.

Finitude, recovery, and transformation, Duns Scotus, Thomas Aquinas, Bonaventure. Such will be the structure of a "tiling" and of a "conversion" of philosophy by theology, not to merely end philosophy in theology but to recognize that the one (philosophy) could not simply remain "on the porch" of the other (theology). Satisfying itself neither with "philosophies of the threshold" (Blondel, Ricœur, etc.) nor with "philosophies of the leap" (French phenomenology in general), the philosopher who is *at the same time* a theologian will agree to go from the one to the other (from philosophy to theology), understanding their mutual fecundity and the possibility of going to it as also of coming back from it. Crossing the river is also touching the banks, and it is by our daring to accomplish this "great crossing" that the two banks that are most often ignored, or at the very least not reciprocally shared, will be joined.

TO EACH HIS WAY

Thinking such a "tiling and conversion of philosophy by theology" will not prevent philosophy and theology from each having their way, and moreover, from respecting their order; quite the contrary. The more we theologize, the better we philosophize, as I have said. What distinguishes philosophy and theology will be maintained, in this sense and paradoxically, less in the nature of the objects than in the mode of arriving at them. Their distance will here be given as a difference in "manners" rather than in "matter."

First, from the point of view of the *point of departure*, it is clear that the two disciplines will not go in the same direction, or even in opposite directions: "problem of facticity—most radical phenomenology, which begins 'from below,'" as Heidegger reminds us.[49] There is no other beginning, therefore, than "the human per se" or "finitude as such" for philosophy. "Nothing human is alien to me," as Terence reminds us. Such will be the philosopher's avowal and opinion [*aveu et avis*], first anchored in our pure and simple humanity. Second, from the point of view of the *mode of pro-*

ceeding, philosophy will follow a heuristic way whereas the theologian will take the didactic way. What is said "at the beginning" regarding philosophy will not necessarily be the same "at the end." As in Descartes' *Meditations*, the doubt posited at the beginning (first meditation) will be lifted at the end (second and sixth meditations). Or also, and to follow my own approach, the finitude discovered *ab initio* in the effigy of man (*The Guide of Gethsemane*) will be "transformed" or "metamorphosed" *in fine* into the figure of the God-man (*The Metamorphosis of Finitude*). There where theology, most often the heir of the German method of the *expositio* (Barth, Bultmann, Moltmann, Kasper, Rahner, Balthasar, etc.), prefers the didactic exposition following the order of teaching, philosophy, in particular in the wake of the Cartesian path, will take the heuristic way of the search, even if it means accepting and even seeking transformations at the end that were not posited at the start. Finally, from the point of view of the *status of the object* to be analyzed, the philosopher will take as "possible" what the theologian will recognize as "actual." The Incarnation, the Eucharist or the Resurrection, being revealed, will not be "believed" by the philosopher, except in the framework of theology itself. As for *the object itself*, it is there, paradoxically, that philosophy and theology differ the least. The same object can indeed be aimed at diversely starting from different disciplines. Liturgy, prayer, and even the Eucharist or the Incarnation, do not belong exclusively to theology. Phenomenology in particular will be able to *describe* what theology exposes and believes. Just as the anthropological, the aesthetic, or the literary could not be excluded from the philosophical field, no more could the religious be exempted from it. No reason, except a badly understood secularity, can paralyze the theological within the only discipline that bears its name, at the risk, conversely, of holding for null and void any contribution that did not come from it; in particular for what concerns the question of God.

In short, and one will have understood this, there where, formerly, one distinguished the disciplines by their "matter," we will now mark their diversity by their "manners." The approach, more than the object itself, is different. Not that there is no proper content of philosophy (man), as also of theology (God), but that Christianity maintains the extremes together, in Him who is the "point of junction" and likewise also the "knot" (the God-man). Each person certainly has his way, on the sole condition of recognizing this "difference between the ways" as so many possible, and different, aims directed on the same object. A sort of eidetic or imaginative *variation* here operates on the object, such that the apprehension of the thing counts at least as much, if not more, than the thing itself. The existence of God "in himself" (*in se*) will have no, or little, importance, if it is not also existence for me, or "for us" (*pro nobis*). The famous "proofs" or, better, the "ways" of Thomas Aquinas do not have as their goal to show that *God is* (the ontological argument) but rather to show *how to access* what he is (cosmological ways)—in which they remain today entirely current: "Therefore I say that this proposition, 'God exists,' *of itself is self-evident,* for the predicate is the same as the subject. . . . Because we do not know the essence of God, this proposition is not *self-evident to us,* but needs to be demonstrated by things that are *more known to us,* though less known in their nature," namely, by the *works* of God.[50]

ON METAPHYSICS

The "link" here made between philosophy and theology will, in this sense, make the aforementioned hypothesis of onto-theology misfire. Apart from the fact that such a model does not exist (unless in the corpus of Thomas of Erfurt, pseudo Duns Scotus, to whom Martin Heidegger devoted his qualifying thesis in 1915), it has in reality no other goal than to disqualify the theological discipline itself in order to prefer to it a discourse supposedly "pure" of all contamination by tradition. French phenomenology, including that of Catholic inspiration, paradoxically shares with Protestant theology that ideal of a "pure faith" or of a "pure discourse," free of all overlaying between the orders. Everything happens as if the *theo*-logical, as a discourse *of* God, had nothing to do with the theo-*logical* as a discourse *about* God, as if all natural theology should be de facto disqualified in the name of an absolute of directly given relation. The rupture between the orders—order of the "flesh," order of the "spirit," order of "charity"—certainly has enough to fascinate. Such an interpretation of the Pascalian division does not, however, do justice to the Christological possibility of unifying the orders, in Him who however does not denigrate anything that is contrary, and even foreign, to him. Moreover, nothing, even in Pascal, ensures that what is a "rupture" cannot also be interpreted here in terms of a "figure," leading us to believe and to think that an order can announce another order rather than simply being opposed to it: "the infinite distance between bodies and minds is a figure of the infinitely more infinite distance between minds and charity," as we must specify with the philosopher of Port-Royal.[51]

The "overtaking of metaphysics" is thus somewhat overtaken; that is the least one can say. Husserl himself had foreseen its blunder, before Heidegger accomplished its aim: "Finally, lest any misunderstanding arise, I would point out that . . . phenomenology indeed *excludes every naïve metaphysics* that operates with absurd things in themselves, but *does not exclude metaphysics as such.*"[52] It remains that we will not today return, conversely, *toward* metaphysics *against* phenomenology, as phenomenology in its day wanted to liberate itself from metaphysics. Rebounds are also backlashes. A co-penetration and transformation of the fields will here be required, at least if we are not to remain with the simple vis-à-vis that can only rigidify, and also even sterilize. Ceasing to send the matters away equal, back-to-back—and, as it happens here, "metaphysics" and "phenomenology"; we will accept, if not that they co-penetrate each other, at least that they return to each other and both look at each other, recognizing thereby that they are not so foreign to each other as we have wanted to believe, and also have thought.

Metaphysics as a "crossing of the physical or of nature (*meta-phusis*)," such is therefore the meaning of the term that it is now suitable to claim, rather than disqualifying it from all permanence. Such a "trek" as the *crossing of nature* does not belong only to man, even though it is first his proper task to perform. God also makes himself its heir, and even its *Passeur*, that is, its Guide, Ferryman, or Crosser, by whom our burden is taken on board to be transported "with him." *Suffering [pâtissant]* from the world (*phusis*) to *pass [passer]* it to the Father (*meta*), the Son accomplishes in himself this same "breach," insisting not only on accompanying us on it but also on carrying us on it, while letting us be transformed this time. The crossing of the ford, precisely in "meta-physics," is not a *leap into a beyond* but a *transformation of our here below*, and a *recognition of our own weight*.

"Finally theology," the die has therefore been cast—*alea iacta est*. It is right to recognize this. We can here heave a "sigh of relief." The "great crossing" that goes from philosophy to theology, and vice versa, ensures their mutual fecundity, as well as the possibility of their counterblow. By redefining the conditions of "interpreting," unto calling for a so-called Catholic hermeneutic of the "body and the voice," by finding the sense of the act of "deciding" unto founding the "philosophy of religious experience" in the existentiality of a "common belief," and by claiming the act of "crossing" as an "overlaying and a conversion" of the relation between philosophy and theology unto the definition of "metaphysics" as a "crossing of the world or of the *phusis*," it is the entire structure of the stony stare in which the disciplines have been locked that I wished to question here. It does not suffice to look at each other, nor even to appreciate each other, nor even to offer one's own expertise, to truly fertilize each other. The mutuality of the encounter is the condition of any true transformation. Thus it is for that "being in common" of man and God that causes one to advance all the more "with uncovered face" as one is freer to not, or no longer, calculate: "Philosophy is the *servant of theology*—Mary is indeed the servant of the Lord" (Lk 1:38), as we must recognize with Charles Péguy. "But may the servant *not pick a fight* with the mistress and may the mistress *not reject* the servant, for a stranger would soon come who would bring them *quickly to agreement*."[53]

NOTES

1. This text was translated from French by Sarah Horton.

2. Gottfried W. Leibnitz, "Discourse on Metaphysics," in *Philosophical Essays*, translated by Roger Ariew and Daniel Garber (Indianapolis: Hackett, 1989), 45.

3. Emmanuel Falque, *The Metamorphosis of Finitude*, translated by George Hughes (New York: Fordham University Press, 2012); *The Wedding Feast of the Lamb*, translated by George Hughes (New York: Fordham University Press, 2016); and *The Guide of Gethsemane*, translated by George Hughes (New York: Fordham University Press, 2019).

4. Gregory the Great, "Homily VII," in Book I of *The Homilies of Saint Gregory the Great on the Book of the Prophet Ezekiel*, translated by Theodosia Tomkinson and Juliana Cownie (Etna: Center for Traditionalist Orthodox Studies, 1990).

5. Paul Claudel, *The Essence of the Bible*, translated by Wade Baskin (New York: Philosophical Library, 1957), 33.

6. Emmanuel Levinas, "Is Ontology Fundamental?" in *Entre Nous: Thinking-of-the-Other*, translated by Michael B. Smith (London: Continuum, 2006), 1–10.

7. Paul Ricœur, *The Conflict of Interpretations: Essays in Hermeneutics*, edited by Don Ihde (Evanston, IL: Northwestern University Press, 1974), 10.

8. Emmanuel Levinas, *Beyond the Verse: Talmudic Readings and Lectures*, translated by Gary D. Mole (London: Athlone Press, 1994), x and 121, respectively.

9. Vatican Council II, *Decree on the Ministry and Life of Priests: Presbyterorum ordinis*, no. 18, in *Documents of the Second Vatican Council* (http://www.vatican.va/archive/hist_councils/ii_vatican_council/documents/vat-ii_decree_19651207_presbyterorum-ordinis_en.html).

10. This formula is cited and translated by P. Beauchamp, "Sens de l'Ecriture," in *Dictionnaire critique de théologie*, edited by Jean-Yves Lacoste (Paris: PUF, 1988), 1087. English translation taken from Emmanuel Falque, *Crossing the Rubicon*, translated by Reuben Shank (New York: Fordham University Press, 2016), 32.

11. Paul Ricœur, *From Text to Action: Essays in Hermeneutics, II*, translated by Kathleen Blamey and John B. Thompson (Evanston, IL: Northwestern University Press, 1991), 85.

12. Ricœur, *From Text to Action*, 83–84.

13. Ricœur, *From Text to Action*, 84–86.

14. Ricœur, *From Text to Action*, 87–88 (emphasis added).

15. Ricœur, *From Text to Action*, 87.

16. Claudel, *Essence of the Bible*, 34.

17. Claudel, *Essence of the Bible*, 10.

18. All Scriptural quotations are from the English Standard Version (ESV) unless otherwise noted (translator's note).

19. Jean-Louis Chrétien, *Under the Gaze of the Bible*, translated by John Marson Dunaway (New York: Fordham University Press, 2015), 6–22.

20. Bonaventure, *Collations on the Six Days*, translated by Jose de Vinck, Works of Bonaventure 5 (Quincy, MA: Fransciscan Press, 1995), bk. XIII, §12, v. 390.

21. Hugh of Saint-Victor, "La parole de Dieu," in *Six opuscules spirituels*, Sources Chrétiennes, 155, translated by Roger Baron (Paris: Cerf, 1969), 63. English translation taken from Falque, *Crossing the Rubicon*, 54.

22. Hugh of Saint-Victor, "La parole de Dieu," 63. English translation taken from Falque, *Crossing the Rubicon*, 54.

23. I here diverge slightly from the ESV, writing "great voice" rather than "loud voice" to better accord with the original French text (translator's note).

24. Aristotle, *De interpretatione* 1.16a3-5, in *The Complete Works of Aristotle: The Revised Oxford Translation*, edited by Jonathan Barnes, Bollingen Series (Princeton, NJ: Princeton University Press, 1984), 1–25.

25. Saint Augustine, *Discours sur les Psaumes*, vol. 2, (Paris: Cerf, 2007), Ps. 85, 62 (translation modified). [I have translated this quotation following Falque's French wording; the quotation can be found in English, with a different wording, in St. Augustine, "Psalm LXXXVI," in *On the Psalms*, translated by J. E. Tweed in *Nicene and Post-Nicene Fathers*, edited by Philip Schaff, First Series (Buffalo, NY: Christian Literature, 1888), 410 (translator's note).]

26. Blaise Pascal, *Pensées*, edited and translated by Roger Ariew (Indianapolis: Hackett, 2004), 212. [I have modified this translation, rendering *embarqué* as "embarked" rather than as "committed" for consistency with the naval metaphor in Falque's next sentence (translator's note).]

27. Maurice Merleau-Ponty, *The Visible and the Invisible*, translated by Alphonso Lingis (Evanston, IL: Northwestern University Press, 1969), 35 and 3, editor note 1, respectively. [Translation of the footnote modified to follow Falque's wording (translator's note).]

28. Charles Péguy, "Note conjointe sur M. Descartes," in *Œuvres en prose complètes* (Paris: Pléiade, Gallimard, 1992), 1280. English translation taken from Falque, *Crossing the Rubicon*, 80.

29. Edmund Husserl, *Experience and Judgment*, translated by James Spencer Churchill and Karl Ameriks (Evanston, IL: Northwestern University Press, 1973), 30.

30. Ludwig Wittgenstein, *On Certainty*, edited by G. E. M. Anscombe and Georg Henrik von Wright, translated by Denis Paul and G. E. M. Anscombe (New York: Harper and Row, 1972), 60.

31. Maurice Merleau-Ponty, "La nature ou le monde du silence," in *Maurice Merleau-Ponty, La nature ou le monde du silence*, edited by Emmanuel de Saint-Aubert (Paris: Hemann, 2008), 53 (emphasis added). English translation taken from Falque, *Crossing the Rubicon*, 96.

32. Edmund Husserl, *Méditations cartésiennes* (Paris: Vrin, 1980), §16, 33. English translation taken from Emmanuel Falque, *Crossing the Rubicon*, 96.

33. Emmanuel Levinas, *Existence and Existents*, translated by Alphonso Lingis (The Hague: Nijhoff, 1978), 61.

34. Henri Duméry, *Critique et religion, Problèmes et méthodes en philosophie de la religion* (Paris: SEDES, 1957), 18 (emphasis added). English translation taken from Falque, *Crossing the Rubicon*, 104.

35. Martin Heidegger, *Phenomenology of Religious Life*, translated by Matthias Frisch and Jennifer Anna Gosetti-Ferencei (Bloomington: Indiana University Press, 2010), 7 (emphasis added).

36. Heidegger, *Phenomenology of Religious Life*, 237.

37. Soren Kierkegaard, *Kierkegaard's Writings: Either/Or*, Part II, translated by Howard V. Hong and Edna H. Hong (Princeton, NJ: Princeton University Press, 1987), 176 (emphasis added).

38. Martin Heidegger, *Being and Time*, translated by Joan Stambaugh (Albany: State University of New York Press, 2010), 248.

39. Ricœur, *The Conflict of Interpretations*, 382.

40. Claude Romano, *Event and Time*, translated by Stephen E. Lewis (New York: Fordham University Press, 2014), 188. This is a formula pronounced concerning birth but which applies even more, in my eyes, to the act of faith.

41. Karl Barth, *Evangelical Theology: An Introduction*, translated by Grover Foley (Grand Rapids, MI: W.B. Eerdmans Publishing Co., 1979), 104.

42. Thomas Aquinas, *Summa contra Gentiles: On the Truth of the Catholic Faith*, book 3, *Providence*, Part I, translated by Vernon J. Bourke (Garden City: Doubleday, 1956), 220.

43. Karl Barth, *Church Dogmatics* II, edited by G. W. Bromley and T. F. Torrance, translated by G. T. Thompson and Harold Knight (Edinburgh: T&T Clark, 1957), 632 (emphasis added).

44. The French expression is *En passant*, which could also be rendered as "While crossing." The titular phrase "Crossing the Rubicon" is *Passer le Rubicon* (translator's note).

45. Thomas Aquinas, *Supra sententiorum* I. d.8 q.1 a.2 s.c.2; English translation taken from Emmanuel Falque, *Crossing the Rubicon*, 146. As for the two complementary interpretations proposed here (in particular concerning the episode of the disciples on the road to Emmaus), I refer to Jean-Luc Marion, *Prolegomena to Charity*, translated by Stephen E. Lewis (New York: Fordham University Press, 2002), 127–36; as well as to my *The Metamorphosis of Finitude*, 19–20.

46. J. Duns Scotus, "Prologue of the Ordinatio," translated by Peter L. P. Simpson (unpublished manuscript, December 2012), 9, http://www.aristotelophile.com/Books/Translations/

Scotus%20Prologue.pdf. [The English translation does not include the final clause of the French ("nor can"), so that portion of the quotation is my own translation (translator's note).]

47. Thomas Aquinas, "Whether Sacred Doctrine is Nobler than Other Sciences?" *Summa theologica* Ia. q.1 a.5 ad.2 and sed contra (Christian Classics Ethereal Library), 10–11. The final citation follows the phrasing of Falque, *Crossing the Rubicon*, 104.

48. Hans Urs von Balthasar, *The Glory of the Lord: A Theological Aesthetics; Studies in Theological Style: Clerical Styles*, edited by John Riches, translated by Andrew Louth, Francis McDonagh, and Brian McNeil (San Francisco: Ignatius Press, 1984), 290.

49. Martin Heidegger, *Phenomenological Interpretations of Aristotle*, translated by Richard Rojcewicz (Bloomington: Indiana University Press, 2001), 146.

50. Thomas Aquinas, *Summa theologica*, I.a., q.2, a.1, resp. 23 (emphasis added).

51. Pascal, *Pensées*, 92.

52. Edmund Husserl, *Cartesian Meditations: An Introduction to Phenomology*, translated by D. Cairns (The Hague: Nijhoff, 1960), 156.

53. Charles Péguy, "Note conjointe sur M. Descartes," in *Œuvres en prose completes*, 1458 (emphasis added). English translation taken from Falque, *Crossing the Rubicon*, xi.

Chapter Two

Where Is the Philosophical/Theological Rubicon?

Toward a Radical Rethinking of "Religion"

Bruce Ellis Benson

No one knows where exactly the famed Rubicon over which Julius Caesar crossed in 49 BCE stands today—or if it even exists. In 1933, as a way of legitimizing his power by linking himself to the power of ancient Rome, the dictator Mussolini decreed that the Fiumicino River would henceforth be known as the Rubicon. As it turns out, there are two other rivers in the area of the "original" Rubicon that have been proposed as alternatives. Yet the area in which all of them lie has a long history of flooding, meaning that the Rubicon has a long history of changing its course over time. Perhaps we might say that there has never been "the" Rubicon; instead, there have been many Rubicons, none of which can claim priority and all of which are subject to change. We need not cite Heraclitus to realize that one can never step into the same Rubicon twice.

Geography aside, one usually invokes the phrase "crossing the Rubicon" to indicate a crucial decision. As the story goes, in crossing the Rubicon, Caesar was crossing into Italy—foreign territory. That made the traversal momentous. From Suetonius, we get the words that Caesar was supposed to have uttered—*iacta alea est* (usually cited as *alea iacta est*): "the dice have been thrown" or "the die is cast." Although it is clear that Caesar would have had to cross whatever "Rubicon" would have existed in his day, that he said these words or grasped the true significance of his act is unclear; there is no real evidence either way. In any case, the very idea of "crossing the Rubicon" has to do with a historical event or situation that dictates the course of subsequent history. It is an event that cannot be undone. Nothing will ever be the same again.

It is between these seemingly contradictory aspects—the ever-evolving path of the Rubicon and the finality of its crossing—that Emmanuel Falque's *Crossing the Rubicon* must be situated. On the one hand, the very idea of "the" Rubicon is problematic at best and, in the end, is more like an ideal in the Kantian sense. Looking forward, it is a concept that guides our thinking even though it is not grasped and cannot ever be reached. Looking backward, it is a past that was never present. The Rubicon is a kind of ideal object that symbolizes decisions of earth-shattering proportions rather than any actual place. That ideal object simply does not "correspond" to any actual states of affairs, because the contours of the Rubicon are continually being reshaped. Although Husserl never admits that ideal objects can change (they come into being but, once they exist, they never vary), the Rubicon as ideal object has no stability. Where is the Rubicon? One never knows exactly. On the other hand, "crossing" has a "once-and-for-all" sort of quality. Unlike the Rubicon itself, the crossing of it cannot be subsequently changed. Once one has crossed over, there is no reversal possible. Whereas the Rubicon as ideal object has a continually shifting identity, the historical crossing is part of the past. It is, as American slang would have it, "one and done."

So why does Emmanuel Falque appropriate such a famous phrase? He reminds us that, in crossing the Rubicon, Caesar was breaking Roman Senate laws, which forbade passage to Italy. Once one breaks the law, one becomes a lawbreaker. However, the territory that Falque has in mind is neither Roman nor Italian but *French*. On his map, the Rubicon is Le Jardin du Luxembourg and what it separates is the religious L'institut Catholique de Paris (ICP) from the atheistic Sorbonne. Although one traverses just over a kilometer to get from one to the other, each kingdom has its own respective set of "laws." Of course, here is one way in which the analogy breaks down. That particular distance can be traversed over and over; there is absolutely no sense in which it is a one-time, life-altering decision. In that respect, Falque is talking about something quite different from the usual meaning of the phrase, and he is not unaware of that. Indeed, he speaks of "a two-way crossing of the Rubicon—'there and back again.'"[1] One of the central tenets of the text is that this distance must be crossed over and over again, since philosophy and theology have much to learn from one another. On this point—as on so many of the points that Falque makes—I completely agree. The openness of each "side" to the other is to be welcomed, for it signals a welcome on both sides.

Yet the analogy breaks down in another way, precisely along the lines of the geography of the Rubicon. If we can say that ICP represents theism (and, as I will later argue, religion), then the Sorbonne is a metonymy for philosophy and thus atheism. Falque is quite attentive to the way in which these "sides" get labeled. He rightly rejects any neat distinctions between such binaries as "faith" and "reason" or "belief" and "unbelief." Indeed, Falque's writing has a kind of sophistication about it that is rarely found on either side of the divide. Falque does not caricature these worlds in such simplistic terms as "those with a God delusion" versus "the infidels." What he argues is that these worlds interpenetrate each other and that, at least in principal, that interpenetration is healthy and life-giving to both. The result is that locating the philosophical/theological Rubicon is even more difficult than locating the historical one.

In the epilogue to his *discourse on method* (cleverly titled "Epilogue: And Then . . . ?"), Falque tells us that "to cross the Rubicon is not to seek combat but to advance or orient thought otherwise."[2] That strikes me as a most worthy goal, and Falque does a great deal of the heavy lifting to get us there. In what follows, my goal is the same as Falque's, though I suggest a different way of conceiving the "problem" of the two "sides." My goal is to think with and also beyond Falque. While he gives us a vast array of tools to think about the boundaries between philosophy and theology, in what follows I attempt to put in question exactly how we should think about their differences. My contention is that—ultimately—the discussion is not really about faith and religion or belief and unbelief but about *power*.

There are some problems with Falque's account. The first is that he assumes a religious homogeneity. While Falque has an extended discussion of the Protestant Ricœur, he suggests that Ricœur's hermeneutics have "had a greater impact in Catholicism."[3] Falque may well be correct in saying that. Yet he shows remarkably little concern for the multiplicity that is found in world Christianity—which is a splintered, disunified phenomenon if ever there was one. To be sure, in France one can assume that the vast majority of Christians are Roman Catholics and, as a text written for a French reader, that assumption is completely excusable. However, the neat boundaries that Falque sets up between the ICP and the Sorbonne are only possible because the choice is, in effect, "Catholic or non-Catholic." As we will see much later in this chapter, one can only understand Christianity as a "religion" precisely *because* of these religious differences. Or one might simply say that these differences in belief are precisely what have made Christianity into a religion. The second problem is that Falque assumes a philosophical homogeneity. When Falque speaks of "philosophy," he is really speaking of "phenomenology." While one might argue that phenomenology has triumphed philosophically in France (which is, at best, a contentious claim), it is clearly a minority view in the rest of the philosophical world. So it is problematic at best to assume that intellectual space can be carved up by way of drawing a boundary between theology and phenomenology. Given the limitations of space, though, I will not be able to address this problem here.

Instead, my concern here will be with two aspects that Falque never even considers. The first is that the distinction between theology and philosophy is *not* inevitable; it is merely a historical occurrence, one that might never have happened apart from certain developments in Christianity itself. The second is that, while Falque uses various forms of the term "religion," he never considers *why* we even speak in such terms as "religious" versus "non-religious." The reality is that at one time, the distinction that to us seems so obvious simply did not exist. What is at stake—as Mussolini realized—is *power*. Who has the power over whom? Before whom must one bow down? Who has the last word? The reality is that, whether one is in Paris or Jerusalem, in our current intellectual framework the side of philosophy/atheism/unbelieving has considerably more power than the side of theology/theism/believing. When one speaks of two "sides," one is really talking about a power struggle. Of course, the power differential between these two sides is very much like the historical Rubicon: it has always been shifting and any new flood could change its location. In ancient Greece, there simply was no difference between the two: theology was part of philosophy. We might want to say that, if anything, philosophy had the upper hand. Yet even to speak in such a way would be highly anachronistic, because there was no meaningful distinction between the two—which were seen as *one*. In medieval Europe, theology came to be elevated as the queen of the sciences, and philosophy was lowered to become merely her handmaiden. In the modern period inaugurated by the Enlightenment, the situation was drastically reversed: theology falls into disrepute, having been eclipsed in power and prestige by philosophy. The situation today, then, is that philosophy and theology are separated in such a way that to cross from one to the other requires crossing certain boundaries. Each discipline has its own rules or laws. As Falque puts it, "the difference between philosophy and theology consists less in *what is studied* (the object), than in their specific *points of departure* (from below or above), their proper *ways of proceeding* (heuristically or didactically), and the *status* of the objects analyzed."[4] Philosophy and theology often—perhaps even "mostly"—talk about the same things; they just talk about them in different ways. But the key word here is "proper"; what is proper to philosophy versus proper to theology? Or, more bluntly put, which idea of "proper" is more powerful?

MAPPING THE TERRAIN

One wonderful thing about philosophical modernity—the kind that begins roughly with Descartes and comes to something like an end in the twentieth century—is that one knew where one stood. Science was believed (and still is by many) to be the one source of true knowledge. Everything else had to bow before it in one way or another. We only need to remember the huge dominance (at least in English-speaking countries) of logical positivism. As long as logical positivism ruled philosophy, philosophy of religion was suspect. Indeed, even ethical judgments were put into question by the position known as "ethical emotivism," the view that ethical statements are not even worthy of the designation "statement" and instead were simply expressions of one's emotions. For logical positivists, only claims that are tautologically true or empirically verifiable have the right to be called "statements." Such an assertion gave the logical positivists *a great deal of power*. They did not even have to denounce religious and ethical claims as untrue: they could simply designate them expressions of emotion that had no right to be taken seriously.

Although it took quite some time, philosophers finally realized that this statement could not pass its own test. The idea that something was only true tautologically or empirically was itself neither true by tautology nor by empirical verification. As a result, logical positivism came to be seen as the fraud that it was. The idea that scientific knowledge is the only true knowledge is less prevalent today, yet it is still the default mode of many people. The gradual loss of the privilege of science over everything else, though, has made many things possible that had seemed unthinkable fifty years ago. For instance, it is no coincidence that the Society of Christian Philosophers (largely an organization of analytic philosophers—that is, philosophers who are not phenomenologists—with about one thousand members) was founded in 1978, precisely at the time logical positivism was on its last legs. As philosophers rediscovered more pre-modern ways of thinking, studying medieval philosophy suddenly got much more interesting. Not too surprisingly, though, many thinkers decried the loss of the modern consensus for it had provided a map on which everyone could agree. In that paradigm, religious believers were clearly seen as inferior to "secular" thinkers (who supposedly start with no presuppositions). Even Christians in the modern era adapted to the times and cast their defense for their "faith" in typically modern ways—proofs, evidence, etc. Whether we should call the period in which we are living as "postmodern" depends upon what exactly that connotes. But such a debate is merely one over terminology, not substance.

Perhaps this is too strong a statement, but I think Falque's book on *Crossing the Rubicon* could not have been written in the age of modernity. Indeed, while many have found the "return of religion" or the "theological turn in phenomenology" to be a surprise, my reaction is: *mais oui, bien sûr*! Having been dismissed for so long as simply superstition, suddenly thinking as a religious believer became possible—in some cases, even quite respectable. For instance, Alvin Plantinga has long said that starting with the belief that there is no God is in no way more "neutral" than starting with the belief that there is a God: either starting point is a *choice*.[5] Falque speaks of "impossible neutrality" or "the prejudice of the absence of prejudices."[6] The point here is not that you can simply start with any beliefs you like but that there is no neutral starting point. Despite all pretensions to the contrary, philosophy, theology, biology, and every other "-ology" have never been presupposition-free. Further, everything (as Derrida reminds us)[7] has its own set of beliefs. Some of these can be proven but others of them are simply "prejudices." R. G. Collingwood terms these "absolute presuppositions," by which he meant the building blocks of thought or things that pretty much everyone takes to be true. As he puts it, "absolute presuppositions are not verifiable. This does not mean that we should like to verify them but are not able to; it means that the idea of verification is an idea which does not apply to them."[8] Of course, Gadamer, who almost singlehandedly rehabilitated the idea of "prejudice," hardly thinks that anyone is simply entitled to their prejudices without questioning them. He writes: "True prejudices must still finally be justified by rational knowledge," though he goes on to say "even though the task can never be fully completed."[9] His point is that there is no way of simply getting rid of them (which was the opposite of one of the main points of logical positivism—that you *could* and *should* get rid of them).

More fundamentally, Falque thinks that philosophy and theology, while different, are complementary. This means that the distance between the ICP and the Sorbonne is not quite so wide after all. "Theologians make a point of reminding philosophers that they incessantly surpass the boundaries set by reason," says Falque. While he does not put it this way, we might say that many things we believe to be "common sense" or obviously true are things we really do not understand well. We have been speaking of "matter" for centuries, but what exactly is it? Is there really such a thing as a "force" of gravity or a "law" of physics or is this simply our way of talking about the world? Even though theology and philosophy differ in terms of such things as how they proceed and the methods used, they are not really separable in any strong sense. As Falque puts it, "those who believe that they should still engage in the battle between philosophy and theology should now see that this clash would forever be sterile."[10] Philosophy helps us to understand theology: one need only think of how the formulation of the Trinity is founded upon Greek concepts. The task for theologians, according to Falque, is that they find new ways of formulating theological beliefs that speak to contemporaries.

WE ARE ALL BELIEVERS

The day after the terrorist attacks on 9/11, the headline of *Le Monde* read: "Nous sommes tous américains." Falque takes up a somewhat similar refrain by pointing out that we are all believers. At the center of *Crossing the*

Rubicon is a section titled "Deciding." The first subsection is titled "Always Believing." Falque cites the challenge, in effect, issued by Pascal: you can either believe or not believe. You have a choice. Yet this choice is based on what Falque calls the "non-choice," the pressure of having to choose even if one does not wish to do so. Yet this non-choice is even more basic than that in believing in God. For, as Husserl reminds us, we always (already) have an *Urdoxa* or *Urglaube* concerning the world, something like an absolutely basic belief that the world is there and that our senses are trustworthy.[11] Even to question the trustworthiness of the senses is to assume their original trustworthiness (or else such questioning would be utterly futile). Falque quotes Husserl as saying "an actual world always precedes cognitive activity as its universal ground, and this means first of all a ground of universal passive belief."[12] This *Urglaube* or primal belief is central to human existence. What I find particularly interesting about this section is that Falque's attention is really turned in a very different direction than the hermeneutics of suspicion. Of course, given the ubiquity of "fake news" and the seeming possibility of people creating and living in alternative realities, one might think that a "hermeneutics of suspicion" is precisely what we need now. But one can (I think quite rightly) counter that, to a great extent, it is suspicion gone wild that has led to this state of affairs. We forget that, even for the people with whom we most disagree, our shared beliefs—our basic *Urglauben*—far outweigh our differences. Instead, we focus on what separates us, and then wonder why we cannot have any meaningful dialogue. Admittedly, it is hard in this environment of distrust for people (on whatever side) to see that their unity outweighs their disunity. Yet Falque reminds us that belief—of a simple ordinary human sort—is much more basic than disbelief. Even to disbelieve is always already to believe. He puts this very forcefully when he writes: "The idea of an original faith in the world, or rather trust in the belief that I have of the world, makes the world paradoxically the highest and the most certain of truths in an originary attitude of trust rather than mistrust."[13] Thus, one can speak of a "philosophical faith," and Falque goes on to say that "religious faith can only rest upon philosophical faith." Before we ever get to a specific belief like a belief in God, we have a fundamental belief that there is a world and that we are part of it.

If Falque is right, then the difference between the believer and the "non-believer" is already problematic. First, if we are all believers, then this terminology is not particularly helpful (and, often, terminology like "believer" and "non-believer" is simply used as a cudgel against the people we do not like). It ends up being a kind of intellectual tribalism. Second, believing is not something that one does simply on one's own. We are always part of a community of believers, whether this be a theological, philosophical, or scientific community. After all, to "believe" in the scientific method is not to believe in something that can be proven to be true, except by arguing that it produces good results. However, the exact contours of what counts as "good results" are already assumed by anyone who believes in the scientific method. I suspect that believers of any sort think that their respective beliefs produce good results and so have been proven to be right. Similarly, if one believes in the scientific method, then the only way one might put it into question is by *using* it. Third, it is not always clear the extent to which one believes *anything*. Belief and doubt are two sides of one coin. For instance, one can be a religious believer and still have doubts about major aspects of whatever faith is in question. Many Christian churches make the saying of the Nicene Creed a part of their liturgy. Does everyone who says this always believe every line? That would be hard to believe. Indeed, I suspect that the experience of many who say these lines is often "but what does this even mean?" let alone whether one believes it. The dialectic between faith and doubt is such that one is never clearly in the one and not the other. If anything, the "formula" of faith (if there *are* any formulas) is that of the father whose child Jesus heals and who says "Lord, I believe; help thou my unbelief" (Mk 9:24). Belief mingled with disbelief. Or perhaps, it is disbelief mingled with belief.

This aspect of lack of "certitude" extends equally to "non-believers," as even atheists can have doubts. The self-identified atheist Thomas Nagel talks of his "fear" of religion, which he distinguishes from "hostility" toward any particular organized religion from "fear of religion itself." He goes on: "I speak from experience, being strongly subject to this fear myself: I want atheism to be true and am made uneasy by the fact that some of the most intelligent and well-informed people I know are religious believers. It is not just that I do not believe in God and, naturally, hope that I'm right in my belief. It's that I hope there is no God! I do not want there to be a God; I do not want the universe to be like that."[14] Of course, one need only to Google this quote and discover that it comes up on many conservative Christian websites. "Ha!"—one can hear them saying: so the atheists are not always convinced! But this is surely attending to the speck in the eye of the atheist and forgetting the beam in the eye of the theist. The reality of human existence is that we can never be absolutely certain about anything and that, if we are thinking and observing beings (as opposed to closing one's eyes and ignoring any new incoming information), our minds are constantly changing about even quite basic and foundational matters.

Falque (rightly) wants to move away from any kind of dialogue between philosophy and theology that is designed to "convert" the other. He also wishes to get rid of unhelpful stereotypes such as "infidels" versus "believers." Instead, philosophy can learn from theology and theology can learn from philosophy. In our time, theologians do much more in the way of description in their theology than in the past. And philosophers have just as much right to ask questions about theological or holy things. One doesn't have to be a believer in order to have something to say on these topics. So Falque suggests a "philosophy of the threshold," one that gets beyond the model "where the philosopher *opens* and the theologian *fills*."[15] After saying many positive things about Ricœur's contribution, Falque claims that he only opens the threshold, leaving it to theologians to fill in the void. Even Marion, says Falque, keeps his theological texts separate from his philosophical ones. In order to prove his point, he turns to the classic distinction Pascal makes between the "God of the philosophers" and the "God of Abraham, God of Isaac, and God of Jacob." Falque notes that, if one studies the distinction Pascal is trying to make, it is not completely clear that there really is a difference here such that one could label one as true God and the other as an onto-theological God.

"The more we theologize, the better we philosophize," says Falque and comes to a section toward the end of the book with that very name.[16] That statement about theologizing and philosophizing should "serve as the leitmotiv for this liberated theology."[17] Falque calls it the principle of proportionality. He makes it clear that crossing the Rubicon is not a one-way, one-off sort of thing. Instead, it needs to be continually crossed and recrossed. Falque clearly self-identifies as a philosopher. He is not interested in blurring the boundaries between philosophy and theology so that they no longer have their respective identities. But he believes that the time for "conquest" is past and now is the time for a generous spirit on both sides. In contrast to "claims of a liberation of philosophy by theology," Falque proposes a liberation of theology by philosophy that provides an analysis of religious experience. This does not mean that philosophy now becomes simply ancillary to theology. Instead, the goal is to "let themselves be transformed—each by the other." More specifically, he goes on to say that "the [philosopher] will teach the [theologian] about the human journey. The [theologian] will make the [philosopher] see that he cannot refuse to open himself—upon a decision, of course—to the transcendence of the One who comes to 'metamorphose' everything."[18]

RETHINKING RELIGION

Even though Falque moves the conversation between theology and philosophy along to a great degree, I think his account fundamentally overlooks a concept that he mentions more than once but never analyzes: namely, what "religion" is. For instance, he makes a distinction between "philosophical faith" and "religious faith," but nowhere does he pause to think about what religion actually means or how exactly it contrasts with philosophy. On his account, the difference between philosophical faith and religious faith is fleshed out entirely in terms of things one believes. One might respond that it is not too surprising that a philosopher would lay out a conception of religious faith as largely as matter of *belief*. The question, though, is whether belief is truly what is at stake here. Or, to put this another way, if belief is what is at issue, then what is the status of this "belief"? I do not think belief of either a religious or non-religious sort is just—or even *primarily*—propositional in nature. Rather it is something much deeper and more fundamental than simply assenting to propositions or a list of claims. Falque makes it clear that both believer and non-believer "believe": they both have their respective faiths. But what is missing from his account here is the element of *practice*: in other words, how that faith or belief manifests itself in our everyday lives. Falque's account, at the very least, appears to assume a priority of orthodoxy over orthopraxy. What makes that particularly strange is that Falque is elsewhere so highly attentive to liturgy. Indeed, his trilogy (composed of *The Guide to Gethsemane*, *The Metamorphosis of Finitude*, and *The Wedding Feast of the Lamb*) is deeply liturgical in nature. One of the themes that we find time and again in Falque is that of *embodiment*. Again, my goal here is not to "correct" Falque but to cross the Rubicon with him—and then go even beyond that crossing.

If one crosses back to the beginnings of Christianity—before it even becomes "Christianity" and Jesus is just another rabbi—one might be tempted to say, as Gertrude Stein famously said of Oakland, California, "there's no there there."[19] But I think we—as Kierkegaard's disciples at secondhand—tend to have the opposite problem from that of Stein: presuming there was a "there" present when there really was not much there. What "doctrine"—what *theological belief*—was there to believe? No doubt, there was quite a bit of talk and speculation about Jesus. The first gospel—Mark, going back to 66–70 AD—presents the disciples as continually confused about who Jesus is. "Who do people say that I am?" asks Jesus (Mk 8:27). He gets answers such as John the Baptist, Elijah, and one of the prophets. Then he asks "who do *you* say that I am?" (my italics) and Peter answers: "You are the Messiah" (Mk 29). Yet, because the category "Messiah" has always been highly contested, that Peter recognizes him to be such does not—on its own—tell us much more than that Jesus was recognized as someone quite special. But what exactly does Jesus teach? The basic message boils to something like "follow me," even though this gets worked out in markedly different ways within the Gospels themselves. In essence, though, the "faith" that Jesus was speaking about was one that centered on *him*. To have faith in Jesus was to have confidence in him, to trust him to lead one along the way. In the four Gospels there is not *any* hint that following Jesus was about believing a set of doctrines. Think for instance of the thief on the cross to whom Jesus says "today you will be with me in paradise" (Lk 23:43). What *doctrine* could the thief have even been able to have believed had he wished to do so? All he has said to Jesus is "remember me when you come into your kingdom" (Lk 23:42). In that statement, he no doubt recognizes Jesus as having some sort of authority, but the exact content of that belief is highly uncertain. Yet even that undefined belief is all he needs.

For the disciples, as well as those who become Jesus' close followers, what we have is a love story—a story about people putting their trust in Jesus. It is a story about following the One whom they love. Indeed, to follow Jesus was originally designated as being part of "the way." Jesus identifies himself as *"he hodos"*—the way—in John 14:6. In Acts 9:2, Luke tells us that Saul was looking for anyone "who belonged to the Way (*tes hodou*)" (NRSV, capitals in the translation). What, though, is the meaning of this term "*hodos*"? In short, it has a very concrete meaning—in which it can mean such things as road, path, journey, expedition, and way—and one much richer and metaphorical in nature. When Jesus asks the twelve: "Do you also wish to go away?" Simon Peter answers, "Lord, to whom can we go? You have the words of eternal life" (John 6:67–68). Following Jesus was the way to eternal life, the way to the Kingdom of God. So, with some rather significant lapses along the way, they followed him to his death, resurrection, and ascension. So *then* what? We do not know all that much about what exactly Christians believed in these early years, though we do know that beliefs varied widely and that many early beliefs came to be seen as heretical, even though it often took decades or centuries for a specific belief to be identified as a heresy. But we do know that they had liturgy. That term comes from the Greek *"leitourgia"* (a compound of *leito*—public; *laos*—people; and *ergon*—working or service). The seemingly almost universal translation of this term is "the work of the people," though the translations "public service" or "public works" are much more accurate. What was this work? Variants of *leitourgia* in the New Testament are used to describe such actions as "ministering" or "ministry," along with "service" and "serving." For instance, Paul praises the Philippians for their ministry to him (Phil 2:30) and the Corinthians for their financial help (2 Cor 9:12). Luke at one point uses the term in a way that is closer to the way it is used today, for he describes the church in Antioch as "worshipping God" (Acts 13:2). But what exactly was this "worshiping God"? What we find in the earliest account of the church—Acts 2— is that these early followers of Jesus "devoted themselves to the apostles' teaching and fellowship, to the breaking of bread and the prayers" (Acts 2:44). This formula is about as close to the classic Christian idea of "word and sacrament" as one can get. But their "liturgy" does not end there. We are also told that "all who believed were together and had all things in common," that they "spent much time together in the temple," and that "they broke bread at home and ate their food with glad and generous hearts, praising God and having the good will of all the people" (Acts 2:44, 46–47). Luke does not make *any* kind of distinction between the "worship service" bits and the "serving the community" bits. Or, better put, *all of this together constitutes their worship*. Spending time in the temple, breaking bread together, and sharing things in common are all part of their liturgy.

So how did the Christian Church eventually move from this strong emphasis on practice to a strong emphasis on doctrine? Consider the distinction Catherine Bell makes between "orthodoxic" and "orthopraxic" forms of religion:

> Whether a community is deemed orthodoxic or orthopraxic can only be a matter of emphasis, of course, since no religious tradition can promote belief or ritual at the total expense of the other, and many would never distinguish between them at all. Moreover, whatever the overall emphasis in a tradition as a whole, it is easy to find subcommunities stressing the opposite pole. . . . [T]erms like "orthodoxy" or "orthopraxy" cannot be used effectively if accorded too much rigidity or exclusivity.[20]

Having made that distinction, she goes on to say the following: "As a result of the dominance of Christianity in much of the West, which has tended to stress matters of doctrinal and theological orthodoxy, people may take it for granted that religion is primarily a matter of what one believes."[21] Terence Cuneo rightly points out that Bell's characterization of Christianity is, at best, only partly true. He writes: "Christianity comes in many varieties, and not all are all belief-centered in the way that Bell describes. This is certainly true of various forms of the Roman Catholic, Anglican, and Mennonite traditions, for example—and might also be true of so-called non-liturgical traditions such as Quakerism."[22] Cuneo goes on to say that his tradition, Eastern Christianity, is particularly orthopraxic in nature and that it "has much in common with Bell's description of Judaism and Islam" (both of which Bell identifies as largely concerned with practice). But what is most important is how he positions liturgy in the Christian tradition. While he is particularly speaking of Eastern Orthodoxy, I take it that what he says applies—*pace* Cuneo—to many other traditions in Christendom, including the Roman Catholic, Anglican, and Lutheran traditions:

> For Eastern Christians, the liturgy functions as the centerpiece of the Christian way of life. It is the paradigmatic expression of the tradition's *mind*—the sense of the term "mind" referring not simply or even primarily to various doctrines or claims but also to ways of conducting oneself and viewing the world, whose rich character and significance might be difficult and perhaps impossible to capture in wholly propositional terms.[23]

I see three important points in this quotation. First, Cuneo rightly gets that Christianity is a way of life. It's about one's very being. Clearly, that is exactly what it is for those Christians in Acts 2. Second, liturgy is not primarily about doctrines but about ways of seeing and being in the world, which would clearly include doctrines but not be limited to them. Third, and closely connected to the second point, liturgical practices are central to the "mind" of the Christian—they are ways of knowing that perhaps cannot be reducible to propositions. I would simply omit the term "perhaps."

There are multiple problems with using both the word and the concept of "religion." One is simply that the word—in its most original meaning—has to do with virtue or fulfilling one's obligations to one's family and community. In contrast, the definition that we would ascribe to the word today took over a millennium to take shape. *Religio* is first about being a responsible person. In one of Terence's plays (approximately 160 BCE), the word is synonymous with the Latin term "*scrupulus*" (which has more or less the same meaning as the English term "scrupulous").[24] Over time, though, *religio* acquires a range of meanings, from "rule" to "worship practice." In the works of Tertullian, for instance, *religio* means such things as "worship" and "rite."[25] In the Church Fathers in general, the word *religio* has a range of meanings but all of them concern relations to other human beings and/or to God; none of them denote anything even remotely like a set of doctrines. When the word first comes into English as "religion," its use was to denote those who took monastic vows. Indeed, it is only in Hugo Grotius's *De veritate religionis christianae* [On the Truthfulness of the Christian Religion] that Christianity is depicted as primarily a set of doctrines to which one could assent.

Sociologically, as long as the Church remained united, it was quite possible to define someone as being a "Christian" on the basis of that person being part of a social group (namely, the Church). One could even meaningfully speak of a country as being "Christian," because the essential properties of the whole could be meaningfully ascribed to each of its individuals. Yet, once the western Church (i.e., Roman Catholicism) came to be divided, such classification was no longer possible. To be sure, the very idea that one could determine whether someone "counted" as a Christian goes back at least as far as the Roman times, when Christianity was first persecuted as a deviant religious sect and then became the state religion. It is precisely at this time (325 CE) that the emperor Constantine brought various Christian leaders together in Nicaea to produce a document that defined the official doctrines of the Church. Then, in 380 CE, the Roman rulers decreed that citizens were required to affirm the Code of Theodosisus, which was an official articulation of the Trinity. That edict indicated that those who did not affirm the code "shall be branded with the ignominious name of heretics."[26] From that point on, Roman citizens were *ipso facto* Christians. And that state of affairs more or less continued through the medieval period for much of Europe. One can hardly argue that all of those Romans and Europeans were thoroughly versed in the Nicene Creed and understood exactly what it was they were supposed to be affirming on each and every line. Indeed, the vast majority of people in medieval Europe were illiterate and mass was said in a language that they did not understand. They had very little idea of exactly what it was that the Church affirmed. Still, they were part of the Church and through the Church came salvation.

However, the Reformation changed all of that. What had been a system of salvation based on being part of an institution turned into a system based on holding to the right set of doctrines. Personally, I am reminded of this reality every day as I walk through the streets of St Andrews and encounter crosses in the pavement, marking the place where heretics were quite literally burned to death, and the ruins of what was once a magnificent (read: Roman Catholic) cathedral. The sixteenth and seventeenth centuries in Europe were marked by continual war over matters of religion. Yet that was not the only change. With the advent of the marketplace of Christian denominations, religion became—by necessity—a personal, private matter. One could cite the United States and the founders' unwillingness to designate a state religion. But one could simply point to any place where freedom of religion became the norm in Europe.

With religion becoming a private matter—something held inwardly—there arose the distinction of "sacred" versus "secular." If religion can no longer be taken to be a corporate matter, then it must become the province of the individual. One can argue that both the Reformation and the Enlightenment greatly contributed to the idea of the individual, autonomous self—one who is able to choose on her own. Representing what has until very recently been the "standard" view on how religion took shape, Wilfred Cantwell Smith argues that, rather than being a living thing that expresses people's genuine feelings, religion has gradually become "reified," "making religion into a thing, gradually coming to conceive it as an objective systematic entity."[27] In one sense, Smith is correct. Since there were a robust set of competing options in Christendom—and since belonging to one meant that one did not and could not belong to another—the various splinters of Christianity needed to define themselves in concrete ways, most usually by way of doctrine though also by ways of worshiping. Yet Smith misses a crucial aspect in the development of the concept of religion. Talal Asad argues—*pace* Smith—that "'religion' is a modern concept not because it is reified but because it has been linked to its Siamese twin 'secularism.'"[28] The idea that there is something like a "sacred" realm only makes sense if it can be differentiated from something like a "secular" realm. What Falque does not seem to realize is that the distinction between theology and philosophy, faith and reason, belief and unbelief ultimately has a *political* dimension. For the distinction is really between the authority of the Church and the authority of the State. William T. Cavanaugh points out that what was at issue in the so-called wars of religion was actually "the very creation of religion as a set of privately held beliefs without direct political relevance."[29]

All of this puts into question not only the location of the Rubicon but what exactly it is supposed to separate. On Falque's reading, the separation is between philosophy and theology. But it would be more accurate to say that the separation is between the Church and the State. In French society, such a separation has been part of the very bedrock of the social and political order ever since the French Revolution. But if the Sorbonne represents the State and the ICP represents the Church, then the boundary is ultimately a question of authority and power. Who has the authority and the power to determine what is (to use Falque's adjective) "proper"? It is this *political* Rubicon that I do not think can so be easily traversed. For the "authority" vested in the Sacred is fundamentally different from the "authority" vested in Secular.

But the actual situation is much worse than this. As long as believers/religious people live in places where the "law of the land" is secular, then faith/belief/religion/Church will *always* be subservient. The "secular" always wins over the "sacred" precisely because the "secular" is able to set the boundaries of what counts as proper: what "good" science or philosophy looks like. Even to use the expression "Christian philosophy" is already to concede a position of inferiority from the very beginning. The deck has been stacked. It is not just that theologians at ICP are already at a disadvantage in comparison to the philosophers at the Sorbonne; rather, it is that *philosophers* at the ICP (like Falque) are just as disadvantaged as the theologians. Earlier, I mentioned the advent of the Society of Christian Philosophers.[30] If one peruses the names on its list of members, it quickly becomes obvious that many of these folks (some of whom are my colleagues here in St Andrews) are quite worthy of being on a list of the best philosophers of our time. They have proven themselves worthy of the accolades of the "secular" world of philosophy. But note that it is still secular philosophy presiding and deciding who counts and what is "proper" philosophy—not the other way around.

My task in this chapter is, fortunately, not to "solve" this problem. One could, of course, argue that it is not even a problem, particularly if one thinks that secular philosophical authority is overrated. Yet Falque sets up the problematic as if philosophy and theology were on equal footing. But in neither France nor Europe nor the United States nor most of the developed world is that the case. And, as long as the boundaries of the sacred and the secular remain, it cannot by definition ever be the case. In an officially "secular" political context, the "sacred" is always an interloper. Crossing the Rubicon, then, is a much deeper problem than Falque's account would have it. To deal with that problem, though, would require more than writing a book.

NOTES

1. Emmanuel Falque, *Crossing the Rubicon: The Borderlands of Philosophy and Theology*, translated by George Hughes (New York: Fordham University Press), 147.

2. Falque, *Crossing the Rubicon*, 156.
3. Falque, *Crossing the Rubicon*, 40.
4. Falque, *Crossing the Rubicon*, 22.
5. Alvin Plantinga, *Warranted Christian Belief* (Oxford: Oxford University Press, 2000).
6. Falque, *Crossing the Rubicon*, 86.
7. See Jacques Derrida, "Faith and Knowledge: The Two Sources of 'Religion' at the Limits of Reason Alone," in *Acts of Religion*, edited by Gil Anidar (London: Routledge, 2002), 40–101.
8. R. G. Collingwood, *An Essay on Metaphysics* (Oxford: Clarendon Press, 1940), 32.
9. Hans-Georg Gadamer, *Truth and Method*, second revised edition, translated by Joel Weinsheimer and Donald G. Marshall (London; New York: Continuum, 2004), 275.
10. Falque, *Crossing the Rubicon*, 132.
11. See Edmund Husserl, *Ideas Pertaining to a Pure Phenomenology and a Phenomenological Philosophy*, First Book, translated by Fred Kersten (The Hague: Martinus Nijhoff, 1982), 252.
12. Edmund Husserl, *Experience and Judgment*, translated by James Spencer Churchill and Karl Ameriks (Evanston, IL: Northwestern University Press, 1973), 30.
13. Falque, *Crossing the Rubicon*, 83.
14. Thomas Nagel, *The Last Word* (Oxford: Oxford University Press, 2001), 130.
15. Falque, *Crossing the Rubicon*, 139–40.
16. Falque, *Crossing the Rubicon*, 25.
17. Falque, *Crossing the Rubicon*, 148.
18. Falque, *Crossing the Rubicon*, 151.
19. Gertrude Stein, *Everybody's Autobiography* (London: William Heinemann, 1937), 298. Stein's point here is actually that all of the parts of Oakland with which she had grown up were no longer in existence when she returned many years later.
20. Catherine Bell, *Ritual: Perspectives and Dimensions* (New York: Oxford University Press, 1997), 190.
21. Bell, *Ritual*, 190.
22. Terence Cuneo, *Ritualized Faith: Essays on the Philosophy of Liturgy* (Oxford: Oxford University Press, 2018), 8.
23. Cuneo, *Ritualized Faith*, 9.
24. John Barsby, *Terence: The Woman of Andros, The Self-Tormentor, The Eunuch* (Cambridge: Harvard University Press, 2001), 940–41.
25. See Timothy David Barnes, *Tertullian: A Historical and Literary Study* (Oxford: Clarendon, 1985).
26. Henry S. Bettenson, *Documents of the Christian Church* (Oxford: Oxford University Press, 1943), 31.
27. Wilfred Cantwell Smith, *The Meaning and End of Religion: A New Approach to the Religious Traditions of Mankind* (Minneapolis: Fortress, 1963), 51.
28. Talal Asad, "Reading a Modern Classic: W. C. Smith's *The Meaning and End of Religion*," *History of Religions* 40 (2001): 205–22.
29. William T. Cavanaugh, "'A Fire Strong Enough to Consume the House': The Wars of Religion and the Rise of the State," *Modern Theology* 11 (1995): 398.
30. There is a "continental" equivalent of the Society of Christian Philosophers—the Society of Continental Philosophy and Theology, of which I serve as the Executive Director.

Chapter Three

Philosophy and Theology

What Happens When We Cross the Boundary?

Jakub Čapek

As evident from its title, this chapter intends to explore the borderlands of philosophy and theology.[1] If I correctly understand the fundamental intention of Emmanuel Falque, he does not aim only to circumscribe the respective domains of philosophy and theology in order to prevent their eventual confusion. Rather, he aims in addition or, perhaps instead, to encourage border traffic, as his allusion to Caesar's crossing the Rubicon suggests. Yet what precisely does it mean to cross this particular boundary? In what Falque proposes, I have found two different meanings of boundary crossing. According to the first, to cross the boundary means to decide to believe;[2] according to the second, to cross the boundary means to transform one discipline, say theology, by using contributions from another, philosophy, and the other way round.[3] Each meaning of boundary crossing is connected with different concerns. In the first meaning, when focusing on deciding to believe, the question is whether this decision—and the experience of the believer—is something that can be shared by people who have not decided to believe. Falque argues that this experience can at least partly be understood (or "apprehended") by people who have not had it.[4] In the second meaning of boundary crossing, one discipline can be transformed by another. According to Falque, this has happened, at least in France, in a one-way manner: phenomenology from Levinas to Nancy has largely transformed theology. If I understand him correctly, Falque is engaging in the reciprocal "transformation of philosophy by theology." He suggests developing a "philosophy of religious experience," and he phrases the desired transformation in explicitly religious terms when talking about the "*conversion* . . . of philosophy by theology."[5]

This approach can obviously raise questions, and even doubts, about whether Falque's initial promise—not to confound the disciplines—was actually kept. In order to deal with this concern, I will focus on the question: "What happens when we cross the boundary?" Falque gives, I believe, two answers to this question. At one point he says that the two banks of the Rubicon "will be joined."[6] This looks like a synthesis of philosophy and theology. Later, Falque suggests that the final "point of junction" is God. Here, he seems to claim that is is ultimately theology, i.e., a discipline which takes religious phenomena (such as liturgy, prayer, and the Eucharist) for granted, that unites and crowns the disciplines in question.

In the following, I will offer and defend a different answer to the question "What happens when we cross the boundary?" I will argue that we neither synthesize the two disciplines nor do we subsume the one under the other, but, rather, we *change perspectives*. In order to articulate this view, I will make use of some suggestions made by Paul Ricœur. I will proceed in three steps. In step one and two, I will consider the border traffic between philosophy and theology in one sense and the other, and in the third part I will articulate the idea that what we have here are not two river banks to be joined, but two perspectives that can be adopted in turn. Before starting, however, I would make two remarks: I am philosopher, not a theologian, and my references in philosophy will be phenomenology and hermeneutics; I am a Protestant and this personal background might also influence my reflections on our topic.

CHRISTIAN THEMES IN PHILOSOPHICAL REFLECTION, PARTICULARLY PHENOMENOLOGY

A philosopher who is at the same time a Christian can easily be led to introduce into their philosophical thought certain concepts derived from reflecting on the Christian faith, and this may result in conceptual confusion. When doing philosophical work, that is, when analyzing our experience, defining concepts, and examining the cogency of arguments, a Christian philosopher, I believe, should not proceed differently from an atheist or non-Christian philosopher.

This might sound too general, so let us look, for example, at phenomenology. Phenomenology was defined by Husserl as an unprejudiced analysis of experience which refuses any speculative constructions. The key phenomenological concept is, consequently, "intuitive givenness" (*anschauliche Gegebenheit*). As the famous "principle of all principles" states, a phenomenologist accepts as a legitimate basis of knowledge only that which is offered or given in an intuition, be it particular objects in the intuition of something individual or general entities in the eidetic intuition. More precisely, it *"is to be accepted simply as what it is presented . . . but also only within the limits in which it is presented there.*"⁷

In the second half of the twentieth century, especially in French phenomenology, many authors have legitimately pointed out that there are certain experiences or "phenomena" that cannot be "given" as Husserlian phenomenology would wish. Emmanuel Levinas, for instance, shows that the analysis of our experience of the other is insufficiently described by Husserl as a combined experience of presentation and a-presentation. As Levinas points out by using the example of the father-son relationship, the possibilities of my son are not my possibilities, and yet I am deeply concerned. There is a more radical transcendence in our relationship than the one analyzed by Husserl.⁸ The legitimate criticism of the Husserlian emphasis on the given, the present (and the a-presented) is followed by a less legitimate claim. Experiences that escape the Husserlian method are taken to be experiences in which we encounter "absolute alterity." Levinas, the philosopher of "absolute otherness," starts from well-justified doubts. Nevertheless, when he articulates and develops his doubts, he makes use of certain concepts that are—within philosophy—no less problematic. What in Husserl was the "experiencing of the other" (of the "foreing," the *Fremderfahrung*)⁹ was turned into the impossibility of the experiencing of absolute otherness.

In a similar way, the idea of givenness was transposed by Jean-Luc Marion from the epistemological context into a more ethical domain: the fundamental way something can be given is the "pure calling." What a phenomenological analysis aims at is no longer the un-prejudiced description of experience, but the transformation of the one who undergoes an experience into a being that was "called" or "summoned" (*convoqué*). The givenness is a gift. Again, it is obviously a theme borrowed from a religious sphere. I think Dominique Janicaud was right when he famously epitomized the turn in question as a *theological turn of the French phenomenology*.¹⁰

In some of his reflections, Falque does something similar. He reminds us of the idea of Husserl and Merleau-Ponty according to which our everyday trust or reliance on the existence of the surrounding world is a kind of belief, an *Urdoxa*. Falque links this "perceptual belief" (*la foi perceptive*) to the belief in God when saying: "We . . . believe 'in the world' or 'in others' before believing (or not) 'in God.' An originary belief or confidence (*Urdoxa*) precedes and founds all disbelief or all mistrust."¹¹ This might be true, yet even though this belief—called by Falque a "philosophical faith"—comes before religious faith and "founds" it, there are two problems here: (1) philosophical faith ("belief in the world and in others") does not imply religious faith and can exist without it; (2) more importantly, the belief in God is—as Falque clearly states—conceptually different from the perceptual belief. Once we pass from the perceptual belief to the belief in God, the very concept of belief gets transformed: it is no longer me who believes in something (world, others), it is God who "believes *in me* more than . . . I believe *in him*."[12] Again, much as in Levinas (absolute otherness) or Marion (the givenness as a gift), there seems to be a terminological shift due to the introduction of a religious or theological concept into a philosophical reflection. The question is: does phenomenological philosophy *as philosophy* gain anything by this shift? In what follows, I will adduce some ideas that substantiate a negative answer to this question.

By way of anticipation, let us suggest that it might be better to render to Caesar the things that are Caesar's, that is, the concept of the given, the experience of the otherness of another person, and the "perceptual faith," and to God the things that are God's, that is, absolute alterity, givenness understood as a creation and gift, and the faith of God in me. Consequently, let us also render to theology the things that belong to theology: reflections on faith. Certain ideas we find in Levinas, Marion, and maybe also in Falque represent more reflection on faith than philosophy.[13] True, we can take up theological motives and transplant them into philosophical reflection, but there are good reasons to be cautious. Personally, I am inclined to embrace the attitude represented, for example, by Ricœur who resolutely refuses to "mix genres" and to "confuse the two spheres,"[14] and who defends "autonomous, philosophical discourse."[15]

PHILOSOPHICAL (HERMENEUTICAL) THEMES IN REFLECTIONS ON CHRISTIAN FAITH

The Christian faith undeniably needs philosophy in many respects. Nevertheless, philosophy can be a source of confusion when introduced into the reflection of Christian faith improperly. Let us take the example of natural theology, which is—especially in its attempts to provide proof of the existence of God—basically a philosophical endeavor with a clearly defined, non-philosophical task. These onto-theological reflections contributed decisively to articulate philosophical terminology and to circumscribe the capacity and limits of human reason. To give but one example, without the debate concerning the ontological proof of the existence of God, there would not have been the discussion, sparked by Kant, whether being is a real predicate or not.

There is, nevertheless, the remaining question whether the proof of God's existence has anything to do with God. Is it possible to transpose the creed, for instance, the first part of the Apostles' Creed—"I believe in God"—into the statement concerning the existence of a certain entity? The question to be asked is not: Can the truth value of the alleged statement be proven? but, rather: Is the truth claim of the Creed the same thing as the truth value of the statement? Insofar as certain philosophical reflections tend to wipe away this difference, they do not help; rather, they prevent and confuse the reflection on faith. I believe that Rudolf Bultmann tries to alert us precisely to this confusion when claiming that statements of faith (*Glaubensaussagen*) are not universal truths (*allgemeine Wahrheiten*).[16]

But let us not focus only on philosophical themes that may eclipse or deform the Christian faith. It is more important to highlight the different ways philosophy can help to cultivate reflections on faith. To do this, I shall draw attention to philosophical hermeneutics, which uncovers the pre-conditions of our understanding of texts. There are pre-conditions both on the side of the person who seeks to understand—especially the fact that the existence of each of us is a continuous task for ourselves—and on the side of what is to be understood: the statements of the text are to be related to the context of motivation in which they start to give a certain meaning.

This has an obvious consequence for our reading and understanding of texts, including the Bible. It is impossible to maintain the idea that a linguistic unit that can have a truth claim is a statement. When interpreting the New Testament passages on the birth of Jesus, for instance, we try—with Gadamer—to reconstruct the context of the motivation of this message. This background is not defined by questions such as when, where, and how Jesus was born, but whether he is the Messiah the prophets were announcing. True, some parts of the Nativity story were subsequently transformed into dogma, but that does not mean that what we have here is statements with a truth value. What we have is something different, a testimony of faith. I believe that philosophical hermeneutics is well suited to consider this type of speech units, which can be true without being statements of fact.[17]

The attempt to understand testimonies of faith entails, however, a considerable difficulty, and possibly even a boundary that philosophical hermeneutics cannot cross. I have just said that it is in the light of one's own existence which a particular type of texts starts to be understandable. Yet the question arises whether that means that human existence determines the conditions of the intelligibility and understandability of a biblical text? This seems to imply that the word of God is made dependent upon the human capacity to understand. Yet in the case of an authoritative, canonical text, such as the Bible, the dependency relationship should be the other way round. Bultmann does not observe this limitation when he says: "The question of God is identical with the question of myself. Now we have found an adequate way of asking for our Bible interpretation. The question is thus the following: *How does the Bible understand human existence?*"[18] Here, I believe, Bultmann overstates the capacity of existential interpretation. From the standpoint of a theologian, and Bultmann was one, it is difficult, perhaps even impossible, to say that human existence (in a particular Heideggerian or existentialist understanding) imposes on an authoritative text of a religious tradition the criteria of intelligibility which it has to fit in.

PHILOSOPHY AND THEOLOGY

In the third part of my contribution, I develop one suggestion presented by Ricœur according to which the relationship between faith reflection and philosophical reflection is one of a "mutual enveloping" (*englobement mutuel*).[19] From the standpoint of philosophy, of philosophical hermeneutics, understanding texts of the Bible is but one case of the more general procedure of interpretation. Consequently, philosophy comprises reflections on faith and goes beyond it. From the standpoint of reflections on faith, however, philosophical hermeneutics is but one instrument that can be used, for instance, when reconstructing the background of the motivation of biblical texts. Nevertheless, reflections on faith are by far not exhausted by this instrument. Reflections on faith and theology entail philosophy and go beyond it. "By turns, one envelops the other."[20]

It is this idea that I wish to develop in what follows. According to Ricœur, any reflection comprises two moves, as the very title of his book-length interview suggests: a *critique* and a *conviction*. Philosophy and theology are each convinced about something; each accepts something, at least as its starting point, something like a pre-given matter to elaborate on. In its elaboration, reflection, be it philosophical or theological, adopts a critical stance. Critique does not necessarily mean refusing the pre-given; rather, it means making distinctions (*krinein*) and conducting a methodologically controlled investigation.

I would reiterate: theology and philosophy each contain both moves, the accepting of something as pre-given and critical investigation. The claim that reflection on faith is but an uncritical receiving of the word of authority (of Scripture) is untenable, as is the claim that philosophy can only reduce itself to criticism. To quote Ricœur: "philosophy is not simply critical, it too belonging to the order of conviction. And religious conviction itself possesses an internal, critical dimension."[21] The difference between the two kinds of reflection consists in what is accepted as pre-given and what constitutes the object of a critique. I will now try to demonstrate this difference by means of a particular philosophical and theological problem: the freedom of the will.

Philosophical reflections on free will typically take the following idea as their starting point: I am responsible for what I do only on the condition that I could have chosen it, that is, that my will to do this was free. Having considered several possible actions, I have decided, on the basis of certain reasons, to act in this particular way. What is adopted by philosophical reflection is the common belief that things somebody does can be traced back to this individual as being their origin. The move of adoption is sometimes expressed by the philosopher's reference to common use. When, for instance, Aristotle establishes the distinction between the *hekousion* and *akousion*, between the voluntary and the involuntary, he invokes our everyday understanding of things that are praised or blamed on the one hand (voluntary acts), and things that constitute an object of a pardon and pity on the other (involuntary events, *Eth. Nic.* III/1). For philosophy, such an "adoption" is but a start. Proper philosophical work consists in the clarification, critique, and, sometimes, even refusal of what was accepted as a starting point of reflection. We can, for instance with Donald Davidson, object that explaining an action by its reasons is not fundamentally different from explaining it by pointing to its causes and that, consequently, the reasons of an action are no different from the causes of an event, and that, ultimately, the relationship between reasons and actions is causal.[22] On a different level, we can, together with Gilbert Ryle and Ludwig Wittgenstein, mistrust the idea of the will as an inner human capacity that is accessible only to the individual himself or herself, and we can suggest that all the talk about reasons, actions, and freedom constitutes part of a particular language game that has of course its rules and is different, for instance, from the language game of a prediction. Against these critical approaches, attempts were undertaken to philosophically defend the fundamental difference between reasons and causes and also to defend a certain concept of the freedom of the will. By my brief allusions to some important debates in the twentieth-century philosophy, I intend only to point out that it is possible to locate two moves here—adoption and critique.

Reflection on faith can focus on free will, for instance, by commenting on the words of Paul in his Epistle to Romans, "I don't do the good I want to do; instead, I do the evil that I do not want to do" (Rom 7:19). This is something different from the philosophical debate on freedom of will. Here we have a completely new form of unfreedom. This does not seem to be purely the lack of the freedom to act, an external impediment to our intended action. On a certain reading suggested by Paul Ricœur in his early *Philosophy of Will*, it is ultimately the will itself that is unfree, be it in the form of uncontrolled ambition, self-accusation, or envy. In these three cases, the individual aims at something particular—their own success (ambition), their own faults (self-accusation), or the property, partner, or success of others (envy)—and they lack the freedom to do otherwise. Again, this form of unfreedom is not the mere absence of freedom; rather, it is an expression of freedom. Ricœur reads the phrase from the Epistle to Romans along these lines, and he does this as somebody who—so to say—crossed the boundary, as a believer. His reflection at this point is a reflection on faith. It is from this standpoint that he says: "the guilty will is a freedom in bondage" (*la volonté coupable est une liberté serve*).[23] It is not somebody else, but I myself who makes me a slave: "I *impose* on myself the fault which *deprives* me of control over myself." Consequently, "I *am* free and this freedom *is* unavailable" (*je suis libre* et *cette liberté* est *indisponible*).[24] Now, phenomena such as envy, jealousy, hatred, or ambition are obviously not restricted to believers only. What is particular to the perspective adopted by Ricœur as a Christian in this text is one fundamental assumption. It is nothing less than faith in the Transcendence as something that is beyond my reach and is the only chance of my liberation. It is thanks to the re-creating action of Transcendence that I can discover, for instance, my envy or self-accusation as different forms of the enslavement of my freedom.[25] This *"gift of being* which heals the injuries of freedom" enables me to see that my freedom was damaged. The idea of freedom of will as the human capacity for self-determination is now seen as the "illusion of positing of the self by the self."[26] It is precisely by claiming self-sufficiency for itself that an individual becomes unfree and—in a religious sense of the term—guilty.[27] The autonomous self is an alienated self.

Faith reflection on the particular type of unfreedom that we experience in envy, jealousy, or hatred comprises, again, both conviction and critique. With regard to conviction, Ricœur accepts a certain idea of Transcendence, more precisely, the conviction that the will cannot be free if not through the liberating action of God. As for the critique: it consists in a different analysis of phenomena such as envy, hatred, or ambition from the one offered by non-faith reflection. But critique is even more fundamental: if it is true that the independent "self" is but a "self" enslaved by the illusion of independence, then philosophical reflection on freedom of will is limited. This particular type of unfreedom is inaccessible for it. This is why philosophy can never claim to be a universally valid "doctrine of subjectivity."[28] It is unacceptable from the perspective of faith to say, for instance, in the Heideggerian vein, that the self can "win itself" (*sich selbst gewinnen*).[29]

To sum up, I have briefly referred to the problem of free will in order to give one example of the more general claim that there is a relationship of mutual enveloping between philosophical reflection and faith reflection. These two forms of reflection comprise, according to Ricœur, both conviction and critique. What they accept and what they criticize is in each case something different. In some cases, they can direct their criticism one against the other: a philosopher will not accept the idea of the re-creating action of Transcendence upon the will; the theologian cannot accept, at least not without further qualification, the idea of the self-determination of the will. What is more, certain phenomena that are accessible from one perspective may be difficult to access from another. A philosopher *as philosopher* has, for instance, no access to the particular *necessity* related to the enslavement of the will that is blinded by envy or self-accusation and *cannot* break its chains. A theologian, however, often does not have much understanding for a "doctrine of subjectivity" that completely abstracts from faith and tries to explore the only human ways in which one can be oneself.

I have just used the term "perspective" for reflection of both kinds, philosophical and theological. If their relationship is as we have discussed a relationship of mutual enveloping, then there is no synthesis in view. To put it differently, both perspectives are original. What does that imply for our question "What happens when we cross the boundary?" I suggested to use the metaphor of perspectives. We can change perspectives, but once we adopt a different perspective, we have abandoned the previous one. They are not two river banks to be "joined." If I understand Falque correctly, what he undertakes is a faith reflection that takes phenomena particular to one religion (Christianity), or even one denomination (Catholicism), as experiences that can be analyzed with the help of philosophical concepts. I have full admiration for the novelty of his way of describing religious experiences and developing the Catholic hermeneutic of "the body and the voice." As for the crossing of boundaries between philosophy and theology, nevertheless, I think he is somebody who crossed the boundary in one sense—from philosophy to theology—and looks back but does not return. It is only coherent when he does not expect certain philosophers to follow him. He says, for instance, "there is *more* in mankind than the pure and simple evaluation of himself by himself. It is precisely at this point that neither a Martin Heidegger, nor a Michel Foucault, nor a Gilles Deleuze would be able to follow us."[30] Falque opted for *one* perspective. In the first meaning of the boundary crossing, which I mentioned at the beginning of this chapter, he decided to believe. I fully understand that he does not want to be separated—*qua* confessing believer—from his human brothers.[31] Still, they are "human brothers" as seen by a confessing believer, that is, from the other river bank.

NOTES

1. This text is part of a research conducted at Faculty of Arts, Charles University in Prague, and supported by the European Regional Development Fund-Project "Creativity and Adaptability as Conditions of the Success of Europe in an Interrelated World" (No. CZ.02.1.01/0.0/0.0/16_019/0000734). The earlier version of this chapter was delivered at the international seminar "Exploring the Borderlands of Philosophy and Theology" (October 27, 2017, Prague), featuring Falque as the keynote speaker. I am indebted both to Emmaneul Falque for submitting the text that sparked the debate and to Martin Koci for his kind invitation and for having organized the event.

2. Emmanuel Falque, "Philosophy and Theology: New Boundaries" (a chapter included in this volume on pp. 3–24), here 11.

3. Falque, "Philosophy and Theology," 4.
4. Falque, "Philosophy and Theology," 14.
5. Falque, "Philosophy and Theology," 13, 17.
6. Falque, "Philosophy and Theology," 18.
7. Edmund Husserl, *Ideas Pertaining to a Pure Phenomenology and a Phenomenological Philosophy*, First Book, translated by Fred Kersten (Dordrecht: Kluwer, 1983), §24.
8. Emmanuel Levinas, *Le temps et l'autre* (Paris: PUF, 1989).
9. Edmund Husserl, *Cartesian Meditations: An Introduction to Phenomenology*, translated by D. Cairns (The Hague, Boston, and London: Nijhoff, 1960), §49.
10. Dominique Janicaud, *Le tournant théologique de la phénoménologie française* (Paris: Éclat, 2001), 49.
11. Falque, "Philosophy and Theology," 11–13.
12. Falque, "Philosophy and Theology," 15–16.

13. Levinas seems to be well aware of this. At least once, when considering the "intelligibility of the transcendent," he himself takes the "idea of the infinite in ourselves" as constituting part of a "theology." Emmanuel Levinas, "Transcendenz und Verstehen," in *Der Mensch in den modernen Wissenschaften*, edited by K. Michalski (Stuttgart: Klett-Cotta, 1985), 171–84.

14. Paul Ricœur, *Critique and Conviction* (New York: Columbia University Press, 1998), 6, 139.

15. Paul Ricœur, *Oneself as Another*, translated by K. Blamey (Chicago and London: University of Chicago Press, 1992), 24–25.

16. Rudolf Bultmann, *Jesus Christus und die Mythologie: Das neue Testament im Licht der Bibelkritik* (Hamburg: Furche-Verlag, 1964). I believe it is legitimate to read the concluding words of Falque's paper, included in this volume, as a plea for natural theology.

17. Hans-Georg Gadamer, *Wahrheit und Methode*, Gesammelte Werke 1: Hermeneutik I (Tübingen: Mohr-Siebeck, 1990), 352ff.

18. Bultmann, *Jesus Christus*, 60.

19. Ricœur, *Critique and Conviction*, 151.

20. Ricœur, *Critique and Conviction*, 151.

21. Ricœur, *Critique and Conviction*, 139.

22. Donald Davidson, "Actions, Reasons, and Causes," in *Essays on Actions and Events* (Oxford: Oxford University Press, 1980), 3–19.

23. Paul Ricœur, *Freedom and Nature*, translated by E. Kohák (Evanston, IL: Northwestern University Press, 1966), 26.

24. Ricœur, *Freedom and Nature*, 26

25. Ricœur, *Freedom and Nature*, 30.

26. Ricœur, *Freedom and Nature*, 30.

27. "Le soi comme autonomie radicale, non seulement morale mais ontologique, est précisément la faute." Paul Ricœur, *Philosophie de la volonté I: Le volontaire et l'involontaire* (Paris: Aubier, 1950), 32.

28. Ricœur, *Philosophie de la volonté I*, 29.

29. Martin Heidegger, *Sein und Zeit* (Tübingen: Niemeyer, 1993), §9.

30. Emmanuel Falque, *The Metamorphosis of Finitude: An Essay on Birth and Resurrection*, translated by G. Hughes (New York: Fordham University Press, 2012), 18.

31. Falque, "Philosophy and Theology," 12–13.

Chapter Four

Foreign Exchange or Hostile Incursion?

William C. Woody

Although the notion of the "theological turn" in phenomenology initially met criticism, if not open hostility, in the late twentieth century, certain contemporary phenomenologists seem far more willing to press boundaries and even to traverse into the realm of a proper "theological phenomenology."[1] For while thinkers such as Emmanuel Levinas and Paul Ricœur maintained more rigid boundaries between their properly "philosophical" and their decidedly "theological" texts, such scruples were lost in the subsequent generation as thinkers such as Jean-Luc Marion engaged more explicitly with questions of theology and God. A new generation of contemporary phenomenologists presses further still, exemplified in the theological phenomenology of Emmanuel Falque.[2] Falque maintains the mantra that "the more we theologize, the better we philosophize," thus daring to cross openly the disciplines' distinctions in a novel and striking manner.[3] Having demonstrated this maxim in his phenomenological readings of theological texts, authors, and experiences—as in his *Dieu, la chair, et l'autre* or his *Triduum philosophique*—Falque now turns to a methodological justification for his approach. In doing so, Falque offers a new paradigm for understanding the relationship between theology and philosophy in his treatise on method, *Crossing the Rubicon: The Borderlands of Philosophy and Theology*.

Before delving into my assessment of Falque's project and its implications for the relationship between philosophy and theology, I wish to make a few preliminary observations with respect to Falque's perspective and overall project goals. I shall then proceed to offer a brief exposition on his new paradigm for philosophical-theological interaction, and subsequently I propose a central benefit that his project affords in facilitating dialogue across differences (or even dissent). I then conclude with a question, namely: does

Falque's account blithely ignore an essential—and perhaps necessary and productive—hostility between philosophy and theology?

A PRELIMINARY OBSERVATION: AN APOLOGETICAL JUSTIFICATION?

On my reading, *Crossing the Rubicon: The Borderlands of Philosophy and Theology* is not, despite its title, primarily about the relationship between these two disciplines. Certainly this relationship is a central theme, the argumentation for which merits the consideration and debate, but I nonetheless contend that in this text, the philosophical-theological relationship is a secondary or even incidental consideration to Falque's more primary apologetical attempt at justifying his larger project.

While *Crossing the Rubicon* certainly does reframe the relationship between philosophy and theology (or, perhaps better, phenomenology and theology), Falque does so in the service of his larger project and, consequently, we cannot understand his "paradigm shift" for philosophy vis-à-vis theology independent of his more primary, overriding philosophical endeavors and concerns. Thus, I must begin by noting that this text is not so purely a treatise on the relationship of these two disciplines but rather an apologetical justification of his own philosophical perspective over and above the thought of other French phenomenologists (*surtout* his mentor and philosophical sparring partner in a self-proclaimed *combat amoreux*, Jean-Luc Marion).

Those familiar with Falque's writings will recognize two common themes that permeate the majority his works and which, I believe, characterize his contributions to phenomenology: (1) the reclamation of the primacy of the incarnate body, even in its finitude and limitations; and (2) a phenomenological perspective that takes immanence, rather than transcendence, as its point of departure. These two common themes emerge as central claims advocated repeatedly by Falque throughout his *Triduum Philosophique*, his habilitation in *Dieu, la Chair, et l'Autre*, and they unsurprisingly figure prominently throughout *Crossing the Rubicon*. Incidentally, they also represent a stark difference and marked departure from the transcendental phenomenology of givenness, characteristic of Jean-Luc Marion. Thus, if we are to understand and to appreciate Falque's claims regarding the relationship between theology and philosophy in this text, we must first acknowledge these two commitments in his overarching philosophical oeuvre.[4]

Falque goes through great lengths in *Crossing the Rubicon* to defend and to distinguish his "immanent" phenomenology from his philosophical forebears, and he uses such an unabashed traversing of boundaries as yet another aspect to distinguish his phenomenology from his predecessors who failed to make the journey—or, at the very least, those who failed to acknowledge that they made the journey:

> "Crossing the Rubicon" is therefore not a reaction in relation to an assigned problem in some set of subject matters—namely, philosophy and theology—and to the mode of being of their approaches, as described by phenomenology, both of which we can only praise and expand. . . . Rather than dividing philosophy and theology up into two utterly separate worlds, we will practice the one as well as the other, seeking in ourselves a new mode of unity.[5]

As a mode of unity, Falque here implicitly criticizes those accused of the "theological turn" who nonetheless maintained a strict demarcation between their more philosophical from explicitly theological works—Levinas, Ricœur, even perhaps Marion. He further contends that such an endeavor must not only be embraced by phenomenologists, but also made explicit, and to welcome the transformation that it may elicit in their philosophical works. Falque asserts, "the 'crossing of the Rubicon'—from philosophy to theology and vice versa—is for myself, as for anyone, all the more justified insofar *as we make explicit* where we went and are able also to return after having been transformed. The better one theologizes, the more one philosophizes."[6] Here Falque distinguishes himself most explicitly from Jean-Luc Marion, whom he less-than-subtly accuses of engaging in theological projects while nonetheless masquerading as a philosopher, failing to acknowledge his theological tendencies (if not a theological method outright as a phenomenologist from the perspective of transcendence). Falque wryly observes that "the muddying of the boundaries is not a consequence of the return to the philosophy of religious experience, but a result of the mask worn by a philosophy that does not admit to being theological, albeit in the passage of time and in the unity of the same person or researcher,"[7] and still later, "the theological turn is not, in any case, to be either taken or left behind . . . it could well be the case that one is more of a philosopher by being at the same time a theologian, in the unity of the same person, than by always trying to pass as nothing but a philosopher while in fact also practicing theology."[8] Falque thus criticizes this failure to acknowledge the traversal of a boundary, the previous generation's refusal to recognize the potential for transformation in favor of strictly segregating one's oeuvre between the disciplines or clandestinely engaging in one while masquerading in the other. Instead, Falque presses further and boldly makes the crossing.

Unique among the phenomenologists accused of the theological turn, Falque brazenly takes this step, arguing both for the need to embrace theology in philosophy (and vice versa), but also to do so explicitly. Such a step, according to Falque, enables the traversing of a previously *verboten* boundary and consequently opens the door to mutual transformation and revelation. He laments that, "philosophy has restricted itself to the threshold of the theological discipline, which could actually be practiced at the very same time. *This step had to be taken.* Elsewhere I have already undertaken part of the crossing. All that was missing was its justification."[9] In the concluding remarks of *Crossing the Rubicon*, Falque discusses not only the necessity of his traversing this boundary—a move that opens up a new field of phenomena to philosophy and which transforms theology itself—but also the previous lack of a *justification* for this move, which the very conclusion of this text consequently purports to provide (and a term he repeatedly employs).

Beyond the more apologetic aspects of Falque's work, any discussion of philosophy and theology in French phenomenology (irrespective of the theological turn) must acknowledge the cultural and academic milieu in which these debates occur. Much like his phenomenological forebears Levinas, Henry, Chrétien, Marion, and Ricœur, Falque writes from within the climate of the French Academy and wider French culture, marked by rigid boundaries between creedal religious faith and *laïcité* (secularity). Despite such commonalities, while the beginnings of the theological turn met resistance and rejection (notably in the works of Dominique Janicaud in his *Phénoménologie Éclatée* and *Le tournant théologique de la phénoménologie française*), Falque belongs to a younger generation of phenomenologists for whom theology in phenomenology—while by no means mainstream or wholeheartedly embraced—is less polemically charged and more widely disseminated in academic philosophy. A notable difference thus becomes clear between Falque's ability in twenty-first-century France to be engaged more directly with theology without "masquerading" or "muddying the boundaries" from those theological turn phenomenologists of the post-war era.

More significantly, in addition to the generational gap to contextualize Falque's writing within France, I also suggest a geographical and cultural particularity that heavily colors his perspective. I pose the question as to whether these methodological considerations are pervasive and systemic to phenomenology, or rather a more idiosyncratic manifestation of the French academy given the prevailing structures and attitudes of the French system, cultural values, *laïcité*, and espoused secularity—an attitude which does not exist nearly as strongly (if at all) in philosophy of religion or religious experience outside of France.[10]

Nonetheless, I leave such observations aside in favor of more substantial critique. I merely note these prefatory remarks—admittedly somewhat longer than I had wished—as something worth acknowledging to ground the context and climate out of which Falque writes.[11]

POROUS BORDERS: A NEW MODEL

Yet what precisely does Falque propose concerning the traversal of this boundary and the relationship between philosophy and theology? The potential fecundity of the "cross-fertilization" of these disciplines notwithstanding, is there any transformative value in this crossing aside from the exchange of methods, ideas, data, and the respective histories to the disciplines? Falque fervently believes so, advocating strongly for the possibility of mutual transformation and the betterment of theology by philosophy, and philosophy by theology. I make this point briefly in order to use it as a springboard for critique and further conversation. It is critical to understand that Falque's novel contributions to this understanding of the disciplines' relationship as a mode of metamorphosis and transformation are not merely supplementation or an exchange of ideas.

Falque rejects any form of a strict demarcation devoid of contact between philosophy and theology, and equally so the denigration of one in favor of the other (either by secular philosophy of theology as unsubstantiated mere belief or superstition, or by theology of philosophy as banality or a preparatory handmaiden). In order to clarify the singular uniqueness of Falque's position, consider what I discern as the five prevailing historical models for the relationship, all of which Falque rejects:

1. Philosophy serves as a preparatory stepping stone to the more advanced discipline of theology, much as grammar serves as preparatory to rhetoric (Propaedeutic model);
2. Theology enables the consummation or completion of the work begun by philosophy, and theology builds upon the groundwork of philosophy and brings it to the heights it could not otherwise achieve on its own (Handmaiden model);
3. Ultimately there should be no distinction between them, arriving at a complete subsumption or synthesis of the two (Mysticism model);
4. Theology and philosophy, faith and reason, operate on two completely separate spheres and are absolutely distinct—contact is neither desirable nor even possible (Modernism model);
5. A complementary relationship between two irreducible yet mutually supportive disciplines, the "two wings by which the human spirit is raised up toward the contemplation of truth"[12] (Phenomenological Catholic model)

Falque, for his part, rejects all of the above in favor of a transformative model, one of porous boundaries that maintains distinction and yet enables a mutuality. He advocates the maintenance of the boundaries only so that they may be traversed and continually recrossed—"there and back again"—a porous border across which we are neither aliens nor sojourners, neither refugees nor immigrants, but rather a foreign exchange of travelers transformed by the foreign. He asks, "How does Christian belief . . . change [philosophical] belief per se in any way? In other words, does religious faith, or more precisely confessing faith, only extend or complete philosophical faith—or does it not rather transform it?"[13] And Falque decidedly and definitively argues, "Confessing faith changes everything," proposing a model by which new fields of phenomena are opened, former ones transformed, a novel perspective gained, and yet philosophical belief and phenomenological method are neither abandoned nor destroyed.[14] A transformative mutuality thus emerges whereby "each truly comes to make sense only as philosophy offers to theology what it possesses—the weight of humanity—and theology reveals itself capable of receiving and converting its meaning—by the Resurrection."[15]

Thus, Falque's conception of the relationship between philosophy and theology is transformative rather than supplemental, metamorphosed rather than completed, mutual rather than complementary, demarcated, segregated, or antagonistic. With at least this (brief) sketch of the relationship between the two in mind, I now turn to consider the laudatory and beneficial contributions of Falque's perspective.

"NOW MORE THAN EVER": DIALOGUE ACROSS DIFFERENCE

Earlier I have praised the many insightful contributions of Falque's larger phenomenological project, specifically in its reclamation of the dignity (and even the priority) of the body in its incarnate finitude, as well as his attempts in promoting a theological phenomenology grounded in the perspective of immanent human experience. I applauded the ethical and spiritual implications of his thought in the realms of pastoral care, praxis, and prayer. With respect to such points, I merely observe that Falque expands and bolsters his contributions in these areas, further solidifying his position throughout *Crossing the Rubicon*. Yet rather than rehash my positions in these areas I will turn my attention elsewhere. I wish here to highlight yet another contribution of his that will have monumental consequences not only for the relationship between theology and philosophy, but also between other estranged and divided groups.

Given Falque's repeated emphasis on traversing seemingly solidified, unquestionable boundaries, I shall assess how his thought provides a potentially fruitful avenue to foster encounter, dialogue, and even conversion (or "transformation," to use Falque's terminology) across insurmountable barriers—dialogue across difference, encounter in place of estrangement, and mutual recognition overcoming rigid segregation.

Falque accomplishes this forcefully and thoroughly throughout *Crossing the Rubicon* by his repeated emphasis on a commonly recognized grounding in a form of faith—philosophical faith in the experience of the world before any creedal confession or theological faith. In doing so, he emphasizes a shared starting point of immanence and finding a common ground whence to facilitate encounter, dialogue, and mutual recognition. A characteristically Falquean move, this builds upon his previous claims of finding a common ground in human finitude and embodiment as a starting point for dialogue instead of shared transcendent concepts, as he articulates in his *Guide to the Gethsemane*.

Falque makes this most explicit in his exposition of the philosophical (dare I say, *secular*) faith that undergirds not just a theological faith and religious belief, but of necessity all human experience. He thus contends that, even with respect to an atheistic or fully secular philosophy, a common act of faith operates:

> I could never believe that I do not believe in the world. A "universal ground of belief in the world" remains nonreducible . . . the idea of an original faith in the world, or rather trust in the belief that I have of the world, makes the world paradoxically the highest and the most certain of truths in an originary attitude of trust rather than mistrust. That this faith may be philosophical and not only religious is one of the great lessons of phenomenology.[16]

Falque thus highlights an implicit yet oftentimes unrecognized common ground—an "originary attitude of trust rather than mistrust"—that provides a common grounding for seemingly opposed or even contradictory beliefs. This opens up a common space for encounter and dialogue across difference. Of necessity, Falque contends that at the root of any form of theological faith or creedal confession shares a rooted patrimony with philosophical, secular "faith" in the world. A secular philosophical position, similarly, shares in the belief structure of a form of faith—faith in the world, in my own existence, in my experience, in the existence of others. For Falque, this patrimony undergirds both philosophy *and* theology:

> There is no confessing faith outside of an original philosophical faith. A common ground of *believing* always precedes the *decided act* of believing. To recognize oneself as "believing otherwise" is then not to disregard faith or to condemn the so-called unbeliever. This position is neither a kind of ostracism nor a kind of conformism, nor does it aim to relativize . . . believing *theologically* in God rests on first believing *philosophically* in the world or in others.[17]

This shared patrimony of faith in the world serves as a starting point—grounded in Falque's characteristic emphasis on finitude and incarnation—that human beings share *phenomenologically*, irrespective of creedal confession. Rather than starting from irreconcilable opposing tenets of belief—immanence versus transcendence, atheism versus theism, secularism versus creed—Falque uncovers a common ground where estrangement yields to encounter, a commonality to be shared in lieu of differences to be debated that can overcome antagonism from both sides:

> Religious faith, often wrongly mistrusting the world and the ordinary belief of humans, should recognize first the trusting attitude that abides in each and every one's originary philosophical faith—whether a believer or not. The belief of all humans in others and the world, if it is simply sympathy, always leads to the belief that others are rather than they are not, and inclines humans to entrust themselves to the world rather than distrust it.[18]

This act of trust rather than mistrust and a recognition of a common faith removes a certain antagonism or even haughtiness of religious faith over and against secular philosophical faith. By opening up a space for common encounter, an attitude of trust, and a means of dialogue through shared concepts and perspectives, Falque has already overcome a history of remarkable segregation and entrenchment between philosophy and theology. Falque presses even further by actually taking the step—traversing the Rubicon and being the "voyager" to travel into foreign land. In doing so he perceives not only the opportunity, but also the very *necessity* of theology and faith to ground itself in these more immanent philosophical perspectives and concepts:

> Finitude thus serves as the beginning of philosophy as well as theology insofar as no *theologoumenon* has any meaning outside of a lived experience or a philosophical "existential," which gives it meaning . . . the body for Incarnation, anguish for Gethsemane, eros for the Eucharist, birth for the Resurrection, wandering for sin, childhood for the Kingdom. In sum, it should be clear that a phenomenology from below precedes and grounds any theology from above.[19]

Not only does this dialogue overcome differences, for Falque it is absolutely essential to any attempt at theology, "Since God became man . . . it is first through the human that we reach God, only seeing after the fact and with a heart still burning that he was already walking at out side when he was speaking to us along the way (Lk 24:32)."[20] Accordingly, this move to "cross the Rubicon" is not simply a theoretical luxury afforded to more progressively minded philosophers and theologians, but the very condition for theology to unfold in the first place—and for the transformation of philosophy by that very theology. Falque thus succeeds in unearthing a mutual relationship of reciprocity rather than a primordial antagonism or estrangement.

Granted, not all interlocutors will share that position, but the ability to open a common ground for fruitful encounters and dialogue is certainly remarkable over an issue and in an era so heavily polarized—and not just in the realm of theoretical academic debates. I cannot help but wonder whether the implications of such a prospect for dialogue hold untapped potential for other historically estranged or opposed groups: theism and atheism, various and differing creedal faiths, the Church and postmodernism, or even into the realm of contemporary politics, to name a few.

A CONCLUDING QUESTION

Despite this, is there not a necessary hostility—or perhaps a less charged, beneficial antagonism—that we should maintain between theology and philosophy?

Crossing the Rubicon provides an exemplary model that enables dialogue across difference, though such a movement also exposes a necessary inner tension that appears irresolvable in the relationship between philosophy and theology—a mutual necessity but also a mutual hostility or antagonism, or (at best) a mutual opposition and critique.

I fear that, in some cases, Falque advocates an overly optimistic view of the potential for this relationship. He concludes, "*Entente* [in French] has two meanings: listening but also agreement. In this double sense, we should listen for and agree on what such a crossing of the ford might have demanded, or yet led us to believe or think."[21] But should all dialogue and encounter be marked solely by listening and agreement? Is it a breakdown in communication and failure, should disagreement or discord emerge? Can we not have transformative and meaningful relationships which are nonetheless marked by significant discord, disagreement, even correction and antagonism amid respect and mutuality (e.g., parents and children, husbands and wives, even between trusted friends)? Discord need not spell out disgust, and those who disagree need not despise one another.

Falque's use of metaphor on this point is curious, and it gestures toward major themes of contemporary philosophy regarding difference, encountering the other, welcoming the stranger, and the (im)possibility of hospitality. Falque frequently employs the examples of a foreigner visiting a foreign land, crossing borders freely to be transformed by it. As he notes, the ability to let:

> The stranger's country becomes my own land, without confining me to the status of an expatriate. Of course, no one will forget his country of origin. But we will also remember that only our country of origin makes the opportunity to travel possible, and that we must finally oppose patriotism's code of silence and disciplinary boundaries and divisions, the transformation of ourselves by that which is foreign.[22]

While optimistic and merely a metaphor, we know all too well that this is not always the case. What of the foreigner maligned and oppressed, rejected and estranged, or the refugee rejected and deported? Contemporary philosophical considerations of hospitality, hostility, *hostipitality* reveal the nebulous nature of these encounters, while the trope of the oppressed "alien and sojourner" is no stranger to theology either. Perhaps caution is merited, and discernment regarding the value of antagonism and discord.

Such hostility and antagonism are not necessarily evils to be avoided. Mutual critique and accountability prove beneficial, and even necessary, in calling another to account or in fraternal correction. Could not any "hostility" provide the necessary corrective against ideological blindness, or misguided dogmatism?

On this point, I consider the aptness of Falque's title: *Crossing the Rubicon*. The allusion to this monumental and mythologized moment of history captures only partially what Falque advocates and embraces: an irrevocable step that constitutes an act of war against the status quo, one that unsettles and provokes, yet nonetheless one that leads to an unquestioning transformation of both the traverser and the traversed—for neither General Julius Caesar nor the Roman Republic were ever the same after that moment. But let us not overlook the necessarily hostile nature of this exchange—or, better yet, this irrevocable incursion and the Civil War that transpired. Without antagonism and hostility in the relationship, perhaps Falque advocates not so much crossing the Rubicon as the more docile foreign exchange of crossing the Schengen zone.

NOTES

1. This chapter is a revised expansion to remarks originally given as part of a panel discussion at the Society for Phenomenology and Existential Philosophy (SPEP) 56 Conference (Memphis, Tennessee) on October 19, 2017. My thanks to Bruce Ellis Benson, B. Keith Putt, and the Society for Continental Philosophy and Theology (SCPT) for extending the invitation to speak as part of the panel. Likewise, I am grateful to Karl Hefty and Tamsin Jones for their respective contributions to our discussion and this subsequent publication. I am especially grateful to Emmanuel Falque for his friendship and mentorship, and for his work that served as the springboard for the SPEP panel discussion.

2. Christina Gschwandtner provides a helpful genealogy of the "theological turn" of French phenomenologists in her *Postmodern Apologetics? Arguments for God in Contemporary Philosophy* (New York: Fordham University Press, 2013). She observes of Falque that "along with Jean-Louis Chrétien, belongs to the next generation of French thinkers . . . he has degrees in both philosophy and theology and merges the two disciplines far more fully than any of the other thinkers, occasionally even challenging the boundaries between these subject matters as unnecessary and superficial" (184). While I disagree with Gschwandtner that Falque views these distinctions as "unnecessary and superficial," her mapping of a trend in French phenomenology is quite insightful; namely, that in each subsequent generation, the strict separation of philosophy and theology begins to fade and a more porous or permeable boundary progressively emerges.

3. Emmanuel Falque, *Crossing the Rubicon: The Borderlands of Philosophy and Theology*, translated by Reuben Shank (New York: Fordham University Press, 2016), 25.

4. Such comments should not be taken to set up a combative relationship with the text in question, and I caution that I make this observation not as a criticism, but rather as a prefatory note to ground and to frame both Falque's claims and my assessments that follow. In fact, I have written elsewhere in strong defense of Falque's reclamation of the body and his emphasis on an immanent phenomenological perspective. See: William C. Woody, "Embracing Finitude: Falque's Phenomenology and the Suffering 'God with Us,'" in *Evil, Fallenness, and Finitude*, edited by Bruce Ellis Benson and B. Keith Putt (London: Palgrave MacMillan, 2017), 115–34.

5. Falque, *Crossing the Rubicon*, 157–58.

6. Falque, *Crossing the Rubicon*, 107 (emphasis added).

7. Falque, *Crossing the Rubicon*, 107.

8. Falque, *Crossing the Rubicon*, 123.

9. Falque, *Crossing the Rubicon*, 158 (emphasis added).

10. And here I note, while anecdotal and experiential evidence, the observation that for the first two conferences of the International Network for Philosophy of Religion in Paris (2015 and 2017), every paper from a French author or presenter focused on methodological justification, while for the Americans and Australians such justification was taken for granted and moved into the realm of application and description.

11. Attention to this hermeneutic grounding of the subject, or "from where do you speak?" (*D'où parlez-vous?*), is an important point that further distinguishes Falque from Marion on the question of hermeneutics. While Falque by no means makes hermeneutics primary (a point argued at length in the opening chapters of *Crossing the Rubicon*), he nonetheless affords it a necessary place in his phenomenology. Marion, for his part, resists such attention to the grounding of the subject and so heavily emphasizes the primacy of the givenness of the phenomena at the expense of the "subject" (*l'adonné*) that hermeneutics seemingly all but disappears in his phenomenology of givenness. A number of critics have pressed Marion on this point, notably Shane Mackinlay, Christina Gschwandtner, and Richard Kearney, all of whom argue for a greater attention to hermeneutics. See also: Shane Mackinlay, "Phenomenality in the Middle: Marion, Romano, and the Hermeneutics of the Event," in *Givenness and God: Questions of Jean-Luc Marion*, edited by Ian Leask and Eoin Cassidy (New York: Fordham University Press, 2005), 167–81. Christina M. Gschwandtner, *Degrees of Givenness: On Saturation in Jean-Luc Marion* (Bloomington: Indiana University Press, 2014), 14–24. Kearney, much in the spirit of his philosophical mentor Paul Ricœur, makes this question of "from where do you speak?" a central focus. For Kearney's own accounting of his encounter with Ricœur on this very question, see Richard Kearney, "Where I Speak From: A Short Intellectual Autobiography," in *Debating Otherness with Richard Kearney: Perspectives from South Africa*, edited by D. P. Veldsman and Y. Steenkamp (Cape Town: AOSIS, 2018), 36–37.

12. Pope Saint John Paul II, *Fides et Ratio*, §1. Falque still recognizes and advocates a level of complementarity between philosophy and theology, though he also emphasizes a transformative aspect that goes beyond mere complementarity. It is important to note that, while this model of complementarity is espoused by Pope Saint John Paul II in his 1999 encyclical letter *Fides et Ratio* and has similarly been endorsed by Pope Emeritus Benedict XVI (one of the principal architects of the encyclical letter itself), I am reticent to label this model as the singular or definitive *Catholic* view. Such a label is so overarching as to be indefensibly general, and it ignores the variety of perspectives that exist within the Catholic tradition. I am most grateful to the Rev. John Conley for his suggestions and clarifications on this matter. For example, the McInerny Thomist school—while undoubtedly *Catholic*—would nonetheless still adhere more closely to the handmaiden model. Recognizing the diversity within the Catholic tradition and its understanding of the relationship between theology and philosophy, I label the model of complementarity the "Phenomenological Catholic" model in the legacy of John Paul II.

13. Falque, *Crossing the Rubicon*, 99.

14. Falque, *Crossing the Rubicon*, 99.

15. Falque, *Crossing the Rubicon*, 124. These themes of transformation and metamorphosis are a thread running throughout Falque's work, and he explicitly links this with the Resurrec-

tion yet again in the second volume of his *Triduum philosophique*. He plays with the maxim of Merleau-Ponty that "the Incarnation changes everything," to argue rather that "the Resurrection changes everything" and offers an account of the metamorphosis and transformation of human incarnation (and its finitude) through Resurrection. The theological notion of Resurrection plays a similar and transformative role here for Falque as well. Emmanuel Falque, *The Metamorphosis of Finitude: An Essay on Birth and Resurrection*, translated by George Hughes (New York: Fordham, 2012), 62–80.
   16. Falque, *Crossing the Rubicon*, 82–83.
   17. Falque, *Crossing the Rubicon*, 99.
   18. Falque, *Crossing the Rubicon*, 83.
   19. Falque, *Crossing the Rubicon*, 124.
   20. Falque, *Crossing the Rubicon*, 152.
   21. Falque, *Crossing the Rubicon*, 153.
   22. Falque, *Crossing the Rubicon*, 152.

Chapter Five

The Geography of the Rubicon

Philosophy, Theology, and Religious Studies in the American Context

Tamsin Jones

In his "discourse on method," *Crossing the Rubicon: The Borderlands of Philosophy and Theology*, Emmanuel Falque wades where the previous generation of French phenomenologists would not dare: into the space separating philosophy and theology in order to, at once, uphold and traverse the distance between the two disciplines. As Matthew Farley notes in his introduction to the volume, Falque challenges those who "continue to treat philosophy and theology as if they were separated by some ancient Panthalassa, rather than by a mere rivulet in Emilia-Romagna."[1] In order to enable and encourage such a crossing from philosophy to theology and theology to philosophy, Falque will minimize the distance between the shores, while at the same time making it very clear that a border still separates and distinguishes them, however slight a body of water it might be. In this chapter, I will consider whether one need map these shores differently if we are to contemplate such a metaphorical crossing in the American academic context, placing it at the intersection of theology, philosophy of religion, and religious studies. As an academic theologian working in a religious studies department in the United States, I will argue that this context presents a somewhat messier geography in which the demarcations between river banks are less clear and, paradoxically, the river less traversable.

Falque encapsulates his methodological discourse in the following mottos: "The better one theologizes, the more one philosophizes," but also, "the more we theologize, the better we philosophize."[2] The benefits of crossing the disciplinary divide are, in other words, mutual. Falque observes that the benefit has thus far been felt mostly on the side of the theologians enjoying the "immense fecundity of phenomenology" while theology's "counterblow" has not yet made its impact fully known to the phenomenological world[3]— an inequity Falque seeks to remedy, already implicitly in his previous works,[4] and now in full methodological openness in *Crossing the Rubicon*. His hope is for equal opportunity crossings:

> As the philosopher and the theologian cross in the Rubicon, they will have no choice in passing each other but to let themselves be transformed—each one by the other. The first will teach the second about the human journey. The second will make the first see that he cannot refuse to open himself—upon a decision, of course (Chapter 4, §14)—to the transcendence of the One who comes to "metamorphose" everything, to the extent to which he has first assumed it in its entirety.[5]

Crossing the Rubicon from philosophy to theology, or vice versa, brings the opportunity of growth in either direction. Philosophy delivers an exploration of the human being in all its rich complexity, while theology invites (or persuades, or forces—Falque is not entirely clear on this point) an openness to something more, the "transcendence of the One."

Nonetheless, the possibility of mutual benefit requires that each remembers their citizenship in the land from which they travel; in other words, Falque is interested in encounter, not conversion. Indeed, this is one of the markers which, arguably, separates him from a previous generation of French phenomenologists who, by refusing the distance between the two disciplines and claiming certain topics (such as revelation, liturgy, Eucharist) as properly philosophical, also were less explicit about the confessional origin of those topics. Distinctly, Falque has no need to "baptize" philosophers like Badiou, Franck, and Nancy, who might, nevertheless, make use of theology in interesting ways.[6] Despite the fact that Falque employs a militaristic metaphor— Caesar's crossing is a movement into battle—Falque's model of the ensuing encounter, he insists, need not result in "crushing" one's foe, but instead could be understood as an athletic contest in which one encounters an equal adversary against which to test, exercise, and thus strengthen one's own abilities.[7]

Recalling that, in order to make this crossing productively and safely, one must remember and return to the land from which one travels, it is necessary to mark the distinct topography of each shore in order to be able to make that return. Falque argues that philosophy and theology are distinguished "not so much by their respective contents (after all, the Eucharist, the Passion, or the Resurrection can also be approached philosophically) than by their modes of proceeding—heuristic or didactic" and the direction of their approach, specifically whether the object of study is approached from on high or from below.[8] Falque seeks a delicate balance between an over-unification of the disciplines, which would confuse their methods, and an over-separation, which would, prejudicially, exclude legitimate objects of consideration to each. The balance is found thus:

> Between philosophy and theology a *difference* must be maintained between (a) their ways, (b) their modes of proceeding, and (c) the status of the objects to be analyzed, while at the same time recognizing (d) the possible and paradoxical *community* of objects given to thought.[9]

In this schema, although both disciplines may share the same objects to consider, the direction of their approach is distinct: theology proceeds didactically—"what is said in opening must then also be repeated identically at the end"—with dogmatic force and "from above," in order to treat an object it takes as (or claims to be) an actuality. However, philosophy proceeds heuristically; with an open and questioning spirit, it proceeds "from below" to consider *possible* objects.[10] Regardless of discipline, however, Falque insists on the greatest overlap with respect to the object of study itself—whether considering prayer, liturgy, Eucharist, Incarnation, revelation, etc. In this way Falque characterizes theology as a "discourse beginning with God," whereas philosophy can be a "discourse on the God-phenomenon appearing to the human."[11] My question is whether this distinction makes as much sense in the American context.

Falque begins his book with a remark that the "relationship between philosophy and theology in France has recently shifted." In France policies of *laïcité*, which forced theology out of the public university setting, are being challenged, and "locked doors have already given way."[12] What I wonder is if, in the American context, we might observe a self-imposed *laïcité* within, at least, academic theology. To explore this question, I will consider two centers of theological training in the United States: Harvard Divinity School and the University of Chicago Divinity School. These institutions are interesting to consider not only because they are, arguably, among the most influential spheres in which training in theology and philosophy of religion occurs, but more specifically, because both operate on a model that has some interesting parallels to Falque's vision of the crossing of disciplines: they are institutions in which students can train for either ordination or for academia, and centers of research in which the philosophy of religion, religious studies, and theology meet.

At both of the divinity schools at Harvard and Chicago, one can pursue a terminal graduate degree in theology either for the purposes of ordination or ministry (MDiv), or for preparation of academic research and teaching (PhD). Both degrees are pursued in the same set of buildings with the same faculty teaching and advising in the programs. This dual identity distinguishes these institutions from others, like Yale and Princeton, both of which *institutionally* separate theological training from the academic study of religion—they are geographically located in different schools or departments, with separate faculty teaching and advising the programs.

The study of theology in these institutions is also distinguished from the study of theology in either a Catholic seminary or Protestant seminary, both of which can assume a uniformity of religious identity and confession that is not possible in a more diverse or pluralistic setting such as Chicago or Harvard. Depending on the order of the Catholic seminary, philosophy may play a smaller or larger role in the curriculum, whereas in many Protestant seminaries, philosophy will be emphasized less than cognate disciplines such as biblical studies and ethics in theological formation.

A third possible setting in which we can consider the relationship between theology and philosophy would be larger Catholic universities such as Villanova University, Fordham University, Boston College, or the University of Notre Dame, all of which have both strong theology and philosophy departments. These institutions, generally speaking, would be more sympathetic toward the kind of relationship between disciplines that Falque advocates for two reasons: on the one hand, these large Catholic universities historically have been more favorably disposed to the continental tradition within their philosophy departments,[13] and on the other hand, their overarching Catholic identity welcomes the contributions of the theology departments in a way that goes absolutely against the trend in public universities and private, nonsectarian universities which have increasingly forbidden anything that smells suspiciously theological. However, these Catholic institutions are less inclined to consider their theological mandate as one of the theological (or philosophical) study of religions outside of Christianity. Again, on this point, Chicago and Harvard seem to occupy a unique and significantly different position as nonsectarian research institutions that continue to hold a place for the study of theology. However, I would argue that this has been accomplished only through a shift in the understanding of how theology is done.

On its website describing the PhD programs of study, the University of Chicago Divinity School structures the possible trajectories of study into three committees and eleven areas of study. We are concerned here with the committee on the "constructive studies in religion," which includes the three areas of philosophy of religion, religious ethics, and theology. Within this structure, theology is defined as a "concern with the *historical study of the self-understanding of a religious tradition* and with the interpretation of its meaning and truth for the contemporary world."[14] Note the framework of the area is necessarily historical, while there is no specification of which religious tradition can be studied theologically. Faculty teaching on this committee work in Chinese religions, Judaism, Tibetan and Indian Buddhism, as well as Christianity. The PhD at Harvard is jointly offered by Harvard Divinity School and the Graduate School of Arts and Sciences and is administered by the Committee on the Study of Religion (which comprises members of the faculty from both schools). There are many different areas of study into which one can apply to pursue a PhD including theology, philosophy of religion, religious ethics, Islamic studies, religions of the Americas, Jewish studies, African religions, Buddhist studies, Greco-Roman religions, religion, gender and culture, and so on. However, if one is applying to study ethics, religion and society, philosophy of religion, religion gender and culture, *or* theology, the applicant must specify "the religious tradition(s) and/or approximate geographical range(s) or temporal period(s)" upon which the applicant intends to focus.[15] In other words, here too, there is no assumption that one is studying Christianity when one studies theology, while at the same time, there is a recognition that one does not study theology generally, but only within a specific tradition, region, and historical period.

Significant to note in the comparison of these two programs is the fact that the study of theology is defined as a regionally and historically specific discipline. However, these programs make explicit the fact that there is more than one region or historical period in which to study theology. As a result, theology is not uniform, didactic, or proceeding from on high, in the way in which Falque suggests. Rather, theology proceeds from a specific historical context and region, and, most importantly, from a specific religious tradition—that is to say, "from below." The sort of theology that one would most likely encounter in an institution dedicated to the academic study of religion—that is, a properly historicized theology—is, de facto, always regionalized; at the very least, it is always constrained by the boundaries of its own tradition—it is Hindu theology, or Christian theology, or Muslim theology.[16] What does this process of historicization mean for the study of theology?

My doctoral advisor at Harvard Divinity School, Sarah Coakley, occasionally would voice a concern that the study of theology had become a study of "theologology"—that discourse on God had become, in other words, discourse on the discourse on God, a second-order study. If I understand Falque correctly, what Coakley meant by "theologology" is something akin to a process of what Falque calls "vulgarization"—the process of clearly identifying and communicating historical lines of influence and the transmission of evolving interpretations of theological (or philosophical) concepts, which is to be explicitly distinguished from the act of philosophical "thinking."[17] In this case, theology would be best understood as a pursuit within the history of ideas. The point I am making here is that this portrait of the pursuit of academic theology is fairly accurate. Within the academic study of religion, one approach to studying religion—namely, the theological—has accepted (some might say too meekly, others might say appropriately)[18] the limitations of its own discourse: its regional specificity and historical contextualization.

As a result, academic theologians have as their object of study not "*theos*" directly but "discourse on *theos*"—a discourse that is, of course, a human phenomenon and always necessarily placed within its historical context. Moreover, the term "discourse" here is cast most broadly to capture, not merely doctrinal and creedal statements, but also liturgy, hagiography, hymns, poetry, art and architecture, ethical and legal precepts, mythological narratives, etc.

Relatedly, one might delineate the characteristic of what makes academic theology academic, in the following manner: the primary audience of the academic theologian is the academy, and the academy is also the authoritative body determining what counts as evidence and legitimating the discourse as such. In other words, the academic theologian does not speak from, or to, a specific confessional body or institution. While the identity of the academic theologian may be confessionally specific, it also may not. In either case, however, the academic theologian is trained not to rely on a specific confessional identity as the foundational authority for their argument. Rather, arguments are defended and adjudicated based on grounds that are held in common with other disciplines: historical responsibility or acuity and the overall persuasiveness of the theological argument—something that may be judged by a variety of criteria including the ethical and pragmatic implications of the argument, its internal logical coherence, or its use of evidence, etc.

In other words, the study of academic theology, at least as it is found in these two major centers of theological study in the United States, proceeds very much "from below," rather than dogmatically from above. If academic theology is dealing in actuality rather than possibility, as Falque determines, then it is merely the actuality of "theologology"—that is, the intellectual history of thinking about the divine, and the rich varieties of doctrine and practice that represent such thinking, found within a specific religious tradition. Theology is, to borrow Heidegger's term, a "positive (ontic) science"—the disclosure of a given being, a *positum*, which is objectified in its study.[19] According to Heidegger, in the case of the science of Christian theology, its positum is faith.[20] Theology investigates, evaluates, and constructs, then, the varieties of Christian faith that are always recognized first as *human* responses to the divine.

One difference between the theology/philosophy relationship in France and the theology/philosophy relationship in North America is the additional factor of the emergence of religious studies departments in the latter. The study of religion, which historically was borne out of departments of theology, has for the most part banished its parent: theology has been pushed out of most departments of religion. Up until fairly recently, philosophy of religion still held a prominent place within religious studies. However, with the material turn to "lived religion" in the 1990s, and the concurrent radical and thorough historicization of the field that problematized any natural, universal, or ahistoric notion of religion, philosophy of religion also increasingly came under suspicion as a subfield which was seen to be sneaking theology in by the back door.[21] A new crop of American philosophers of religion—with interesting allegiances to both the continental and analytic traditions, but located within departments of religious studies—have more recently pushed back on this marginalization and, in so doing, offered a different perspective on the relationship between theology, philosophy, and religious studies.[22] I will very briefly consider Lewis' work, *Why Philosophy Matters for the Study of Religion & Vice Versa*, as illustrative of this position.

Lewis defines religious studies as "the disciplined examination of religion, including religious thought, people, movements, practices, materials, etc., as well as reflection on the conceptions of each of these terms, without presupposing the validity of or privileging the study of any particular religion or group of religious phenomena"—neither presupposing the truth nor the falsity of any particular religion.[23] In other words, religious studies cultivate a self-conscious discipline of openness. Where does theology fit into this discipline? According to Lewis, theology is too diverse a field to state whether it can be fit as a sub-field within religious studies. Some theology "excludes itself by making conversation-stopping appeals to authorities conceived as unquestionable,"[24] whereas the theology that does not, which continues to proceed "from below" clearly belongs within the academy. Note that for Lewis normativity is not the issue; theology and religious studies can and should make normative claims (just as political science, history, and literature, let alone philosophy do). What is the crucial marker for entry into the academy is "a principled willingness to submit all claims to scrutiny and questioning, to insist that no assumptions, doctrines, or authorities are beyond questioning"[25]—to proceed "from below," heuristically rather than dogmatically. Philosophy of religion, as well as any theology "academic" enough to follow these ground rules, can provide conceptual depth and synthetic ability to the study of religion. Thus, according to Lewis, philosophy is necessary to the study of religion, whereas a nondogmatic theology is permitted as a sub-field. The divinity schools of Chicago and Harvard retain a far more robust and central role for the study of theology within religious studies more broadly, but the nondogmatic restraints are implicitly shared.

One appraisal of academic theology in the United States might be that it has given up its own authority to speak otherwise than according to the standards of the secular academy. This negative evaluation may be correct, but it is not the only way to understand the position of theology within the secular university. It is also possible to understand academic theology's insistence that it too proceeds from below and without the authority of speaking from on high, as itself a theological claim: its own acceptance of the inescapability of finitude, and the appropriate methodological humility of the discipline in recognition of that. Academic theologians might explicitly identify themselves as Catholic, or Eastern Orthodox, Methodist, Mormon or Anglican, or as non-Christian believers (as Falque reminds us we always believe in something),[26] but they cannot rely on that identity as providing access to a particular type of authoritative evidence for the argument they put forth.

In this context, I would argue that it has become more and more difficult to adequately distinguish between the philosopher of religion and the academic theologian. Both seek to investigate the modes of reason-giving in a religious tradition, probing the coherence and rationality of a system of belief and practice, and pondering the human response to transcendence. Moreover, as I have demonstrated, for at least an important segment of theological studies in the American academy, such thinking is not pursued didactically "from on high," but heuristically "from below." Thus, on this side of the Atlantic, the two disciplines are more alike than not. Yet philosophy and theology are precisely what Falque has argued can and ought to be kept clearly discrete in the French academic context in which the Sorbonne and L'institut Catholique are both distinct and yet bridged by the Jardin du Luxembourg. The question remains whether, given the diminishing of the methodological distance between philosophy and theology, we can talk in the same way of crossing this Rubicon in the American context.

NOTES

1. Matthew Farley "Introduction" to Emmanuel Falque, *Crossing the Rubicon: The Borderlands of Philosophy and Theology*, translated by Reuben Shank (New York: Fordham University Press, 2016), 4.

2. Emmanuel Falque, *Crossing the Rubicon: The Borderlands of Philosophy and Theology*, translated by Reuben Shank (New York: Fordham University Press, 2016), 107, 139.

3. Falque, *Crossing the Rubicon*, 21.

4. See *Le Passeur de Gethsémani, Angoisse, souffrance et mort. Lecture existentielle et phénoménologique* (Paris: Cerf, 1999); *Métamorphose de la finitude. Essai philosophique sur la naissance et la résurrection* (Paris: Cerf, 2004); *Les noces de l'Agneau. Essai philosophique sur la corps et l'eucharistie* (Paris: Cerf, 2011). For English translations, see *The Guide to Gethsamane: Anxiety, Suffering, Death*, translated by George Hughes (New York: Fordham University Press, 2018); *The Metamorphosis of Finitude: An Essay on Birth and Resurrection*, translated by George Hughes (New York: Fordham University Press, 2012); and *The Wedding Feast of the Lamb: Eros, the Body, and the Eucharist*, translated by George Hughes (New York: Fordham University Press, 2016.)

5. Falque, *Crossing the Rubicon*, 151.
6. Falque, *Crossing the Rubicon*, 138.
7. Falque, *Crossing the Rubicon*, 139.
8. Falque, *Crossing the Rubicon*, 24.
9. Falque, *Crossing the Rubicon*, 125.
10. Falque, *Crossing the Rubicon*, 126.
11. Falque, *Crossing the Rubicon*, 127.
12. Falque, *Crossing the Rubicon*, 16.
13. The University of Notre Dame is the exception here. However, one might argue that in its marriage of analytic philosophy and theology in the formation of "analytic theology" it follows the same pattern as Falque promotes. On this regard, see *Analytic Theology: New*

Essays in the Philosophy of Theology, edited by Oliver Crisp and Michael Rea (Oxford: Oxford University Press, 2009) as well as the *Journal of Analytic Theology* (Center for Philosophy of Religion at the University of Notre Dame and Baylor University).

14. The University of Chicago Divinity School: https://divinity.uchicago.edu/academics/areas-study/constructive-studies-religion (emphasis added).

15. Harvard University, Committee on the Study of Religion: https://studyofreligion.fas.harvard.edu/pages/research.

16. This statement ignores the reality of the porosity of the borders between religious traditions and the overlapping paths of inter-religious definition in the ongoing construction of religious identity. Nonetheless, it stands as a statement of the domain a theologian *claims* to investigate: that is, a Jewish theologian claims only to speak authoritatively within the domain of Judaism, and not, for instance, about Buddhist doctrine.

17. Falque, *Crossing the Rubicon*, 17.

18. I recognize that there is a real debate between those thinkers who believe theology rolled over too quickly to the demands of the secular academy in order to keep its foot in the door, and those who would argue that theology is hard-wired to accept such a humbling diminishment of its domain as the nature of its study has always required it. I will leave that judgment for others to fight over. My argument here is less about how theology ought to be, than about how it actually *is* taught and studied within institutions that study religion more generally.

19. This definition of theology is found in a lecture by Heidegger, "Phenomenology and Theology," which was originally given on March 9, 1927, and subsequently translated and published in *Pathmarks*, edited and translated by William McNeil (Cambridge: Cambridge University Press, 1998), 39–62.

20. Heidegger, "Phenomenology and Theology," 52.

21. For a recent expression of this suspicion see Timothy David Knepper, *The Ends of Philosophy of Religion: Terminus and Telos* (New York: Palgrave, 2013).

22. See Thomas A. Lewis, *Why Philosophy Matters for the Study of Religion & Vice Versa* (Oxford: Oxford University Press, 2016); Kevin Schilbrack, *Philosophy and the Study of Religions: A Manifesto* (Malden: Wiley-Blackwell, 2014); Tyler Roberts, *Encountering Religion: Responsibility and Criticism After Secularism* (New York: Columbia University Press, 2013).

23. Lewis, *Why Philosophy Matters for the Study of Religion & Vice Versa*, 7.

24. Lewis, *Why Philosophy Matters for the Study of Religion & Vice Versa*, 7–8.

25. Lewis, *Why Philosophy Matters for the Study of Religion & Vice Versa*, 8.

26. Falque, *Crossing the Rubicon*, 78.

Part II

Emmanuel Falque in Comparison

Chapter Six

At the Confluence of Phenomenology and Non-Phenomenology

Maurice Blondel and Emmanuel Falque

William L. Connelly

The capacity, or incapacity, of Husserlian method to fulfill its own inspiration has been well shown, whether it be in the "return to the things themselves," in attaining for philosophy the status of "rigorous science," or in delivering a means for a methodical description of personal subjectivity with the phenomenological reduction; in any case, it would appear that by now Husserlian phenomenology has come near the point of reaching a state of *full philosophical consciousness*. Critiques against Husserlian method have been well cast throughout the development of the phenomenological tradition, certainly for Emmanuel Levinas, Michel Henry, and Jean Luc-Marion in terms of the "theological turn" but also for Maurice Merleau-Ponty in terms of the "barbarian principle," where he asserts that "the ultimate task of phenomenology as philosophy of consciousness is to understand its relationship to non-phenomenology."[1] In the end, these challenges to Husserl's phenomenological method have led to a certain confluence perhaps best understood in terms of how "non-phenomenology" must find its place within phenomenology; at this precise convergence, we may situate both Maurice Blondel and Emmanuel Falque within the phenomenological tradition.

The recognition of a gap between the realm of phenomenality proper to phenomenology and that of *another realm* absent to any direct phenomenolization is brought to expression by Falque in his book *Nothing to It* (2020), where he claims that psychoanalysis can help in overcoming this divide by way of the so-called backlash of psychoanalysis upon phenomenology.[2] The backlash of Freudian psychoanalysis upon phenomenology materializes in two ways, first by challenging the a priori of phenomenolization in phenomenological method, and then secondly by reconciling the method of phenomenology with "this never interrogated a priori of manifestation and its possible signification."[3] What this confluence ultimately leads to is the development of a "phenomenology of force," centered on the Freudian Id, the powers of the will, and the realm of instincts and of drives, as all of these appear in such a way that challenges the traditional paradigm of manifestation as it has been typically construed within the phenomenological tradition. The shift toward this paradigm of "force" is a task that Falque considers to be *necessary* in order to accomplish this "ultimate task for phenomenology" despite such affirmations as given by Jacques Derrida of its inaccessibility: "Now, one would seek in vain a concept in phenomenology which would permit the conceptualization of intensity or force."[4] The present chapter will seek to highlight this movement in phenomenology by tracing out the French phenomenological tradition in terms of *counter-intentionality* as pioneered by Emmanuel Levinas, and then to that of the intentionality of the flesh as brought to the fore with Maurice Merleau-Ponty, as both of these trends converge in their being rooted in and yet breaking away from the original phenomenological paradigm as established by Edmund Husserl—and finally, this French development of the phenomenological tradition will be viewed as leading toward a certain confluence or even paradigm shift in the phenomenological landscape which can be best understood in light of Emmanuel Falque's call toward a phenomenology of force, though this time *not* as a result of the backlash of Freudian psychoanalysis or Nietzschean philosophy upon phenomenology, but rather in terms of a consequent though more fundamental backlash of an already operative though subterranean influence that is now coming to the surface: the thought of Maurice Blondel, which while historically preceding Husserlian phenomenology, nevertheless conceptually succeeds the tradition in France in its capacity to respond to this "ultimate task" of phenomenology—as Blondel's philosophy of action is centered upon the constructive dynamism of the will and its connection to the mind, in what he later describes as an ontogenesis.

THE FRENCH PHENOMENOLOGICAL TRADITION: TRACING THE STREAMS

In order to understand the intricacies of this development in phenomenological method, it is helpful to assess two distinct streams in French phenomenology, here taking as a starting point the critique offered by Dominique Janicaud in his classic text *The Theological Turn in French Phenomenology* (1991), where he describes the "rupture with immanent phenomenality" of Emmanuel Levinas and the concomitant pushing of phenomenological limits with Maurice Merleau-Ponty.[5] From here we can discern the first steps toward the confluence and merger of these phenomenological impulses, which serves to define the philosophy of Emmanuel Falque, and is assisted by and corresponds to the heritage of Maurice Blondel; in sum, this edges the phenomenological tradition toward a promising new paradigm of descriptive methodology—here centered upon the constitutive faculties of the will.

FROM INTENTIONALITY TO COUNTER-INTENTIONALITY

At the root of Levinas' thought there is a critique that brings to light *the incapacity to bring to light* a darkness beyond any sense of meaning, hidden in the shadows beyond all signification but yet somehow still implicating a certain mode of existential expression, which is described by Levinas in terms of "the night," and given succinct articulation in terms of the generic appellation of the *il y a* (there is):

> We could say that the night is the very experience of the *there is* [*il y a*]. But this universal absence is in its turn presence, an absolutely unavoidable presence. . . . The mind does not find itself faced with an apprehended exterior. The exterior—if one insists on the term—remains uncorrelated with an interior.[6]

Here in his *Existence and Existents* (1947), in the movement toward "this universal absence," that is nevertheless "an absolutely unavoidable presence," with the proclaimed notion of the "night" and the *there is* [*il y a*], we find Levinas deliver a challenge (at least conceptually) to Husserlian phenomenology in terms of the a priori of direct phenomenolization with the reduction to intentionality.[7] The definitive break away from Husserl's phenomenological paradigm was decisively announced in *Totality and Infinity* (1961), which appeared some fourteen years *after* these initial demands began to stretch phenomenological method up to a breaking point. This process is brought to completion in his treatment of "the ethics of the face" where is found a resounding blow against the notion of intentionality, which in turn opened up the counter-intentional shift in phenomenology: "The relation between the Other and me . . . issues neither in number nor in concept. The Other remains infinitely transcendent, infinitely foreign; his face in which his epiphany is produced . . . breaks with the world that can be common to us."[8] For Levinas, the idea of the infinite is not merely an abstract principle, but instead represents a profoundly manifest expression, where in the face of immanence there is found a radical transcendence.

In this sense Levinas leveled a challenge to phenomenology as a method, particularly as a method situated in the mode of consciousness in terms of eidetic elucidation and the intuition of essences.[9] The reduction of phenomenology to the eidetic structure situates both being and thought in terms of *adequation*, which according to Levinas leaves *non-adequation* unaccounted for phenomenologically, such as with *the other*, the *il y a*, or in terms of the idea of the infinite, and as Janicaud suggests, this results in an essential *violence* to the very notion of *intentionality* and thus leads to "considerable distortions" and even to the "abandonment of the phenomenological *method*."[10]

FROM COUNTER-INTENTIONALITY TO THE INTENTIONALITY OF THE FLESH

It is noteworthy that both Levinas and Merleau-Ponty were developing their research not only at the exact same time, but also as Janicaud notes, on "resolving the same problem in and responding to the same deficiency of Husserlian phenomenology"—a body of research that would culminate concomitantly in 1961, the year of Maurice Merleau-Ponty's death, and with the apparition of Levinas' *Totality and Infinity* and the still wet ink of Merleau-Ponty's *The Visible and Invisible*. Dominique Janicaud draws another important parallel between Emmanuel Levinas and Maurice Merleau-Ponty in his assertion that they both respond "in two different and on the whole divergent directions" to the "metaphysical question par excellence: the paradoxical revelation of Transcendence in a source at the heart of phenomenality."[11] As Janicaud continues to note, "where Levinas is concerned, aplomb is the categorical affirmation of the primacy of the idea of infinity, immediately dispossessing the *sameness* [*mêmeté*] of the I, or of being [*être*]."[12] It is just this notion of *aplomb* that Janicaud places in immediate juxtaposition to that of *intertwining*—the chiasm, or the *Ineinander*—which is "at the heart of Merleau-Ponty's research."[13]

Where Levinas places intentionality in terms of the Other that "breaks from this world," Merleau-Ponty remains faithful to phenomenological method in coming to terms with the question of transcendence from within the horizon of the world, and here in terms of the flesh. The *flesh* represents a new form of intentionality that is part of the "tissue" of existence—both interior and exterior to the individual—described as "the formative medium of the object and the subject."[14] Engaging these themes in terms of the "system of equivalences between the inside and the outside,"[15] Maurice Merleau-Ponty sought to lay the groundwork for an ontology of nature, a topic he chose to thoroughly develop, even making it the "sole topic" for nearly half a decade during his teaching at the Collège de France (1956–1960).[16] The writing of *The Visible and the Invisible* interrupted this agenda, perhaps functioning as a kind of preface to this larger project. Despite postponing his effort to produce an "ontology of nature," he was still able to generate a wide body of material including several finished essays on the subject, to be later published as *In Praise of Philosophy and Other Essays* (1963). This is in addition to a large body of notes and drafted material that remains largely unpublished, though the depth and content of what here can be considered his "later work" has been well surveyed, most notably by Emmanuel de Saint-Aubert.[17]

It is here in Merleau-Ponty's later work that we find his concept of the flesh [*chair*], "toward which all his philosophy converges" and something which "is geared toward a never abandoned methodological challenge to understand the total life of human beings, starting from his most elementary corporeal modes of expression."[18] Responding to this task, we find that Merleau-Ponty leads his phenomenological investigations of the flesh into a more ontological register: "we must think of it . . . as an element, as the concrete emblem of a general manner of being."[19] In this sense we find Merleau-Ponty developing a phenomenological correlate to this theme of brute being, and with the introduction of this theme we can come to see what is at stake for phenomenology: "If being is to disclose itself, it will do so before a transcendence, and not before an intentionality, it will be the engulfed brute being that returns to itself."[20]

Between Emmanuel Levinas and Maurice Merleau-Ponty, we find there are certain existential realities of life of which phenomenology is methodologically incapable of describing, leaving open the question: how effective is phenomenological method in its description of life, in getting after the lived experience and the "things" themselves? In these two diverging movements, prompted by the same block in Husserlian method, we could find a shift "towards another paradigm" or even a kind of *system breakdown* for phenomenology itself, as the shock of this blast against the most stable ground in phenomenology—in either uncovering meaning (Heidegger) or bringing a meaning into expression (Husserl)—clears away a place to reveal *a deeper level*, a new fundament and more profound substratum, or at least an alternative spectrum of experience for phenomenology to grapple with.[21] It is here along with Levinas where we find Falque leading us along the drift toward "the night of phenomenology" or even the "extra-phenomenal."[22] Yet at the same time, Falque leads us along with Merleau-Ponty in terms of "a phenomenology of the underground" and with his task of uncovering "brute being."[23] Here Falque assimilates Levinas' ultimate critique and breaking up of phenomenological method *in addition to* Maurice Merleau-Ponty's challenge and deepening of it; from this position we find Falque's deployment of certain positive responses to these assembled negative critiques against phenomenology.

From this vantage point, the philosopher of the borderlands helps us to closely define the phenomenological dimensions of a transcendental presence which breaks in upon the phenomenal order of existence; it is here with the development of the concomitant traditions in French phenomenology of counter-intentionality and the intentionality of the flesh that we can begin to chart out the move from phenomenology to non-phenomenology. Besides furnishing certain *positive responses*, Falque also delivers his own *negative critiques*, in such terms where "contemporary phenomenology suffers from a triple hypertrophy—of the flesh over the body . . . of meaning over chaos . . . and of passivity over activity or weakness over force."[24] These themes overlap in the notion of the body, and in this sense Falque comes to anticipate the arrival of a certain "existential analytic of the body" that he asserts would "turn the human body, including its animal and biological dimensions, into the 'transcendental' that could serve as the starting point for the appearance of the world (Nietzsche)."[25]

FROM THE FLESH TO THE BODY

The phenomenological terrain thus charted out helps us to see how Falque views the Rubicon separating the realm of phenomenology proper with that of the obscure domain of non-phenomenology. The key point here is that this passing need not be a *de facto* crossing from philosophy into religion—therefore representing *a second crossing*—but rather, we find in psychoanalysis inroads into the obscure region of the Freudian Id, "the dark inaccessible part of our personality."[26] For Falque, it is this aspect of human life, the "'chaos of passions and drives' at the limit of the somatic and the mental"[27] that will bequeath a phenomenology of force, helping to serve as a better philosophical proxy zone in establishing a more sensitive philosophical connection to the transcendental domain specific to religion. As Falque remarks:

> Spirituality and psychoanalysis thus have something to exchange here, if only we do not confuse the aspirations of the first (the tension of the soul towards God and its turning away into sin) with the specificity of the second (the quest for the unique depths of the human).[28]

The so-called backlash of psychoanalysis upon phenomenology, in such a meditation upon the Id, functions as a sort of bridge that Falque suggests will help to incorporate these non-phenomenal elements—inaccessible to phenomenological method—back into phenomenology. This represents a necessary step in order to bring description of certain powers at work *which lead* toward and become *implicated* in a certain phenomenolization present in human life, least of all within the domain of religious experience; this effort bypasses the theological structures leveled against phenomenology by Dominique Janicaud as this backlash preempts dealing with the question of God and religion through focusing upon *other* non-phenomenal elements which are operative at the same subterranean inter-subjective and metaphysical milieu of existence—this in turn situates religion within the purview of a so-called *psychology of the depths*:

> We must go down into our own chaos created by these drives and passions with the help of either a psychology or a phenomenology of "the depths," in order to find the power of the force that constitutes us, instead of always being satisfied with the (certainly necessary but not sufficient) requisites of passivity and alterity that make us forget what there is of the "will" and its own power.[29]

The central strategy of this move is not to induct certain transcendental elements into phenomenology as if they were proper to phenomenology itself, but rather to show the *insufficiency* of phenomenology to equate itself to these "things" whose "phenomenality" exists as an extra-phenomenal presence, and yet whose essence phenomenology need not remain silent in the face of. This again calls into question the very notion of phenomenology itself, as it runs counter, if not acting in immediate contrast, to the constitutive feature of phenomenology—with the a priori of direct phenomenolization.[30] In this sense we can better appreciate Merleau-Ponty, who served in the vanguard of a true paradigm shift within phenomenology, and which Emmanuel Falque is now moving toward fully realizing. One way to understand this paradigm shift can be found in the focusing upon the constitutive powers of the will—in terms of forces, instincts, and drives, but also the ontological ground which renders them operative. These elements were given concerted focus in a distinct phenomenological tradition with undeniable bearing to this question, here found in the work of Maurice Blondel, who in fact acts as an inconspicuous beam of support for these thinkers.[31]

THE BACKLASH OF MAURICE BLONDEL UPON PHENOMENOLOGY

Maurice Blondel's connection to phenomenology can be seen and has been articulated in a variety of substantial ways, though the question has remained in terms of how his philosophy relates not only to the contemporary scene of French phenomenology, but to the tradition more broadly speaking.[32] With Falque renewing the challenge set out by Maurice Merleau-Ponty, and in drawing attention to the role of psychoanalysis in developing phenomenological method, we see that such a structural shift reveals the ground whereby a deeper sense of phenomenological meaning can be articulated. Blondel's thought grants a sufficient philosophical paradigm to support the terrain now being trod in the development of the French phenomenological tradition. This can be articulated in terms of three distinct contributions (or shocks) that Blondel offers to phenomenology.

THE FIRST SHOCK:
THE CHALLENGE TO IMMANENT PHENOMENALITY
(LEVINAS)

Blondel holds that to understand the constitution of consciousness, or even of being itself, there is required a move to go "beyond what seems directly presented to consciousness, and beneath, behind, . . . for a reality even more real."[33] This philosophical need is postulated by Blondel without overlooking "a first movement to take our immediate representations for real truth."[34] This dynamic tension between a realist and idealist tendency in philosophy is articulated in his essay "The Idealist Illusion" (1898), which illustrates how "it is just as impossible to define as to really choose either one of these attitudes to the exclusion of the other."[35] The basic premise of this essay, "that the content of consciousness should be unfurled as it appears, by withdrawing from any idealist or realist prejudice, before judging the consistency of its content as a whole," should be considered as follow-up support for the "phenomenological method" used in Blondel's 1893 thesis "Action."[36]

Blondel would agree with Janicaud against Levinas that the theological dimension of these transcendental elements (whose presence Blondel would affirm along with Levinas) are "phenomenologically untenable" and whose truth "could only be secured in an alliance with another order."[37] This is a critique that Maurice Blondel anticipated, even establishing from the start as the north star to orient his entire philosophical enterprise: "The essential thing is to show the possibility and necessity for man of the supernatural, *while asserting its independence and inaccessibility*."[38] Just as Blondel is affirming the need to equate the existential facts of life to our consciousness, the philosopher of Aix would just as much agree along with Emmanuel Levinas that the manifested chain of phenomenon available for reduction to the level of consciousness is not entirely sufficient *in itself* for describing existence—as there are nocturnal elements that do not immediately appear within the direct register of consciousness.

These themes are more fully developed and characterized in Blondel's *The Starting Point for Philosophical Research* (1906), where he breaches the problem of adequation such as it would be posed later by Levinas, though here Blondel furnishes a method to affirm the role of consciousness in philosophically relating to any such radical transcendence despite the impossibility for it to ever be made equal [*adaequatus*] to one's own consciousness, but here instead he suggests the possibility of equating it to one's own life:

> Substituted in place of the abstract and nebulous *adequatio speculative rei et intellectus* [the speculative adaequation of thing and intellect] is the methodological research of the *adaequatio realis mentis et vitae* [the real adaequation of mind and life].[39]

Maurice Blondel qualifies a phenomenological method for situating the relation of transcendental elements—that appear only *indirectly* and are *implicit* to consciousness—in "the methodological research of the real adequation of mind and life," and in principle, this serves as a corrective to the critique leveled by Levinas against phenomenology, as it allows for the transcendental elements of life (which escape phenomenological reduction) to be *placed* within the phenomenal chain of consciousness through a method of *equation*. For Blondel, these philosophical themes directly bear upon the question of religion and apologetics, leading him to clarify the parameters for having a credible philosophy of religion where he makes the distinctions necessary for respecting the integrity of any such "immanent phenomenality" in accommodating the domain of immanence, while also understanding the role of philosophy in touching upon the presence of a *necessary* though *inaccessible* transcendence which breaks with the realm of any such immanent phenomenality.

THE SECOND SHOCK: GROUNDING THE NON-PHENOMENAL (MERLEAU-PONTY)

As if under the influence of a kind of quicklime, once Merleau-Ponty was exposed to Blondel's ontological treatise, *L'Être et les êtres* (1935), he began to transform and rework his own thinking, not only making liberal use of peculiar terms and concepts that come directly from this text, but he largely follows the general spirit behind Blondel's thinking, as Emmanuel Saint-Aubert remarks:

> *L'Être et les êtres* adopts in places an unusual terminology to describe a transcendence no longer retrospective, attributed from the outside by transgression of previously separated ontological layers, but a transcendence of departure that becomes one with an original implication—and this unity would make the very paradox of being. . . . Under these descriptions, Merleau-Ponty spontaneously retains along with Blondel that which resists the neo-Platonizing dimension of the *analogia entis*, and that which runs parallel to his philosophy of the flesh.[40]

The basic idea of Blondel's ontology is seen to be assumed by Merleau-Ponty in substantial measure: "We are going to Being by passing by beings. 'All attraction toward the height passes by the low.' There is a circulation between Being and beings."[41] Merleau-Ponty even goes so far to note that: "The idea that the world is neither first nor second. This is what Blondel thinks at bottom [*au fond*] (This is the true idea of Nature)."[42] The text *L'Être et les êtres* represents the middle volume of Blondel's metaphysical trilogy, and it is here where he speaks of "the assaults of phenomenology in attempting to arrive at an ontology."[43] The philosophical contributions Blondel provides in his critiques against phenomenology are directly taken up by Merleau-Ponty from the earliest stages in the development of his own ontology of nature. His later development of "the flesh" represents a phenomenological correlate that implicitly sustains not only Blondel's critique of phenomenology, but also the fundamental problem of the ontological double, typified in the philosophical research of the link or bond, which is the starting point of Blondel's philosophy in the Leibnizian *Vinculum*, and stands as the central theme at the apex of Merleau-Ponty's thought in terms of the *chiasm*. This touches on what Merleau-Ponty describes as "the most difficult point, that is, the bond between the flesh and the idea."[44] Blondel would develop upon a similar theme with his concept of ontological diplopy (or double vision), which is predicated by the following idea:

> In fact, and independently of any theory, thinking has three meanings that cannot be isolated, reduced to unity, or simply juxtaposed. In turn, it is what is thought or at least conceivable, it is what is thinking, producing, acting, and it is this mysterious relationship between what seems to be the two previous data; but these data themselves are only affirmed as such by an abstract elaboration whose scholarly reflection has so far failed to discover the primitive elements and to justify their progressive steps.[45]

This "mysterious relationship" generates an *intrinsic* "conflict" that constantly appears in mental life, manifesting as "two conceptions of being."[46] This constitutes an "oscillatory dichotomy" that must be conceded as an "inherent duality in mental life" that he asserts is "impossible to fulfill except in infinity."[47] It is just this sense of being that Merleau-Ponty would come to affirm: "Could we not find what has been called an 'ontological diplopy' (Blondel), which after so much philosophical effort we cannot expect to bring to a rational reduction and which leaves us with the sole alternative of wholly embracing it, just as our gaze takes over monocular images to make a single vision out of them."[48] Blondel asserts that this disparity [*inadéquation*] exists as a "propulsion."[49] This is expressed as functioning as a "centrifugal" and "centripetal force," described as a "rhythmic undulation" and "vibratory rhythm."[50] These relations in turn form the ground of what Blondel calls a "cycloidal movement"[51] and "cycloidal ontogeny."[52] It is precisely this whole "cycloidal" ontological complex that Merleau-Ponty would turn toward his idea of the flesh, and come to evoke in his mature critique of Husserl:

> It is necessary to take up again and develop the . . . *latent* intentionality which is the intentionality within being. That is not compatible with "phenomenology," that is, with an ontology that obliges whatever is not nothing to *present*

itself to the *consciousness*. . . . It is necessary to take as primary, not the consciousness . . . with its distinct intentional threads, but the vortex, . . . the spatializing-temporalizing vortex (which is flesh and not consciousness facing a noema).[53]

We find that this same ontological paradigm appears in his *The Visible and Invisible*, "the unique Being, the dimensionality to which these moments, these leaves, and these dimensions belong, is beyond the classical essence and existence and renders their relationship comprehensible."[54] It is just this sense of the distinction of essence and existence that Blondel would articulate, asserting that "instead of taking this distinction as a principle of analogy between Being and beings, is it not necessary to find the true point of reference in the one in whom 'essence' and 'existence' are but one, in a transcendence that defies any denomination, any analogy, any ambiguity and even any reciprocity?"[55]

The immanent sense of transcendence that Merleau-Ponty articulates is already found in Blondel's own *philosophical* work, and besides considering this as an *accidental* occurrence we must take it as a *contingent* reliance, which should not only cause us to pay due to the master whose work "from the pious stillness of Aix" goes largely uncredited, but to find in it a pillar of support in the ongoing work of French phenomenology.[56]

THE THIRD SHOCK:
TOWARD A PHENOMENOLOGY OF FORCE
(FALQUE)

What Edmund Husserl only hinted at, only to leave undeveloped and uninterrogated, is precisely what Maurice Blondel was to fully develop and thoroughly investigate in his own philosophical enterprise; this is found in the question of the genesis of consciousness and the dynamism at work in its constitution. This point could be understood with reference to Husserl's own words where he asserts a lack of "centrating ideas" and he expresses his desire to "reference back to the phenomenological primordial sources of all knowledge, the deepest founding of all objective sciences arising from the universality of knowing consciousness."[57] This element of Husserl's work, in "the description of primordial dimensions of experience"[58] is focused upon the unconscious elements of life, considered variously as affective, instinctual, and drive related, and it is here where Husserl speaks of a "systematic [phenomenology] of genesis."[59] Husserl remarks this would require the development of a new phenomenological method situated upon what he describes as the "impressional," and on "the genesis of intentionality," about which Husserl disjunctively notes: "The 'chaos' of 'impressions' becomes organized—the impressions are still not objects, elements [won by] the reduction, genetic primordial elements; dismantling intentionality and the genesis of intentionality lead back to them. Unarticulated affinity, unarticulated 'objects.'"[60] Here we find that Husserl's initial paradigm—of intentionality and the eidetic reduction—is insufficient for touching upon this aspect of the primordial experience of life, and this in turn pushes toward the postulation of an "intentionality of the drive," as Husserl notes:

> Shouldn't we or musn't we posit a universal intentionality of the drive which unifies every original presence as permanence of a temporalization which concretely moves it forward from presence to presence in such a way that all content is the content of the realization of the drives and it is determined by the goal toward which the drive aims.[61]

Didier Franck comments upon this element of Husserl's work, stating that "intentional acts and the intentionality of consciousness owe their constitution to the activity, to the force, to the intensity of the originary impression—in a word, to the energy of absolute transcendental life."[62] Franck notes how "Husserl indeed led . . . back to a universal drive intentionality."[63] Though despite this, Franck continues "Husserl found himself compelled to presuppose a pre-intentional and pretemporal driveness [*pulsionalité*], he never proceeded to an analysis of the drive, let alone explained the way a drive could give rise to intentionality—in short, how sense and phenomenality stem from force."[64] With Blondel, we find a fully articulated system of thought adapted to this primordial realm. There is yet to be a complete reckoning between these two paradigmatic thinkers who each acted as progenitors of their own mutually distinct and yet complementary phenomenological paradigms, however with Emmanuel Falque we find inroads toward a genuine philosophical rapprochement between these two thinkers.

The explicit impact of Blondel's thought upon phenomenology (in the Husserlian sense) is discernable in the three volumes of Falque's *Triduum Philosophique*. In the last of his triptych, *The Wedding Feast of the Lamb* (2016), we find the sustained—though methodologically unarticulated—application of Blondel's "method of immanence" to a phenomenological account of Roman Catholic ritual practice in the Eucharistic celebration.[65] As Falque develops his trilogy, we find the blending together of Husserlian phenomenological method with that of "the immanent affirmation of the transcendent," making what is present in this text an undeniable blending together of Blondel's method of immanence with the Husserlian phenomenological tradition. This approach seems to have been prompted by the elder Jean-Luc Marion, who gave a challenge to continue developing Blondel's method of immanence in terms of "describing phenomena specific to Christianity."[66] Emmanuel Falque explicitly makes reference to this challenge in the first chapter of the middle volume of the trilogy, *The Metamorphosis of Finitude* (2012):

> We need then along with Maurice Blondel, and not in opposition to him, to develop the method of immanence further—that is to say, we need to *push it to its limits*, just as one works at a thesis in radicalizing it further.[67]

Blondel wished to probe the philosophical conditions necessary for establishing an integral understanding of rationality, with the task "to fix the relation between the order of knowledge with that which surpasses it, without abusing either the known or the unknowable."[68] In this manner he committed himself to establishing the foundations for a genuine philosophy of religion, endeavoring to survey and clearly define the parameters and methodological demands with the rigor of a concrete science. Under the initiative to position his own Catholic faith in such a way that it would not interfere with his properly *philosophical* work, Blondel would come to write his classic text, *A Letter on the Requirements of Contemporary Thought and on Philosophical Method in the Study of the Religious Problem*, coming to be known as his *Letter on Apologetics* (1896). In this text, where Blondel provides his renowned "method of immanence," a unique phenomenological method comes into clear relief, suited in order to critique "the phenomena which make up our inner life, each one in the light of the others, to adjust them, to study the connections between them, to show all their implications, to discover what principles are presupposed by thought and by action."[69]

Blondel does not forsake the integrity of what may be considered immanent phenomenality, but rather *enshrines* a method for respecting it and with an eye on transcendence. What Blondel's method *uniquely* accomplishes is found in its capacity to equate the non-conceptual content of life to the intellect and chain of consciousness. This is accomplished by bringing volitional and drive or instinct based content into the orbit of philosophical reflection: "We must consider our own action . . . and also the initiative by which our instincts, our desires and our intentions are expressed in everything else."[70] Blondel develops a vitalist phenomenology and anchors it in what he terms a "panlogism" that he articulates in order "to recover for rationality areas which the philosophy of the idea—not to be confused with intelligence or intelligibility excludes because it has restricted itself to what is only a virtual source of light while abstracting from real conditions and vital sources."[71] From here he ultimately arrives at a panpsychic philosophy centered upon the dynamic faculties of the will: "This is why I have insisted on the noetic and pneumatic origins of a world where, from the lowest origins, thought is already constitutive of materiality itself."[72]

For Blondel, the ultimate question is, at its core, one of *dynamism* and power. These themes are thoroughly developed in his own later work, as suggested in the first of two essays entitled *The Problem of Catholic Philosophy* (1931–1932), where he asserts that "the debate's entire vital knot" is to be found in the "the religious drive [*élan*]."[73] It is just this impulse, impetus, or drive that Blondel claims "arises from the very ground of nature and of man" and is something "implied in the entire movement of our thought" where he conceives it as an "internal dynamism that has nothing imprecise or merely supplementary [*facultatif*] to it."[74] This binding activity and consequent relational dynamic represent Blondel's central philosophical focus, and are perhaps most succinctly expressed in his *Le procès de l'intelligence* (1922), where he states that "the emphasis is on the internal or reciprocal relationships of beings rather than on their intimate nature and their substantial truth, which our concepts are not enough to bring us into possession of."[75] He adapts his methodology to attend to this relation and conceives of *two* primary forces in this dynamic: considered as the noetic and pneumatic—representing division and unification, analysis and synthesis, the one and the many, binding and loosening, *solve et coagula*. Most importantly, these are considered as much ontological movements as cognitive processes. It is just this distinction that has been proclaimed as "one of the most original and valuable contributions of Blondelian philosophy to *philosophia perennis*."[76]

For the backlash of psychoanalysis upon phenomenology, we find in Blondel first of all support for articulating what is in principle outside the reach of immanent phenomenality, and, secondly, we gain the means for describing how the content of the will relates to consciousness—seeing this as much from an ontological as epistemological point of view.[77] In the end, this moves away from the initial phenomenological paradigm of immediate and direct phenomenolization, and instead offers a method of implication, or even an indirect ontology—perhaps the best philosophical approach for attuning to this "barbarian principle" or the primordial domain of "brute" being. The work of Emmanuel Falque helps to open up the debate to move beyond the first paradigm of phenomenology as typified by Husserl and Heidegger, to a more accommodating methodology for an explication of certain powers at work in the process of phenomenolization—a movement that could be considered the first steps toward a genuine paradigm shift, here centered around the powers of the will, of instincts and drives—or, in other words, toward a paradigm oriented toward energy, forces, and powers, and how these are to be situated in terms of a philosophy of mind or consciousness, and therefore to phenomenology, or the science of describing human experience. Perhaps issuing a final blow toward the fulfillment of Blondel's own philosophical inspiration:

> We'd see it even better if, instead of studying the superficial subjectivism of the phenomena of consciousness, we entered into the real intimacy of souls, where the task of a doctrine of thought would indeed be one of always bring-

ing us back to ourselves, without taking either a literary and romantic psychology, or an abstract psychoanalysis or phenomenology, for a complete and legitimate science of the living mind [*l'esprit vivant*].[78]

NOTES

1. Maurice Merleau-Ponty, "The Philosopher and His Shadow," in *Signs*, translated by Richard C. McCleary (Evanston, IL: Northwestern University Press, 1964), 178.
2. Emmanuel Falque, *Nothing to It: Reading Freud as a Philosopher*, translated by Robert Vallier and William L. Connelly (Leuven: Leuven University Press, 2020), 28.
3. Falque, *Nothing to It*, 105.
4. Jacques Derrida, "Force and Signification," in *Writing and Difference*, translated by Alan Bass (Chicago: University of Chicago Press, 1978), 27.
5. Dominique Janicaud, *Phenomenology and the "Theological Turn": The French Debate*, translated by Bernard G. Prusak (New York: Fordham University Press, 2000), 17.
6. Emmanuel Levinas, *Existence and Existents*, translated by Alphonso Lingis (The Hague: Nijhoff, 1978), 53.
7. This is not to overlook Martin Heidegger's "phenomenology of the inapparent," but rather to suggest a *different* line of development that occurred in France, of a similar (if not the same) theme. For a contemporary study of Heidegger's phenomenology of the inapparent and its relation to the theological turn, see Jason W. Alvis, *The Inconspicuous God: Heidegger, French Phenomenology, and the Theological Turn* (Bloomington: Indiana University Press, 2018).
8. Emmanuel Levinas, *Totality and Infinity: An Essay on Exteriority*, translated by Alphonso Lingis (The Hague: M. Nijhoff Publishers, 1979), 194.
9. Janicaud, *Phenomenology and the "Theological Turn*,*"* 36–37.
10. Janicaud, *Phenomenology and the "Theological Turn*,*"* 36–37.
11. Janicaud, *Phenomenology and the "Theological Turn*,*"* 23.
12. Janicaud, *Phenomenology and the "Theological Turn*,*"* 25.
13. Janicaud, *Phenomenology and the "Theological Turn*,*"* 24.
14. Maurice Merleau-Ponty, "The Intertwining—The Chiasm," in *The Visible and the Invisible; Followed by Working Notes*, translated by Alphonso Lingis (Evanston, IL: Northwestern University Press, 1968), 147.
15. Maurice Merleau-Ponty, "Nature and Logos," in *In Praise of Philosophy*, translated by John Wild and James Edie (Evanston, IL: Northwestern University Press, 1963), 197.
16. Merleau-Ponty, "The Concept of Nature, I," in *In Praise of Philosophy*, translated by John Wild and James Edie (Evanston, IL: Northwestern University Press, 1963), 131.
17. See in particular Emmanuel de Saint-Aubert and Maurice Merleau-Ponty, *La nature ou le monde du silence*, Hermann Philosophie (Paris: Hermann, 2008).
18. Emmanuel de Saint-Aubert, "Rereading the Later Merleau-Ponty in the Light of His Unpublished Work," in *The Oxford Handbook of the History of Phenomenology*, edited by Dan Zahavi (Oxford: Oxford University Press, 2018), 381.
19. Merleau-Ponty, "The Intertwining—The Chiasm," in Merleau-Ponty, *The Visible and the Invisible; Followed by Working Notes*, 147. For a contemporary phenomenological account of such an elemental ontology, though here in regard to the "milieu," see Taylor Knight, "In a Mirror and an Enigma: Nicholas of Cusa's De Visione Dei and the Milieu of Vision," *Sophia* 59:1 (2019): 113–37.
20. Merleau-Ponty, "Note from September, 1959," in Merleau-Ponty, *The Visible and the Invisible; Followed by Working Notes*, 210.
21. Falque, *Nothing to It*, 42, 44.
22. Emmanuel Falque, "The Extra-Phenomenal," *Diakrisis Yearbook of Theology and Philosophy* 1:1 (2018): 9, 11.
23. See Emmanuel Falque, "A Phenomenology of the Underground: Maurice Merleau-Ponty," in *The Loving Struggle: Phenomenological and Theological Debates*, translated by

Bradley B. Onishi and Lucas McCracken (London; New York: Rowman & Littlefield International, 2018), 45–76.

24. Falque, *Nothing to It*, 64.

25. Emmanuel Falque, "Toward an Ethics of the Spread Body," in *Somatic Desire: Recovering Corporeality in Contemporary Thought*, edited by Sarah Horton et al. (Lanham: Lexington Books, 2019), 91.

26. Sigmund Freud, "The Dissection of the Psychical Personality," from "New Introductory Lectures on Psycho-Analysis (1933 [1932])," in Sigmund Freud, *The Standard Edition of the Complete Psychological Works of Sigmund Freud*, translated by James Strachey, volume XXII (London: The Hogarth Press and the Institute of Psycho-Analysis, 1986), 73.

27. Falque, *Nothing to It*, 83.

28. Falque, *Nothing to It*, 75.

29. Falque, *Nothing to It*, 75.

30. For a particularly concise expression of this paradigm see, Martin Heidegger, §7 The Phenomenological Method of Investigation, in *Being and Time*, translated by John Macquarrie and Edward S. Robinson (Blackwell, 1967), 59. "To have a science of phenomena means to grasp its objects in such a way that everything about them which is up for discussion must be treated by exhibiting it directly and demonstrating it directly."

31. While I choose to describe Blondel's philosophy as a "distinct" or "parallel" phenomenology, Emmanuel Gabellieri has chosen to describe it as an "alternative" phenomenology. See his *Le phénomène et l'entre-deux: pour une métaxologie* (Paris: Hermann, 2019).

32. See in particular, Christian Dupont, *Phenomenology in French Philosophy: Early Encounters* (Dordrecht: Springer, 2014); Clara Mandolini, "Blondel and the Philosophy of Life," *Analecta Husserliana: The Yearbook of Phenomenological Research* 53 (2009); Michael A. Conway, "A Positive Phenomenology: The Structure of Maurice Blondel's Early Philosophy," *Heythrop Journal* 47:4 (2006).

33. Maurice Blondel, "The Idealist Illusion," in *The Idealist Illusion and Other Essays*, translated by Fiachra Long, Studies in Philosophy and Religion (Dordrecht; Boston: Kluwer Academic Publishers, 2000), 75.

34. Blondel, "The Idealist Illusion," 75.

35. Blondel, "The Idealist Illusion," 75.

36. See the penetrating analysis offered by translator and commentator Fiachra Long in Blondel, "The Idealist Illusion," 8.

37. Janicaud, *Phenomenology and the "Theological Turn,"* 45.

38. Maurice Blondel and Emmanuel Tourpe, *"Mémoire" à Monsieur Bieil: discernement d'une vocation philosophique* (Paris: CERP, 1999), 90–91. See also in Emmanuel Falque, *The Metamorphosis of Finitude: An Essay on Birth and Resurrection*, translated by George Hughes (New York: Fordham University Press, 2012), 16–19, 159.

39. Blondel, "The Starting Point for Philosophical Research (1906)," in *The Idealist Illusion and Other Essays*, translated by Fiachra Long, Studies in Philosophy and Religion (Dordrecht; Boston: Kluwer Academic Publishers, 2000), 135.

40. Emmanuel de Saint-Aubert, *Vers une ontologie indirecte: sources et enjeux critiques de l'appel à l'ontologie chez Merleau-Ponty* (Paris: J. Vrin, 2006), 123.

41. Maurice Merleau-Ponty, "Second Course: The Concept of Nature, 1957–1958. Animality, the Human Body, and the Passage to Culture," in *Nature: Course Notes from the Collège de France*, translated by Robert Vallier (Evanston, IL: Northwestern University Press, 2003), 134.

42. This is an excerpt from Merleau-Ponty's unpublished manuscript, *La nature ou le monde du silence*, reproduced in Saint-Aubert, *Vers une ontologie indirecte: sources et enjeux critiques de l'appel à l'ontologie chez Merleau-Ponty*, 124.

43. Maurice Blondel, *L'Être et les êtres* (Paris: Félix Alcan, 1935), 370.

44. Merleau-Ponty, *The Visible and the Invisible; Followed by Working Notes*, 149.

45. Maurice Blondel, *La pensée*, volume I (Paris: F. Alcan, 1934), X.

46. Blondel, *L'Être et les êtres*, 368.

47. Blondel, *L'Être et les êtres*, 368.

48. Merleau-Ponty, "Existence and Dialectic," in Merleau-Ponty, *Signs*, 154.

49. Blondel, *La pensée*, I, 13. What is particularly noteworthy here is the correspondence to the ancient Persian dualism that would later be taken up in Manicheism and then become one of the central intellectual points of focus for St. Augustine. See Guy Stroumsa and Paula Fredriksen, "The Two Souls and the Divided Will," in *Self, Soul, and Body in Religious Experience*, edited by A. I. Baumgarten et al. (Leiden: Brill, 1998), 198–217.

50. Blondel, *La pensée*, I, 31. One thought-provoking contemporary work that helps to show the fruitfulness of "rhythm" as a theological category can be found in Lexi Eikelboom's *Rhythm: A Theological Category* (Oxford: Oxford University Press, 2018). Though her treatment of Blondel's notion of immanence could be viewed as incomplete, where she asserts: "The limit proposed by Blondel ends up being simply the limit between consciousness and the world. . . . He identifies two realms and a limit between them." Ibid., 114–15. This reading is challenged in light of Blondel's later work, where far from separating consciousness and the world he articulates their solidarity. In this sense, his notion of immanence expresses a transcendence that is internal to consciousness: ". . . the whole world is penetrated and already constituted by a real and dynamic thought, the higher life of the spirit, even in its apparent independence, remains in part conditioned, supported, thwarted or guided by the forces which it implements and which, conversely, it helps to direct, complete and spiritualize." Blondel, *La pensée*, I, 56.

51. Blondel, *L'Action*, volume I (Paris: F. Alcan, 1936), 402.

52. Blondel, *L'Être et les êtres*, 376.

53. Merleau-Ponty, "Note from April, 1960," in Merleau-Ponty, *The Visible and the Invisible; Followed by Working Notes*, 244.

54. Merleau-Ponty, "Note from April, 1960," 117.

55. Blondel, *L'Être et les êtres*, 370.

56. Merleau-Ponty, "Existence and Dialectic," in *Signs*, 154.

57. Edmund Husserl, "Preliminary Considerations for the Lecture on Transcendental Logic," in *Analyses Concerning Passive and Active Synthesis: Lectures on Transcendental Logic*, translated by Anthony J. Steinbock (Dordrecht; Boston: Kluwer Academic Publishers, 2001), 5.

58. As described by translator Anthony Steinbock, in Husserl, "Preliminary Considerations for the Lecture on Transcendental Logic," 15.

59. Husserl, "The Phenomenon of Affection," in Husserl, "Preliminary Considerations for the Lecture on Transcendental Logic," 197–98.

60. Husserl, "Appendix 19," in Husserl, "Preliminary Considerations for the Lecture on Transcendental Logic," 515–16.

61. Husserl, "Universal Teleology," in *Husserl, Shorter Works*, edited by P. McCormick and F. Elliston (South Bend, IN: University of Notre Dame, 1981), 336.

62. Didier Franck, "Beyond Phenomenology," in *Nietzsche and Phenomenology: Power, Life, Subjectivity*, edited by Élodie Boublil and Christine Daigle (Bloomington: Indiana University Press, 2013), 283–84.

63. Franck, "Beyond Phenomenology," in *Nietzsche and Phenomenology: Power, Life, Subjectivity* (Bloomington: Indiana University Press, 2013), 284.

64. Franck, "Beyond Phenomenology," 285.

65. Emmanuel Falque, *The Wedding Feast of the Lamb: Eros, the Body, and the Eucharist*, translated by George Hughes (New York: Fordham University Press, 2016).

66. Jean-Luc Marion, "Lettre postface," in *L'action, une dialectique du salut* (Paris: Beauchesne, 1994), 291.

67. Falque, *The Metamorphosis of Finitude*, 19, 160.

68. Maurice Blondel, "Lettre à la Revue de metaphysique et de morale (1894)," in *Oeuvres complètes, Tome II 1888–1913*, edited by Claude Troisfontaines (Paris: Presses universitaires de France, 1997), 49.

69. Blondel, "Letter on Apologetics," in *The Letter on Apologetics, and, History and Dogma*, translated by Illtyd Trethowan and Alexander Dru (Grand Rapids, MI: W.B. Eerdmans Publishing Co., 1994), 157.

70. Blondel, "Letter on Apologetics," 181.

71. Blondel, "Letter of Blondel to Lalande (1902)," in André Lalande and Société française de philosophie, *Vocabulaire de la Société française de philosophie*, sixth edition (Paris: Presses universitaires de France, 1951), 1231; reproduced in Henri Bouillard, *Blondel and Christianity*, translated by James M. Somerville (Washington: Corpus Books, 1969), 21.

72. Blondel, *L'Être et les êtres*, 524.

73. Blondel, "The Problem of Catholic Philosophy," in *Reason Fulfilled by Revelation: The 1930's Christian Philosophy Debates in France*, translated by Gregory Sadler (Washington, DC: The Catholic University of America Press, 2011), 201.

74. Blondel, "The Problem of Catholic Philosophy," 201.

75. Blondel, *Le Procès de l'Intelligence* (Paris: Bloud & Gay, 1922), 232–33.

76. A. de Jaer and Albert Chapelle, "Le noétique et le pneumatique chez Maurice Blondel. Un essai de définition," *Revue Philosophique de Louvain* 59 (1961): 611. Another key insight into this contribution is observed by Oliva Blanchette: "What Blondel does that has never been done by other philosophers who have reflected on the irreducible duality of human thought, is to show how it hangs from the very alternative that is presented in our consciousness regarding the final end of our existences, which defines our very being." Oliva Blanchette, *Maurice Blondel: A Philosophical Life* (Grand Rapids, MI: W.B. Eerdmans Publishing Co., 2010), 457.

77. It is especially noteworthy that Blondel's philosophical paradigm connects together with that of Carl Jung, perhaps finally helping to open the port for a broader philosophical consideration of his work. As one contemporary thinker recounts that Paul Ricœur once said, "I haven't read Jung. He's on the Index in France." Recounted in Jordan Peterson, *Maps of Meaning: The Architecture of Belief* (London: Routledge, 1999), 411. The relevance of Jung's connection is particularly apparent in regards to the "energetic viewpoint in psychology" that is understood as not being "founded on substances themselves, but on their relations." Carl Jung, *Contributions to Analytical Psychology*, translated by H. G. and Cary F. Baynes (London: Kegan Paul, Trench, Trubner & Company, 1942), 2. To go further, Jung's thought represents another parallel tradition that would terminate at a similar point, upon the body and the ontological powers of mind, which for him is expressed in such terms where "the structure and function of the bodily organs are everywhere more or less the same, including those of the brain. And as the psyche is to a large extent dependent on this organ, presumably it will—at least in principle—everywhere produce the same forms. In order to see this, however, one has to abandon the widespread prejudice that the psyche is identical with consciousness." Carl Jung, *Mysterium Coniunctionis: An Inquiry Into the Separation and Synthesis of Psychic Opposites in Alchemy*, translated by G. Adler and R.F.C. Hull, volume 14, Collected Works of C. G. Jung (Princeton, NJ: Princeton University Press, 2014), 25. Kevin Corrigan proposes Gregory of Nyssa as a patristic thinker more innovative than Augustine on this topic, as he provides a model that "proposes a complex physical basis for consciousness," in terms of a "psycho-psychical interactionism" that may be seen to complement modern cognitive perspectives; and in particular, Corrigan describes the basis of this interaction in terms where "psychic energy" is "a major feature of the physical universe." Kevin Corrigan, *Evagrius and Gregory: Mind, Soul and Body in the 4th Century* (New York; London: Taylor & Francis, 2016), 38, 207.

78. Blondel, *La pensée*, I, 152.

Chapter Seven

A Friendly Tussle between Hermeneutics and Phenomenology

From Ricœur to Falque and Beyond

Katerina Koci

Over the past two decades, the field of philosophical hermeneutics has been augmented by the work of the French phenomenologist Emmanuel Falque, whose *Crossing the Rubicon: The Borderlands of Philosophy and Theology*[1] is considered the clearest exposition of the author's philosophical hermeneutics and a natural extension of his lifelong endeavor to ensure that philosophy engages with theology (and vice versa), that is, to cross the metaphorical Rubicon. Such a scholarly enterprise is respectable and admirable, especially as the current state of the academic debate makes it almost impossible to bring scholars from related fields to the same table. The careful reader or passionate hermeneutist could not, however, escape the impression that Falque reveals the hermeneutical path only for it to be overcome, ultimately, by the seemingly more complex path of phenomenology. This point has been pointed out by Jean Greisch in his general critical assessment of Falque's hermeneutics.[2] In what follows, I will focus on questions that arise from the role of the reader/addressee in Falque and the ambiguity of his understanding of that role in the hermeneutical process. Such a perspective will allow me to ask whether hermeneutics must be superseded by phenomenology or whether the discourse can be framed within the sphere of "phenomenological hermeneutics."

The first part of this chapter will critically assess Falque's reading of "the" textual hermeneutics of Paul Ricœur and will highlight those aspects omitted from both Falque's assessment and Greisch's review. The second part will discuss Falque's "hermeneutics of the body and voice" and make a comparison with Gadamer's hermeneutics of play. In bringing Gadamer into the discussion, I aim to point out that Falque's hermeneutics, while expertly promoting the role of the voice as opposed to the usual dominance of language (Ricœur) or speech (Levinas), quietly dropped the *active* and *conscious* role of the "ear" (the reader/addressee). The active partner who listens, understands, and interprets makes an appearance in Falque's account only after he has finished with hermeneutics (part I of *Crossing the Rubicon*) and moved on to phenomenology (part II).[3] The final section will explore the role of the reader/addressee (the interpreting subject) and the complementarity (or otherwise) of phenomenology and hermeneutics. Although the relationship between these two disciplines appears somewhat confused throughout Falque's book, the author does eventually seem to come down on the side of separating them and giving preference to phenomenology. My aim is to suggest that the "active ear," which not only hears but also listens, understands, and interprets, is a natural component of hermeneutics. Moreover, if the active ear were to be postulated before the hermeneutics of the body and voice rather than after (thus Gadamer), hermeneutics would not have to be overcome by phenomenology and the reader/addressee would not have been erased from the process of interpretation (Falque).

"THE" PROTESTANT HERMENEUTICS

Emmanuel Falque opens his discourse on method by distinguishing his hermeneutics from traditions arising from his two French-speaking compatriots Paul Ricœur ("the" Protestant hermeneutics) and Emmanuel Levinas ("the" Jewish hermeneutics). While paying tribute to both authors and their respective confessional allegiances, Falque nevertheless seeks to demonstrate the greater complexity of his own hermeneutics, which he calls "Catholic" and defines as the *hermeneutics of the body and voice*. In the introduction to *Crossing the Rubicon*, Matthew Farley allows such a reading by stating that:

> Falque's work is Catholic in its attempts to reconcile hermeneutics and phenomenology: Falque yokes the Protestant "sense of text" (Ricœur) with the Jewish "body of the letter" (Levinas) under the broader rubric of a Catholic "phenomenality of text." . . . Falque argues for a thicker "hermeneutics of the body and voice."[4]

Greisch is skeptical of such a distinction and finds the categories of "Protestant," "Jewish," and "Catholic" hermeneutics simplistic, schematic, and potentially dangerous, especially given the many centuries of inter-confessional strife.[5] As a Protestant reader of Falque's Catholic thought, I do not find it offensive, but I agree entirely with Greisch's conviction that such a categorization is indeed both simplistic and schematic. Furthermore, while Ricœur's hermeneutics is discussed at length in *Crossing the Rubicon*, that of Levinas is mentioned only in passing. Readers are left to deduce the meaning of Falque's term "the hermeneutics of the body of the letter" from their knowledge of Judaism, however limited that knowledge may be.

Falque's account on the Protestant hermeneutics is more detailed but not without problems. At the beginning of chapter 1, where he discusses the issue of confessional hermeneutics, Falque asks "whether (specifically written) linguistic voices are the only ones through which the Word becomes incarnate?"[6] By the end of the chapter, he has provided his own answer:

> Although the text cannot serve as a unique basis for interpretation, we should, however, recognize its exemplary structural modification of theology understood as the identification of its "object" (discourse about God [theo-*logy*] and its subject (discourse of God [*theo*-logy]), provided that we pay more attention to the epiphany internal to the text or to its own phenomenality than to its sole mediation by language.[7]

Falque's observation that the text should not be the main or only source of hermeneutics is undoubtedly valid. The Word of God in Christian theology is embodied: the Word of God is Jesus Christ, not scripture alone.[8] However, this doctrinal conviction is shared by both Catholics and Protestants and bears no relation to the Reformers' creed "sola scriptura," as Falque seems to suggest.[9] Moreover, the creed deals with the interpretation of scripture (*sola scriptura sui ipsius interpres*—scripture interprets itself), not the interpretation of the Christian faith as a whole. In liturgical praxis, Lutheran tradition clearly represents the "two tables": the liturgy of the Word proclaimed and the liturgy of the Eucharist.[10] Falque's claim that Protestant hermeneutics represents "the meaning of the text" is therefore overstated. It is not possible to draw conclusions about "Protestant hermeneutics" from a single author representing a single Protestant tradition, but in speaking of "Protestant hermeneutics," Falque is arguably referring to the Reformed tradition (L'Église réformée de France) as represented by Paul Ricœur. Furthermore, Ricœur's hermeneutics, interpreted by Falque as "the meaning of the text," is not itself completely justifiable.[11] Greisch insists that:

> we face a wide range of [hermeneutical] approaches that may hardly be reducible to the simple designation of textual hermeneutics. Each of these approaches has a universal (fundamental) claim.[12]

In responding to Greisch, Falque acknowledges that Ricœur's hermeneutics is broader and richer and cannot simply be reduced to the hermeneutics of the meaning of the text. He admits, moreover, that speaking about "the" hermeneutics in general might even be misleading.[13] In confining himself to a single aspect of Ricœur's hermeneutics, Falque is seeking to come to terms with his own context, Paris, where hermeneutics and phenomenology barely acknowledge one another's existence. Falque's teachers and colleagues, some of them influential figures in French phenomenology, did not, he claims, refer to Ricœur at all. Ricœur's hermeneutical genius was received rather in the context of biblical exegesis:

> In *Crossing the Rubicon*, I decided to focus my polemic with Paul Ricœur on his "textual hermeneutics." This decision was made not out of ignorance of his other approaches to hermeneutics (e.g., the hermeneutics of evil) but because of the way his hermeneutics was received in France, specifically his reception in [biblical] exegesis and catholic theology.[14]

This may well explain why Falque sought to select Ricœur's textual hermeneutics as "the" example of Protestant hermeneutics but it does not legitimize such an approach, especially as the greater part of international scholarship does not see the particularity of the late-twentieth-century French context as a decisive factor. It is a misleading approach and one that does not, I will argue, serve Falque's purpose well.

Falque's polemic with "Protestant hermeneutics" also concerns the issue of the reader. Falque's assertion is that, "*Readers* do not grow in reading scripture. The opposite is true: *scripture* grows as it is read. . . . *I* am not the one transformed by reading the text. Rather *the text itself* grows by virtue of my reading; *it lives from my life*, rather than exclusively my living from it."[15] It is certainly important that postmodern hermeneutics acknowledges this transformation of the "objective" and "unchangeable" literary text of romantic hermeneutics. It is not clear, however, why the interpreting subject should be deprived of any potential spiritual, emotional, aesthetic, or intellectual growth that could result from an encounter with the text. On the basis of dialogical/dialectical hermeneutics, one might ask why scripture should live in us and not us in scripture; why scripture should change from being read rather than we by reading scripture. Logic suggests it should function both ways. The direction suggested by Falque—that scripture changes by being read—is the more challenging.[16]

The idea that the reader breathes life into the dead text entered the hermeneutical discourse with reader-oriented approaches and was certainly not welcomed by mainstream literary and biblical scholarship. The first reader-oriented approaches—formalism in continental Europe and New Criticism in the Anglo-Saxon tradition—acknowledged the role of the recipient only to show up the "fallacious" nature of the addressee's subjective response.[17] For the formalists, the reader legitimizes the existence and relevance of the text through the act of reading, but could also misinterpret the text and thus also change its meaning for or impact on the reader. Dialogical/dialectical approaches acknowledge the role of the reader, who is assigned an equal role in the hermeneutical process. In our discourse, this means both that the reader is changed by the text and that the text is changed by being read.[18]

A hermeneutic based on the mutual interaction of the reader and the text appears the most feasible. Readers/addressees intentionally grasp the subject of their interpretation and are changed by such an experience; equally, however, they imprint their own understanding on the subject, which is thus naturally changed. The experience of every reader is that they are changed by reading a text. In many cases, this is the very reason for the encounter with the text, especially with sacred texts. Literary scholars such as Hans Robert Jauss and Harold Bloom have constructed lists of influential books (the so-called Literary or Western Canon) which map the influence of "great novels" on our Western culture.[19] If it is not us but only the text that is changed, why then, we could ask Falque, would such efforts be made and why would people read the Bible or "great novels" at all? Falque's account of the relationship between reader and text cannot be justified even by his own argument, which seems to undermine the complexity of literary and biblical hermeneutics and its essential role in Christian hermeneutics.

Elsewhere, where Falque exposes the "four senses of scripture," he ascribes the literal meaning to historical-critical method but the moral/tropological sense to textual hermeneutics.[20] For the two other senses, the allegorical (what to believe) and the anagogical (what to aim for), that is, the organic aspects of hermeneutics, Falque finds no place in the current praxis of biblical hermeneutics and ascribes them to phenomenology. It is highly problematic, however, to ascribe the "literal meaning" to historical-critical method. Surely, what was meant by the "literal meaning" of a biblical text in the Middle Ages, when the concept of the four senses of scripture was formulated, would be considered "fundamentalist" today. What the historical-critical method aims for is the "original" meaning of the text rather than its "literal" meaning. Although there is a certain relevance to the concept of the four senses of scripture, the idea can be misleading when used outside its original context. It would be more appropriate to refer, with Ricœur, to the "hermeneutical circle,"[21] a concept formulated in our historical horizon and not biased therefore by the historical horizon of the Middle Ages.

Regarding the original meaning, no thorough hermeneutist would think of passing over the historical-critical method. Indeed, Ricœur, Gadamer, and others consider the original meaning of the text (the world behind the text; contextualization of the text) to be an indispensable part of any genuine hermeneutics. Re-contextualization (the world in front of the text; or understanding oneself in front of the text) can take place only when de-contextualization (the world of the text itself) and contextualization have been carefully conveyed.[22]

In this opening section on Falque's polemic with Ricœur, I have set out some of the ways in which Falque may have misinterpreted the French hermeneutical master. Some flaws were acknowledged and "corrected" by Falque himself in his response to Greisch's review, but other equally important points were neither addressed by Greisch nor revoked by Falque. I will discuss some of these points in the next section.

BODY, VOICE, AND EAR

Much recent hermeneutical debate, including that involving Gadamer and Ricœur, has been framed by the relationship between the reader and the text and how each participates in the hermeneutical process. In Falque's hermeneutics, that relationship is ambiguous to say the least. Dialogical/dialectical hermeneutics suggests the relationship is more or less equal. As we have just seen, by placing himself in opposition to the formalists, who leave almost no space for the reader,[23] Falque has shifted the equilibrium well over toward the recipient: "*Readers* do not grow in reading scripture. The opposite is true: *scripture* grows as it is read."[24] The reader is therefore the more powerful figure: the text is changed; the reader remains untouched. However, in what follows, I will argue that in his own hermeneutics of the body and voice, Falque seems to leave the reader/addressee out of the process of interpretation.

Falque's suggestion that Ricœur's textual hermeneutics is "the" (Protestant) hermeneutics fails to justify the frequent appearance of Ricœur in the pages of his book and the relative absence of Gadamer, whose hermeneutics is not mentioned outside the context of Ricœur until Falque moves on from hermeneutics to phenomenology. This is all the more surprising because, as Falque himself admits, Gadamer's hermeneutics is fundamentally phenomenological[25] and should therefore be closer to Falque's phenomenology. Greisch describes Gadamer's attitude as "hermeneutics which focus on the experience of understanding."[26] In Falque's definition, "experience" disappears and Gadamer's hermeneutics become "the hermeneutics of understanding."[27] The word experience is key, however, as it designates the "phenomenologicality" of Gadamer's hermeneutics. When Falque moves on from his polemic with others and begins his own formulation of the hermeneutics of the body and voice, it is difficult to find any role in the process of interpretation for an "experience" or "effect" that may lead to a "response." Falque's intimate and recognizable voice (a masterful concept, which assumes the embodied nature of its producer) has no counterpart in an "active" ear on the part of the addressee. The response evoked by the voice is described as "joy,"[28] but no further interpretation is offered. By way of explanation, Falque puts forward two verses from the Bible: Song of Songs 2:14 ("Let me see your face, let me hear your voice; for your voice is sweet, and your face is lovely") and John 3:29 ("The friend of the bridegroom, who stands and hears him, rejoices greatly at the bridegroom's voice"). The Greek verb ἀκούω used in these two verses means both to hear and to listen, and figuratively perhaps to understand. Falque chooses the meaning to "hear," which assumes neither the content (message) of what is heard nor an active role for an addressee who will listen, understand, and interpret. His use of "hear" therefore assumes no active response to the call of the beloved or the bridegroom.

In contrast, Matthew 11:15 and Revelation 2:29 ("Let anyone with ears listen!" New Revised Standard Version), which also use ἀκούω, and in the imperative meaning, do assume the content of what is listened to, namely the message. Some English translations of the Bible suggest "Whoever has ears, let them hear" (New International Version) or "He that hath ears to hear, let him hear" (King James Version; American Standard Version). However, some more modern English versions suggest using "listen" rather than "hear." As already quoted above, the NRSV reads, "Let anyone with ears listen!"; the more lay-oriented New Living Translation suggests "Anyone with ears should listen and understand!" These scriptural references clearly assume an active interpretive partner. Furthermore, the use of ἀκούω ("to hear," "to listen," "to understand") together with the participle ὁ ἔχων ὦτα (whoever has ears/anyone with ears) allows an interpretation not only of "to have the physical bodily organ that enables hearing," but also "the readiness and intention to listen and understand." The ear stands for the reader/addressee and is a natural part of the interpretive process. These verses therefore represent an invitation to begin a dialogical/dialectical hermeneutics and set up a dialogue with Gadamer, whose hermeneutics is essentially dialogical/dialectical.[29]

Gadamer begins his explanation of his hermeneutics with the interpretation of artistic works and artifacts, a process which always includes two partners, or co-workers, who "play" together.[30] In Gadamer's terminology, these co-workers are called "players." They are (1) the author in the process of creation and (2) the interpreter in the process of its recognition or re-creation. To these is added (3) the work itself.[31] "Play" here means an exchange between the partners and the medium of the hermeneutical process. The play grounds the interpretation and the interpretation takes place during the play. Only when we have both the text and the reader can we talk about literature: "A drama really exists only when it is played, and ultimately music must resound."[32] Westphal paraphrases Gadamer and provides a useful link to the hermeneutics of interpretation of the text: "If we are talking about a play, the spectator belongs to it essentially. If we are talking about a text, it is the reader who is essential."[33] It is the reader who changes the unread or "dead" text into a "living entity" that is able to convey a message:

> Just as we were able to show that the being of the work of art is play and it must be perceived by the spectator in order to be actualized (*vollendet*), so also it is universally true of texts that only in the process of understanding them is the dead trace of meaning transformed back into living meaning.[34]

Here, Gadamer appears to be in accord with Falque, but as we saw above, for Falque it is only the interpreted that is changed, not the interpreter, who remains untouched.

Gadamer, however, believes that the subjectivity of the reader/addressee and the text dies in the process of playing: "What no longer exists is the players—with the poet or the composer being considered as one of the players. None of them has his own existence for himself, which he retains so that his acting would mean that he 'is only acting.'"[35] Gadamer therefore believes that the interpreting subject grows into the process of interpretation and for the time being forgets its subjectivity. In Gadamer's hermeneutics, the interpreter and the interpreted merge in the process of interpretation: each influences the other and eventually loses itself in the other in order to grasp the essence of what is interpreted. In literary hermeneutics, what is in view is the meaning of the text. Gadamer is not that specific, however, as his theory of understanding is to a large extent taken from Heidegger.

As suggested in the introduction, this study is framed by the role of the reader/addressee in Falque's hermeneutics. That role is far from clear in Falque's account: it is overstated when he is setting his hermeneutics in opposition to that of Ricœur; it is undermined during his exposition of the body and voice. This review of Falque's polemic with Ricœur and my own perspective arising from my methodological background in Gadamer's hermeneutics bring us to the final part of this study, namely the "combat amoureaux," to use Greisch's term for Falque's somewhat tentative exchange between hermeneutics and phenomenology.

HERMENEUTICS AND PHENOMENOLOGY
(OR VICE VERSA)

The question of the relationship between phenomenology and hermeneutics is the golden thread running through Falque's *Crossing the Rubicon*, although parts I and II focus on each in turn (first hermeneutics, then phenomenology). In this final section, I will problematize Falque's distinction between phenomenology and hermeneutics and his decision to prioritize the former over the latter.

The relationship between hermeneutics and phenomenology is a delicate issue. What Gadamer describes as natural and organic partners, co-workers, co-players, Falque appears to keep apart. In part I (interpretation), Falque makes no great distinction between phenomenology and hermeneutics:

"Without attacking the distinction or relation between phenomenology and hermeneutics, the exact character of their relation can be made explicit such that one may even decide between the two."[36] In part II (deciding), he seems to differentiate between them:

> On the one hand, Heidegger advances a notion of understanding without history; on the other, Gadamer sets forth the historicity of understanding. This is probably the greatest dividing line between phenomenology and hermeneutics: the short way, on the one side, with Husserl and Heidegger, and the long way, on the other, with Gadamer and Ricœur.[37]

Falque eventually makes a clear distinction between phenomenology and hermeneutics and even prioritizes the former over the latter, although it is not clear why he chooses the "short way" over the "long way." In part II of *Crossing the Rubicon*, Falque sets out his interpretation of the conditionality of understanding and the concept of prejudices. Prejudices condition and determine our understanding and arise from the historical nature of every understanding (Gadamer), or the horizon of expectation (Jauss). Like Gadamer, Falque pleads for their rehabilitation, but although he prioritizes the short way over the long, he never succeeds in offering an alternative to Gadamer's long way "through the historical horizon."

Gadamer speaks of a "hermeneutical triad" of understanding, interpretation, and application. Likewise, Falque's approach includes interpretation, deciding, and crossing. Although Gadamer describes the triad as three "steps," he insists these steps occur simultaneously. Falque presents three progressive steps and suggests that only interpretation belongs to the realm of hermeneutics, while the other two aspects belong to phenomenology: "[t]he hermeneutic of the body and voice . . . opens unto 'phenomenology of believing' that grounds it."[38] The phenomenology of believing begins with the believing subject but is no longer part of the process of interpretation. It is difficult to understand such a move. Falque seems to suggest in his discourse on method that we should begin with hermeneutics and proceed to phenomenology, which nevertheless conditions the hermeneutics: "Where hermeneutics drew out meaning, albeit anchored in the body rather than in the text, phenomenology describes a mode of being-there rooted in believing."[39] All well and good. But why not, therefore, begin with the phenomenology of believing and move on to the hermeneutics of understanding faith? This would feel more natural and straightforward. Indeed, Falque is also convinced that:

> The previously stated choice of the primacy of the short way over the long way and thus phenomenology over hermeneutics should not obliterate the very question of obliteration. Any lived experience of consciousness—the focus of

phenomenology—always gives itself in a story or a history—the concern of hermeneutics. [40]

As mentioned previously, in his hermeneutics of the body and voice, Falque seems to undermine the role of the reader/addressee, who is marginalized in the process of interpretation. By contrast, his discussion of phenomenology begins with the reader/addressee, and suggests, for example, that whereas God's relation to us is subject to interpretation (hermeneutics), our response to this relation is phenomenology. Our decision precedes our own understanding: it is pure phenomenality and is thus excluded from hermeneutics.

Falque's approach to hermeneutics and phenomenology could be summarized in the following way. First, Falque's preferencing of phenomenology over hermeneutics appears to contradict his praxis. Falque confesses that the "focus of phenomenology [the understanding of our faith] always gives itself in a story or a history." He clearly sees, therefore, the merits of the hermeneutical path and acknowledges the historical nature of understanding (Gadamer). Secondly, there is no need to decide or even distinguish between hermeneutics and phenomenology. Gadamer's triad of understanding, interpretation, and application clearly begins with the phenomenality of "being-there" (an existential encounter with prejudices) and proceeds to understanding (a continual process during which we rid ourselves of those false prejudices that prevent us from understanding and hold onto the right prejudices that help us to understand). The three "steps" of understanding, interpretation, and application are all parts of a single hermeneutical process. They occur simultaneously and continuously, and an active reader/addressee is involved at each point.

Unlike his teachers and colleagues in the French phenomenological tradition, Falque decided to invite hermeneutics—that is to say, Ricœur's textual hermeneutics—into his research into the interface between theology and philosophy. While respecting such an enterprise and drawing on the existing hermeneutical discussion as set out by Greisch, I have dared to point out some of the ways in which Falque might have misinterpreted Ricœur. My aim was not simply to review Falque's hermeneutics or discuss his reading of Ricœur, but to explore and assess his larger project of "crossing the Rubicon." Here, my focus was on those matters I see as having contributed to Falque's decision (1) to separate phenomenology and hermeneutics, and (2) to prefer phenomenology over hermeneutics.

Falque opens his discourse on method with a friendly polemic with Ricœur's textual hermeneutics. This polemic should be understood as a way of drawing hermeneutics, and Ricœur in particular, into the French phenomenological context, as Falque himself admits in his discussion with Greisch. Such a move cannot, however, provide a convincing argument for preferring phenomenology before hermeneutics. "Phenomenology then hermeneutics" is the most natural, plausible sequence: phenomenality precedes its interpretation, and this is the path carefully set out by Gadamer in his phenomenological hermeneutics. However, interpretation is a continuous process that happens at all levels of hermeneutics and always includes the reader/addressee/interpreter. In postulating the phenomenality of being-there, Gadamer introduced the reader/addressee/interpreter and avoided the risk of this interpretive partner being omitted from any level of interpretation, which is something Falque fails to achieve in his hermeneutics of the body and voice. As a contribution to the discourse on the philosophy of religious experience, his account of hermeneutics and phenomenology does nonetheless offer theoretical hermeneutics some well-defined material that invites further research in the fields of both philosophy and theology.[41]

NOTES

1. Emmanuel Falque, *Crossing the Rubicon: The Borderlands of Philosophy and Theology*, translated by Reuben Shank, Perspectives in Continental Philosophy (New York: Fordham, 2016).

2. Jean Greisch, "Où passe le Rubicon? Un problème de géographie spirituelle," in *Une analytique de passage: Rencontres et confrontations avec Emmanuel Falque* (Paris: Editions Franciscaines, 2016), 315–40.

3. "It was necessary to interpret. . . . It is now time to decide." Falque, *Crossing the Rubicon*, 77.

4. Falque, *Crossing the Rubicon*, 11.

5. Greisch, "Où passe le Rubicon?," 325–27.

6. Falque, *Crossing the Rubicon*, 19.

7. Falque, *Crossing the Rubicon*, 52.

8. "In a Catholic mode, we will thus no longer content ourselves with the ark of speech, which runs the risk of losing sight of the distinction of Christianity's 'Word become flesh in the Son' amid Judaism's 'speech become body in the text.' I will suggest that 'the ark of the flesh' may be understood both as 'a body of speech to be recited'—that is, mouthfuls of scriptural verses—and a 'Eucharistic body' to be assimilated—that is, partaking of a meal or even as contemplation and adoration." Falque, *Crossing the Rubicon*, 49.

9. Falque, *Crossing the Rubicon*, 55.

10. "Thus, the written text is primary in Protestantism and Judaism according to a truly necessary 'liturgy of the Word,' but in a Catholic structure it designates only one of the 'two tables'—the other being the Eucharistic table—where we consecrate as well as celebrate." Falque, *Crossing the Rubicon*, 55.

11. Greisch insists that the hermeneutics of the twentieth century, not to mention earlier, is much more complex and cannot be reduced to the "meaning of the text." Greisch sees Ricœur's hermeneutics as "a hermeneutics which seeks to understand symbols in order to prevent evil." Greisch, "Où passe le Rubicon?," 322.

12. Greisch, "Où passe le Rubicon?," 323 (translation mine).

13. "We do not speak about the hermeneutic (in singular), but about hermeneutics (in plural): hermeneutics of the 'historical consciousness' of Dilthey, hermeneutics of the 'lived facticity' of Heidegger, the hermeneutics of 'understanding' of Gadamer, the hermeneutics of 'evil' of Ricœur, the hermeneutics of the 'self' of Foucault, etc." Emmanuel Falque, *Parcours d'embûches: S'expliquer* (Paris: Editions Franciscaines, 2016), 126 (translation mine).

14. Falque, *Crossing the Rubicon*, 129.

15. Falque, *Crossing the Rubicon*, 30.

16. Traces of the superiority of the reader over the text can be found in the literary scholarship of Stanley Fish and therefore in the biblical scholarship of David Clines. Fish introduced the influential concept of "interpretive community," which is the decisive factor in the process of creating the meaning of a text. As Fish argues: "At this point it looks as if the text is about to be dislodged as a center of authority in favor of the reader whose interpretive strategies make it; but I forestall this conclusion by arguing that the strategies in question are not his in the sense that would make him an independent agent. Rather, they proceed not from him but from the interpretive community of which he is a member." Stanley Fish, *Is There a Text in This Class? The Authority of Interpretive Communities* (Cambridge: Harvard University, 1980), 13–14; see also Stanley Fish, "Literature in the Reader: Affective Stylistics," in *Reader-Response Criticism: From Formalism to Post-Structuralism*, edited by Jane P. Tompkins (Baltimore: Johns Hopkins University Press, 1980), 70–100; or as Clines puts it: "Whatever a text may mean in one context, it is almost bound to mean something different in a different context." David Clines, *Interested Parties: The Ideology of Writers and Readers of the Hebrew Bible* (Sheffield: Sheffield Academic Press, 1995), 178.

17. W. K. Wimsatt and M. C. Beardsley, "The Affective Fallacy," *The Sewanee Review* 57:1 (1949): 31.

18. Louise Rosenblatt, *The Reader, the Text, the Poem: The Transactional Theory of the Literary Work* (Carbondale: Southern Illinois University, 1978), 41, 52, 89–90.

19. Hans Jauss, "Literary History as a Challenge to Literary Theory," in *Toward an Aesthetic of Reception* (Minneapolis: University of Minnesota, 1982), 3–46; Harold Bloom, *The Western Canon: The Books and School of the Ages*, first Riverhead edition (New York: Riverhead Books, 1995).

20. Falque, *Crossing the Rubicon*, 34–35.

21. Paul Ricœur, *Hermeneutics and the Human Sciences: Essays on Language, Action and Interpretation*, edited by John B. Thompson (Cambridge: Cambridge University, 1981), 165.

22. Paul Ricœur, *From Text to Action: Essays in Hermeneutics, II*, translated by Kathleen Blamey and John B. Thompson (London: Athlone Press, 1991), 84–88.

23. In the French context we could name, for example, Michael Riffaterre and Georges Poulet.

24. Falque, *Crossing the Rubicon*, 30.

25. Falque, *Crossing the Rubicon*, 39.

26. Greisch, "Où passe le Rubicon?," 322 (italics mine).

27. Falque, *Parcours d'embûches*, 126.

28. "The lover in the Song of Songs begs his spouse in a vocal expression of conjugality, which everyone may experience: 'let me hear your voice' (Sg 2:14), which can be heard echoed in the Gospel of John, where this time, the friend of the bridegroom 'is full of joy when he hears the bridegroom's voice' (Jn 3:29)." Falque, *Crossing the Rubicon*, 63.

29. Jonathan Roberts, "Introduction," in *The Oxford Handbook of Reception History of the Bible*, edited by Michael Lieb and Emma Mason (New York: Oxford University Press, 2011), 3.

30. Hans-Georg Gadamer, *Truth and Method* (London: Sheed and Ward, 2004), 102.

31. "In a certain sense interpretation probably is re-creation, but this is a re-creation not of the creative act but of the created work, which has to be brought to representation in accord with the meaning the interpreter finds in it." Gadamer, *Truth and Method*, 118.

32. Gadamer, *Truth and Method*, 115; Davies describes the hermeneutical relationship in much the same way as Gadamer: "The subject (reader) and the object (text) were indivisibly bound together, and the relationship between them was a dynamic process, for texts only became alive and meaningful when people became involved with them and responded to them." Eryl Davies, *Biblical Criticism: A Guide for the Perplexed* (London: Bloomsbury, 2013), 14.

33. Merold Westphal, *Whose Community? Which Interpretation? Philosophical Hermeneutics for the Church* (Grand Rapids, MI: Baker Academic, 2009), 82.

34. Gadamer, *Truth and Method*, 156.

35. Gadamer, *Truth and Method*, 111.

36. Falque, *Crossing the Rubicon*, 39.

37. Falque, *Crossing the Rubicon*, 86. Cf. "Where hermeneutics drew out meaning, albeit anchored in the body rather than in the text, phenomenology describes a mode of being-there rooted in believing." Falque, *Crossing the Rubicon*, 77.

38. Falque, *Crossing the Rubicon*, 77.

39. Falque, *Crossing the Rubicon*, 77.

40. Falque, *Crossing the Rubicon*, 86.

41. This text was written with the support of Charles University for the project PRIMUS/HUM/23.

Chapter Eight

Hoc est corpus meum

Kenosis, Responsibility, and the Ethics of the Spread Body between Levinas and Falque

Lorenza Bottacin Cantoni

In *Crossing the Rubicon: The Borderlands of Philosophy and Theology*, Emmanuel Falque refers several times to Emmanuel Levinas marking a distance between the "Jewish hermeneutic of the body of the letter" and the "Catholic hermeneutic of the world or the body."[1] On the battlefield, the Christian theologian and philosopher who crossed the Rubicon lines up against the "Atheist" Jewish philosopher Levinas.

Levinas himself claims to be "atheist" and affirms that philosophy must be atheist in order to avoid the dangerous drift of the primacy of ontology and its subsequent transformation into onto-theology. Nevertheless, in *Of God Who Comes to Mind*, Levinas collects some of his most relevant essays on the question of God, or, more precisely, the meaning of the word "God."[2] This collection gravitates toward an interrogation that Levinas explicitly raises in the essay "Useless Suffering":[3] is it still possible, after Auschwitz, to speak about God in a theological sense, or, on the contrary, is it necessary to find another meaning and another address to the word "God"?

The problem is not the *existence* of God: Levinas aims to find the phenomenological concreteness in which the word "God" could gain meaning, even in contrasts with phenomenality. Such a contrast does not lead to an apophantic negation, whereas it describes phenomenologically the "circumstances" in which transcendence concretely manifests itself. God becomes the mark of transcendence that must be taken into account from a strictly philosophical (and secular) point of view. The "signification of meaning," according to a Levinasian concept of transcendence, surpasses knowledge and ontology. Transcendence, in fact, represents an *excess* and a *surplus*, which means a call from the *outside* (*ex*-cess) and from above (*sur*-plus of the height of God). Above and outside the ontological ground and the paradigm of knowledge, Levinas finds *another* source of meaning—otherwise than being—as ontology is not fundamental,[4] and otherwise than the equation of God and Being of onto-theology. Nevertheless, God "comes to the mind" of Levinas in an obsessive way and his profession of atheism seems to be a shield to safeguard his "first philosophy" from the accusation of being a pseudo-religious or quasi-theological position.

Levinas, instead, aims to redefine the vocabulary of philosophy and to outline new categories suitable to give meaning again to the embodied self in his responsibility for the other. Both Levinas and Falque take into consideration the matter of the subject and the redefinition of the self and, despite the discrepancy between the "Jewish" body of the letter and the Christian voice of the body, both the thinkers revalue the body as a key element to re-signify the self. Therefore, it is not sufficient to consider philosophy as the *ancilla theologiae* nor as some privileged knowledge; on the contrary, philosophy must find a new path, which is at the same time grounded in materiality and orientated to (and by) transcendence. Both Falque and Levinas fight to keep philosophy far from the throes of onto-theology. Falque points out that a true onto-theology does not properly exist as a philosophical position nor as a theological one;[5] Levinas criticizes the theory of knowledge based on the symmetry between being, language, and truth where the transcendence of God legitimates knowledge as an attempt to adapt thought (and its expression) to the Truth represented by God. Onto-theology, thus, does not take into consideration the call coming from the other, while every movement of consciousness leads back to the self and is not addressed to any true otherness. At a first glance, the Levinasian position seems to distrust reason. Yet Levinas aims to find another way of meaning, different from the theoretical dimension of representation and capable of addressing and "speaking" transcendence without reducing it to *adequatio*: "can a discourse or a word mean otherwise than meaning in a theme?" Can a "said" be said outside of a system of meaning?[6]

The answer to this question can only be given beyond intentionality and outside representation, and it leads to another meaning of the Transcendence of God since the idea-of-the-Infinite-in-me as my relation to God comes to me in the concreteness of my relation with the other in society as responsibility for the neighbor. In this sense, transcendence is expressed in the commandment "thou shalt not kill," which does not simply provide prevention against homicide, but means rather that it is impossible to justify, make justice, or give meaning to the death of the other and to their suffering. The commandment marks once for all the end of theodicy and establishes another relation with God, which is "already ethics, or, as Isaiah 58 would have it, the proximity to God, devotion itself, is devotion to the other man."[7]

"Thou shalt not kill. Is this not, through the face of others, the very significance of the word of God, the unheard-of significance of the Transcendent that immediately concerns and awakens me? Revelation—circumstances or kenosis—in which the 'abstract' truth of monotheism is thought *concretely*."[8] Here lies the meaning of a kenotic ethics of the face: a commandment is not expressed in words or letters, so any exegesis comes afterwards, as a response to what the face is *silently asking*. Ethics is shaped on the model of God's kenosis, and it is a form of *kenosis* of the subject that depends on the suffering of the other and on my responsibility for the other. Three elements, here, contribute to develop a "kenotic" ethics of the body (devotion to the other) *as* the hermeneutic of the body of the letter, namely: God is not a concept, the commandment is not a prescription, and the other is not an abstraction or an object of knowledge. The concreteness of such a complex relationship emerges in suffering. Suffering is meaningless and unjustified: it is impossible to *use* it with a purpose. Levinas roughly highlights that physical pain is useless: while psychological suffering is noble,[9] the body in pain is just miserable, ugly, and weak. Nevertheless, the suffering body *reveals* something.

Beyond the words, the body in pain is the source of a revelation that does not come from the "body of the letter," but from the all-human concreteness of suffering. So, even if Falque labels Levinas' philosophy as Jewish hermeneutic of the body of the letter, the Lithuanian thinker addresses the letter (namely the problem of language) as a trace of God in the flesh of the Other. Divine incarnation remains "foreign to Jewish spirituality," but human flesh is the concrete place where transcendence can have place. "The Other is not the incarnation of God, but precisely by his face, in which he is disincarnate, is the manifestation of the height in which God is revealed."[10]

Falque points out that the problem of God comes to mind for Levinas not only on the basis of the written text (as for Derrida and Blanchot), but also first and foremost as the deployment of the oral interpretation of the Talmud.[11] This is certainly true as far as the problem of the language is concerned, so Falque uses this argument to explain the differences between Ricœurian and Levinasian positions on written and spoken word. Nevertheless, Levinas does not separate body and word. The "Saying," the possibility of language, lies in the body. My body is the only vehicle I have to respond to the other, so the structure of responsibility is at the same time the transcendence of the Saying and embodiment, it is both carnal and verbal. Embodiment is crucial in Levinas' philosophy from the articles *Reflections on the Philosophy of Hitlerism* to *Otherwise than Being*. The young scholar of Husserl focuses more on the body as self-perception:

> But the body is not only something eternally foreign. Classical interpretations relegate to an inferior level, and regard as a stage to be overcome, a feeling of identity between our bodies and ourselves, which certain circumstances render particularly acute. Not only is it the case that the body is closer and more familiar to us than the rest of the world, and controls our psychological life, our temperament, and our activities. Beyond these banal observations, there is the feeling of identity. Do we not affirm ourselves in the unique warmth of our bodies long before any blossoming of the Self that claims to be separate from the body? . . . In a dangerous sport or risky exercise in which gestures attain an almost abstract perfection in the face of death, all dualism between the self and the body must disappear. And in the impasse of physical pain, is it not the case that the sick man experiences the indivisible simplicity of his being when he turns over in his bed of suffering to find a position that gives him peace? Can we not say that analysis reveals in pain the spirit's opposition to this pain, a rebellion or refusal to remain within it and consequently an attempt to go beyond it? But is it not the case that this attempt is characterized from the very beginning as desperate? Does not the rebelling spirit remain ineluctably locked within pain? And is it not this despair that constitutes the very foundation of pain?[12]

Whether considered trivial or as a tool for the purification or self-empowerment of the mind such as in ascetical practices, physical pain is inescapable. It is impossible to detach ourselves from physical suffering, which affects us with the harshness of a brute fact: the body, writes Levinas, nails us to the world. The *strength* of the body is not at all due to the power of an incarnating *ego*, but to an excess of self-consciousness. We are constantly subjected to power and unable to control it, as shown in the condition of weakness, illness, nausea, insomnia, etc. For Levinas we are always in the *Stimmung* of being-held to the body:

> Need becomes imperious only when it becomes suffering. And the specific mode of suffering that characterizes need is malaise, or disquiet. Malaise is not a purely passive state, resting upon itself. The fact of being ill at ease is essentially dynamic. It appears as a refusal to remain in place, as an effort to get out of an unbearable situation.[13]

Levinas describes a rebellious body that exceeds the boundaries of the will and the unity of the subject. The body gives evidence to the otherness in ourselves. Suffering keeps *Körper* and *Leib* together, however, testifying to the otherness in me. It consequently imposes upon me to accept the other in name of the law of hospitality. Levinas, then, moves from a phenomenological approach to the body to an embodied ethics. Suffering itself becomes an "offering" that receives a sense, an orientation, toward the other and only by accepting the other. Levinas and Falque, at this point, can be compared through the base notion of the active force of the body that "says" something outside the order of the said, or better that becomes a source of meaning. The institution of meaning in a language depends on the force of the Saying, which is the condition of possibility for whatever is said. The Saying is the sign of openness of the body itself. Falque writes that suffering because of pains [*maux*] comes along with the struggle to express suffering in words [*mots*].[14] The passage from the experience of pain into a definition or a diagnosis represents, then, the transition from the strength of the body to a formal order to control the chaos, according to Falque.

Levinas claims that "the least one can say about suffering is that, in its own phenomenality, intrinsically, it is useless: for nothing" and this leads to

> [t]he ethical problem of medication, which is *my duty*. Is not the evil of suffering—extreme passivity, helplessness, abandonment and solitude—also the unassumable, whence the possibility of a half opening, and, more precisely, the half opening that a moan, a cry, a groan or a sigh slips through—the original call for aid, for curative help, help from the other me whose alterity, whose exteriority promises salvation? Original opening toward merciful care ... the anthropological category of the medical, a category that is primordial, irreducible and ethical, imposes itself.[15]

By witnessing the suffering of the other, I am called in the first person: a medical answer is an ethical response that goes beyond the diagnosis of the illness. By taking care of the suffering body, we help to give expression to the strength of pain that delivers an access to understand human corporality both for Falque and for Levinas. It is not possible to reduce the power of the organic to a diagnosis or to a rational narration. Nevertheless, according to Falque, it is possible to expose suffering by painting, sculpting, feeling, seeing, or touching the material body through either an artistic representation or the ethical dimension. The discourse on pain comes as a consequence. Also for Levinas the said (the meaning) comes afterwards, and suffering is the condition of possibility of any representation: the un-representable otherness exposed by the body in pain, as the face of the Other, interrupts the totality of meaning, breaks the rules of representation, and leads to another order of meaning. Transcendence qualifies flesh as human body and marks the difference, the *décalage*,[16] between the human body capable of and obliged to responsibility for the other and the animal body.[17]

Similarly, Falque explains that the sufferings affecting the material flesh are at the same time the words [*mots*] used to express the pain and the sufferings [*maux*] according to which the body lives. Language and concrete phenomenality coincide in an almost perfect way, and the act of consciousness stems from the *kinesthesias* of the body. The suffering body struggles to break any boundary. A force rises from the suffering body and dismantles and abandons any formal structure of the self. Falque does not aim to affirm the "surplus of sense over non-sense" or absence of sense in phenomenology, nor the "hypertrophy of the flesh" against the body, nor the "overdetermination" of passivity on activity. The body itself is an activity that cannot be entirely traced back to consciousness, even if it is intimately welded to it.[18]

Flesh, thus, can be considered as a burden weighing on the self, on *myself*, a bedrock I constantly try to transform by overcoming its resistance. The body affirms its power through suffering. The unjustified suffering destroys my existential horizon and crumbles the totality of knowledge. Both Levinas and Falque go beyond the phenomenological distinction between *Körper* and *Leib*. Yet while the first puts in brackets this distinction to highlight the primacy of ethics and thinks incarnation as hospitality, Falque openly addresses the problem of the junction between the organic body [*corps étendu*] and the lived body [*corps vécu*]. "I *have* and *am* a body in a new way, that of the 'spread' body [*corps épandu*] on this side of any signification, all the way into the depths of its interior chaos."[19] As a *spread body*, I do not live *my* body, but rather it lives me; I become the object of a force expressed by a suffering I refuse to undertake, and I am destroyed by action of this power. The spread body represents the acme of the active power of the flesh, both as an animal strength of the *viande* doomed to be slaughtered and to putrefy, but also blessed (as *chair*) as divine flesh that can actually mean and *say* something. The *pathology* of diseases unifies *pathos* to *logos* and allows the passage from one to the other. Falque's notion of the *spread body* on the one hand comes from the threshold of Husserlian phenomenology (and of Cartesian *res extensa*). Yet, on the other hand, it involves a new problem: an aesthetics of the body is developed as a privileged heuristic way to define the connection between *viande* and *chair*. And here an ethical appeal demands a concrete answer.

The manifestation of suffering occurs before any effort to explain and express the pain in a symptomatology: language is a way to give meaning to the exhibition of pain, but first and foremost it is an ethical command. The spread body is exhibited in *extreme* suffering when "there is nothing to do" to heal the patient and every project is vain. Falque recounts his experience in a palliative care hospital, and he describes the spread body as the body of the terminally ill person.[20]

To look at a patient's suffering, as to see the other suffering for Levinas, transforms the phenomenological approach into ethical demand. The other's pain requires me to understand without words of explanation (outside of the Levinasian said) the passivity of the human body, which means to be exposed (as in the Levinasian Saying) to the material expression of the body. Yet it also imposes upon us to take care of the ill person. The strength of the organic flesh is not entirely due to the organic body: the chaos of the pain is not just the lack of energy of the self, it is rather the outbreak of a force exceeding the form, geminating in cancerous cells, in suppurations and gangrene. Flesh as *viande* keeps consciousness in check; the self-destruction of the spread body dismantles the principle of identity and attests, nevertheless, that there is still a *chance* for redemption. A generous offer of the self must be at the core of an *aesth-ethical* interpretation of the spread body by which *aesthesis* as sensibility is part of the ethical dimension. *Eros*, desire, and fecundity become pivotal notions that Falque and Levinas use to develop their approach to the suffering body. Generosity (rooted in the body) *transforms* animal flesh in *my body for the other*:

> In saying suffering signifies in the form of giving, even if the price of signification is that the subject run the risk of suffering without reason. If the subject did not run this risk, pain would lose its very painfulness. Signification, as the *one-for-the-other* in passivity, where the other is not assumed by the one, presupposes the possibility of pure non-sense invading and threatening signification. Without this folly at the confines of reason, the one would take hold of itself, and, in the heart of its passion, recommence essence. How the adversity of pain is ambiguous! The *for-the-other* (or sense) turns into *by-the-other*, into suffering by a thorn burning the flesh, but for nothing. It is only in this way that the *for-the-other*, the passivity more passive still than any passivity, the emphasis of sense, is kept from being for-oneself.[21]

Paradoxically, the annihilation of the self in suffering shows how to give meaning to incarnation, and it leads to a re-appropriation of the body as my own offered to the other: "To say 'here I am.' To do something for the Other. To give. To be human spirit: that's it. The incarnation of human subjectivity guarantees its spirituality."[22]

In this perspective "*hoc est corpus meum*" and the *kenosis* of self-sacrifice become the paradigm for Falquean and Levinasian reinterpretation of the plexus *Körper/Leib* in light of transcendence. The annihilation of the self represented by the spread body must be assumed as a commandment, a call to the impossible task of take care and substitute the other in his suffering, which is the only way to rebuild consciousness and ego. Embodiment entails that flesh is *significant*, which means that it literally *makes (facio) signs (signum)*. Christ becomes human assuming our finitude; therefore, he assumes also the animal part of flesh. As Merleau-Ponty recalls: "it is a little too much to forget that Christianity is, among other things, the recognition of a mystery in the relations of man and God, which stems precisely from the fact that the Christian God wants nothing to do with a vertical relation of subordination. . . . Christ attests that God would not be fully God without becoming fully man."[23]

As Falque demonstrates, *kenosis* means that Christ accepts the "the condition of a servant" (Phil 2:7) but indicates also that God inhabits materiality and redeems the flesh, or, better, transforms the carnal body: "*hoc est corpus meum*." According to Falque, through artistic representations such as the *Crucifixion* by Grünewald or the *Slaughtered Ox* by Rembrandt, suffering of the spread body reveals in the most vivid way the connection between animality and divinity in the human flesh.[24]

The Isenheim altarpiece testifies that a true adoration and cult of the incarnation also in the atrocious spread body is possible. Such a conception, grounded in the "stoicism" of the Fathers of the Church,[25] lies in Falque's notion of spread body and leads to the cult of the suffering body. *Kenosis*, therefore, means that God accepts human finitude and the ugliness of pain, giving meaning to "useless" suffering. Also Levinas affirms a *kenotic* movement at the basis of his Jewish ethics as first philosophy,[26] following Rabbi Haim of Volozhin's book on study of the Torah. Besides the notion of God as the unsayable tetragram, infinite and absolute, there is another notion of God as the source of all power and justice, called Elohim who, "like a soul of the world" creates the world continuously:

> But it so happens . . . that this God, master of power, is powerless to associate himself with the world he creates and recreates, enlightens and sanctifies and maintains in being by that very association, without a certain behavior of man—a being created, but ontologically extra-ordinary. The vocation, or *raison d'être*, of humanity is precisely to provide the necessary conditions for the association of God with the worlds, and thus for the being of the worlds ("being" that also means holiness, elevation and light), as if being could not, *qua* being, in its pure persistence-in-being, constitute its own justification for being, such as would suffice in the eyes of God.[27]

The hermeneutics of the letter, at this point, receives a full investiture in the ethical task of echoing the continuous creation, and of transforming the *kenosis* or powerlessness of God in a generous production of words that make *kenosis* visible and understandable. God *naturally depends* on the human:

> this is the ethical meaning of human activity: its conformity with God's order in the Torah, or the transgression of that order, has a significance that transcends, of course, the natural effects of the act, as well as whatever it could mean, morally, for a self. It counts first and foremost for the others. That is its gravity. It causes "to live or to die" not just myself, but others besides myself. In his acts, man is responsible for all the other worlds and men.[28]

The powerless, *kenotic* God that depends on man becomes the model for an ethic as the care for the powerless, suffering other "to the degree that the suffering of each person is already the great suffering of God who suffers for that person, for that suffering that, though 'mine' is already his, already divine."[29] Finally, Falque's ethics of the spread body can be put into comparison to Levinasian ethics as first philosophy on the basis of a transcendence that is not simplified as an act of faith, yet it is the complication or co-implication of animal, divine, and human components. Suffering (*sub-ferre*) with the other means to be exposed to the *chaos* of the spread body to which we must offer (*ob-ferre*) ourselves as a servant, "caressing" the body in pain, hand-in-hand (or *corps à corps*) with the other. Face to face is not enough and Levinas, at this point, is interested in transcendence not as a vertical relationship with God but as a concrete, wounded relationship with the other person, who becomes the witness of God and embodies the trace of God.

For Levinas, responsibility for the other is the only way to confer meaning to human finitude outside a regime of signification. Anarchic responsibility implies responding to the others and to care for the others without a particular purpose. Palliative ethics is an ethics of compassion: even if it is impossible to substitute the other in suffering, we must *be there* and suffer with the other.

The practice of the ethics of the spread body can be associated to the Levinasian caress:

> The caress is the not coinciding proper to contact, a denuding never naked enough. The neighbor does not satisfy the approach. The tenderness of skin is the very gap between approach and approached, a disparity, a non-intentionality, a non-teleology. Whence the disorder of caresses, the diachrony, a pleasure without present, pity, painfulness. Proximity, immediacy, is to enjoy and to suffer by the other. But I can enjoy and suffer by the other only because I am-for-the-other, am signification, because the contact with skin is still a proximity of a face, a responsibility, an obsession with the other, being-one-for-the-other, which is the very birth of *signification beyond being*.[30]

Levinasian notion of caress is similar to the "palliative" practice to ease pain sketched by Falque, who develops the concept of palliative ethics as *ethos*, as a *way* of being and acting where embodiment involves wound and exposure to the chaos of the matter. Palliative care involves entirely the body, also the carnal dimension. *Eros* becomes a pivotal element because it represents the threshold between *viande* and *chair*. As for Levinas desire is infinite (as opposed to "need," which ends once it is fulfilled). Desire and eros mean that the spread body is desirable, still "beautiful." Ethics becomes a *cultus* that allows cultivating the flesh as *chair*, not as *viande* (food that fills a need). Embodiment is not just a biological fact, it is desire and fecundity: incarnation involves being engendered. Without fecundity, the body can be reduced to a carcass or to a machinery: fecundity, thus, avoids the complete annihilation of what can be defined as humanity in the virtual age, and keeps human beings (or our humanity) safe from any upload of the self, the mind, the memory online.[31] The desiring subject is not only "needy." Desire is not some weakening lack, but an intensive, strengthening production of *values* by which we set something as *good* because we want it, and not vice versa. Keeping alive the desire, which is nothing other than an expression of vitality, then, becomes crucial also in the palliative ethic. Due to the transfiguration of the *viande* operated by transcendence and assured by the figure of

Christ, the body is more than a carcass (spread body) and it is still an object of desire, still unfolded to the future and grafted onto the past of memory and not only riveted to pain and suffering.

Palliative care means the nurturing of the spread body: no mechanic device can perform an ethical care far from any functional purpose or project that involves desire, generation, and carnality. Palliative care, similarly to a Levinasian caress, touches and reveals an entirely human texture of the flesh rooted in the organic desire and in its tension to transcendence in the extreme urgency of a situation in which there is nothing to do to save the other:

> Extreme urgency is the modality of obsession—which is known but is not a knowing. I do not have time to face it. Outside of conventions (so many poses of theatrical exposition), no welcome is equal to the measure I have of a neighbor. Adequation is impossible. Obligations are disproportionate to any commitment taken or to be taken or to be kept in a present. In a sense nothing is more burdensome than a neighbor. Is not this desired one the undesirable itself?[32]

The neighbor who could not leave me indifferent is an undesirable desired and the extreme suffering of the body concretely shows and imposes the ethical bond that Levinas calls responsibility. Transcendence is given only in the interhuman dimension of the infinite desire. Therefore, an ethics of the body of the other arises side by side and fulfills the hermeneutic of the body of the letter.

To suffer and to give, a "subjectivity that suffers and offers itself before taking a foothold in being"[33] also entails being in the abyss of inexorable desperation and before the menace of death, namely without cutting the suffering other out of the inter-human plot of sociality. The Jewish hermeneutic of the letter is not an act of comprehension grasping a matter, it is a tender touch of the hand. Following Chalier's reflection on the Jewish alphabet, the idea of the caress as an ethical gesture toward the spread body is echoed in Psalm 146:8: "the Lord gives sight to the blind, the Lord lifts up those who are bowed down [kefufim], the Lord loves the righteous."[34] The Jewish letter Kaph symbolizes the hand. My hands, the left guided by justice and the right associated with pardon and generosity, are called from the other to take care of the suffering of the dying other, of the most "insignificant" pain of the terminally ill person. As Moses—surrounded by darkness in the cave—understands, he cannot be face to face with God. Yet he nevertheless perceives transcendence by the lightest "touch" of the palm of the already withdrawn hand (kaph) of God. The strong kindness of the caress gives meaning to suffering, and an orientation within the chaos of the body in pain.

Levinas and Falque both call us to our responsibility and both point out the primacy of transcendence perceived in the body and through the body. *Hoc est corpus meum* means that this body, the body in pain, the spread body of the other is my own as a task: I have to take care of the other's body more than if it were my own. *Hoc est corpus meum* is a silent command to the "kenosis" of the self before any hermeneutic or phenomenology—coming from God or from the other—that transcends the horizon of finitude and makes it crumble with the unperceivable touch of a caress: "To this command continually put forth only a 'here I am' [*me voici*] can answer, where the pronoun 'I' is in the accusative, declined before any declension, possessed by the other, sick, identical. Here I am—is saying with inspiration, which is not a gift for fine words or songs. There is constraint [astriction] to give with full hands, and thus a constraint to corporeality." [35]

NOTES

1. Emmanuel Falque, *Crossing the Rubicon: The Borderlands of Philosophy and Theology*, translated by Reuben Shank (New York: Fordham University Press, 2016), 44.
2. Emmanuel Levinas, *Of God Who Comes to Mind* (Stanford: Stanford University Press, 1988).
3. The essay "Useless Suffering" was originally published in *Giornale di Metafisica* 4 (1982): 13–26, then collected in Emmanuel Levinas, *Entre nous: On-thinking-of-the-other*, translated by M. B. Smith and B. Harshav (New York: Columbia University Press, 1988), 91–102.
4. Emmanuel Levinas, "Is Ontology Fundamental?" in *Entre nous*, 1–12.
5. Falque, *Crossing the Rubicon*, 134.
6. Levinas, *Of God Who Comes to Mind*, 55–57.
7. Emmanuel Levinas, *"It Is Righteous to Be?" Interviews with Emmanuel Levinas*, edited by J. Robbins (Stanford: Stanford University Press, 2002), 243.
8. Emmanuel Levinas, "From Ethics to Exegesis," *In the Time of the Nations*, translated by M. B. Smith (Bloomington: Indiana University Press, 1994), 111.
9. "While in moral pain one can preserve an attitude of dignity and compunction, and consequently already be free; physical suffering in all its degrees entails the impossibility of detaching oneself from the instant of existence. It is the very irremissibility of being. The content of suffering merges with the impossibility of detaching oneself from suffering. . . . In suffering there is an absence of refuge. It is the fact of being directly exposed to being. It is made up of the impossibility of fleeing or retreating. The whole acuity of suffering lies in the impossibility of retreat. It is the fact of being backed up against life and being!" Emmanuel Levinas, *Time and the Other*, translated by R. A. Cohen (Pittsburgh: Duquesne, 1987), 69.
10. Emmanuel Levinas, *Totality and Infinity: An Essay on Exteriority*, translated by A. Lingis (Pittsburgh: Duquesne University Press, 2013), 79.
11. Falque, *Crossing the Rubicon*, 44–45.
12. Emmanuel Levinas, "Reflections on the Philosophy of Hitlerism," *Critical Inquiry* 17:1 (1990): 69.
13. Emmanuel Levinas, *On Escape*, translated by B. Bergo (Stanford: Stanford University Press, 2003), 58.
14. Emmanuel Falque, "Toward an Ethics of the Spread Body," in *Somatic Desire Recovering Corporeality in Contemporary Thought*, edited by S. Horton, S. Mendelsohn, C. Rojcewicz, and R. Kearney (Lanham: Lexington Books, 2019), 91–116.
15. Levinas, "Useless Suffering," 93.
16. Such a difference is related to desire and enjoyment: "The happiness of enjoyment is stronger than every disquietude, but disquietude can trouble it; here lies the gap between the animal and the human." Levinas, *Totality and Infinity*, 149.
17. Levinas does not completely refuse the face of the animal, but the priority, for him, is the human face. See Tamra Wright, Peter Hughes, Alison Ainley, "The Paradox of Morality:

An Interview with Emmanuel Levinas," in *The Provocation of Levinas: Rethinking the Other*, edited by R. Bernasconi and D. Wood (London: Routledge, 1998), 168–80.

18. Falque, *Crossing the Rubicon*, 149.
19. Falque, *Crossing the Rubicon*, 149.
20. Falque, "Toward an Ethics of the Spread Body," 92.
21. Emmanuel Levinas, *Otherwise than Being: Or Beyond Essence*, translated by A. Lingis (Pittsburgh: Duquesne University Press, 1998), 50.
22. Emmanuel Levinas, *Ethics and Infinity* (Pittsburgh: Duquesne University Press, 1985), 97.
23. Maurice Merleau-Ponty, *Signs*, translated by R. McCleary (Evanston, IL: Northwestern University Press, 1964), 70.
24. Huysmans, in *Down there [Là-bas]* describes the picture in quite explicit words, that fit perfectly the notion of the spread body presented by Falque. Huysmans words read: "Ah, this coarse, tear-compelling Calvary was at the opposite pole from those debonair Golgothas adopted by the Church ever since the Renaissance. This lockjaw Christ was not the Christ of the rich, the Adonis of Galilee, the exquisite dandy, the handsome youth with the curly brown tresses, divided beard, and insipid doll-like features, whom the faithful have adored for four centuries. This was the Christ of Justin, Basil, Cyril, Tertullian, the Christ of the apostolic church, the vulgar Christ, ugly with the assumption of the whole burden of our sins and clothed, through humility, in the most abject of forms. It was the Christ of the poor, the Christ incarnate in the image of the most miserable of us He came to save; the Christ of the afflicted, of the beggar, of all those on whose indigence and helplessness the greed of their brother battens; the human Christ, frail of flesh, abandoned by the Father until such time as no further torture was possible; the Christ with no recourse but His Mother, to Whom—then powerless to aid Him— He had, like every man in torment, cried out with an infant's cry. In an unsparing humility, doubtless, He had willed to suffer the Passion with all the suffering permitted to the human senses, and, obeying an incomprehensible ordination, He, in the time of the scourging and of the blows and of the insults spat in His face, had put off divinity, nor had He resumed it when, after these preliminary mockeries, He entered upon the unspeakable torment of the unceasing agony. Thus, dying like a thief, like a dog, basely, vilely, physically, He had sunk himself to the deepest depth of fallen humanity and had not spared Himself the last ignominy of putrefaction. Never before had naturalism transfigured itself by such a conception and execution. Never before had a painter so carnally envisaged divinity nor so brutally dipped his brush into the wounds and running sores and bleeding nail holes of the Savior. Let the observer know that realism could be truly transcendent. A divine light played about that ulcerated head; a superhuman expression illuminated the fermenting skin of the epileptic features. This crucified corpse was a very God, and, without aureole, without nimbus, with none of the stock accoutrements except the bloodsprinkled crown of thorns, Jesus appeared in His celestial super-essence, between the stunned, grief-torn Virgin and a Saint John whose calcined eyes were beyond the shedding of tears. These faces, by nature vulgar, were resplendent, transfigured with the expression of the sublime grief of those souls whose plaint is not heard." Joris Karl Huysmans, *Down There*, translated by K. Wallis (Chicago: The Black Archer Press, 1935), 10–13.
25. Michel Spanneut, *Le Stoïcisme des Pères de l'Église* (Paris: Seuil, 1957).
26. "The fact that kenosis, or the humility of a God who is willing to come down to the level of the servile conditions of the human (of which St Paul's Epistle to the Philippians [2:6–8] speaks), or an ontological modality quite close to the one this Greek word evokes in the Christian mind—the fact that kenosis also has its full meaning in the religious sensibility of Judaism is demonstrated in the first instance by biblical texts themselves. Terms evoking Divine Majesty and loftiness are often followed or preceded by those describing a God bending down to look at human misery or inhabiting that misery." Levinas also gives proofs of a form of kenosis in the study of Old by a Lithuanian rabbi, Haim of Volozhin (1759–1821). Emmanuel Levinas, "Judaism and Kenosis," in *In the Time of the Nations* (Bloomington: Indiana University Press, 1994), 114, 119–21.
27. Levinas, "Judaism and Kenosis," 122.
28. Levinas, "Judaism and Kenosis," 126.
29. Levinas, "Judaism and Kenosis," 128.

30. Levinas, *Otherwise than Being*, 90.

31. Since the early decades of our century, the idea of uploading "identity" or mind is one of the most controversial, yet interesting themes in neuroscientific and cognitive sciences, as reported by Anders Sandberg and Nick Boström, *Whole Brain Emulation: A Roadmap* (Oxford: Oxford University, 2008). The notions of incarnation and embodiment become fundamental in order to avoid simply transforming humanity in some sort of computing capacity, to avoid losing the ethical grip of philosophy and, most importantly, to avoid the risk of extinction through a sterile virtual immortality. Michel Carrouges (also quoted by Deleuze and Guattari in *Anti-Oedipus*) already pointed out the importance of desire and fecundity to define the boundary between man and machine in his study on Marcel Duchamp's *Le Grand verre. La mariée mise à nu par ses célibataires, même*. Michel Carrouges, *Les machines célibataires* (Paris: Arcanes, 1954).

32. Levinas, *Otherwise than Being*, 90.

33. Levinas, *Otherwise than Being*, 105.

34. Catherine Chalier, *Les lettres de la Création. L'alphabet hébraïque* (Orbey: Arfuyen, 2006) 49.

35. Levinas, *Otherwise than Being*, 142. The French word "astriction" does not indicate only a constraint or a binding, and it is actually used in medicine to mean an astringent action, therefore a contraction of an organic tissue.

Chapter Nine

God's Word and the Human Word

Philosophy and Theology in Emmanuel Falque's Phenomenology

Francesca Peruzzotti

The entire production of the French philosopher Emmanuel Falque corresponds to an interesting and creative statement on the theoretical intertwining between philosophy and theology. What he realizes throughout all his works is rigorously formalized by epistemological and methodological considerations in the text *Crossing the Rubicon*. The analysis of that book, therefore, makes it possible to verify the theological discipline's status and role, which can never be separated from its interlacing with philosophy.

Among the many marks offered by the solution provided by Falque, we will follow the one that operates through the analysis of the speculative form attributed to the text. In fact, it can be shown that the hermeneutic thesis set out in the first two chapters of *Crossing the Rubicon* contribute in a decisive manner to the setting of the whole work; they can be considered as the premises for the final chapter. It seems that in Falque's proposal, although decisive, the relationship between philosophy and theology is defined by a radical dichotomy between the two. This separation is built on a theory of faith that is not deprived of a certain extrinsicism with respect to reason rooted in this initial separation between body and voice, experiential and theoretical approach. A binary structure affecting the entire work of the philosopher is highlighted, and it sometimes appears as the opposite of a harmonious and integrated description of the cognitive and existential phenomenon of human being.

The investigation of textuality is fruitful because it indicates the possibility of a different synthesis, in which the starting point chosen by Falque—the consideration of finitude as the only viable way to ponder theological questions as well—is earned by a unitary and non-dichotomous description of its faculties. This can be achieved by means of Falque's phenomenological research, which in *Le livre de l'expérience* brings to light the role of the act of reading. The relationship to the word taking place in the act of reading is not limited to a partial moment, but it is a synthetic image that defines the entire human-world relationship and—in the theological sphere—the sacramental dimension of the Holy Scripture rooted in Christ's definition as *God's word*. It remains, however, a question of whether the sacramentality of the word can serve—even in the contemporary world—to identify the theoretical aspects that allow us to understand the uniting nexus between voice and body. This analysis can point out that both philosophical and theological expressions are based on a common belonging to critical reason, consequently the subject that pronounces them is not dichotomycally defined by the separation between the act of faith and that of reason.[1] The investigation concerning word and scripture in Falque's proposal, enabling an evaluation of theological and philosophical speeches, allows to determine which kind of human measure follows and in which way the *duplex ordo cognitionis* can be overcome.

THE DUPLICITY OF THE BODY AND THE VOICE'S HERMENEUTICS

The first part of *Crossing the Rubicon* is dedicated to investigating the peculiarities of hermeneutic thought. Hermeneutics is described as an initial form of the "Rubicon's crossing"[2] because, through considering Paul Ricœur, it is possible to recognize that religious texts, especially the Christian one, are decisive in order to achieve universal philosophical questions. Falque's intent is related to broaden and deepen the role of hermeneutics, that is to define that its fundamental role does not originate in the single word of sacred Scripture, but is highlighted from its intrinsic carnal dimension.

The author's aim concerns a "hermeneutic of the body and voice," obtained by developing his argument through progressive demarcations. In fact, considering the limits of a definition of the text only obtained by the vocal or written dimension, Falque attributes Ricœur the role of representative of protestant Christianity, whose emphasis on *Sola Scriptura* would be detrimental to reflections upon the bodily dimension. According to Falque a fundamental difference is established with respect to the Catholic approach that, on the contrary, would have many resources to recognize the decisive role of the body, thanks to the primacy of the Eucharistic sacrament.

Although Falque takes care to clarify his disinterest in the confessional dispute in order to preserve the theoretical questions underlying it,[3] he defines a reasoning that operates through the establishment of successive distances, obtained with a very radical *pars destruens*. This approach is not impromptu, but determined by a theory recognizing the dynamics of separation, given by the dispute, the possibility of better exposing its own positions.[4] This approach has the undoubted merit of better exposing issues, yet at the same time it runs the risk of over-polarizing standpoints, which would entail losing the possibility of a subsequent synthetic integration of both the poles emerging from the dispute and a more detailed analysis.

What is now of interest is not only to evaluate the opportunity of a reduction to the disincarnated speech,[5] but the consideration of the word as such. In fact, if it is defined through a development of contrasts, by favoring the bodily aspects compared to the vocal and written one—rather than by defining the unity of the two, the theory risks to miss some fundamental features. More precisely, verifying the peculiarity of the speech in the religious dimension—that is, both in the sacred writing and in the body—introduces the possibility of considering the inextricable interweaving of philosophical and theological speech. Otherwise the theological discourse, as it is by Falque constantly defined by difference from the philosophical one, risks being recognized as non-essential. The threshold that the text *Crossing the Rubicon* proposes takes a chance in persisting as a constant source of estrangement if we do not define the commonality of the critical speech through which both disciplines operate. Investigating the aspects that make up Falque's approach to hermeneutics—then defining the structures that define the text in his theory—allows a first useful check to evaluate the most general and decisive approach that accompanies the theological word.

According to Falque the theoretical investigation concerning the role of speech is appropriate if the priority of the body is considered over the text: "should not the hermeneutical *relief*, as understood in its Catholicity, move in the direction of *corporality* rather than *textuality*?"[6] To corroborate his hypothesis Falque points out that in the speculative tradition of Catholicism there already have been thinkers who recognized and articulated this notion. More broadly, it can be defined as a priority of the experiential aspect over the purely speculative one: the believer's relationship with Holy Scripture is absolutized, reducing it to a theoretical bond, unable to liven up the experience. In particular, Falque quotes Bonaventure, recalling how he documented the non-necessity of the written text in the prelapsarian condition. The Franciscan thinker notes that the second chapter of Genesis describes the Edenic condition where the encounter of man and woman with God happened. In that situation there was no need for a text: "no scripture was needed in Eden; nature spoke fluently of itself,"[7] while in the book of Exodus, Moses needs a writing in order to accomplish his mediation between God and the Jewish people (first of all the Tables of the Law and then the text of the Torah itself, of which he was considered the author).[8] The privilege of the bodily dimension—typical of the Edenic situation, on the written one—resulting from sin, is rooted in the form of God's word. It is given by favoring experience and not vocality, as Falque defines following Bonaventure again:[9] "for God, *speaking* . . . is identical to *acting*, to *doing*: God speaks not only by word *(non tanquam loquitur per verba)*, but also by deeds *(verum etiam per facta)*. For to speak, for Him, is to do, and to do is to speak *(quia ipsius* dicere *facere est, et ipsius* facere *dicere)*."[10]

The overcoming of the mediation of the wordily signs is a mark of a more general structure that sometimes affects Falque's proposal. Falque is only a little interested in the most detailed interweaving between the text and the word. In his philosophy the reality is clearly structured in a binary way and by consequence it is necessary to choose for one of the two poles, without considering their relationship. This relationship can be harmonious or dramatic, but never overcoming. Rather, there is a parallelism that becomes a simple mirroring, devoid of opacity and thus of relationship. Proposing anew the classical image of the two books through which God speaks, that of Scripture and that of nature, it is suggested that both are God's speaking, but they do so in a self-sufficient form. Each one is the happening of a complete definition; at least, the book corresponding to the world, declared in particular as the book of experience, has priority.

This structure highlights two aspects: the first is the difficulty of Falque's thinking in proposing an anthropology capable of considering the opacity given by the weight of sin, thus to highlight the form of freedom.[11] The second aspect is related to the first: it is hard to argue the role played by Christology in the understanding of the world. Christology, as we shall see, establishes a double nexus, that is a ternary form of the bond, between the world and the text.

JESUS CHRIST AS THE UNIFICATION OF BODY AND VOICE

To introduce Falque's position regarding the relationship between Christology and hermeneutics, it is good to return to the other philosophers to whom he compares his position. First of all, the author considers the hermeneutics dependent on the Jewish faith summarized by Emmanuel Levinas. For Levinas the biblical text is considered to be divine incorporation, an institution of God's kenotic connection to the world through the abandonment of the divine form, in order to establish finitude. Although Falque considers this moment as a fundamental theoretical step, he does not find it to be sufficient to achieve a fully Catholic hermeneutics. Even if the body is projected as an indispensable dimension, it is still the body of the text. There is no possibility of defining the "text of the body." The meaning of the "kenosis of the text" is therefore immediately replaced by "the abandonment of the divine prerogative." For this reason, Catholic hermeneutics finds its center in Jesus, he is the "text of the body," which does not correspond to an ark of the word, but to an ark of the flesh. Falque believes that the former exposes himself to the risk of losing the Christian structure concerning "Word become flesh in the Son."[12]

This passage can be understood by dedicating special attention to the comparison with Jean-Louis Chrétien,[13] from whom Falque draws the image of the ark of the word, immediately overturned in the ark of the flesh. Chrétien's hermeneutics is considered inadequate for reestablishing the Catholic idea of the body to its central role. This difficulty is generally due to what Falque calls the *preemption of the infinite*;[14] that is, the difficulty he attributes to thinkers such as Jean-Luc Marion, Michel Henry, and Chrétien himself of forgetting and overlooking the dimension of human finitude. According to Falque, this entails both a speculative aporia, unable to fully honor the phenomenological method, as well as a deeper difficulty in returning to the founding nucleus of Christianity—a singular facticity whose corporeity is an unsurpassed experience. Falque's investigation, mentioned in *Crossing the Rubicon*, interprets the phenomenology of call and response, which, according to Chrétien, finds its privileged purpose in the speech. Again, this is still limited by its lack of prominence attributed to the body.

To understand this essential step it is good to refer to Falque's[15] detailed analysis of the phenomenology of the voice: he recognizes the peculiarity of Chrétien's proposal and points out that "the text itself 'is' the body, a locus of intercorporeity rather than a simple means of linguistic exchange."[16] Although the cognitive priority of the body over that of the word is immediately pointed out, this alternative shows that only the former is adequate to fully give the complexity of human measure.

However, through a more generous reading of Chrétien's work, it is perhaps possible to find a valid structure for completing Falque's argument.[17] In fact, Chrétien demonstrates how the phenomenological structure of call and response operates in the totality of experiences characterizing the human being. Thus, both the flesh and the text are manifestations of this structure. Therefore, not only does the voice simply become incarnate, as only a simple and finite expression of a singular body, but it is peculiar when it is structured in a writing. The voice, in fact, is arranged in an intersubjective form, collecting intentionalities involving the many voices with which it speaks. This is the case even more for biblical scriptures, which overturn the correlation with the subject that approaches it: he is no longer a mere interpreter, but he's implicated in the need for a response. He is called to freedom because his existence is interpreted by the story he reads.[18]

Falque, however, builds his own interpretation in order to signal how the outcome of Chrétien's phenomenology is a naked voice, deprived of the flesh. This danger is due—according to his interpretation—to Chrétien's insuperable bond to the Heideggerian notion of consciousness' voice in *Being and Time*,[19] which is disembodied and marked by solipsism.[20] In Falque's vision, therefore, only the ark of flesh, establishing a priority of the body over the voice, is adequate to describe human beings, as it can be understood by direct consideration of Jesus as the perfect figure of man and at the same time the embodiment of the Word of God.

THE ACT OF READING AS THE ENCOUNTER OF THEORY AND EXPERIENCE

Falque therefore aims to gain theoretically a hermeneutic that not only safeguards the bodily dimension, but also that corresponds to a hermeneutic of the body. This all is in order not to fall into reliance upon the priority of the text, from which the forgetfulness of the body necessarily follows. In order to establish how this is possible, starting from the Christian experience, Falque considers the Eucharistic celebration, insisting on the patristic image of the two tables, that of the word and that of bread, making it clear that only the latter realizes the body of Christ in a radical way.[21] The two tables do not have the same importance, although the first finds its meaning only by leaning on the second. Falque corroborates his thesis by interpreting the Gospel of Luke 24:21–35: from the evangelical description of the resurrected Christ's meeting with the disciples of Emmaus, Falque substantially prioritizes the breaking of the bread. The listening to the Scripture—becoming possible because Jesus himself performs their hermeneutics—has only a chronological and not a substantial precedence. Likewise, in the liturgical celebration, the "table of Scripture" would only be introductory to that of the body. At the same time, it is necessary to ensure that it is not considered autonomous, otherwise the historical dimension given by the founding reference to the body would be lost. Falque recalls that only after recognizing Jesus as Risen are the disciples able to find a meaning in the interpretation of Scripture and to be reminded of the moment of the first breaking of bread, during the last supper. According to the author's interpretation, this dynamic is the basis of the unique development that binds the two tables and that more generally links the body to the word: the bread's table gives sense to the Scripture, but it is impossible to reverse the direction. If not mediated by the celebratory act where the body itself is received, the writing would remain speechless, unable to lead to the body, and therefore also to life.

Falque explicitly states that he wants to "deliver the voice, or to no longer treat it as a voice possessed by the message it bears (conscience, call, debt, being), [and this] entails disengaging it from language (*logos*)—more specifically, from writing (*gramma*)."[22] This statement still operates according to a binary distinction through which he has structured his entire analysis: in order to preserve the vital and experiential dimension, he renders almost alternatively the body and the voice, and the written and bodily dimension.

The claim supporting this basis is built by investigating the Eucharistic dimension, expressed in its Christological roots. The interweaving between body and speech, experience and reading, is then deepened by Falque's attendance to the analysis of medieval thought. This peculiar age in the history of thought allows us to consider the role of theology in its relationship with philosophy. During the medieval period, in fact, the investigation of human experience as such is philosophically delineated by virtue of the contribution of theological data. This structure consists, according to Falque's approach, in a mostly unexplored repository of issues considered by phenomenologists in the last century.[23]

Even to understand the text's hermeneutics and its connection with experience, therefore with the flesh, Falque develops some fundamental instances described by medieval authors: a brief incursion to what is expressed in *Le livre de l'expérience* can therefore illuminate the structure he proposed in *Crossing the Rubicon*.

Medieval reflection returns a fundamental interweaving between the act of reading and experience as such. The two dynamics are mutually linked, as there is no experience without reading nor is reading alien to experience. Following Hugh of Saint Victor, Falque recalls that the ability to read is founded by the divine creative act: the latter is described as a writing. God communicates himself, and his creatures can decipher who he is through the encounter with the world he created. The creator is known through his work, the world is a symbolic writing, offered to be decoded. Once again, however, the act of writing is immediately understood in a figural sense, while the first sense of writing, determined by the Bible as the Holy Scripture, remains put aside. The primacy of nature's book over that of writing is therefore established, which risks determining the negligible relevance of the Bible and the relationship to it. In fact, "the act of reading, far from being reduced to a simple following of the writing's trace, is extended to the whole reality, to the world itself."[24] As a result, the author states that "reading in the Middle Ages is not first and foremost a way of relating to a writing or to the Scripture (*liber Scripturae*), but to the creatures (*liber creaturarum*), to the world (*liber mundi*), to Christ (*liber Christi*), or to one's own life in general (*liber vitae*)."[25]

Falque's interpretation, unbalanced on the side of experience, does not forget, however, what the act of reading in the Middle Ages means, remembering that it also is a form of experience. This explanation is disproportionate, however, because it insists on the primacy of the world's interpretation, over that addressed by Scripture, without highlighting their intrinsic nexus. Above all, what Falque overshadows is that the interpretation of the world is achievable only if intimately linked to the first, recognized as its vital nucleus.

Reading the world and reading Scripture cannot remain in a parallel dimension: the style configuring the reading of the Bible is that of the monastic *lectio divina*. It is a non-intellectualistic act, which would reduce the text to its technical, cognitive, and informative dimension, but it is built as a real experience of otherness, of both the divine and humans. In fact, the formally impossible experience of bringing from the pages the encounter with God out[26] is an intersubjective, therefore experiential, act: it happens only when the reader is able to reproduce the same connection to experience that led the Bible being written. Hagiographers recognized divine revelation in their history and decided to bear witness to it by writing it; so, those who read the text produced by their activity will interpret it only if they are able to put it back into dialogue with experience, historically rooted.[27] Moreover, the medieval experience of reading, especially in the monastic context, was quite different from modern individualistic and quiet activity, carried out through the mental reading of the signs. The sacred page resonated and called everyone not only in a spiritual sense, but also in a physical one. The text was the subject of a public reading; books were not a private but a communitarian possession.[28] The reading is therefore not silent, nor does it take place alienated from reality. It is the real and vital act of decrypting the text enabled by the bond with experience. By consequence it lets its call resonate in experience as such.

SACRAMENTALITY OF THE WORD AS A SYNTHESIS OF BODY AND VOICE

Falque defines the experience of Scripture implemented during medieval times using a term that only recently entered the theological and ecclesiastical lexicon, that of the *sacramentmentality of the word*.[29] The expression allows the author to explain the connection of the voice with the body to which he has already hinted, that is, the Eucharistic form. An analysis of that term provides a way of definitively understanding the importance he attaches to the hermeneutics of the word, and it opens up the possibility of understanding what the weight of the theological word can be toward the philosophical one.

The theme of the sacramentality of the word allows the author to recognize that the biblical writing is not reduced to the material support of a speech, but in the first instance it is "Word of God." The analogic link between the historical body of Christ and his taking shape in Scripture as its hermeneutic center discloses the living dimension of Scripture. This theoretical resource, which Falque could deepen again on the kenotic dimension of the writing—anticipated by Levinas and made explicit by Chrétien—would allow the expression of the duplicity of the body and the word as unified in a single source, that is, Christ himself. However, following the procedure already highlighted, Falque opts for an immediate understanding of the sacramental form referring to the breaking of bread, recognized as the only and true sacramental event.

This valuable indication is immediately overdetermined. The reading of the Word is a medium that ferries beyond itself, as it opens to a more general form of listening that can open up to vision. Vision, understood as the possibility of deciphering the sense of the world, is understood as the definitive point, which swallows the previous ones, and thus the Bible has only a temporary and not definitive role. The author dwells on the image found in the book of Revelation (10:8), which describes the authentic connection to the book: it is not read, but eaten. For this reason Falque comments that "it does not matter that the monk can read a text, if he has the keys to interpret his life . . . he will learn to collect the book of his own life in the Book that is God himself in his Wisdom, in a heart-to-heart rather than in a text-to-text."[30]

The sacramentality of the word is immediately deferred to the Eucharistic dynamic, leaving in the background what concerns the vital link given by a confrontation with the text. In short, the two tables, of the bread and of the word, are not only ultimately extrinsic to each other: they also do not have equal importance. Sacramental celebration would in fact have only one center, the breaking of bread that gives access to the sacrificial body of Christ, while the proclamation of Scripture finds its meaning only in relation to the breaking of bread itself, so that it is considered as a mere moment of passage. The primacy of the body is therefore earned to the detriment of the text.

Precisely the idea of sacramentality of the word, however, can lead to a different restitution of the matter. It not only allows us to verify the fundamental role played by the speech in the Christian experience, but also to interpret otherwise the relationship between the two tables. From this, we add, one can draw a valuable indication to interpret the role of the theoretical word that corresponds to theology and consequently to its role according to philosophy.

WHAT KIND OF DIMENSION FOR THE THEOLOGICAL EXPRESSION?

Falque's proposal establishes a clear parallelism between the conception of hermeneutics and the status attributed to theology. In both cases their re-evaluation is the result of a sort of distortion of some qualifications, which can be summarized according to the primacy of experience on the theoretical and critical dimension. In fact, according to Falque's position, hermeneutics is authentic when it refers to the body rather than to the speech. Similarly, theology has a valuable role to play for philosophy if it intercepts the facticity of religious experience, rather than providing a critical reflection on faith and revelation.[31]

The positive interest in a link between philosophy and theology, theorized through the image of the shock of return provided by theology to philosophy, also establishes the irreducible difference between the two disciplines: it is difficult to recognize a common belonging to critical reason.

The deepening proposed by Falque, however, suggests a different reconstruction: starting from the unitary link between body and voice in the hermeneutic dimension, it is possible to reconsider the relationship between faith and reason at the anthropological and gnoseological level and finally to present the unitary epistemology that binds philosophy and theology.

In the analyses related to hermeneutics and in the explicit use of biblical commentary to provide valid examples for his own phenomenology, Falque seems to be reducing theological and biblical knowledge to a necessary but partial exposure of some significant and paradoxical experiences.[32] Thus, there is not a very deep epistemological difference, from theology to any other discipline, such as psychoanalysis or art.

Nevertheless, the formula relating to the sacramentality of the word he proposes suggests a different development: the theologian Louis-Marie Chauvet provides a valuable indication to interpret the figure of the tables of the word and bread.[33] These are not to be understood as two different tables, but as the one and only Eucharistic table, determined by the body of Christ that manifests itself in sacramental form, both in bread and wine as found in Scripture. In fact, only through this interpretation is it possible to fully enhance what the monastic tradition has theorized about the *lectio divina*. It enlightens the inextricable connection with historical and singular experience, rooted in the decisive relationship to Christ, met through the Bible, making it meaningful for one's own existence. Otherwise the Eucharistic celebration would remain extrinsic to free and personal determination, not concomitant to history.

Significantly, it was precisely the monastic experience during the Middle Ages that favored an approach to speculation not separated from life. Theology was at the same time a vital practice able to inherit all the aspects of classical culture, formulating a speculative synthesis with the ability of being transformed by history.[34]

The role of theology, as a critical interpretation of faith, can be founded precisely in the form of biblical writing, which is neither merely narration, nor the container of exemplary or moral examples, but rather is the call of humans to answer with all the resources of their universal reason. On the contrary, it proposes a specific form of revelation, which, paradoxically, is singularized in history. The Bible, defined as attested revelation,[35] shows the measure and the definitive role of both history (intersubjective and testimonial) and written text.[36] The Bible's inner dynamics, opening up to an history of accomplishment, shows that the speech has a non-negligible role because it implies a living, intersubjective determination of life that cannot in any way be overcome or set aside.

The theoretical speech derives its role from the same dynamics as the theological word. The idea of crossing the Rubicon from theology to philosophy can reach a definitive dimension and open a new field of research in Falque's theory if theology is understood not simply as an expression related to mere experience, but rather as a speech defined according to the anthropological dimension rooted in history and universalized by reason.

NOTES

1. Benoit Bourgine, "Philosophie et théologie en procès d'alliance," *Recherches de science religieuse* 102 (2014): 519–538, here 528.
2. Emmanuel Falque, *Crossing the Rubicon: The Borderlands of Philosophy and Theology*, translated by Reuben Shank (New York: Fordham University Press, 2016), 29.
3. Falque, *Crossing the Rubicon*, 30.
4. Emmanuel Falque, *The Loving Struggle: Phenomenological and Theological Debates*, translated by Bradley B. Obishi and Lucas McCraken (London; New York: Rowman & Littlefield, 2018), 1–15.
5. Benoit Bourgine, "Récension de Emmanuel Falque, Passer le Rubicon," *Revue théologique de Louvain* 46 (2015): 100–04.
6. Falque, *Crossing the Rubicon*, 40.
7. Falque, *Crossing the Rubicon*, 43.
8. This reference shows a possible different approach hidden in Moses' role: as Exodus, Genesis is part of the Torah, so the both are written by Moses. By consequence, in the universal postlapsarian condition the link to the description of absence of text in Edenic condition is mediated by the necessary use of the text.
9. See Bonaventure, *Breviloquium*, Prol. 4, No. 4 (V, 206a).
10. Emmanuel Falque, *Saint Bonaventure and the Entrance of God into Theology. Afterword: Saint Thomas Aquinas and the Entrance of God into Philosophy*, translated by Brian Lapsa (St. Bonaventure, NY: Saint Bonaventure University, Franciscan Institute Publications, 2018), 84.
11. Concerning the theme of sin dimension's lack, see Manuel Belli, *Al di là del limite. Filosofia e teologia nella proposta di Emmanuel Falque* (Milano: Glossa, 2015), 69–71.
12. Falque, *Crossing the Rubicon*, 49.
13. See Jean-Louis Chrétien, *The Ark of Speech*, translated by Andrew Brown (New York; London: Routledge, 2004), 1–8.
14. Emmanuel Falque, *The Metamorphosis of Finitude: An Essay on Birth and Resurrection*, translated by George Hughes (New York: Fordham University Press, 2012), 16–19.
15. See Falque, *The Loving Struggle*, 175–91.
16. Falque, *The Loving Struggle*, 175.
17. In order to find a totally different appreciation of Chrétien's work, whose aim is to show how difficult is to take Falque's interpretation, see Jean Greisch, "Bulletin philosophie et christianisme," *Recherches de science religieuse* 102 (2014): 129–55, here 153.
18. Jean-Louis Chrétien, *Under the Gaze of the Bible*, translated by J. M. Dunaway (New York: Fordham University Press, 2015), 6–22.
19. Falque, *Crossing the Rubicon*, 60–61.

20. In Francesca Peruzzotti, *Lo scritto e il suo lettore. In ascolto di Jean-Luc Marion, Martin Heidegger, Jean-Louis Chrétien* (Milano: Mimesis, 2015), 161–98, I attempted to show how the structure proposed by Chrétien is an overwhelming of Heideggerian troubles, just in reason of the main reference to the Bible as a paradigmatic and exemplar writing.

21. This idea had been reconsidered at Vatican II. The Dogmatic Constitution on Divine Revelation Dei Verbum claims: "The Church has always venerated the divine Scriptures just as she venerates the body of the Lord, since, especially in the sacred liturgy, she unceasingly receives and offers to the faithful the bread of life from the table both of God's word and of Christ's body" (§21).

22. Falque, *Crossing the Rubicon*, 67.

23. Emmanuel Falque, *God, the Flesh, and the Other: From Irenaeus to Duns Scotus*, translated by William Christian Hackett (Evanston, IL: Northwestern University Press, 2015), 5–19.

24. Emmanuel Falque, *Le livre de l'expérience. D'Anselme de Cantorbéry à Bernard de Clairvaux* (Paris: Cerf, 2017), 163.

25. Falque, *Le livre de l'expérience*, 165.

26. Jean-Yves Lacoste, *Recherches sur la parole* (Peeters: Leuven, 2015), 226.

27. Enzo Bianchi, *Praying the Word: An Introduction to Lectio Divina*, translated by J. W. Zona (Athens, OH: Cistercian Publications, 1998), 18.

28. See Ivan Illich, *In the Vineyard of the Text: A Commentary to Hugh's Didascalicon*, translated by V. Borremmans (Chicago; London: University of Chicago Press, 1993), 54–57.

29. Falque, *Le livre de l'expérience*, 172. The first explicit employ of this term in an ecclesiastic document is in 2008, with Benedict XVI, Verbum Domini, *Post-Synodal Apostolic Exhortation* (London: Catholic Truth Society, 2010), §56; see Enzo Bianchi, "La sacramentalità della Parola," in *Il vangelo celebrato*, edited by E. Bianchi and G. Boselli (Milano: San Paolo 2017), 191–217.

30. Falque, *Le livre de l'expérience*, 183.

31. Falque, *Crossing the Rubicon*, 101–07.

32. Concerning Falque's employment and interpretation of the Bible—sometimes reduced to a common text and not considered in its status—see Paul Gilbert, "Ecriture phénoménologique et méthode patristique. Les frontières de la philosophie et de la théologie selon Emmanuel Falque," in *Une analytique du passage. Rencontres et confrontations avec Emmanuel Falque*, edited by C. Brunier-Coulin (Paris: Editions Franciscaines, 2016), 386–87; and "L'attenzione del pensiero. Emmanuel Falque, la filosofia, la teologia e la fenomenologia," in *Emmanuel Falque. Tra fenomenologia della finitezza e teologia dell'incarnazione*, edited by C. Canullo and P. Gilbert (Firenze: Le Lettere, 2014), 21.

33. Louis-Marie Chauvet, *Symbol and Sacrament: A Sacramental Reinterpretation of Christian Existence*, translated by Patrick Madigan S.J. and Madeleine Beaumont (Collegeville, MN: The Liturgical Press, 1995), 213–26.

34. Jean Leclercq, *The Love of Learning and the Desire of God: A Study of Monastic Culture*, translated by Catharine Mirashi (New York: Fordham University Press, 1982), 191–235.

35. For the first time in 1993 the Bible was defined as *attested revelation* in Pontifical Biblical Commission, *The Interpretation of the Bible in the Church*, edited by J. L. Houlden (London: SCM Press, 1995).

36. Pierangelo Sequeri, "La struttura testimoniale delle scritture sacre: teologia del testo," in *La rivelazione attestata. La Bibbia tra Testo e Teologia*, edited by G. Angelini (Milano: Glossa, 1998), 6.

Part III

Constructive-Critical Engagements

Chapter Ten

Oportet transire

How "Crossing" Becomes *a* quaestio de homine

Carla Canullo

OPORTET TRANSIRE: FALQUE'S READING OF MEISTER ECKHART

Regarding knowledge of God, Meister Eckhart wrote in his *Sermo 24:2* that "the intellect resolves [what it apprehends] into being, [yet] it behooves the intellect to pass by and leave it [this conception]."[1] Commenting on this sentence, theologian and philosopher Vladimir Lossky wrote that it is the intellect that grasps God "in a contentlessness and total anonymity" and that this *Oportet transire* (this necessity that "we behoove to pass by") points toward how we are "to go beyond being" or "to go beyond God" in order to find God himself "in the bottomless ocean of this infinity."[2]

Far from this Eckhartian mystic, it is not such a *transire* that Emmanuel Falque investigates on his own philosophical path. Instead, he focuses on the *conversion* that he reads as an *Abgeschiedenheit* (*disinterest* or *detachment*), thus linking it to the phenomenological reduction. After all, the reading of medieval thought is, from a phenomenological perspective, the essence of Falque's work *God, the Flesh, and the Other: From Irenaeus to Duns Scotus*.[3] Starting from the phenomenological point of view, he interprets Meister Eckhart's depiction of the story of Martha and Mary in the *Sermons*. This paragraph elucidates Falque's understanding of these two women from the Gospel, overruling the most classical reading by identifying Mary's "Natural Attitude" and Martha's "Phenomenological Epochē."[4] Falque writes:

> There is nothing here that excludes the fact that Martha, taken up with "the multiple cares of serving her guests" (Lk 10:40) is actually not listening, as it

were, to that which listening signifies, that is, obedience: "In true obedience," Eckhart emphasizes, "she has completely *exited from herself into God*." To hear or to obey, since they share the same root (*akouô*), is primarily understood by Eckhart as *to climb out of* or *to undo* the self—or better, as a certain *mode of self* in its relation to the world. Who is the one who truly hears and obeys in this passage from the Gospel? That is, who discards more of the conception of God as "thing" and understands him as act of a "life in itself"? Not Mary, who sits, far from quotidian occupations, absorbed in God as "thing," but rather Martha—who stands "*with or close to* things" without being "*in* things."[5]

Continuing with his reading of Meister Eckhart, Falque further writes, "Mary remains in some sense beholden to the natural attitude and therefore 'perceives the world, and lives there, in a completely natural way being interested in it'—that is: here, in the world of God. Mary, when she is transfixed and absorbingly listening to the Lord, loses herself in him, with a 'sensible delight'—she gets 'lost in the world,' according to Eckhart, 'lost in things, lost in ideas, lost in the plants and the beasts . . . outside, diverted.'" Falque augments:

> The apprenticeship of Mary led by Martha becomes in a sense the phenomenological *epochē*: "Martha says 'Lord order her to help me' (Lk 10:40), as if she had said: my sister believes that she can do what she wants as long as she is *sitting close to you* in consolation. Let her see if all is well and order her to *rise up* and *leave you*." Martha . . . desires that her sister be *detached* from the Lord as "thing" (*Abgeschiedenheit*), a sort of phenomenological reduction. . . . Eckhart, in producing the necessary detachment that makes it impossible for God to be identified within the mode of being of "substance," portrays man as a receptor of a non-reified divine. . . . It is not sufficient simply to confirm that God is not "some thing" (*non est quid*); again it would be necessary that this non-reification attains the *practical modality* of man himself in his apprehension of God. . . . It is Martha's task to teach her sister this "conversion of self" as a mode of phenomenological *epochē*, operating already from herself and on herself, that is, according to Eckhart's remarkable formula, teaching her "no longer to take God as if you would wrap his head in a coat and stuff it under a bench."[6]

This paragraph clearly depicts, through a unique interpretation, Falque's proposal of the German mystic and Thuringian theologian. However, we will not be able to investigate further, as doing so properly, would require not only "reading Falque" but also going back to the texts of the Dominican thinkers that he interprets and uses. Yet before moving on from the interpretation of the phenomenological reduction through the interpretation of Meister Eckhart, it is worth highlighting that, in those pages, Falque puts at stake also the second matter that fundamentally characterizes phenomenology: intentionality.

The "main phenomenological theme," as Husserl defines *intentionality* in §84 of *Ideas I*, is introduced in this case through Falque's reading Eckhart:

> Articulated in Eckhart's terms, Martha is detached from "work" in no longer being in things but remains nevertheless in the "activity" by remaining with things: "work [*Werk*] is when one is exercised *exteriorly* in works of virtue; but 'activity' [*Gewerk*] is when one is exercised *interiorly* with reasonable discretion." An identical and first step is accomplished therefore in the phenomenological *epochē* as in religious conversion. It is in the *inner* transformation of the self (activity [*Gewerk*]) that the world is suspended or one is converted to God, and not in the simple obedience to external rules (work [*Werk*]). Such a return above the self does not imply that God or the world are not able to exist independently of the I. It indicates only that the *lived experience of the world* like the *lived experience of God* designate for me the "thing itself"—the act of my consciousness by which the world and God are seen at once.[7]

Falque emphasizes his phenomenological reading by claiming that

> the world does not disappear in Eckhart, as it does for the Cartesian *dubitatio* (doubt), but it is in some way "bracketed" or "reduced" in order to leave the mode of objectivity behind. *Abgeschiedenheit* is a mode of the *epochē* as "detachment" diverting consciousness from its relation to things in order to show its lived experience of things. . . . God is not *objectively given exteriorly* but is *intentionally engendered interiorly*. Such is the message of Eckhart who shows his originality—inasmuch as he is reread in light of the concept of intentionality.[8]

Reducing our reading to those two themes of course does not do the text justice. The first paragraph (introduced in "The Reduction to the I: The Apprenticeship of Mary of Bethany")[9] is actually followed by two other important sections devoted to "The Constitution of God: The Fecundity of Martha"[10] and to "The Reduction to Nothing: The Vision of Paul."[11] Nevertheless, as Falque needs Meister Eckhart to connect the first part of his work (God) with the second part (The Flesh), we leave the comment of the Dominican Father to *transire* to other works by Falque, following his ideal, connecting the two, demonstrating the way Eckhart serves *as a passage* toward the second section: "It would be *of little value for me that 'the Word was made flesh' for man in Christ*, Eckhart indicated in the conclusion of his *Commentary on the Gospel of John*, 'unless he was also *made flesh in me personally* so that I too might be God's son.'"[12]

Here it is shown that Meister Eckhart is undoubtedly an important author for Falque (even if the invitation to *oportet transire* is not for him as central of a theme as it is for other French authors such as Stanislas Breton or Pierre Gire); the latter employs especially the *Treatise* concerning *Abgeschiedenheit* from the former.[13] Yet even if this motto of Eckhart is not expressly quoted, the passage is umbilical also for Falque. He would, perhaps, not deflect the idea that "we must cross over," *oportet transire*.

THE POSSIBLE PASSAGE

Oportet transire could therefore be a theme found in Falque, due to the role that the passage has had since his first work, *Le passeur de Gethsémani. Angoisse, souffrance et mort. Lecture existentielle et phénoménologique*.[14] This book is a central key by which Falque's thought might be accessed. First, because of the phenomenological method that is explicitly summoned in it, and, second, because it clarifies a demeanor in Falque's thought, namely, that we must approach the passage and cannot avoid or *escape* it. We could, in fact, affirm that the crossing from one problem to another is the attitude that Falque maintains throughout his entire oeuvre. For Falque, it is neither about avoiding nor eluding any components of a human *indépassable* finitude. Therefore—and in order to talk about human finitude—he proposes an "existential reading" of the One who crosses and *passes* through Gethsemane without *running away* from his existential condition.

It is only when the patient crossing toward existence is *possible* that the matters demanding such crossing gain significance and weight. This crossing makes us unavoidably human. "Unavoidably" not because this weighs on the human so heavily as to make her wish her own death, but rather because the possibility of her "authentic" human *existence* relies upon these moments of crossing. In these moments, the human is shaped into an image. For "the image of God in us," Falque writes, "can be read today in the profundity of our nature."[15] That is why "Christ teaches us first of all to be human beings—that is, precisely, not to flee from our own finitude. He teaches us how we can also, with him, 'abandon' ourselves in death."[16] Therefore, in a very intense chapter,[17] Falque insists on the moment of "suffering the world" to "pass to the Father." Since Christ passed *from* this world to the Father, yet, simultaneously, also passed his sorrow *to* the Father. It is a sorrow that, as our author establishes, is not the outcome of a sinful experience, but actually a natural one. Therefore, "in suffering this world the Son conveys to the Father (a passage) the weight of finitude experienced in his death," up to the point of begging the Father to allow him to avoid the sorrow.[18]

In this passage the proposal is not a replacement of Christ as the human sacrifice. The emphasis here is not Christ's bearing our suffering upon himself, but rather how he faces his own suffering. In this passage, the impossible becomes possible: hence, it becomes possible that the human is not simply subjected passively to suffering, or must necessarily run away from it. Instead it becomes possible for humans to choose it and go through. At first sight, one could wonder how that is possible for humans. This matter is answered by Falque in a neither simple nor evident way, as he declares that this is *made* possible by the Son. The path, as already mentioned, is not evident because, firstly, it is not clear where Christ's sufferance lay in His flesh, as each one of us must live through suffering on his or her own. That is to say: Christ's suffering in His human flesh enables the passage of suffering to God. Yet evidently it is His suffering. What can *every human* get from such a passage?

Falque refers to Jürgen Moltmann's claim that "Jesus suffered and died alone." Moltmann however, then goes one step further: "But those who follow him suffer and die in fellowship *with him*."[19] Now, the meaning of the *possible passage* lies in this "with." The fact that the suffering of Christ *passes* to the Father does not imply a replacement (as our suffering is inherent to each one of us as uniquely ours) but rather the opening, and the disclosing of a *possibility*: the possibility of not living the experience of sorrow and suffering in isolation, and of *living-with* it. "To suffer and die 'with' the Son does not mean that one does not any longer suffer and die, nor does it take away the 'mineness' of suffering and death," as indeed nothing can take away from human condition, "nor does it take away the "mineness" of suffering and death."[20] Falque continues, "Christ suffers and dies *for* me and *with* me: he does not suffer and die in my place. . . . Like a guide or ferryman [*Passeur*] taking in charge the one who passes or whom he guides [*le passant*], Christ transforms, starting from today, the meaning of my suffering, so that I am able to make it (along with him) the modality of my own life. It becomes, as it were, the place of reception of an *else-where* or an *other* of my life."[21]

Here ripens the ideas of the possible passage of the image of the "other," which one inherently has, and which Christ enables us to discover to reveal. This passage is about oneself and the alterity dwelling in the "self." It is about one's finitude not to run away. And while this conception does not necessarily contradict a Heideggerian ontology, it does go beyond it: it is possible to discover a radical alterity at the root of the self. Falque refers to this dynamic of discovery and revelation as a *non-substitutable substitution*,[22] meaning that Christ comes not to take away suffering but to bear it *with* man (and in this Christ is the *Passeur*). Losing this *non-substitutable substitution* exposes one to the risk of *closure* "in the pure unbreakable solipsism of suffering and dying flesh."[23] The possible passage, therefore, allows for the discovery—in finitude and most of all in the suffering finitude—of the intimate opening of existence in which "suffering remains." This suffering and opening is "that which tears me apart rather than, as the untenable alternative has it, something that reveals me to myself in my own,"[24] revealing the radical alterity that dwells in me; the "other," in front of whom my existence discovers its possibilities.

Passage and crossing is also at the heart of the second work of Falque's trilogy, *The Metamorphosis of Finitude*.[25] In this work, Falque makes us pass from the awareness of suffering and of death *to* faith in resurrection. Jesus' dialogue with Nicodemus is a sign of this possible passage, as is the double birth in the flesh and in the spirit.

Falque, commenting upon the dialogue reported in John 3:4 writes:

> Just as you know for yourself what birth is from the birth of your own flesh from your "mother's womb," or you know because in your turn you also have begotten by your own flesh, so, in the same way, you understand today what the "rebirth of the spirit" is, starting from the first experience of the birth of your flesh, or by your flesh. In other words, as flesh is born of flesh in the act of filiation, or of begetting, so spirit is born of spirit in the act of baptism and even more in the final resurrection.[26]

Now, if on one side of this dialogue is "a motif . . . to justify the philosophical, and therefore human, interrogation of what is our actual experience of the birth of the flesh,"[27] then on the other side is "the passage from death to birth invites us to a 'rebirth' that can never skip over the meaning, first of all phenomenological and descriptive, of the act of birth—because the act of birth serves as its guide and model."[28]

In this passage, a great deal is mentioned regarding the human's relationship with God and the relationship between theology and philosophy. In fact, in the recurring statement that "We have no other experience of God but human experience,"[29] the attempt to show the necessity of the thought that humanity is the beginning of the world, is abridged. Further, in this book, starting from the *datum*, according to which theology and the Holy Scriptures show how in the Trinity a real transposition of the sufferance of the Son to the Father—the humanly impossible—is realized.[30] We ought to—starting from the theological event of Christ's resurrection—attempt to think "that what philosophy holds legitimately to be impossible."[31] One could almost say that theology states the possibility of entering in an area that, philosophically, is impossible to explore, and, therefore, to think. Finally, in the statement that is often repeated, namely that "Nothing happens to mankind that did not first happen to God, except sin,"[32] Falque declares his intention of highlighting how the Trinitarian incorporation of man in the advent of resurrection transfigures the human condition so much as to legitimate a new reading of human finitude, and, as a consequence, of the world in which man lives.

In the first part of *The Metamorphosis of Finitude*,[33] he highlights that by saying "human," one means to say finitude. Falque unmasks this way of practicing a certain naive optimism of any theology that conveys the experience of the human, simply trying to produce a thought that takes away the natural limits of the human in order to conceive of the human as limitless.

The French philosopher instead attempts both to describe human experience as one that is really *human*, and to show the plausibility of theology, identifying it with its Christology. In fact, for Falque the claim concerning our insurmountable anthropological finitude is not reduced to the minimalistic and "feeble" tale of human existence, but instead, seeks to demonstrate how such finitude is necessarily the first word (as the beginning of thought) and not the last one, given the final Christological transfiguration of this same finitude.[34] Therefore the resurrection—as Falque states—"changes everything": it realizes, in fact, the possible passage to a radical novelty.[35]

Here it is highlighted that the resurrection can be thought as that which gives itself, because of its event-like character (namely, as a birth). Further, after this occurrence the event determines a radical novelty, as it faces the possibilities of thought as the realization of something that, without this event, would and could not even be considered. As a consequence, if taking finitude seriously requires the acknowledgment of an insurmountable immanence that does not allow for the possibility of remaining open toward God's transcendence (indeed a kind of immanence that cannot claim anything, not even the revelation of creation), then we must see how the events of the incarnation and the resurrection open a radical novelty also in the possibilities of the thought itself. Falque motivates such a novelty through a rereading of the inner dynamics of the Trinity, carrying out such a reading with the tools of phenomenology. This rereading leads him to state that within the Trinity the Son really *passes* the burden of his carnal finitude to the Father, realizing through Trinitarian life what in the worldly plan seems *necessary* and *impossible* at the same time: *necessary* because the acknowledgment of the alterity of the other requires the awareness of that which "I myself could also experience *if* I were in the other's place";[36] *impossible* because "the other is other not because I could put myself at his/her place, but because if I want to take his/her place, I understand I will never take it."[37] In the inner life of God by Jesus Christ, this necessary though impossible transposition occurs, giving life to what we could call substitutionary atonement or vicar representation, *Stell-vertretung*, taking the place. Such a divine singularity is the core matter of the Trinitarian event of Jesus' resurrection, and that, according to Falque, really represents the beginning of any relationship God has with the world and with man, even before creation and incarnation.[38] This is a relationship according to which any other passage becomes *possible*.

In this way the possible passage becomes a true human undertaking. This finitude, in the eye of God, comes simultaneously with a transfiguration and a metamorphosis of man in God, which gives man himself his sense and his ultimate goal: a sense and a goal that neither man nor philosophy, in their insurmountable finitude, neither have nor expect. But, since *in man nothing can be realized that is not already realized in God* (except sin), then, starting from the event of the Trinitarian incorporation of man in Christ's resurrection, it is possible to interpret human finitude beyond what—on the pure immanence plane—is humanly impossible to imagine. And perhaps most of all, one can even talk about the desire of God. The Father, under the power of the Spirit, gives birth to the desire of Him and of our resurrection. "God only puts in me the *desire of Him*—in which absence I can be 'without Him,' until he calls me to let me transform myself 'with Him.'"[39] If then *the only experience we have of God is the one of human*, it is necessary to acknowledge that, because God made the human and showed Godself as a man also in the resurrection, then it is through the humanity of man (namely, of Jesus Christ the man) that everyone (and, therefore, philosophy) always had the access to this God within. This is for the sake of establishing that every man can be transfigured, or also metamorphosized in God (and, thus, somehow also philosophy is transfigured in theology).

Through this, one discovers in oneself a possibility that was not known before: one acknowledges that one is able to receive God, not because one lowers God to the level of our finitude, but because God Godself has received, and transfigured in Godself our finitude. The same is true for philosophy, metamorphosed or transfigured by theology, which finds itself able to go into the deep places where I would otherwise have never imagined nor thought to go. Philosophy finds itself transfigured, converted by theology in a way similar to a resurrection: it rediscovers its sense and its ultimate goal, even if is aware of that for which it awaits. Therefore, in the same way that one is "eschatologically" surprised by the capacity of waiting and wishing for God, philosophy also can be "eschatologically" surprised by God's resurrection, receiving an offer that philosophy could have neither imagined nor felt the need for. An offer, instead, which would even enable us to "cross the Rubicon."[40]

Crossing, finally, is the title of the third part of the work with the same title (*Crossing the Rubicon*). Choosing the verb of "crossing" and not a noun, Falque shows the *verbality* of his work, which is what his work "does"— working just like a verb is used to express action within a sentence. He in fact does not limit himself to hermeneutic description, demonstrating the possible effects that would follow from the truth of that which he describes. Therefore, when he finally gets to the matter that interests him, namely believing, he does not talk about belief or faith but rather about the decision to believe. He shows that believing in action highlights not only its being a "religious category" but, even before that, declaring its irreducibility.[41] Certainly, the confessing faith, the faith that "has decided," is not a mere philosophical faith. Believing is at the base of being in the world.[42] Faith follows an existential structure by which "one believes" firstly in the world, and one first begins with faith.

After having acquired and discussed the distinction between the different ways of believing, which he receives from engagements with Husserl, Heidegger, Bultmann, Merleau-Ponty, Ricœur, Wittgenstein, and Gadamer, Falque makes also a step forward and, maybe, *beyond* this distinction. His step forward (or *beyond*) is not in order to invite the philosopher or the theologian to bear in mind the particular "faith" of the other (*scilicet* of the originary "belief" and of the confessing faith), nor in the fecund interpretation that Falque proposes about the meaning of phenomenology's methodological "atheism"[43] (which even Levinas must address).[44] This step forward and *beyond* is found in the "philosophy of decision" Falque addresses in the chapter "Kerygma and Decision."

If the *kerygma* is the announcement of a person and not only a letter, the decision of believing will not be limited to stating another form of faith. Rather, it will be transformative, as it will produce those effects that encounters with the other(s) cause. In others words, the decision of believing, the decided belief (expression where the *Entschlossenheit* by Heidegger echoes), has a *transforming* power. This is not just a "philosophy of religion" but a depiction of the religious experience in which the decision turns from a decision made by someone *about* something into a "kerygmatic decision of the believer is consecrated as an entry and incorporation into the Decision of God."[45] Once again: "In passing from the philosophical to the theological and then from the theological to the philosophical, we must agree now to descend, and no longer uniquely to ascend; that is, to begin with 'God's decision in relation to the human' and not to dwell uniquely on the human decision before God."[46] Here we encounter the great transformation of the experience of believing: deciding in the face of the *kerygma*. One makes the experience of the paradox one's own authentically. This amounts to a paradoxical authenticity, as it is authentic in so far as it is inauthentic, as it comes from the Other and from the decision that this One, first, has made regarding every human. However, in being faithful to the motto that crosses the book from the beginning to the end—"the better one theologizes, the more one philosophizes"—he also accounts for the necessity of a counter-movement from theology to philosophy. Here we are to look for traces of the change that occurs in philosophy, as no passage worthy of the name can be accomplished without leaving a trace that such an experience necessarily would bring about.

The "authentic" religious and philosophical experience that one has is therefore the discovery that being oneself is a "being with," as being chosen by another person. And again, it is the discovery that one's possibility of deciding *belongs* to her because someone has already decided—*for* her. In the final paragraph of the second section, a number of passages devoted to this idea follow one another and unfold rapidly: in accordance with Nicholas of Cusa, Falque writes that the decision for God can be recognized only if assessed and witnessed by a third person, who confirms what paradoxically one could doubt; that is, that God has taken a decision *for him* (and therefore *for me*). One departs from the doubt that such a decision was actually made *for* me, only because a witness has seen what I also have seen and that we can share in this together:

> [If] belief in God (*fides quod*) certainly does pass through God's belief in the human (*fides qua*), but this time united and reinforced by the unique trust of a human in another human, such that I have faith in another in order to also have faith in God (*fides cum*). The "in-common of believing" the kerygma joins up with—even as it returns to—the "believing-in-common" of the human per se, inasmuch as the Trinity establishes in an original and eternally determined way a fellowship in faith, which is at the same time a fellowship of the self.[47]

This philosophical-religious experience that believing makes possible leads to a rediscovery of the self. The more this rediscovery is transformed by the Other, the more authentic it becomes for the one who has decided, namely by enabling the decider to decide *for himself while he also decides for the Other and for any other*. Through leading one to rediscover what one did not know—even though it was already there—a transformation happens thanks to the "crossing of the Rubicon." This is a passage that—as mentioned earlier, just as in any passage—*must* produce effects of transformation, transforming first of all the present experience.

Now, therefore, experiencing is irreducible to being merely *Erlebnis* or *Erfahrung*: experiencing now is what changes and transforms us, like a crossing that enables us to go back and forth, like a bridge that connects two shores and makes the passages in two directions ever-possible. These passages are made by Falque between §13 ("Philosophy of the Decision"), where he debates the meaning of the transformation that the experience of believing brings about, and §20 ("The Principle of Proportionality"), where he evaluates the outcomes of such a transformation, confirming the fact that "the better one theologizes, the more one philosophizes" in a way that does not compromise the finitude of the human, which is so dear to Falque.

The overall aim of this work, which is expressed in its general framework, is to overcome the ancillary role of philosophy in comparison to theology, and to free theology through philosophy. And this is the intended outcome of crossing the Rubicon: that the two disciplines maintain their autonomy (as they each hold a different status), while simultaneously discovering their heuristic power to give one another a unique intelligibility; a power that is accessible only when the disciplinary barriers are overcome. Through such crossing, one can be personally transformed. And, if philosophy frees theology, becoming strictly heuristic before assuming *tout court* the real and revealed data, theology "receives itself from philosophy at the same time as it opens onto it and offers to it the actuality of an act of faith that only the revealed and its 'in-common' can at once provoke and accompany."[48] This demonstrates that experience itself is able to transform not for what *it does* but for *Who* makes it happen and *pass*.

OPORTET TRANSIRE, IN FINE

Concluding, these reflections upon "crossing" become the *quaestio de homine*. This is because we believe that Falque never, even when he translates the "lavartus prodeo" by Descartes in "Larvatus pro Deo" by Jean-Luc Marion, abandons his passionate questioning about the human condition. Even his *endurante* reflection about flesh, and more recent engagements with Freud, never forget "the one who makes philosophy." Differently from what Meister Eckhart invited us to do, encouraging us to *transire*, in Falque there is no proposal to "to go beyond God." In fact, Falque always invites us to go to the heart of the human. Yet a passage (*transire*) still is necessary to discover the human, to grasp the folds of his heart and flesh. Such a passage is necessary, in other words, because that which is known (that is, that heart and that flesh we call "ours"), also is not known, to paraphrase Hegel. Speaking of the human and God, about theology and philosophy, does not require any leap, as Kierkegaard invited us to do, for between them both we might pass. Falque's thought invites us to accomplish this passage, and he demonstrates up to which point man questions himself, as Augustine from Hippo wrote in the *Confessions*: "I have become a question unto myself."[49] Put differently, it is the passage *between* God and man, theology and philosophy that gives man back to himself without his being reduced to "something." Instead of remaining trapped and masked as *larvatus*, the passage makes one an ongoing and never-ending passing, leading one to live more openly.

It is in fact "with an unveiled face" that Falque interprets French phenomenology, also in *The Loving Struggle*,[50] and with no ambiguity, because from the beginning of his book Falque shows us the limits of his research regarding the human, as the fight among philosophers is a *struggle* among humans who think. Or, perhaps any philosophical research is but a struggle with an angel, as the story goes in Genesis 32:22–31.[51] This way Falque calls upon us to fight with him so that the human always remains a question unto itself. And perhaps indeed this is more than a "philosophical matter": it is a task the French philosopher leaves to his readers because every "quaestio de homine" is set only to and for the *specific* human who poses it, and therefore to and for everyone among us who, together with Falque, do so repeatedly.

NOTES

1. "Item cum intellectus resolvat ad esse, oportet et hoc transire." Meister Eckhart, *Die Lateinischen Werke*, Band 1,1 hgg. von Konrad Weiss et al. (Stuttgart: Kohlhammer, 1965), *Sermo* XXIV, 2, 226.

2. For Vladimir Lossky the intellect grasps God "dans un dépouillement et anonimat total." *Oportet transire*, therefore to "dépasser l'être" but also to "dépasser Dieu" in order to find God himself "dans l'océan sans fond de son infinite." Vladimir Lossky, *Théologie négative et connaissance de Dieu chez Maître Eckhart* (Paris: Vrin, 1960), 195 for both quotations.

3. Emmanuel Falque, *God, the Flesh, and the Other: From Irenaeus to Duns Scotus*, translated by W. C. Hackett (Evanston: Nothwestern University Press, 2015).

4. Falque writes: "By contrast to a hasty reading of this passage from the Gospel, the natural attitude, or in other terms that which entertains the most ordinary relation to things and to beings, is signified by Mary of Bethany rather than Martha—especially as Mary herself would with all her heart 'remain sitting at the Lord's feet listening to his word' (Lk 10:39)." Falque, *God, the Flesh, and the Other*, 83.

5. Falque, *God, the Flesh, and the Other*, 83.
6. Falque, *God, the Flesh, and the Other*, 83–84.
7. Falque, *God, the Flesh, and the Other*, 91–92.
8. Falque, *God, the Flesh, and the Other*, 92–93.
9. Falque, *God, the Flesh, and the Other*, 82–90.
10. Falque, *God, the Flesh, and the Other*, 90–101.
11. Falque, *God, the Flesh, and the Other*, 101–12.
12. Falque, *God, the Flesh, and the Other*, 112.

13. Pierre Gire, "Métaphysique, théologie et Mystique chez Maître Eckhart," in *Penser la religion. Recherches en Philosophie de la Religion*, edited by J. Greish (Paris: Beauchesne, 1991), 99.

14. The English title perhaps loses the meaning of the French word *Passeur*. The English translation: *The Guide to Gethsemane: Anxiety, Suffering, and Death*, translated by George Hughes (New York: Fordham University Press, 2019).

15. Falque, *The Guide to Gethsemane*, 13.
16. Falque, *The Guide to Gethsemane*, 13.
17. See chapter 9, "From Self-Relinquishment to the Entry into the Flesh" in Falque, *The Guide to Gethsemane*.
18. Falque, *The Guide to Gethsemane*, 77.
19. Falque, *The Guide to Gethsemane*, 54.
20. Falque, *The Guide to Gethsemane*, 102.
21. Falque, *The Guide to Gethsemane* 102.
22. Falque, *The Guide to Gethsemane*, 102.
23. Falque, *The Guide to Gethsemane*, 102.
24. Falque, *The Guide to Gethsemane*, 104.

25. The first book is *The Guide to Gethsemane* (the French original published in 1999), the second *The Metamorphosis of Finitude: An Essay on Birth and Resurrection*, translated by George Hughes (New York: Fordham University Press, 2012). The third is *The Wedding Feast of the Lamb: Eros, the Body, and the Eucharist*, translated by George Hughes (New York: Fordham University Press, 2016).

26. Falque, *The Metamorphosis of Finitude*, 5
27. Falque, *The Metamorphosis of Finitude*, 6
28. Falque, *The Metamorphosis of Finitude*, 6.
29. Falque, *The Metamorphosis of Finitude*, 15.

30. "*Cur Deus resurrexit*? The challenge would be impossible were it not that theology . . . and the Holy writ has made us see how much of what is impossible *for human beings* is precisely fulfilled *in God*—particularly, the accomplishment of the apperceptive transposition to the other." Falque, *The Metamorphosis of Finitude*, 72.

31. Falque, *The Metamorphosis of Finitude*, 72.
32. Falque, *The Metamorphosis of Finitude*, 83.

33. Falque, *The Metamorphosis of Finitude*, 11–90.

34. "The first words of Christianity (the impassable horizon of the finitude of man, or of his Being-there) are not its final word (the transfiguration through Christ of this same finitude)." Falque, *The Metamorphosis of Finitude*, 18.

35. See especially the chapter "The Resurrection Changes Everything" in Falque, *The Metamorphosis of Finitude*, 62–81.

36. Falque, *The Metamorphosis of Finitude*, 68.

37. "The other is other, not because I could put myself in his place but because, while wishing to occupy his place, I realize that I can never do so" (Falque, *The Metamorphosis of Finitude*, 68).

38. "At the origin or the beginning not simply the *Creation* . . . not even when it is along with the *Incarnation* . . . but we need also and above all the *Resurrection* as *transformation*." Falque, *The Metamorphosis of Finitude*, 24.

39. "God alone places that *desire for him* in me. And it is in the absence of such a desire that I can be 'without him'; so much so that he does not then call me to be transformed 'with him.'" Falque, *The Metamorphosis of Finitude*, 87.

40. Emmanuel Falque, *Crossing the Rubicon. The Borderlands of Philosophy and Theology*, translated by Reuben Shank (New York: Fordham University Press, 2016).

41. Faith in God cannot precede nor separate from believing in the world, as Falque repeatedly insists. See, for example, Falque, *Crossing the Rubicon*, 77.

42. Falque calls this faith or belief "originary belief in the world" (Falque, *Crossing the Rubicon*, 80); that is, believing the world is, that it is there irreducibly as a residual of any doubt and *epochē*. On this topic see the third chapter, "Always Believing," which does not mean "believer forever" but rather points out that the constant rooting in the world requires a philosophical faith that could benefit the theologian.

43. For example, see Falque, *Crossing the Rubicon*, 90. Yet the reader will easily find other places that confirm this position. Here, Falque distinguishes life "without God" and life "against God."

44. Falque, *Crossing the Rubicon*, 91.

45. Falque, *Crossing the Rubicon*, 110.

46. Falque, *Crossing the Rubicon*, 110.

47. Falque, *Crossing the Rubicon*, 116–17.

48. Falque, *Crossing the Rubicon*, 151.

49. Augustine, *Confessions*, translated by Henry Chadwick (Oxford: Oxford University Press, 1998), 57 (translation modified).

50. Falque, *The Loving Struggle: Phenomenological and Theological Debates*, translated by B. Onishi and L. McCracken (London; New York: Rowman & Littlefield, 2018).

51. "That night Jacob got up and took his two wives, his two female servants and his eleven sons and crossed the ford of the Jabbok. After he had sent them across the stream, he sent over all his possessions. So Jacob was left alone, and a man wrestled with him till daybreak. When the man saw that he could not overpower him, he touched the socket of Jacob's hip so that his hip was wrenched as he wrestled with the man. Then the man said, 'Let me go, for it is daybreak.' But Jacob replied, 'I will not let you go unless you bless me.'"

Chapter Eleven

Phenomenology and the Metaphysics of Conversion

Andrew Sackin-Poll

This chapter is an interpretation of the following passage toward the end of *Crossing the Rubicon*: "The crossing of the Rubicon not only joins the two banks (philosophy and theology) by a single thread but also 'casts the rope' (in the nautical sense of the phrase) to metaphysics itself. Phenomenology and metaphysics can thus discover, if not a place for *conciliation*, at least terms for the *discussion*."[1] In order to begin exploring this passage, the first two parts of this chapter outline the following central claims. The first is that metaphysics and embodied experience find themselves interwoven through the crossing between philosophy and theology within a trinitarian monadology. The second is that phenomenology, far from overcoming metaphysics, plays an expressive role in the crossing, articulating embodied experience within a trinitarian figure. A phenomenology of embodied life, its suffering, its joy, thus articulates and finds itself articulated within this novel construal of the relation between phenomenology and a trinitarian metaphysics.

I suggest that this reciprocal relationship between phenomenology and metaphysics found within this crossing provides the figure within which to think the terms for this "rope cast" for discussion. Note that the rope is cast to "metaphysics itself." If a trinitarian metaphysics joins philosophy and theology by a "single thread," and if this casts the rope toward metaphysics, then this suggests that the rope is cast out toward another site for discussion. This discussion takes place, not between phenomenology and theology, which the crossing outlines and draws together, but between phenomenology and metaphysics understood from out of this crossing. I approach this possibility from the perspective of a metaphysics of conversion. The emphasis upon embodied finitude and its traversal demands that this dialogue take place at the point where, through the body, the self reaches a point of conversion or entrance into the divine from out of phenomenology and philosophy, suspended by the nautical rope from the crossing.

METAPHYSICS

In order to engage with this passage, I need, first of all, to clarify how Emmanuel Falque understands the term "metaphysics" and its difference from other contemporary formulations. My engagement with this question takes seriously Falque's comparison of *Crossing the Rubicon* with Bonaventure's *Breviloquium*, wherein the seraphic doctor describes steps taken long beforehand.[2] In the same way, then, the crossing comes at the end of a long trodden itinerary, gathering and reflecting upon it. This book is read as a portal through which to view and interpret his *Triduum philosophique* and other works.

In my view, Falque's crossing concerns, first and foremost, the establishment of finite, embodied experience as the common site for both theology and philosophy. This forms the common thread throughout this and other works. Part of the motivation for this stems from Falque's earlier engagement with the Church Fathers (Ireneus, Tertullian, among others) and Medieval theologians (Bonaventure, Aquinas, Meister Eckhart, among others), each of whom understands, in one way or another, their work to be an exposition of their living faith in the form of a response (to another) or a confession (to God).[3] Drawing upon the historical insights of Pierre Hadot, Falque claims that the modern distinction between the construction of a theoretical system or metaphysics and a spiritual life of faith is simply not made within such works: "Christianity presents itself as a *philosophia* inasmuch as it assimilates the traditional practices of spiritual exercises" into its theology and metaphysics.[4] In this model, the metaphysical edifice articulates a Christian spiritual experience, with the latter nourishing the former (and vice versa) in a speculative exposition of a living faith.[5]

Such an experience reveals from within metaphysics its "vivifying support," that is, the living experience that sustains it.[6] This reciprocal relation between metaphysics and experience informs the way in which Falque approaches the relation between theology and contemporary phenomenology in the crossing. There is no longer any hard and fast distinction between metaphysics and phenomenology. The relation between the two disciplines is understood, instead, in terms of an overlay, whereby phenomenology finds itself inscribed within and interpreted through a theological metaphysics, on one side, but the content and living sense of this metaphysics is "fleshed out" in phenomenology, on the other.

What sustains this overlay is the trinitarian axiom that "nothing is produced in the human that is not first produced in God, except for sin."[7] In the context of the crossing in contemporary thought, this could be parsed in the following terms: *no human experience, from suffering to joy, passes through the self that does not already pass in and through God.* What this axiom articulates is the intimate relation between the finitude of human experience and the divinity within which it is inscribed.

The cornerstone of this axiom is the mystery of the risen Christ, through whom human and divine experience are drawn together in a reciprocal metamorphosis. Through the risen Christ, the finitude of human experience finds itself transformed by the Father, while the Father, through the incorporation of human finitude, finds Himself transformed, too. This reciprocal transformation produces a peculiar Christocentric "monadology without pre-established harmony," which overcomes the separation of worlds, that is, the human and the divine, replacing it with two different ways of living the same world. There is thus no separation of the two worlds: material and ideal, body and spirit, flesh and word.[8] To think within such a metaphysical figure, as I attempt to do, means neither to forget the density and thickness of embodied experience nor to evaporate into an ideal and diffuse mystical or negative experience.[9]

This monadology is not, therefore, merely a dogmatic axiom or metaphysical hypothesis, which comes from outside human experience "from on high," so to speak, but articulates and motivates the traversal of embodied experience from within this figure. This informs the definition of metaphysics within the crossing. For Falque,

> Metaphysics as the act of *traversing* across the physical or natural—*meta(trans)physical*—entails agreeing to plunge into the Heraclitean river in which one can never bathe in the same way twice, and thus to suffer from the world and finitude—in philosophy—in order to pass it to another, the Father, the only One capable of bearing it with me—in theology.[10]

The term "metaphysics" is taken in the sense of passing through (*meta*) nature (*phusis*), rather than transcendence in its ontological significance, that is, whatever lies beyond the horizon of physical entities. This definition of metaphysics as an act of traversing experience introduces, however, an ambiguity into the meaning of the term. On the one hand, there is dogmatic metaphysics, namely the trinitarian axiom and its profoundly Christological basis. On the other, there is metaphysics as an *experience* of passing through nature. This remains, however, consistent with the refusal to distinguish a pure metaphysics from pure appearing or experience. The metaphysics of the crossing articulates neither a static objective theory nor merely the imposition of (speculative) dogma upon experience, but rather a dynamic traversal and transformation of human finitude through it.

The definition of metaphysics as, first of all, the traversal of experience places the starting point for it within the human per se, that is, the finitude of embodied experience, before its transfiguration through the risen Christ. This commitment to "starting from below" is, perhaps, clearest in *The Guide to Gesthemane*, where Falque draws upon existential philosophy and phenomenological descriptions of incarnate experience (e.g., Martin Heidegger, Emmanuel Levinas, and Michel Henry) in order to articulate an account of the finitude of Christ's own embodied life. Drawing upon such resources, the passage is thus shown, for both the living self as for Christ, to submit or be put to the test (*l'épreuve*), that is, "to suffer (from) this world in its incompressible finitude and not to take flight in a fugitive passage."[11] In the face of embodied life, one either attempts an impossible flight, leading only into despair (Kierkegaard), or immerses oneself in the *pathos* of life's suffering (Henry and Falque). What incarnate experience shows is that there is simply no possible escape or flight from "the ineluctable immanence of this world and the radical traversal of its own corruptible nature (*meta-phusis*)."[12] Without this traversal through experience, the "burden of (human) finitude" would not be transfigured in the subsequent Resurrection and the trinitarian axiom would be emptied of all living content, reduced to a mere speculative axiom of dogmatic faith.[13]

In this manner, the trinitarian monadology finds its phenomenological explication through attention to the finitude of embodied experience shared by the human and the divine incarnate. Whatever the finite and embodied self experiences, from jubilation to sorrow and despair, can and must be understood, as Falque makes clear in *The Metamorphosis of Finitude*, as being fully in the Father, who, through the risen Christ, gathers together and transfigures such experience. "By the operation of the metamorphosis of God [through the risen Christ], it is no longer the soul of man who alone 'wants the world inscribed within it' and 'it in God' (Bonaventure), but its entire body, which, taken up [with Christ] into the divine fabric, is also, through this, metamorphosed."[14] Through the risen Christ, the body forms the apex around which experience and metaphysics turn. The two worlds are thus drawn together: spirit and body, flesh and word. Whatever passes in the living self, passes in the Father, through the risen Christ.

The possible interlacement between phenomenological description of embodied experience and metaphysics takes place within and through the risen Christ, understood within this monadological figure. This interlacement distinguishes Falque's understanding of metaphysics from its modern ontotheological figure. The defining mark of this modern figure of metaphysics is the way in which it accounts for the entrance of the divine into philosophy in terms of speculative metaphysical concepts (e.g., *summum ens, causi sui*). To refuse the separation between metaphysics and experience, as Falque does, and, consequently, to start from below in the finite body means that the entrance of the divine is no longer understood in terms of the onto-theological figure of metaphysics. The divine enters, not through the metaphysical language of *causa sui*, as Heidegger argues, but through the mystery of the risen Christ.[15] With this departure from the onto-theological figure of metaphysics and its trinitarian substitute, Falque's trinitarian monadology looks beyond onto-theology toward a spiritual and embodied *apex affectus* that transfigures the life of human finitude.[16] Such a claim necessarily precipitates changes in the relation between phenomenology and metaphysics.

PHENOMENOLOGY

In this part, I examine the way in which the reformulation of the relationship between phenomenology and metaphysics through this crossing leads to a transformation of the very idea of phenomenology itself. Drawing upon Hadot, Falque notes that "theology and philosophy have always been 'spiritual exercises'"[17] and forgetting this fact has led to the hasty separation of phenomenology and metaphysics. I suggest Falque's recollection of their union entails that phenomenology restricts itself neither (1) to an inquiry into the conditions of appearing per se nor (2) to an effort to overcome metaphysics, understood as onto-theology. In the place of this idea, phenomenology becomes part of a spiritual ordeal, describing the "great traversal" of embodied experience through the suffering (of this) world.

In order to illustrate this alteration in the idea of phenomenology, I will briefly outline recent articulations of the relationship between phenomenology and metaphysics. I turn my attention in particular toward the debate around the so-called theological turn, initiated by Dominique Janicaud.[18] The central claim made by Janicaud is that the "theological turn" sees phenomenology favor excessive transcendence and the infinite over and above the finitude of the living self and the limited nature of intentional acts, thus departing from the initial impetus of phenomenology, at least as Edmund Husserl understood it. This move toward the infinite is one expression of a latent tension within the phenomenological project as a whole between (1) the effort to grasp the things themselves in their pure and simple appearing and (2) the retrospective account of their formal conditions or foundations.[19] In Husserl's phenomenology, the first term in this relationship accords well, of course, with the famous "principle of principles," which restricts phenomenological attention to whatever presents itself in intuition strictly within the limits of its presentation.[20] When the reduction to phenomena as given in their specific mode of presentation is complete, an eidetic analysis of its structure, conditions, and constitution is possible.[21] The pure and simple appearing of a thing and its conditions are bound tightly with the finite activity of consciousness. Both poles of Husserl's phenomenological inquiry revolve around the intentional life of consciousness and the general essence that underpins this or that region of its experience. But this bond between finite intentional acts and appearing is broken in the theological turn and replaced with a "pure appearing" that exceeds such finite conditions.

In contemporary phenomenology members of the so-called theological turn (Jean-Luc Marion, Jean-Louis Chrétien, and Michel Henry) think the way Husserl articulates this tension is too restrictive. What Jean-Luc Marion, for example, finds problematic about Husserl's formulation of this follows from the way in which it restricts phenomenological inquiry to intuition and regional analyses of discrete domains of phenomenal appearing. Such a restrictive approach determines phenomena as existing only insofar as constituted in their phenomenal appearing with respect to the intentional life of consciousness. By restricting the problem of appearing to the (eidetic) constitution of this or that phenomenal object, Husserl loses appearing as such, keeping it, as Marion says, "in metaphysical detention."[22] The first pole, pure and simple appearing, is diminished for the benefit of the second, finite conditions. In order for phenomenology to surpass the restrictive horizons of intentionality, according to Marion, it must employ the reduction in a much more radical fashion, leading back beyond any condition or horizon. This forms the "third reduction," which sets aside all such restrictions. Going beyond even Heidegger's ontological reduction, through an analytic of *Dasein*, Marion sets appearing free from any restriction, even ontological. Through this reduction, appearing is thus "unbound" from the limits of the (metaphysical) language of intentionally constituted objects (Husserl) and the ontological horizon (Heidegger). Beyond such horizons can be heard, through this radical reduction, the pure call, that is, "the originary schema . . . [that] plays before all specification, even of being."[23] The second pole of the tension—the search for conditions—is thereby set aside for the benefit of the first—pure appearing.

What Janicaud finds troubling about this theological turn toward pure appearing concerns the way in which this effort to surpass the intentional or ontological horizon nevertheless leads to another form of obfuscation. While the conditions for appearing are no longer understood in terms of the constitutive acts of intentional consciousness (Husserl) or the clarification of the ontological question (Heidegger), the active self is lost beneath the blazing luminosity of pure appearing. This is troubling because the qualifying terms for the superabundance of this blazing light are neither human nor finite.[24] While this pure call does, indeed, address itself to another, the respondent is nevertheless stripped down to being almost a pure receptacle, an index, for the negative appearing of this call.[25] In the crossing, Falque echoes Janicaud's concern, noting that "the purification of the subject nearly leads to its elimination, except for its frame as pure receptacle or simply passivity."²⁶ The finitude of human experience, its obscurity and density, is thus left behind in Marion's third reduction for the benefit of a pure, transcendent call. But rather than draw phenomenology back to Husserl, as Janicaud does, Falque's approach offers a means for phenomenology to retain a sensitivity to the finitude of embodied experience at the same time as engage with and draw lessons from theology for understanding human experience.

What Falque finds problematic about this and other aspects of the theological turn is the separation of what is always given as mixed. "In claiming to separate boldly what gives itself first as mixed by means of a 'leap' into pure faith (or philosophy), we sometimes forget," Falque observes, "the obscurities and oscillations in all humans . . . [forget] the wild trails upon which God can also reveal himself through humanity this time."²⁷ This is the quiet revelation of Christ at Emmaus, within the human finitude of His risen body, eating with the disciples, rather than a blinding revelation from on high.

In contrast to the image or idea of phenomenology described thus far, whereby the life of the self is either (1) lost through abstraction from experience and reduction to essences and constitutive acts (Husserl) or (2) overwhelmed from beyond the finite horizon (Marion), Falque's reformulation of metaphysics in terms of passage and transformation within and through the finite horizon retains throughout a focus upon the finitude of embodied life. Within the trinitarian figure of metaphysics, phenomenology becomes a description of the burden of suffering and effort within the immanent finite horizon of experience, starting from below, without seeking either its formal condition(s) or to inscribe it within a neutral and indeterminate horizon of the pure call.

The interlacement of metaphysics and experience that Hadot observes (noted previously) finds itself vivified through the crossing between philosophy and theology. The purpose of starting "from below" within the immanent horizon of finite, embodied experience avoids the imposition of a speculative metaphysics from outside the common experience of the embodied self and, in doing so, retains its density and thickness. With the body forming the apex around which phenomenology and metaphysics turn, the notion of a phenomenological "overcoming" of metaphysics or a "leap" from human finitude into pure theological discourse is itself overcome, and a sense of the obscure emergence of the divine within finitude is recovered. Phenomenology can thus form part of a spiritual ordeal or exercise, drawing upon Hadot's insight into the early unity between experience and metaphysics noted previously. The role phenomenology now plays plunges the self into the flowing river of experience in order to encounter and undergo the traversal of life. Through the "self-apprenticeship" of suffering, felt through embodiment, an experience of a singular, irreducible life, without equal, is given here in human finitude.²⁸

PHENOMENOLOGY AND THE SPIRITUAL ORDEAL

With the figure of metaphysics and the image of phenomenology this entails now in hand, I am able to turn toward an interpretation of the passage under discussion. Crossing the Rubicon refuses to separate what is, first of all, given in obscurity into pure phenomenology, wholly detached from metaphysics, on one side, and pure theology, beyond human finitude, on the other. The admixture of phenomenology and theology motivates the way in which I interpret the following passage, already quoted in the introduction: "the crossing of the Rubicon not only joins the two banks (philosophy and theology) by a single thread but also 'casts the rope' (in the nautical sense of the phrase) to metaphysics itself." I suggest that the reciprocal relationship between phenomenology and theology described earlier provides the basis upon which to think the terms for this "rope cast" between phenomenology and metaphysics itself. The terms of engagement and dialogue must be dynamic, however, intertwining metaphysics and phenomenology. To seek to characterize such a dialogue between phenomenology and metaphysics as between two static domains of inquiry, wholly extrinsic to one another, without interlacement, would overlook the basic union between the two that underpins the crossing.

My first question is, then, what figure or form of engagement might this cast rope create? Where are the terms for this engagement to be found? There is no question that this crossing draws philosophy and theology together around the apex of embodied experience. The rope cast from within this crossing is toward some form of metaphysics that concerns, at least in part, the embodied self. On this basis, I suggest that some of the terms for this discussion can be found in a spiritualist metaphysics. "Spiritualism is," as Jean-Louis Vieillard-Baron defines it, "a metaphysics that thinks the relation between mind and body: spirituality is incarnated."[29] Drawing inspiration from René Descartes' reflections in his *Méditations métaphysique*, spiritualism reflects upon the inner life of the self and the relation between the mind and the body. To this extent, spiritualist insights into the incarnate life of the self may offer the terms needed in order to make sense of this cast rope.

But the terms for this dialogue must also pertain to the passage. The two pivotal moments in Falque's crossing are (1) the traversal of finite experience and (2) the transformation or metamorphosis of this finitude through the risen Christ. This raises questions. How does the self pass through experience? How could the self encounter the divine through the "great traversal" within philosophy and phenomenology? While a spiritualist metaphysics could certainly be understood in terms of conversion, nevertheless such a conversion or transformation is not necessarily religious or confessional. Another term is needed, I suggest. This can be found in the recovery of what Étienne Gilson calls a "metaphysics of conversion."[30] The metaphysics of conversion is distinct from what Alain de Libera calls a "metaphysics of Exodus," which, according to him, forms the starting point for onto-theological determinations of the divine, drawing such determinations from the identification of God and Being made in the well-known divine utterance: "I am who I am" (Ex 3:14). The metaphysics of conversion, by contrast, determines God as the pole toward which the soul is drawn back.[31] The movement back toward God leads to the recognition within the soul of that which is more intimate and interior to the self than itself (*interior intimo meo*).[32] Such a metaphysics describes the dynamic movement of passage and conversion within the life of the self, which consists, in some form or another, in a transgression or excess (over its speculative and representational thought) toward what is most secret and interior to it.

What Falque's reformulation of phenomenology makes clear is that there is a need for immersion in the *pathos* of life, that is, its suffering, in order to recognize the transfiguration of the embodied self by the divine.[33] In the context of the crossing and cast rope, a recovered and revised metaphysics of conversion could articulate precisely the way in which the self immerses itself in life, drawing back to that which is most interior to it, and thereby become transformed through embodied experience. To begin "from below" demands also to sink into the below, that is, immerse into embodied life on the phenomenological side of the borderland between philosophy and theology. Such an immersion, described in terms of a metaphysics of conversion, qualifies as another step along the *itinerarium* that is the crossing and marks another "wild way" through the obscurity and thickness of embodied life toward the divine.

My first step along this wild trail begins with Michel Henry's philosophy and phenomenology of life, which draws upon a spiritualist philosophy of the body. A key element to spiritualist thought is the notion of abundance or excess within the incarnate spirit, and this trail toward conversion, through philosophy and phenomenology, depends upon such excess, felt within the singularity of embodied life. It is, therefore, important to identify the ways in which embodied life, in some way, opens the way toward transgression. There are two ways in which this happens: (1) the feeling of embodied effort and (2) the experience of bodily suffering.

The first excess can be understood through (1) the inner experience of embodied effort. From Pierre Maine de Biran's philosophy of the body, Henry articulates the excess of the body over representational thought and the (phenomenological) obscurity this entails. The *ego* experiences itself and knows itself, first and foremost, according to Maine de Biran, through the feeling of embodied motor effort and resistance.[34] Between the active movement of the body and the resisting force that marks the terminus and limit of its power a tension arises that constitutes the *ego*'s way of appearing to itself. What distinguishes the way in which the feeling of embodied motor effort appears from other modes of appearing is the fact this feeling of tension is felt and experienced, not like an empirical fact, as if from outside, but, instead, within an inner sense.[35] This feeling is neither an image nor representation but a hidden inner experience of embodied life.[36] This hidden experience is, Henry asserts, the subjective body, that is, the living singular body beneath the visible objective one, which conceals, "not from the living man, but from the philosopher or psychologist," the primitive fact of immediate, inner experience.[37] This body is not understood in terms of an object in the world or the anatomical structure and organic unity of the body but in purely phenomenological terms: the inner life of the body is an irreducible phenomenon that shows itself within the immanent and immediate sphere of the life of the self in a non-representational, imageless way.

This inner experience of tension indicates an excess of embodied experience. In contrast to the Cartesian *cogito*, whose inner life consists almost exclusively in *cogitata*, which, in principle, admit of clarity and distinctness, the *biranienne cogito* consists in an embodied effort and tension, which can never be brought to light within a clear and distinct idea.[38] In the experience of embodied effort, the self experiences how this effort exceeds its capacity to think it in images or representations, perceiving how it can neither possess itself nor found itself within speculative thought.

The second excess of the body can be understood through (2) suffering. In addition to the feeling of embodied effort, the body is felt and experienced (in a hidden, non-representational way) though passive experiences, such as illness or injury. In such experiences, there is a sense in which the body exceeds and penetrates the *ego* when this body suffers in some way. The presumption of the self's efficacy and the dependency of this upon the body that supports its practical possibilities is felt most keenly when this body becomes, for example, tired, injured, or unwell. Through the disappearance of certain, if not all, bodily capacities, the suffering of this body shows that I *can* no longer, that is, I am incapable, and so, in this embodied experience, I feel an inescapable bond between my being and my suffering body. What such experiences reveal is, as Levinas notes, "the impossibility of flight and recoil" before my own embodiment.[39] I cannot escape my body nor, therefore, can I avoid my own existence. If I am sick, then I suffer from it, of course, but I also suffer from being unable to avoid doing so. This experience of the indissoluble bond between the *ego* and the body shows the way which I am this body exceeds my capacity to exit from it.

What the foregoing indicates is that the self cannot reach its embodied life through speculative thought or escape from its embodied suffering. In both ways, the body exceeds its grasp. Yet, even within this experience of an elusive embodied life, Henry identifies a more fundamental experience: the inner experience of the self alone with itself in its immanent embodied life. Both the action of embodied motor effort and the passive invasion of bodily injury derive in some way or another from the body's relation to the world, whether in the form of an intentional effort or passive reception of injuries, illness, or fatigue. But Henry notes that "what situates our original body itself is subjectivity."[40] There is, within the obscure experience of bodily life, a subjective life, which makes this body precisely a singular living and embodied self. This life is not found, first and foremost, within its relation to the world, but within a sphere of immanence. In order to reach this immanence, the self must sink within its singular embodied life and in what follows I show how Henry's methodological approach to this immanent and singular embodied life constitutes a kind of conversion through an immersion in the *pathos* of life.

FROM REDUCTION TO CONVERSION

A close reading of Henry's phenomenological method reveals that the reduction is no longer simply a leading back from the natural attitude toward, for example, the pure appearing of the *ego* (Husserl) or toward a clarification of the ontological question (Heidegger) but rather leads to its conversion into life's own immanent appearing within itself. The methodological difference between Husserl and Henry lies between a reduction to the pure *ego* and a conversion of the *ego*. Henry articulates his own phenomenological method using categories drawn from Meister Eckhart's mystical theology. In *The Essence of Manifestation*, Henry describes his eidetic analysis, using the following categories: humility and impoverishment, virginity, and solitude. While such categories are chiefly ethical or spiritual in their import, Henry draws from them a phenomenological use. The most important categories, for the purposes of this chapter at least, are poverty and humility. The methodological significance of impoverishment stems from its capacity to "lay bare the structure of the essence."[41] But this "laying bare" does not involve the removal of whatever covers the essence or any other sense of disclosure, whereby the hidden essence is revealed or unveiled, nor does this retreat involve simply a stepping back from the natural attitude or *quotidian* life toward an original essence of some kind. The exclusion undertaken through impoverishment lays it bare by entering directly into the inner movement of the essence.

Humility and poverty do not intervene in an eidetic analysis as a stage or prior condition, like Husserl's "bracketing" or "setting in parenthesis," but rather seek direct immersion in the inner movement of the essence itself.[42] This identity of the reduction with the inner movement is precisely what, in my view, makes it a conversion. Entrance into the inner movement and structure of the essence involves less a "leading back" (*reducere*), more a "turning with" (*converso*) or "passing into" (*metanoia*) that marks a conversion into life's involute movement.[43]

This characterizes what I call a "phenomenological method of mystery," whereby the reduction does not seek to unveil or clarify but, instead, enter into and remain within the opacity of living experience.[44] As Henry outlines early in his phenomenological project: "it suffices that [phenomenological ontology] be conscious of the basic *obscurity* which *in principle* belongs to the essence, not for the purpose of surmounting it . . . but in order to live it as such, in mystery."[45] In other words, mystery is not a veil to be rend asunder in order to disclose whatever lies beneath; rather, it is to be lived as such. The "way of mystery" is, for Henry, a specific phenomenological mode of eidetic analysis that precludes any notion of phenomenological "clarification" or "elucidation" of the essence yet retains a rigorous experiential foundation. This is not, then, a phenomenology of clarity but one of density, thickness, and obscurity. To turn into this movement deprives the self of the world of (discrete) images and representations, immersing it, instead, within the solitude of a singular embodied life, without aspect, gap, or restriction.

With Henry's reformulation of reduction as conversion and mystery, a phenomenology of embodied life, which draws from spiritualist insights, can be put in dialogue with a metaphysics of conversion. On this point, I suggest that such a reduction as conversion is analogous, in part, to the *itinerarium in mentis deum* of the Augustinian tradition insofar as what such a reduction, understood as conversion, recovers is that which is more intimate to the self than the *ego*. In the inner life of the embodied self, the body exceeds the *ego*, but more interior still than the feeling of embodied motor effort (Maine de Biran) or the invasion of embodied suffering (Levinas), which surpasses representation and image, is the inner appearing of the living self in mystery. This is the intimate "secret of the soul (*abditum mentis*)" deep within the singular life of the body.[46] Through the reformulation of reduction as conversion, Henry's own *abditum mentis* articulates a phenomenological experience of this inner life, which shows its very opacity and density.

What makes this analogy between phenomenology and a metaphysics of conversion compelling is the way Henry identities this most inner life with God: "Being and life, the life of God himself, an absolute life."[47] If this embodied experience of life can be identified with God in this way, then, to access this life, through the involute movement of impoverishment, is, therefore, to enter upon the divine. The phenomenological conversion of the *ego* into the inner movement of embodied life is, therefore, comparable to an inward journey toward the divine along the lines of Gilson's metaphysics of conversion.

Taking this trail through Henry back toward the crossing, recall that metaphysics, for Falque, "entails agreeing to plunge into the Heraclitean river in which one can never bathe in the same way twice, and thus to suffer from the world and finitude."⁴⁸ Within Henry's phenomenological method, such a plunge is taken from the side of phenomenology, through the traversal of embodied experience up until its conversion in Life (or God). Immersion into the *pathos* of life is, as Henry describes, drawing upon the young Hegel, like plunging into the liquid element, water, which "knows no gap, no restriction, no multiplicity, no determination."⁴⁹ The phenomenological immersion into this water confers upon reduction a sense of conversion or, perhaps even, renaissance. To plunge into Falque's Heraclitean river with Henry is, then, to immerse oneself in a peculiar living baptismal water. With this phenomenological rendering of conversion, the metaphysics of conversion, alluded to earlier, finds within Henry a contemporary and embodied figure: it is the life of the *embodied* self, not simply its spiritual life, that forms the site for transformation and immersion. In line with the crossing, the turn back toward God, toward the origin, which characterizes the metaphysics of conversion, is not only spiritual but also incarnate. What makes a Henrian conversion is precisely immersion of the *embodied* self in the *pathos* of its own singular life. Thus the spiritualist concern with embodied life along with a phenomenology of the body finds its own *apex affectus* within a metaphysical figure of embodied conversion similar to the crossing.

The excess of embodied life through the feeling of embodied effort or the invasion of the body through some inescapable (contingent) suffering is drawn, through an immersion in *pathos*, around the singularity of this most intimate life of the living self (*interior intimo meo*). Along this wild trail, the phenomenological reduction stumbles upon the divine through immersion in the embodied self's own *pathos* from the hitherside of the crossing between philosophy and theology. In following Henry, another step is thus taken through the obscurity and thickness of embodied life along Falque's *itinerarium* toward the divine. The terms for this step, suspended by the nautical rope thrown from the crossing, are found within a phenomenology of the body, drawing from the spiritualist tradition, and a metaphysics of conversion.

NOTES

1. Emmanuel Falque, *Crossing the Rubicon: The Borderlands of Philosophy and Theology*, translated by Reuben Shank (New York: Fordham University Press, 2016), 157.
2. Falque, *Crossing the Rubicon*, 16.
3. Emmanuel Falque, *Dieu, la chair, et l'autre, D'Irénée à Duns Scot* (Paris: PUF, 2008), 31.
4. Pierre Hadot, *Exercices spirituels et philosophie antique* (Paris: Études augustiniennes, 1981), 56.
5. Falque, *Dieu, la chair, et l'autre*, 31–32.
6. Falque, *Dieu, la chair, et l'autre*, 39.
7. Falque, *Crossing the Rubicon*, 132.
8. Emmanuel Falque, *Triduum philosophique: Le Passeur de Gesthsémani, Métamorphose de la finitude, Les Noces de l'Agneau* (Paris: Les Édition du Cerf, 2015), 299.

9. Emmanuel Falque, *Saint Bonaventure et l'éntrée de Dieu en théologie* (Paris: VRIN, 2000), 77.
10. Falque, *Crossing the Rubicon*, 135.
11. Falque, *Triduum philosophique*, 118.
12. Falque, *Triduum philosophique*, 118.
13. Falque, *Crossing the Rubicon*, 132.
14. Falque, *Triduum philosophique*, 288.
15. Martin Heidegger, *Identity and Difference*, translated by Joan Stambaugh (New York: Harper & Row, 1969).
16. Falque, *Crossing the Rubicon*, 24.
17. Falque, *Crossing the Rubicon*, 24.
18. See Dominique Janicaud's *Phenomenology and the "Theological Turn": The French Debate* (New York: Fordham University Press, 2000); and *Phenomenology "Wide Open": After the French Debate* (New York: Fordham University Press, 2005).
19. Janicaud, *Phenomenology "Wide Open,"* 19–20.
20. Edmund Husserl, *Ideas Pertaining to a Pure Phenomenology and to a Phenomenological Philosophy*, First Book, translated by Fred Kersten (The Hague: Martinus Nijhoff, 1982), §24, 44.
21. Husserl, *Ideas*, §3, 10-11.
22. Jean-Luc Marion, *Réduction et donation* (Paris: PUF, 1989), 62.
23. Marion, *Réduction et donation*, 343.
24. Janicaud, *Phenomenology and the "Theological Turn,"* 63.
25. Marion, *Réduction et donation*, 347.
26. Falque, *Crossing the Rubicon*, 113.
27. Falque, *Crossing the Rubicon*, 144.
28. Falque, *Crossing the Rubicon*, 24.
29. Jean-Louis Vieillard-Baron, "Spiritualisme et spiritualité," *Laval théologique et philosophique* 69:1 (2013): 57.
30. Étienne Gilson, *L'Espirt de la philosophie médiévale* (Paris: VRIN, 1932), 138.
31. Alain de Libera, *La Mystique rhénane, d'Albert le Grand à Maître Eckhart* (Paris: Édition du Seuil, 1994), 36.
32. De Libera, *La Mystique rhénane*, 37.
33. Falque, *Crossing the Rubicon*, 69–70.
34. Michel Henry, *Philosophy and Phenomenology of the Body*, translated by Girard Etzkorn (The Hague: Martinus Nijhoff, 1975), 12–13.
35. Henry, *Philosophy and Phenomenology of the Body*, 15–17.
36. Pierre Maine de Biran, *Oeuvres*, III, 72n1.
37. De Biran, *Oeuvres*, III, 72n1.
38. Henry, *Philosophy and Phenomenology of the Body*, 54–55.
39. Emmanuel Levinas, *Le temps et l'autre* (Paris: PUF, 1979), 55 (my translation).
40. Henry, *Philosophy and Phenomenology of the Body*, 195n4.
41. Michel Henry, *The Essence of Manifestation*, translated by Girard Etzkorn (The Hague: Martinus Nijhoff, 1973), 314.
42. Henry, *The Essence of Manifestation*, 317.
43. Henry, *The Essence of Manifestation*, 316.
44. I reformulate this "method of mystery" with respect to the "opacity of living experience" through the invention of the "ordinary body" in my forthcoming book *Le grammaire de l'âme* and another eponymous publication (in English) "The Ordinary Body" that was first presented at *Penser en phénoménologue* seminar of the International Network in Philosophy of Religion and L'institut Catholique de Paris, Paris (May 2019).
45. Henry, *The Essence of Manifestation*, 18.
46. De Libera, *La Mystique rhénane*, 44.
47. Henry, *The Essence of Manifestation*, 670.
48. Falque, *Crossing the Rubicon*, 135.
49. Henry, *The Essence of Manifestation*, 289n4.

Chapter Twelve

Transforming Heideggerian Finitude?

Following Pathways Opened by Emmanuel Falque

Barnabas Aspray

What is the relationship between philosophy and theology for Emmanuel Falque? Does he annihilate all distinction between them? "The thesis of a passage toward theology," he concedes, "could offer the impression that I am ready to confuse everything."[1] However, it would be a gross misunderstanding of Falque's project to consider it as one of confusion. Falque is not a transgressor of boundaries but a marriage counselor; he calls for us to overcome the *divorce* between philosophy and theology. His aim is to break down the artificial barrier of separation between the two disciplines that was erected in twentieth-century France. Just as a marriage makes "one flesh" out of two individuals without destroying the uniqueness of each, so Falque's reuniting of philosophy and theology does not homogenize them but rather restores their right mutual relation. Falque's new marriage keeps the discourses distinct in their *methods*, but united in their common concern.[2] Philosophy and theology can enrich each other precisely because they offer mutually complementary perspectives on the same object.

No more timorous keeping to our chosen discipline, fearful of trampling on someone else's expertise, says Falque. To cross the Rubicon means for a philosopher to dare to be also a theologian, and for a theologian to dare to be also a philosopher: "the more we theologise, the better we philosophise" and vice versa.[3] The happy marriage of philosophy and theology should take place inside each of us, our thought being enriched by participation in both.[4] This is the clearest way Falque departs from the famous *philosophes croyants* of the last century, Maurice Blondel and Paul Ricœur;[5] not that he is criticizing them from some superior atemporal position—they did the right thing for their time, but the "times have changed,"[6] and a more liberating approach is called for.

This remarriage of philosophy and theology is bad news to anyone who imagined their own discipline to be hierarchically "upstream," in an untouchable pristine purity, determining the other without being affected in turn. Philosophers, says Falque, must abandon their "hegemonic pretention . . . to resolve everything better than everyone else, including general theological questions."[7] But theology, also, is not the highest level of a "terraced fountain" (borrowing the vivid metaphor of Gilles Deleuze), pouring revelation down to a lower level.[8] Each discipline is transformed by the other without thereby losing its core identity or its distinctive contribution.

The first part of this chapter outlines key features of Falque's views on philosophy, finitude, and theology, with a focus on how finitude binds the disciplines together and creates a much needed "common grammar" for discourse. The second part seeks to follow where Falque has led by using his methodology to question philosophy from within. Should contemporary philosophy's definition of finitude be taken as an unquestioned point of departure? Does sin, like the Resurrection, also transform our finitude, and if so, in what way? Can theology say anything of its own about plain and simple humanity (*l'homme tout court*) or is it fully dependent on contemporary philosophy?

SPEAKING THE SAME LANGUAGE: FINITUDE AS FUNDAMENTAL STARTING POINT

Philosophy for Falque begins with human finitude. As we shall see, this finitude is defined as impassable immanence, temporality, and death, meaning that we are initially "without God in the world," but also without the need for God or any sense of absence or lack that would deny the positivity of our finitude. All of this is true, for Falque, *without bringing sin into the picture*. On the contrary, the original sin of Adam and Eve was to reject their finitude in wanting to be like God, free of the limitations that come with created fleshly existence.

All of this begins, however, with Falque's concern for a common language between Christians and non-Christians. Falque often quotes the words of Pope John Paul II to the Bishops of Canada in 1999:

> We need a new apologetic, geared to the needs of today. . . . Such an apologetic will need to find a common "grammar" with those who see things differently and do not share our assumptions, lest we end up speaking different languages even though we may be using the same tongue.[9]

This quote can be taken as a programmatic statement of Falque's own concern and his method. It is based on the premise that Christians extend Christ's love toward non-Christians by listening first and foremost to what they have to say. Taking them seriously on their own territory means learning their language, rather than denouncing them from haughty dogmatic principles which they do not share, or criticizing their unbelief as an atheist "drama" (as did Henri de Lubac).[10] Only by understanding others on their own terms will we have something to say that they will be either able or willing to hear.

Therefore, we must accept that philosophy is whatever our contemporaries say it is. When Falque uses the word "philosophy," he does not have any fixed atemporal definition in mind, a sort of *philosophia perennis* or abstract rationality untouched by the currents of history and discourse. No: "philosophy" means twenty-first-century phenomenology, and, more precisely "where we currently are" in the conversation.

Where, then, is contemporary philosophy? For Falque, it begins with Martin Heidegger's conception of finitude. Heidegger has replaced Aristotle as "the philosopher" *par excellence* in France, being the point of departure for Maurice Merleau-Ponty, Jacques Derrida, Jean Greisch, Jean-Luc Marion, Jean-Yves Lacoste, and many others besides. That Falque is no exception to this list is evident, for example, when he gives his total agreement to Philippe Nouzille's suggestion that "*Being and Time* should be the first chapter of every theology book," and then adds, "even every philosophy book."[11]

Heidegger is the *first* word, but not the *last*, at least not for theology. Falque makes it clear that we must pass *through* and not *around* Heidegger precisely because his philosophy represents the contemporary "common grammar": "The fact that we cannot and must not remain at the level of Martin Heidegger's existential analytic, however, does not exempt us from passing *through* it. Otherwise we risk entirely losing touch with modernity, whose primary insight was the necessity of recognising ourselves as limited beings."[12] For these reasons, Falque begins to philosophize with the philosophical "grammar" provided by Martin Heidegger (and, following him, also Merleau-Ponty, Deleuze, Sartre, Camus, and Foucault). He never challenges this dominant "grammar," because to do so would be to take a different point of departure than that of his contemporaries, which would destroy the common language that John Paul II called for, rendering communication impossible.

Within this shared language, philosophy begins with our concept of finitude, which for Falque is the foundation on which all else is built. Falque affirms with Foucault that "modern man is possible only as a figure of finitude."[13] Following Heidegger, Falque uses the term "finitude" not to describe objects in the world, but rather the condition of plain and simple humanity (*l'homme tout court*, to use one of Falque's favorite expressions).

Finitude means "impassable immanence,"[14] the fact that whatever we know or see or experience or talk about, we never do so in any other way than as embodied, limited, and finite human beings. Finitude is "not an accident of the 'immortal' essence of man, but the foundation of man's existence," says Falque, quoting a Heidegger scholar.[15] Even more strongly, Falque insists that the Heideggerian definition of finitude is not even up for debate, as if it was a philosophical conclusion that could be overturned: "Finitude doesn't summarise a doctrine, but simply sums up the most ordinary existence of all human beings."[16] As the ground of common human experience, finitude cannot be fruitfully questioned or doubted.

Now the question is: what characterizes human finitude, according to Falque? Three points must be mentioned.

First, finitude is a *positive standalone category*, emphatically *not* related to infinitude in some Hegelian dialectic. It would be a great mistake, Falque tells us, to define finitude negatively as a falling short of the "infinitude' of God."[17] Finitude is not merely lack, incompleteness, or imperfection. Finitude has its own "thickness," its own positive substantiality. "Only the *positiveness of finitude*," says Falque, "independent of all considerations of the finite (the insufficiency of man) or the infinite (the plenitude of God), can tell us what there is of the being-there of man (*Dasein*)—man described as one whose 'future itself is closed' and who exists in his 'ownmost nullity.'"[18]

Far from being a threat to theology, Falque sees this view of finitude as coinciding perfectly with the Christian doctrine of creation. Our created nature, the fact that we are *not God*, is not a flaw or a failing. Quite the reverse: our failing and sin is in refusing to recognize our finitude, in *wanting to be like God*, to be infinite, to escape our created limits and gain divine power and insight.[19] Theologians should gratefully accept the doctrine of finitude as a great support to their cause, says Falque: "where finitude is only observed in philosophy, it is, on the contrary, *sought* and *desired* in theology."[20]

Second, because finitude is positive and not negative, not simply an emptiness waiting to be filled, this means for Falque that the plain and simple human (*l'homme tout court*) does not naturally desire God. It is not as if there were a "God shaped hole" in everyone, to which the only remedy was to become religious. The modern person is simply "non-theist," or "atheist" if one defines atheism, with Emmanuel Levinas, as "a position prior to both the negation as well as to the affirmation of the divine."[21] Falque supports this conception with reference to Edmund Husserl's phenomenological *epochē* of the "'absolute' and 'transcendent' being," Heidegger's elaboration of philosophy as "fundamentally atheistic," and Jean-Yves Lacoste's assertion that "the disturbing hypothesis of a humanity satisfied with existing 'without God in the world' (Eph 2:12) must therefore be taken seriously. Atheism is neither simply nor in the first place a theoretical problem: it is first an a priori of existence."[22] That is why Henri de Lubac's concept of a "drama of atheist humanism" (the French term *drame* can have its more original meaning of a tragedy or catastrophe) is an insult and offense to the likes of Merleau-Ponty, whose complaint Falque wishes to take seriously.[23] With Merleau-Ponty, Falque wishes to see philosophy as more than simply "antitheism"—it has more positive concerns and contributions than to reject religion. This indifference toward God, Falque says, is not the result of sin or evil, but simply part of our natural created finitude. Our "impassable immanence" is sufficient to itself and initially closed in on itself, says Falque, "as opposed to any supposition of an immediate opening up to transcendence."[24]

This means there can be no natural theology. God may not enter philosophy as an a priori metaphysical guarantee, because he is not *necessary* to explain anything we see or experience. However, God may be still described philosophically as an *a posteriori* phenomenon: "a *descriptive phenomenology* and not a natural theology," that is, "a discourse on the God-phenomenon appearing to the human."[25]

Third, again following Heidegger, Falque defines human finitude as being-toward-death in its very essence, and not the result of sin (this refers only to *biological* death; *spiritual* death, or separation from God, is another matter). The scientific discovery of evolution shows us that death was always part of life, not a subsequent curse for Adam and Eve's transgression. We would have died even if sin had never entered the world.[26]

In Falque's view, this picture of finitude as impassable immanence, temporality, death, and non-theism must not be questioned or challenged but rather accepted as the point of departure for all thought, both philosophical and theological. We cannot pretend that philosophy is not saying what it is, in fact, saying, or else we break communication and lose our "common grammar" with our contemporaries.

What does all of this mean for theology? Falque insists first and foremost that theology must accept philosophy's definition of finitude as its conceptual starting point: "The contemporary theologian, like the philosopher, needs to take finitude as the first given."[27] Theology begins *through* and *by* our finitude because the Incarnation, the central doctrine of Christianity, affirms that God comes to meet us in our finitude: "Finitude . . . simply sums up the most ordinary existence of all human beings, including that of the Son of God, who precisely was 'made man.'"[28] The Incarnation, then, rather than only being a response to sin, marks the crucial point of contact between philosophy and theology: "The God-man carries out the 'tiling' or overlaying of the human and the divine. Thus, philosophy and theology come to 'overlay' or 'cover' each other in Christology."[29]

The Resurrection transforms our finitude, giving us access to transcendence and God for the first time. That is why theology must begin, but not end, with Heideggerian finitude. Theology begins properly with the Resurrection because it is by the Resurrection that our finitude is transformed, such that we then and only then desire God and gain access to eternity. There is, after all, such a thing as desire for God, but only for Christians, whose finitude has been transformed by the Resurrection of Jesus. "If there is an *opening here to transcendence* and *desire for God*," writes Falque, "it is simply because God himself, by his metamorphosis and by our metamorphosis in him, transfigures the structure of the world, and places a desire for him in us."[30]

In sum, for Falque, theology must *begin* with finitude, defined in whatever way current philosophy defines it—which at the moment, following Heidegger, means impassable immanence, non-theism, temporality and death as *originary* and essential to human existence, *not* consequences of sin. Nonetheless, theology goes beyond this starting point to a new conception of finitude given by the Incarnation and Resurrection. Our participation in Christ, who in his hypostatic union is the overlap between immanence and transcendence, transforms our finitude, freeing us from death, opening us to transcendence, and making us desire God.

ANOTHER WAY OF ENGAGING CONTEMPORARY PHILOSOPHY

Emmanuel Falque is first and foremost a true *listener*, reaching out across the barricades to engage in serious and honest dialogue with people who "see things differently" than Christians. This listening attitude is laudable, because it shows love and respect for the humanity of the people to whom he listens. It is not my intention to challenge this listening position of Falque's, which is to be celebrated for opening fresh possibilities for dialogue. However, I would like to suggest another way for Christians to engage with contemporary philosophy. Rather than accepting its starting point wholesale as an unalterable fact, this alternative approach consists of questioning philosophy on its own terms. My proposed approach takes the route of first entering the philosophical debate around what constitutes finitude *as philosophers*. Having done this, we may then, *as theologians*, critically appropriate the philosophies of our time, rather than accepting them without question.

Falque's insistence on a "common grammar" between believers and unbelievers is without doubt an essential part of the Christian calling, especially for theologians. As Jesus entered a particular culture and used the language and concepts of the time, so Christians, if they are to communicate effectively and with relevance, must "incarnate" the gospel message by making it understandable and credible for their age. This is no one-way communication, as if we needed only to download the gospel into our culture without risk of transformation on our part. Theology is not an impenetrable fortress of correct answers, but a living and growing dialogue that bears the marks of its passage through history. The principle of doctrinal development teaches that theology is continually renewed by serious engagement with the objections and critiques of every age, discovering new areas of thought and even weaknesses in itself that it may have previously failed to see.

But the division believers/unbelievers does not map neatly onto the division theologians/philosophers. As Falque is keen to underline, not all philosophers are unbelievers. He has wonderfully demonstrated how both philosophers and theologians may cross disciplinary boundaries and do genuine work on the other side of the Rubicon. To take this insight seriously means that *theologians may also do philosophy*, maybe even transform philosophical discourse from within. *As philosophers*, believers may question the currently accepted starting points of finitude: death, temporality, and being initially "without God in the world."

The problem is that when a believer makes a philosophical argument about matters that concern theology, they are invariably accused of having apologetic motivations. "You say that because you are a theologian/Christian," they are told. But this is an ad hominem slander that does not respond to the arguments themselves. Of course believers will be motivated by their faith, but they are no exception. *No philosopher* is free of non-philosophical motivations. Who can claim that their philosophy is neutral, absent of outside influence or motivation? Such a claim would violate the conditions of our finitude, which philosophy is so keen to uphold. To have non-philosophical motivations is essential to our finitude; therefore the unbeliever has no superior standpoint to the believer when doing philosophy.

But the impossibility of motivation-free philosophy does not mean that all philosophy is invalid, falling under the hammer of the philosopher's own autobiography. The distinction between motivation and argument is crucial here and was invoked by Paul Ricœur when he was accused of being a crypto-theologian whose philosophy was compromised by his faith-commitment. "I do not claim that at the deep level of motivations these convictions remain without any effect on the interest that I take in this or that problem," he wrote, "but I think I have presented to my readers arguments alone, which do not assume any commitment from the reader to reject, accept, or suspend anything with regard to biblical faith."[31] Ricœur insisted that his arguments be judged on their own merit, rather than dismissed due to any presumed theological motivation. That was, for him, precisely why he was a philosopher and not a theologian: "in none of my works do I use any arguments borrowed from the domain of Jewish or Christian biblical writings. And, if one does use these writings, it is not an argument from authority."[32]

As philosophers, we need not accept without question the contemporary definition of finitude for use in theology. It would in fact be unphilosophical to accept Heideggerian finitude as an unquestionable fact of reality ("the first given"[33]), even to call it *not a doctrine* but *ordinary everyday existence*. Such a posture turns Heidegger into a sort of *philosophia perennis* whose conclusions will never be overturned by future philosophical investigation. This is particularly ironic given that some of Heidegger's most penetrating insights concerned the temporally bound nature of human thought. This means that our conception of the "ordinary existence of all human beings"[34] is itself temporal, shaped by our particularity and subject to constant revision. In other words, is *our conception of finitude* not itself finite, heuristic, changeable? Does Heidegger himself, then, not give us license to challenge his "fundamental starting point" *on its own terms*?

I shall give two examples of places I think Heidegger's conception of finitude may be questioned philosophically. First, is philosophy naturally "without God in the world"? Doubtless contemporary philosophy is, if we are speaking *descriptively* of the position of most philosophers today. But *must* it be? To say so would seem to imply a dogmatism that is quite foreign to the spirit of philosophy. This question does not deny the positivity of finitude. Does a conception of finitude as positive, not a mere lack or absence, abolish the coherence of an idea of God as the Infinite? A positive finite number in mathematics does not, by its positivity, abolish a positive infinite number. On the contrary, an infinite number may contain any finite number without destroying either its own positivity or the positivity of the finite number. Why should the two be seen as a threat to each other's internal consistency?

The second way I would question Heideggerian (and thus Falquean) finitude is in the domain of ethics. It is well known that Heidegger's philosophy is an ethics-free zone. Falque, following this, has insisted that his description of human finitude is essential to the plain and simple human (*l'homme tout court*), prior to any entry of sin into the scene. Not that Falque has no place for sin: but for him, sin is dissatisfaction with our finitude and desiring to be infinite. But what is the *ontological* effect of sin? If the Resurrection transforms our finitude ontologically and not simply ontically, as Falque has emphasized, might not original sin do the same?[35] Can we really be so sure that death, temporality, and being "without God in the world" are fundamental features of non-sinful humanity and not consequences of sin? If the word "sin" sounds already too theological, we may use the word "guilt," which Heidegger himself was happy to employ.

This is not the place to answer such questions or provide an alternative account. My point is merely that Falque's (Heideggerian) conception of finitude *can be disagreed with*, and *from within philosophy* without making recourse to any dogmatic theological impositions "from above." Anything that can be disagreed with is no longer a starting point but is open for debate, mutual correction, and progress in understanding.

Although Falque is keen not to see one discipline as "upstream" from the other, having an effect without being affected in turn, there is one particular way in which he puts philosophy upstream from theology. His conception of finitude *comes from* philosophy and yet *determines* theology, requiring acceptance without pushback. Because finitude, for Falque, is the fundamental point of departure for both theology and philosophy, it occupies the role of an immovable rock, the foundation on which all thought is built. Consequently, theology can say nothing about the finitude of the plain and simple human (*l'homme "tout court"*). Theology may only enter to describe finitude *after* it has been transformed by the Resurrection. But theology must still accept philosophy's depiction of finitude.

Falque is right not to protect theology from being transformed by developments in philosophy, as if all divine revelation was pristine and unaffected by the currents of human thought. The truth of revelation is always articulated through the language and concepts of a particular age, and indeed cannot be known in isolation from them.

But if philosophy has such a large impact on theology, as Falque rightly insists, it becomes all the more important that philosophy is correct in its account of the human condition. Falque's picture of the human is the one given to us by contemporary phenomenology, especially the figures Falque most often quotes (Heidegger, Merleau-Ponty, Foucault, Deleuze). But is it the *correct* picture of the plain and simple human (*l'homme tout court*)? Should theology allow itself to be *unilaterally determined* by contemporary phenomenology? Such a position would open theology to be led about by the trends of philosophy like a dog on a leash that must follow wherever its master goes.

Two things are being confused here. First, there is the *concept of finitude* in contemporary phenomenology, in which finitude is characterized by impassable immanence, being-toward-death, temporality, and non-theism. It is an unalterable fact that this is what philosophy is currently saying, and theologians would fail in their calling to a "common grammar" if they ignored it. But secondly, there is the *true state of human finitude in reality*, regardless of what anyone in any age, believer or unbeliever, says or thinks about it. Theology is not required to accept the first (contemporary concept of finitude) as if it were the second (reality about finitude). Indeed, to do so might introduce into the heart of theology any mistakes or imperfections in the concept of finitude that currently prevail among our contemporaries.

If theology had something to say about the plain and simple human, it would affect theology's own doctrines and conclusions. For example, Falque has rightly noted that the Nicene Creed can be read as saying that Jesus came from heaven "for us" independently and even if it had not been so, also "for our salvation."[36] For him, this means that both the Incarnation and the Crucifixion would have happened even without sin. But if it turned out that death, even biological death, was a consequence of sin and not a natural part of God's created order, then it would change the picture: the Incarnation might have happened anyway, but the crucifixion might not. Jesus came down from heaven "for us" but nonetheless was crucified, died, and was buried only "for our salvation."

Similarly, if it turned out that being "without God in the world" was due to sin and not God's original created intention for our finitude, then a philosophical conception of God could be sought prior to revelation and the transformation of finitude by the Resurrection. The plain and simple human (*l'homme tout court*) might have been meant to know God from the beginning, not like the angels, but in his or her fleshly existence, *as human*. This philosophical God need not be the God of ontotheology, an epistemological proof in the apodictic sense, a "ground" of Being that guarantees the basis of all argument. He might be more like the God of Plotinus (taken up and used by Denys), whose brilliance surpasses our philosophical systems and conceptual grasp. Nor need we start using this philosophical God as an apodictic argument for apologetics, a strategy which leaves much to be desired in its conformity to the spirit of Christ. Nonetheless, the possibility of natural theology, even as an ideal of sinless finitude that sin has now made impossible, would have its own hidden and subtle impact both on theology itself and on dialogue between believers and unbelievers in philosophy.

In sum, Falque's reconciliatory efforts have undoubtedly helped advance the relationship between philosophy and theology from the rigid entrenchment into which it had stagnated. No longer is either discipline "safe," locked away in its fortress of watertight conclusions, invulnerable to questioning and transforming from the other. The new dialogue will take directions that cannot be predicted in advance.

This chapter asks more questions than it answers, because its purpose is to walk in the path opened up by Falque's work, and to show the possibilities that arise from the true dialogue and good listening that he exemplifies. May the generous spirit which pervades Falque's philosophy continue to stimulate friendships and growth of mutual understanding between believers and unbelievers.

NOTES

1. Emmanuel Falque, *Crossing the Rubicon: The Borderlands of Philosophy and Theology*, translated by Reuben Shank (New York: Fordham University Press, 2016), 147.
2. Falque, *Crossing the Rubicon*, 126.
3. Falque, *Crossing the Rubicon*, 147.
4. "Rather than dividing philosophy and theology up into two utterly separate worlds, we will practice the one as well as the other, seeking in ourselves a new mode of unity." Falque, *Crossing the Rubicon*, 158.
5. Falque, *Crossing the Rubicon*, 140–41.
6. Falque, *Crossing the Rubicon*, 139.
7. Falque, *Crossing the Rubicon*, 123.
8. Falque, *Crossing the Rubicon*, 131.

9. Cited in Falque, *Crossing the Rubicon*, 133. See also Emmanuel Falque, *The Metamorphosis of Finitude: An Essay on Birth and Resurrection* (New York: Fordham University Press, 2012), 34; and *Triduum philosophique: Le Passeur de Gethsémani, Métamorphose de la finitude, Les Noces de l'Agneau* (Paris: Les Édition du Cerf, 2015), 218–19.

10. See chapter 3, "Is There a Drama of Atheist Humanism?," in Falque, *The Metamorphosis of Finitude*, 30.

11. My translation: "nous acquiescerons ainsi tout à fait à la formule du conférencier selon laquelle *Être et temps* 'devrait constituer le premier chapitre de tout livre de théologie' [sic.], voire aussi de philosophie." Emmanuel Falque, *Parcours d'embûches: S'expliquer* (Paris: Editions Franciscaines, 2016), 155. For Nouzille's original quote, see his contribution in *Une analytique du passage: Rencontres et confrontations avec Emmanuel Falque*, edited by Claude Brunier-Coulin (Paris: Editions Franciscaines, 2016), 357.

12. Emmanuel Falque, *Saint Bonaventure and the Entrance of God into Theology*, translated by Brian Lapsa, revised by William C. Hackett (St Bonaventure, NY: Saint Bonaventure University, Franciscan Institute Publications, 2018), 230. Translation modified: "Qu'on ne puisse ni qu'on ne doive en demeurer à l'analytique existentiale de Martin Heidegger . . . ne saurait donc nous exempter d'y passer, sauf à tout manquer de notre modernité, et d'abord de la nécessité de nous reconnaître comme des êtres limités." Emmanuel Falque, "Limite théologique et finitude phénoménologique chez Thomas d'Aquin," *Revue des sciences philosophiques et théologiques* 92:3 (2008): 533–34.

13. Cited in Falque, *The Metamorphosis of Finitude*, 14.
14. Falque, *The Metamorphosis of Finitude*, 15.
15. Falque, *The Metamorphosis of Finitude*, 21.
16. Falque, *The Metamorphosis of Finitude*, 13.
17. Falque criticizes theologians for whom human finitude is "so often seen as simply the deficient mode of the uncreated." Emmanuel Falque, *The Guide to Gethsemane: Anxiety, Suffering, Death*, translated by George Hughes (New York: Fordham University Press, 2019), 119.

18. Falque, *The Metamorphosis of Finitude*, 18.
19. Falque, *Guide to Gethsemane*, 12, 15.
20. Falque, *Crossing the Rubicon*, 146.
21. Cited in Falque, *Crossing the Rubicon*, 92.
22. Falque, *Crossing the Rubicon*, 91–92.
23. Falque, *The Metamorphosis of Finitude*, 33; *Triduum philosophique*, 217–18.
24. Falque, *The Metamorphosis of Finitude*, 14.
25. Falque, *Crossing the Rubicon*, 127.
26. Falque, *Guide to Gethsemane*, 10.
27. Falque, *The Metamorphosis of Finitude*, 13.
28. Falque, *The Metamorphosis of Finitude*, 13. Translation modified: "le 'condensé' non pas d'une doctrine, mais de l'existence la plus ordinaire de tout homme, y compris de celle du Fils de Dieu précisément 'fait homme' (*et homo factus est*)." Falque, *Triduum philosophique*, 187.

29. Falque, *Crossing the Rubicon*, 131.
30. Falque, *The Metamorphosis of Finitude*, 97.
31. Paul Ricœur, *Oneself as Another*, translated by Kathleen Blamey (Chicago: University of Chicago Press, 1992), 24.

32. Charles E. Reagan, *Paul Ricœur: His Life and His Work* (Chicago: University of Chicago Press, 1996), 125. "Dans aucun de mes ouvrages philosophiques j'emploie d'arguments empruntes aux domaines des écritures bibliques juives ou chrétiennes. Et, si je le fais, c'est sans argument d'autorité." Charles Reagan, "Interview avec Paul Ricœur," *Journal of French and Francophone Philosophy* 3:3 (1991): 158.

33. Falque, *The Metamorphosis of Finitude*, 13.
34. Falque, *The Metamorphosis of Finitude*, 13.
35. Falque himself insists that attempted descriptions of the perfection of humanity's perfection in the Garden of Eden are fanciful speculations without grounding: "We have no knowledge whatsoever of the first Adam." Emmanuel Falque, "Evil and Finitude," in *Evil, Fallen-*

ness, and Finitude, edited by Bruce Ellis Benson and B. Keith Putt, translated by Christina Gschwandtner (Cham: Palgrave MacMillan, 2017), 85. But do not his own attempts to describe finitude-without-sin come close to claiming knowledge of a "first Adam"?

36. Falque, *Guide to Gethsemane*, 10. This does not mean questioning the results of biological research or imposing theological insights onto science. But what science tells us may always be interpreted theologically in more than one way.

Chapter Thirteen

The Sense of Finitude in Emmanuel Falque

A Blondelian Engagement

Victor Emma-Adamah

In his thought-provoking book, *The Metamorphosis of Finitude*, the second installment of his philosophical triduum,[1] Emmanuel Falque challenges and invites the religious and the non-religious reader alike to consider the raw experience of human finitude in its most basic and ordinary mode of brute fleshiness. In the same spirit as the other texts of the triduum, Falque thematizes finitude by unpacking the content of an ordinary human existence, an inescapable given (*homo factus*) of experience as lying in brutish animality ("the animal that I am"). To speak of finitude is to define a "closed up horizon of our existence."[2] Falque's call is for the deepening of the meaning and implications of the truth of human finitude and a concomitant rejection of any hurried transposition of this finitude into a transcendent accomplishment or other beatific fulfillment. As a result, he pushes back on any undue theological or philosophical gesture that preempts a supernatural fulfillment of finitude without being duly rooted within the horizon of the immanence that circumscribes the ordinary lived experience. In his *Guide to Gethsemane*, Falque further elaborates this question of finitude on a broadly Heideggerian register as the "anguish of death" and as the foundational fact that traverses all human experience.[3] In this he takes a decided *parti pris* with the analytic of the human condition as finitude as represented by Martin Heidegger, Jean-Paul Sartre, Albert Camus, and Gilles Deleuze, against what he sees as a paradigmatically Cartesian project (*Cartesian preemption*) of deducing the finite by way of a negation of the infinite, as it is expressed by the likes of Emmanuel Levinas, Jean-Luc Marion, Michel Henry, Maurice Blondel, Karl Rahner, or Hans Urs von Balthasar.[4] In other words, essential to Falque's work in the entire triduum, and most prominently seen in the *The Metamorphosis of Finitude*, is the program of understanding, philosophically, the common experience and shared analytic of finitude, and then of showing, theologically, the transformation or metamorphosis that this finitude *as finitude* undergoes according to the Christian revelation. But in so doing, we have before us two competing understandings of finitude: one defined by the Heideggerian tradition and the other represented by Blondel. Falque's presentation in the *The Metamorphosis of Finitude* allows for this opposing juxtaposition of paradigms, with decisive consequences for how both philosophy and theology are ultimately construed.

In *The Metamorphosis of Finitude*, Falque aims to develop a concrete phenomenological account of resurrection—the transformation of *flesh* that Jesus Christ undergoes and which, in Christian teaching, is the anticipated destiny of human existence. He conducts this exploration by an account of the phenomenon of birth and death—events that both bound the reality of my existence at its two extremities but to which I have no experiential access *as such*. In order to understand something of the resurrective transformation that is held out for me, there must first be insight into Jesus' lived bodily existence, which my own embodied reality shares in. Resurrection can only be understood to the extent that I situate myself before the "anguish of death."[5] It is important to note that when Falque addresses finitude and its metamorphosis in *The Metamorphosis of Finitude*, it follows a detailed prior treatment in the *Guide to Gethsemane* of finitude as the anguish of death. In that previous text, he poses the question "is there a '*Christian sense*' of the anguish of death?"[6] This consideration sets off the investigation for Falque: In order to say something tangible about the resurrection, what is the question and experience of life in the face of death? In other words, the question of "finitude." The constraints of space would not here allow the proper appreciation of Falque's entry point into the question of the resurrection nor yet the scope of the transformation or metamorphosis he affords it in the *The Metamorphosis of Finitude*. Rather, more manageably, we must focus on the notion of finitude as Falque explores it within his larger project of understanding the resurrection, but specifically doing so against the backdrop of his counterpoint notion of finitude in Blondel.

In what follows, I shall explore the case Falque makes for his decision for a Heideggerian analytic of finitude in rejection of a broadly Blondelian one. I shall evaluate the interpretation Falque makes of Blondel on this question and explore the merits and limitations of his proposal of finitude as a "closed horizon" of immanence. I shall then make a case along with recent interpretations of Blondel for a fresh understanding of the *phenomenon* of finitude. In this attempt, early German Romantic understandings of finitude, as we find it in the likes of Friedrich Schlegel, Friedrich Hölderlin, and Novalis, provide us with a helpful perspective that expresses a native orientation of finitude to the infinite, but without falling into a hasty religious philosophical preemption, as Falque fears. I shall then conclude prospectively with the need to thematize afresh "the horizon" of finitude along with Blondel. Instead of its function as a bounded closure on finitude, as Falque has it, Blondel would prefer the indication of a "limit" and the announcement of a new opening.

THE PRÉCIS OF FINITUDE

"The contemporary theologian, like the philosopher," Falque affirms, "needs to take finitude as the first given. Finitude does not summarize a doctrine, but simply sums up the most ordinary existence of all human beings, including that of the Son of God, who was exactly 'made man' (*et homo factus est*)."[7] The conviction with which Falque upholds this foundational position bears underscoring for how it informs, in the first instance, the kind of non-bordered traversing he is able to effect between theology and philosophy.[8] In order to recover a proper starting point for philosophy and theology, one rooted in the universal ordinary experience of humanity, it is to a notion of finitude, without any supernatural preemption or aspiration, nor yet any hidden "access" to the infinite, that one must appeal. This place of an irreducible human experience is thematized as *l'homme tout court*: the human being standing in the face of death and therefore as defined by the reality of anxiety. The Heideggerian determination of the existential analytic of facticity here is clear.[9] For Falque, along with Heidegger, the task today is to do philosophy from within the matrix of our existence. And the key requirement of this stipulation is to understand my existence within the structure of the world—the "sealed off horizon of my existence."[10] This, for Falque, drawing on Michel Foucault, is what defines a key requirement of modern thought.[11] Among other things, it is principally in the name of meeting the requirements of "our modernity" that Falque insists on the shared starting point theology must make in reimagining finitude.

But what is the specification of this notion of *l'homme tout court*? Its essential determination is what Falque captioned in the *The Metamorphosis of Finitude* as an "impassable immanence." That which is "opposed to any supposition of an immediate opening to transcendence, the avowal of an infinite temporality as opposed to its impossible derivation from an eternity of some kind, and the recognition of the *possible depth of man without God*."[12] This is the point at which Falque's decisions enter into confrontation with Blondel. But it is a contention aimed at pushing forward the understanding of immanence to meet new requirements.[13] What is the "immanence in question"?

To the extent that Blondel in his famous 1896 essay, "Lettre Apologétique," was concerned with opening a discourse between philosophy and theology that would meet the "exigences of contemporary thought," he and Falque share a concern for reaching a methodological common ground between both disciplines. Hence, we find in Blondel that the shared starting point between philosophy and theology is the "method of immanence."[14] But for Falque, it is clear that there is a different account of "immanence" that is to be reckoned with *today*. It is no longer the immanence that defined the "apologetics" context of the late nineteenth and early twentieth centuries, as we see in Blondel, Léon Brunschvicg, and Émile Boutroux, for example, but in standing resolutely with Heidegger within the "*horizon* of finitude and its impossible overcoming" (*impossible dépassement*).[15] Falque here plays off a Heideggerian "immanence" (precisely, the horizon of finitude) against what he identifies as a Spinozist *immanentism*, though leaving this latter vaguely defined. This comparison invites the important consideration that Blondel, too, was deeply interested in the philosophical question of immanence and this through a reading of Spinoza. Acquaintance with Blondel reveals the extent to which the "method of immanence" was appropriated from Spinoza, mediated through the insightful studies of his close friend and Spinoza specialist, Victor Delbos.[16] Hence, the proposed engagement between Falque and Blondel is not an opposition between, on the one hand, a thinking on immanence versus its complete exclusion, on the other, but of the precise nature of the "immanence" at work.

The point of contention with this Blondelian immanence, in Falque's assessment, is its invariable derivation from a "secret postulate"—"as though the *horizon of finitude* had always to be resolved 'to' something else."[17] Falque's opposition is born out of his concern (not unlike Blondel himself) to address the hasty and direct way by which the "infinite" is derived preemptively from the "finite" by a prefigured presence of the transcendent within the structures of human experience—*the preemption of the infinite*.[18] The Blondelian preemption, in Falque's reading, is defined by the understanding of the supernatural by the author of the *Action* as a movement of the will that is driven by a natural "insufficiency," which leads its unending movement toward a fulfillment in the infinite. Thus, Blondel's affirmation of a supernatural option at the end of human action requires its construal in terms of an openness to the infinite—an infinite that is already given. As Falque further understands it, this philosophical-theological gesture is itself an expression of the Cartesian program found in the *Meditations*: "In a way, I have within me, first, the notion of the infinite, than of the finite, that is, of God than of myself."[19] This "preemption of the infinite over the finite" is the constituting method operative in "a large part of contemporary phenomenology (Lévinas, Marion, Henry) as well as in theology (Blondel, Rahner, Balthasar)."[20] For Falque, this is the very surreptitious theological infinite (*postulat secret*) within philosophical speculation that may have informed Émile Boutroux's critique of Blondel's thesis defense.[21]

But the calling into question of this way of thinking finitude and immanence (*ce tour de pensée*) by the tradition represented by Gilles Deleuze, Martin Heidegger, Albert Camus, and Jean-Paul Sartre, for Falque, initiates a new philosophical sensibility for our current intellectual context, where finitude must be thought and lived *as such*. In other words, for example, contrary to the French Jesuit theologian, Henri de Lubac's reading, by which he characterizes as programmatically atheistic ("a drama of atheist humanism") those philosophies that suspend or reject any opening to a transcendent fulfillment, Falque, by what could be seen as a pastoral and irenic sensibility, understands these philosophies of immanence as genuine attempts to reimagine finitude and meaning within a horizon and a temporality that is accessible to all and free of supernatural accomplishment. In the wake of new exigencies and an intellectual climate manifestly different from Blondel's, new challenges must be surmounted. Furthermore, a philosophy of immanence so conceived poses a new set of challenges to theologians that serves as an invitation for theological reflection to engage from within a "purified atheism," to invoke a similar call made by Simone Weil.[22] The call of Blondel's project, insofar as it claims to meet "the exigences of contemporary thought . . . in the [appropriate] philosophical method for the study of the religious problem," would seem to seal the fate of its own surpassing since the very conditions of "contemporary thought" in Blondel's time can no longer be taken for granted today.[23] By this, Falque calls into question not only Blondel but the entire philosophical and theological tradition by which "finitude" or creaturely existence is read as the dynamism of a native desire; a desire that is the expression of some account of "insufficiency." The very way of being of self-transcending desire is what seems to be in question. As Falque states it pointedly, "What cannot go without question today is the assumption that our dissatisfaction, or our predisposition toward happiness, is such that human beings have no other 'way of being' than for us to open ourselves to God (who becomes *necessary*) or that God has no other way than to give himself to human beings (showing himself in the process as *inaccessible*)."[24]

We must, however, be careful to underscore certain nuances of Falque's proposals. Within the scheme of the treatise on resurrection, his Heideggerian and Deleuzian interpretation of finitude as an unsurpassable immanence is "not the last word" in Christianity. There remains a metamorphosis of finitude to be effected. The implication of the foregoing is captured by Falque's insistence, both in the *Guide to Gethsemane* and in the *Metamorphosis of Finitude*, on a decoupling of the notion of finitude from its entanglement with the ideas of the "finite" and "infinite," and, by extension, from the immediacy of the polemic between transcendence and immanence.[25] In other words, the question of "finitude," as he makes the point, is not necessarily that of the "finite" and thus not the counterpoint of the Christian infinite. Finitude, then, does not as such decide (negatively) the question of transcendence. However, this proviso granted, what is evident is that Falque nonetheless decides the *means* by which the transcendent relates to finitude—that is, by way of the transformation (metamorphosis) and assumption of finitude, *not* through aspiration or prefiguring presence.

THE BLONDELIAN QUESTION

Because so much hinges on Falque's thematizing and rejection of the described paradigm of "immanentistism" (because the infinite is understood to be in some fashion immanent in the finite), and because he places Blondel as so centrally emblematic of this position, let us look closer at Blondel's account, assess what is at stake, and the merits or not of Falque's reading.

In engagements with Falque's work by an impressive selection of colleagues, admirers, and more critical readers, we find an instructive Blondelian "confrontation" initiated by Emmanuel Gabellieri's chapter on a similar question.[26] Gabellieri calls into question Falque's proposal of a recovered Heideggerian and Deleuzian notion of finitude as the unsurpassable universal horizon of human experience (*l'homme tout court*).[27] Under Falque's project, the price of admission of Blondel's thought into the currency of contemporary discourse would be for it to forego its purchase on finitude as already somewhat intended for the infinite and the retroactive working of this position into the analytic of finitude itself. But it is this account of finitude as *necessarily* bounded by a closed horizon, circumscribed in pure immanence, that Gabellieri pushes against. He raises the question—suspending for now the alleged preemption of the Christian infinite—of whether this Heideggerian analytic of finitude in fact takes full account of the phenomenon in question. That is, even while granting Falque the moment of the Christian metamorphosis, we must pose the question of whether the proposed determination of finitude as this new immanence is adequate to the experience of finitude itself. Has the analytic of finitude fully brought to light the phenomenon at work? In a most recent book, Gabellieri has given an even clearer formulation of the questions at hand by challenging the main thesis of Dominique Janicaud's watershed book, *Phenomenology and the "Theological Turn."*[28] The question to be posed is not so much that of a worrisome (for Janicaud) "turn" to theology but of whether phenomenology, in the reductions that constitute its Husserlian *eidetic* and Heideggerian existential heritage, is adequate to what human finitude experiences.[29] Gabellieri's questioning, before any conclusive sealing off, in the name of the pure phenomenon, of finitude within a determination of "pure immanence," calls for, *also in the name of the phenomenon,* a re-evaluation of the very conditions of appearing. That is, it problematizes the determination of the phenomenon of finitude as "closed."

A NEW PHENOMENON OF FINITUDE

This brings us to the consideration that there is a nuance of reading to be made of Blondel's account of the immanence that defines "finitude" and, in the same vein (though to a lesser extent), of Henri de Lubac. We may ask the question: Is it possible that the dynamism of the phenomenon of action and its elaboration of insufficiency, as we meet it in Blondel, does not fall into Falque's charge of the preemption of the infinite but is instead the reality and experience true of a phenomenon? Preliminarily, we must answer in the positive to these hypotheses, to which Blondel and de Lubac give support by a brief revisit of the "analytic of desire."

Within philosophy, theology, literature, music, and more, there is an entire tradition of the analytic of desire as the essential experience of human willing and action that is to be reckoned with. Even before the theological determination of the Thomist *desiderium naturale,* popularized in the twentieth century by de Lubac himself, the analytic of desire brings to visibility a phenomenon of the will as constantly willing beyond its own capacity.[30] The drama by which the will's appetite always surpasses its own powers comes to intense clarity, for example, in the thought of Friedrich Nietzsche and Fyodor Dostoevsky's *Brothers Karamazov,* both of whom de Lubac in his *Drama of Atheist Humanism* submits to a comparative analysis.[31] This drama is in fact one of the mainstay analyses of the Augustinian tradition, through Pascal, which Blondel so consistently held as the unity of that tradition.[32] As Gabellieri has suggested, what Falque's analysis, along with others, misses in Blondel's phenomenon of action is the radical discovery, through systematic exposition, by which he comes to a determination of action as the dynamism of two irreconcilable polarities doubly present in the phenomenon. In other words, the essence of the phenomenon is an insufficiency that is the result of the impossibility of the will to equate with its own appetites, and the impossibility of "satisfying" its natural appetites with the objects within its reach in finitude. In Blondel's well-known account, it is only through the idolatrous absolutizing of finite objects of desire that the will feigns this adequation. This procedure is what informs Blondel's analysis of "superstition": the attempt to resolve an infinite orientation of action by an appropriation of finite objects.[33] The first transcendence, then, is the natural disposition of self-surpassing within the phenomenon of desire.[34] This is the point at which the intellectual heritage of Blondel's phenomenon of action to be found in early German Romanticism is instructive.[35] Blondel's understanding of action and desire draws on the elaboration within this tradition of the coincidence of the finite and the infinite and the double movement that allows for this interpenetrative presence (*Übergang des Unendlichen ins Endliche*), as it is found in no less than Novalis, for example.[36]

Crucially, this insufficiency, or impossibility for desire to be self-sufficient and equal to itself (*s'égaler*), this infinite and unresolvable overlap (*décalage*) *is* what for Blondel defines the phenomenon itself.[37] The analytic of desire, then, brings to the analytic of finitude the *experience* of an infinite surpassing, and the analytic of finitude within this horizon of desire manifests in the phenomenon a tensional incommensurability with itself.

The foregoing analytic of desire opens up to the specificity of Gabellieri's reading of Blondel. It rests on the insight that if the phenomenon of finitude reveals this constant surpassing of itself, then there is the crucial need to thematize this "meta" dimension of the phenomenon itself, along the lines envisaged, for example, by Stanislas Breton, as the phenomenon of an ascensional surpassing of itself.[38] In this vein, instead of a closed immanence, the phenomenon of finitude proposes for its structure what Gabellieri along with Romano Guardini has referred to as the "structure of polarity."[39] This lodges into the heart of the concrete the double presence of what can be considered polar extremes. And it is the differential between these two that accounts for the dynamism of the phenomenon Gabellieri indicates. This thought of the dual presence of opposition and the dynamic mediation between them no doubt goes even further back, to the kind of polarity to be found in Aristotle between the *dunamis* and *energeia* and the dynamism that exists between their different actualizations. This phenomenon, too, we find as underlying Simon Weil's elaborate philosophy of the *metaxu*.[40]

Ultimately expressed here is the idea that there is a reckoning of the "infinite" as immanent and this sense must not be hastily resolved to the Cartesian foundationalist sense. The infinite here would suggest not something "present" within a so-called finite (even if hidden), but rather the sense of incommensurability of polarities. So that, there is a necessary question of an "immanent" mediation within individual existences in such a way that does not necessarily preempt the theological question of the infinite, as Falque fears. This framework of an infinite non-coinciding of polarities and of the internal dynamism this difference allows is what we find insightfully elaborated by Gabellieri as "alternative phenomenologies," represented by the philosophies of Henri Bergson, Gabriel Marcel, Blondel, and Weil.[41]

This philosophical élan of insufficiency is one of the key arguments for the much-needed re-evaluations of Blondel's philosophical Trilogy, beyond the polemics of the "Modernist Crisis" that defined the early reception of *L'Action* (1893) and derailed its essential philosophical thrust.[42] In the Trilogy, Blondel constructs an elaborate edifice of a "philosophy of insufficiency" as the structure of creaturely existence. In other words, his equivalent of an "analytic of finitude" is defined by incommensurability, a pillar of thought that has been further systematized, for example, by Claude Tresmontant.[43]

This way of understanding the infinite as the phenomenon of immanence, instead of leading to Descartes, may more accurately lead to the early German Romanticism of Schlegel, Hölderlin, Novalis, in its rich inspiration from Nicholas of Cusa and Giordano Bruno, among others.[44] The infinite then defines the fundamental experience of finitude. This sense, furthermore, applies not only to a human finitude, but following the transformations of early modern physics, becomes the key determination of the order of the cosmos, as we find it in the mathematical transformations of the period.[45]

In conclusion, Falque's notion of finitude represents insightful efforts at bringing the event of the resurrection into a certain experienced phenomenality of transformation, or, simply, a metamorphosis of lived finitude. But in so doing, it still raises the crucial question of whether a Heideggerian-Deleuzian-Camusian determination of finitude as a closed horizon is the only or even most enlightening option for this experience of something beyond finitude. The caution of not preempting the theological transformative event duly taken, might it not be the case that the Heideggerian option itself is not innocent of a certain dogma of immanence? Could it be that to seal off the horizon is also to take a philosophical stance on how things *should* be, and may betray the innocent but enquiring agnosticism that sometimes seems to inform Falque's reading? Furthermore, if we should take seriously the weight of the image of "horizon," as Didier Maleuvre has suggested in his rich study, then perhaps we are before a reality for which the boundary is merely apparent and not "real" or "hard." This image of the horizon, therefore, is "a boundary turned outward rather than inward" and is ultimately "inseparable from a theology of finitude."[46]

This therefore brings us to the conclusion that there is more to be read from Blondel and the "other phenomenologies" explored by Gabellieri as alternative accounts for finitude, yet without thereby preempting the question in a Cartesian way. The direction opened for such alternatives must turn to a rich tradition informed, since ancient Greek philosophy, by a thought of an internal polarity in individual things and a resistance to coincidence. This guarantees that a kind of infinite aspiration is without completion, a fundamental insufficiency is the very grammar of finitude, and the satisfaction (if ever) of that insufficiency is the very event of metamorphosis we find in Falque.

NOTES

1. Three volumes constitute Falque's philosophical triduum: *The Guide to Gethsemane*, *The Metamorphosis of Finitude*, and *The Wedding Feast of the Lamb*. The original French titles

have been published as a single, three-part volume: Emmanuel Falque, *Triduum philosophique: Le passeur de Gethsémani; Métamorphose de la finitude; Les noces de l'Agneau*, Triduum Philosophique (Paris: Cerf, 2015). In this chapter, I reference the English translations of the individual books under consideration, notably Emmanuel Falque, *The Guide to Gethsemane: Anxiety, Suffering, and Death*, translated by George Hughes (New York: Fordham University Press, 2019); and *The Metamorphosis of Finitude: An Essay on Birth and Resurrection* (New York: Fordham University Press, 2012), 15–19.

  2. Falque, *The Metamorphosis of Finitude*, 187.
  3. Falque, *Guide to Gethsemane*, 10–21.
  4. Falque, *The Metamorphosis of Finitude*, 193–96.
  5. Falque, *Guide to Gethsemane*, 8.
  6. Falque, *Guide to Gethsemane*, 7.
  7. Falque, *The Metamorphosis of Finitude*, 13.
  8. Emmanuel Falque, *Crossing the Rubicon: The Borderlands of Philosophy and Theology*, translated by Reuben Shank (New York: Fordham University Press, 2016).
  9. Martin Heidegger, *Kant and the Problem of Metaphysics*, translated by Richard Taft, fifth edition (Bloomington: Indiana University Press, 1997), 153–62.
  10. Falque, *The Metamorphosis of Finitude*, 14.
  11. Michel Foucault, *The Order of Things: An Archaeology of the Human Sciences* (London: Routledge, 2006), 340–47.
  12. Falque, *The Metamorphosis of Finitude*, 14.
  13. Falque, *The Metamorphosis of Finitude*, 19.
  14. Maurice Blondel, "Lettre sur les exigences de la pensée contemporaine en matière d'apologétique et sur la méthode de la philosophie dans l'étude du problème religieux," in *Œuvres Complètes. 2: 1888–1913: La philosophie de l'action et la crise moderniste*, edited by Claude Troisfontaines (Paris: Presses universitaires de France, 1997), 97–173.
  15. Falque, *The Metamorphosis of Finitude*, 16. Modified translation, added emphasis. For a historical account of the Modernist context of these accounts, particularly in the Catholic engagement with it, see Gabriel Daly, *Transcendence and Immanence: A Study in Catholic Modernism and Integralism* (Oxford: Clarendon Press, 1980).
  16. Maurice Blondel, "Une Des Sources de La Pensée Moderne: L'Évolution Du Spinozisme," in *Œuvres Complètes. 2*, 61–88. For the work that influenced Blondel's account of modern philosophy and the exigences of its method, see Victor Delbos, *Le problème moral sans la philosophie de Spinoza et dans l'histoire du spinozisme* (Paris: Félix Alcan, 1893). Blondel insists upon a *method* of immanence (as opposed to an "order" of immanence), with the former defining a kind of monadic understanding (but upon very realist foundations) of how everything is included or "enfolded" within everything. See Blondel's definition in *Œuvres Complètes. 2*, 647–51.
  17. Falque, *The Metamorphosis of Finitude*, 17.
  18. Falque, *The Metamorphosis of Finitude*, 16–19.
  19. C. Adam and P. Tannery, eds., *Œuvres de Descartes*, revised edition, volume 9 (Paris: Vrin/CNRS, 1898), 36 (translation mine).
  20. Falque, *The Metamorphosis of Finitude*, 16–17.
  21. Blondel, *Œuvres Complètes. 2*, 701; Falque, *Métamorphose de la finitude*, 193. "Vouloir l'infini, n'est-ce pas le point de départ et comme la pétition de principe de toute votre recherche? Et, avec l'infini en main, est-il surprenant ensuite que vous leviez toutes les contradictions du fini?"
  22. Simone Weil, *Gravity and Grace* (London; New York: Routledge, 2002).
  23. Falque, *The Metamorphosis of Finitude*, 17.
  24. Falque, *The Metamorphosis of Finitude*, 17.
  25. Falque, *The Metamorphosis of Finitude*, §5; Falque, *Guide to Gethsemane*, §7. See account of modern debates and the postmodern transformation of the core questions: Regina M. Schwartz, ed., *Transcendence: Philosophy, Literature, and Theology Approach the Beyond* (New York: Routledge/Taylor & Francis Group, 2004).

26. Emmanuel Gabellieri, "Entre 'vérité du monde' et 'vérité de Dieu,' 'l'homme tout court'?" in *Une analytique du passage: Rencontres et confrontations avec Emmanuel Falque*, edited by Claude Brunier-Coulin (Paris: Éditions Franciscaines, 2016), 191–218.

27. Gabellieri, "Entre 'vérité du monde' et 'vérité de Dieu,'" 191–218.

28. Dominique Janicaud, *Phenomenology and the "Theological Turn": The French Debate*, translated by Bernard G. Prusak (New York: Fordham University Press, 2000).

29. Emmanuel Gabellieri, *Le phénomène de l'entre-deux: Pour une métaxologie* (Paris: Hermann, 2019).

30. Gabellieri, "Entre 'vérité du monde' et 'vérité de Dieu,'" 202–06.

31. Henri de Lubac, *The Drama of Atheist Humanism* (San Francisco: Ignatius Press, 1995), 277–308.

32. Maurice Blondel, "Le quinzième centenaire de la mort de Saint Augustin (28 Août 430): L'unité originale et la vie permanente de sa doctrine philosophique," *Revue de métaphysique et de morale* 37:4 (1930): 423–69; "Les ressources latentes de la doctrine augustinienne," *Revue néo-scolastique de philosophie* 27:2 (1930): 261–75.

33. For analysis of Blondel and superstition, see Cathal Doherty, *Maurice Blondel on the Supernatural in Human Action: Sacrament and Superstition*, Brill's Studies in Catholic Theology, Volume 4 (Leiden; Boston: Brill, 2017). I shall not here unpack Blondel's philosophy of action, as it is not in its entirety immediately central to the present task. Cf. Oliva Blanchette, *Maurice Blondel: A Philosophical Life* (Grand Rapids, MI: W.B. Eerdmans Publishing Co., 2010), 63–94.

34. For a philosophical account of the dynamism of Blondel's phenomenon of action, see Koen Boey, "Blondels Metaphysica van de Wil," *International Journal for Philosophy and Theology* 62:3 (2001): 317–38.

35. Peter Henrici, *Hegel und Blondel: Eine Untersuchung über Form und Sinn der Dialektik in der "Phänomenologie des Geistes" und der ersten "Action"* (Munich: Berchmanskolleg, 1958).

36. John H. Smith, "Religion and Early German Romanticism: The Finite and the Infinite," in *Brill's Companion to German Romantic Philosophy*, edited by Elizabeth Millán Brusslan and Judith Norman (Leiden: Brill, 2018), 61; Frederick C. Beiser, *The Romantic Imperative. The Concept of Early German Romanticism* (Cambridge, MA: Harvard University Press, 2003).

37. Maurice Blondel, *Action (1893): Essay on a Critique of Life and a Science of Practice*, translated by Oliva Blanchette, new edition (Notre Dame, IN: University of Notre Dame Press, 2004), 148, 274, 283, 284, to indicate a few instances.

38. Stanislas Breton, "Réflexions sur la fonction *méta*," *Dialogue* 21:1 (March 1982): 45–56. We can retain several important points of Breton's powerful short essay. The "meta" prefix of metaphysics finds its role within the specific task of Analogy, within which its "vocation" is to be a link (*lien*), a function of stability and continuity within an understanding of *cosmos* defined by instability, movement, and of perpetual becoming. It describes an ontological structure of the universe traversed by a double movement of ascent and descent between its constituents. "C'est que tous les niveaux de l'univers communiquent, que les coupures de la métaphysique ne sont point l'étagement bureaucratique de substances séparées, et que tout être, sur la ligne ontologique où il se trouve, traverse, et doit traverser, pour aller jusqu'au bout de lui-même, un 'intervalle d'univers.'" We can finally underscore in Breton's words the "meta" function as an operator of analogy: "En raison de son universalité vraiment transcendantale, il est possible de la retrouver, comme lien commun et pouvoir de transgression, dans les choses comme dans les mots, dans les pierres comme dans les esprits. D'un mot leibnizien, hérité de Suarez, disons qu'elle serait le *vinculum substantiale*, le *nexus* substantiel d'un univers." Cf. Stanislas Breton, *Du Principe: L'organisation contemporaine du pensable* (Paris: Cerf, 2011).

39. Gabellieri, *Le Phénomène de l'Entre-Deux*, 173–202. Cf. Romano Guardini, *La polarité: Essai d'une philosophie du concret vivant* (Paris: Cerf, 2010). For philosophical history of the notion of polarity, see Geoffrey E. R. Lloyd, *Polarity and Analogy: Two Types of Argumentation in Early Greek Thought* (Cambridge: Cambridge University Press, 1966).

40. Emmanuel Gabellieri, *Être et don: Simone Weil et la philosophie*, Bibliothèque Philosophique de Louvain 57 (Louvain-la-Neuve: Editions de l'Institut, Supérieur de philosophie;

Peeters, 2003). More concisely, Gabellieri, *Le phénomène de l'entre-deux*, 149–66; "Blondel, S. Weil et le Panchristisme. Vers une 'métaxologie,'" in *Maurice Blondel et la quête du sens*, edited by Marie-Jeanne Coutagne (Paris: Beauchesne, 1998), 53–65.

41. Gabellieri, *Le Phénomène de l'entre-deux*, 95–166.

42. The Blondelian philosophical Trilogy comprises: Maurice Blondel, *La pensée: La genèse de la pensée et les paliers de son ascension spontanée*, volume 1 (Paris: Félix Alcan, 1934); *La pensée: La responsabilité de la pensée et la possibilité de son achèvement*, volume 2 (Paris: Félix Alcan, 1934); *L'être et les êtres: Essai d'ontologie concrète et intégrale* (Paris: Félix Alcan, 1935); *L'action: Le problème des secondes causes et le pur agir*, volume 1 (Paris: Félix Alcan, 1936); *L'action: L'action humaine et les conditions de son aboutissement*, volume 2 (Paris: Félix Alcan, 1937).

43. Claude Tresmontant, *La métaphysique du christianisme et la naissance de la philosophie chrétienne* (Paris: Seuil, 1961); *Introduction à la métaphysique de Maurice Blondel* (Paris: Seuil, 1963).

44. Smith, "Religion and Early German Romanticism: The Finite and the Infinite," 60–96. For a rich discussion of this kind of determination of the infinite, see Didier Maleuvre, *The Horizon: A History of Our Infinite Longing* (Berkeley: University of California Press, 2011).

45. Michel Serres, *Le système de Leibniz et ses modèles mathématiques: Etoiles, schémas, points*, third edition, Épiméthée (Paris: Presses universitaires de France, 1990); Alexandre Koyré, *From the Closed World to the Infinite Universe* (Baltimore, MD: The Johns Hopkins Press, 1957).

46. Maleuvre, *The Horizon: A History of Our Infinite Longing*, xix.

Chapter Fourteen

The Power at Work within Us

Steven DeLay

> To yield and give way to our passions is the lowest slavery, even as to rule over them is the only liberty.
> —Justin Martyr[1]

The body is the *I can*, as Husserl has taught us. So understood, it is what opens a field of possibility, and what thus in turn presupposes the most intimate and immediate features of that condition, including the ability to move, touch, and feel. As phenomenology has never ceased to emphasize, this incarnate capacity is entwined with the world to which it responds, to the world, not when understood as a naturalistic collection of atoms and the void, but the human world, a lifeworld exemplifying a sensible logic of both practically and theoretically meaningful solicitations and affordances. Contrary to what the dogmas of naturalism and scientism assert, the real world simply is the perceived one that we all encounter and know, and no other. As Merleau-Ponty made clear in *Phenomenology of Perception*, any assertion contrary to that effect will only contradict itself by affirming the identity between them it wishes to deny. In short, it must be admitted: the world *is* the perceived world. As for our condition of embodiment, it is determined by parameters that are themselves determined, at least initially, not by any originary choice of our own, but by the body's natural rhythms and patterns as well as the features of its surroundings. I cannot jump to the moon, breathe under water, or stop digestion by thinking. The heart beats on.

To be embodied, thus, is not only to be empowered, but also to be constrained by the thresholds we encounter at the limits of that power. There always is an element of constraint at work shaping the surrounding space of possibilities we explore by exercising our bodily powers. The body opens us to the real, yet the fact remains that we thereby are limited. Just as the body is not omnipotent, so too in that sense it is finite.

We have noted that the world is a perceived world. Many of the things around me (we may ignore what is present in memory or imagination) are made intelligible in their sensibility; they are matters of sight, taste, touch, smell, and hearing. But even here, there is an inescapable deficit or lack at work with the body's capacities. For even when considering circumstances in which things are readily accessible to the senses (a rose we touch or a sunset we see), what lies within our powers of reach, influence, or detection appears against a background horizon that itself is determined, not in terms of what we can encounter, but instead what must remain inaccessible to or impossible for us. Our powers of perception and movement, inherently limited as they are, render certain feats and encounters unattainable. Take, as an example, an afternoon hike on a park trail. The face of Pilot Mountain looks daunting. And it is imposing objectively even if that effect is due in part to the fact that, as I approach it, I can do so only as I do, from down below rather than on high as a bird. I am, after all, the height I am, not that of a giant. What are we to make of this perceptual situation rooted in our embodied situatedness? Anyone still in thrall to to what Merleau-Ponty called "objectivist thought" will try to explain away the described state of affairs as not being what it is. One might, for instance, insist on saying that the perceptual situation is in fact subjective, a matter of *mere* perception. But that cannot be right. Disregarding one's perception would be to do so at one's peril. That the mountain looks to me tall is no illusion. For if I fall, I will be badly injured or maybe even die. Here, perception does not occlude or otherwise distort the reality of the situation, but to the contrary reveals it. Even if one characterizes the perceived world as something perspectival (and hence subjective), when I do not heed what I experience, the consequences are not based upon perception. Naturalism's or objectivism's philosophical mistake of equating perception to sheer subjectivity is evident, then, not only in the abstract arena of the logical *non sequitur*. There is more. The fact that perception reveals what truly is the case explains why, if it is ignored, there are real consequences for not acknowledging what it shows. Far from perception being illusory or subjective, the injury or death inevitably awaiting me, should I neglect what it reveals, is most objective.

As for the mountain trail itself, it circles gently to the top, soliciting my steps. It is cut to my measure, with a human hiker's frame in mind. And if it guides me so surely, helping me reach a summit that would otherwise be inaccessible on foot, it does so because it was configured always keeping the possible (and impossible) in view. For what is impossible to me but that which exceeds my bodily capacities and accordingly frustrates the desires of my will or imagination? When walking, seeing the hovering hawks above only reinforces my own incarnate condition's limitations for what they are. I am earth-bound. Indeed, that the trail matters to my purposes is because, as I walk it to reach the top, I cannot leap there all at once but must get there one step at a time. And when I do get there, the scenic view available to me will have been won by an exertion the hawks do not know. For them, the view is not a goal but a matter of course. Hence, the range of options available to me (or anybody else who finds himself in the same position) implicates, in the technical sense of that term Merleau-Ponty borrowed from Husserl, a horizon of possibilities itself set against a background of impossibility, of what is *not* open but closed to me. If I hike the mountain, it is because I am neither hawk nor giant, but a man.

These observations could not be more obvious. Further reflection, however, reveals a situation more intriguing than the one we have preliminarily described might suggest. For we may ask whether the limitations we come up against in everyday embodied existence, including lacks such as hunger and thirst, susceptibilities to the aches and pains of injury or aging, weaknesses demanding a need for protection from the elements, urges for sex or rest, and daily necessities such as urination, defecation, and dental hygiene are merely that: are they simple limitations? Are they only bonds that shackle? The history of philosophy supplies no shortage of those who have answered the question affirmatively. Probably the most famous among them is Plato and his teacher Socrates. As Plato's *Phaedo* recounts, shortly before taking the hemlock, Socrates compares the body to a prison. To view the body's limitations this way, in a purely negative or quasi-gnostic register, is to understand the constraints responsible for determining the scope of our embodied capacities as limits that are imposed from without. They are constraints experienced as external to our choice. In short, they are impositions. And the form the imposition takes is twofold, entailing as it does distinguishable yet mutually reinforcing consequences. As already mentioned, first, there is the non-choice regarding those constraints associated with what I can or cannot do because the body's capacities simply are what they are. But there is also a second form of non-choice, one consisting in the further limitation that it was never up to me to determine the thresholds of these constraints. The powerlessness is striking. We are so weak that we have no say even over the extent to which we are weak.

To be limited in this way means that the *I can* is determined first and above all from without. Its limitations, which do not originate from within the body schema's own reservoirs of power, are experienced as extraneous constraints, to the point that sometimes they become obstacles to our will. To view the *I can* aright, thus, is to acknowledge, if only in the thinnest of outlines, the presence of a determining power beyond what the body by itself possesses starting from itself. There is a *transcendence* hovering over the very mode of power through which we experience that bodily power. What exactly, we must ask, may be said of this power?

It is in attempting to answer this question that we shall turn to the thought of Emmanuel Falque, which, perhaps more so than any phenomenologist's work in recent memory, has taken up the problem of the body, with particular emphasis on the origin and limit of the body's power. In doing so, we shall linger on a question Falque himself has posed: when it comes to the body, and hence the limits of the *I can*, what is (or can be) the power at work within us? Is there more at work in us through the body than what I myself alone can give? And if so, how is such power to be understood? It is by asking these questions, we shall see, that questioning is led to confront a fundamental question of method: does not a proper accounting of the body (and its power) require a reevaluation of traditional divisions thought to hold between philosophy and theology? The answer is "yes": the problem of the body, as Falque shows, explodes traditional partitions between philosophy and theology.

Now, if it was Husserl and Merleau-Ponty who originally conceptualized the flesh or lived body (*Leib*), it is Falque who has radicalized that notion of the *I can*. Doing so, in turn, calls for an expansion of phenomenological method as it was formulated by transcendental phenomenology. Thinking on the body will henceforth take place along the borderlands between philosophy and theology. In the preface to the English translation of the *Metamorphosis of Finitude*, for instance, Falque characteristically observes, "It has at last become possible, at least in certain places and in certain circumstances, to describe oneself as 'at the same time' philosopher and theologian, and to take on due responsibility for such a claim."[2] That very approach, notably, is also at work in *Crossing the Rubicon*. As Falque explains there, the body is not just what opens the perceived world, but also, and no less so, what opens us to the revelation of God in Christ. A recognition of this experiential fact is significant methodologically for obvious reasons, as we have already mentioned. For it mobilizes an account of the body whose task becomes the exploration of what is now the fluid interface between philosophy and theology. In fact, as that same text notes, the stated goal is not only to approach theology phenomenologically, but to reconfigure phenomenology itself through theology. As Falque emphasizes repeatedly, the cornerstone phenomenon of that approach is the Resurrection, for, as he says, "the resurrected Christ alone has the means to open [finitude's] immanence to a dimension of eternity."[3] The suggestion is audacious, but it is not baseless as some might contend. It follows from a recognizable and intelligible *logos*, one typifying the texture of the human condition as we all experience it. Who, after all, is without a body or does not know what it is to be embodied?

The *logos* is a human *logos*, for to be human is to be embodied, to be thrust into a time whose finitude initially is burdened by anxiety, suffering, and a fear of what we feel is death's ineluctable arrival. It is this forlorn condition, that of finitude, which the Resurrection transforms, at least for anyone who has appropriated the event personally. As Falque explains, *"The*

Resurrection changes everything: it is the place of philosophy's conversion by theology—that is, the place of the passage of the aforementioned finitude to the resurrected Christ."[4] The transformation, as we have remarked, does not reconfigure just how we mark the intellectual divisions of labor between theology and philosophy. It does so, but it also does more. More importantly, the transformation brought about by the Resurrection occurs at the most basic levels of the perceived world itself. Altering the horizon of time so that time no longer is determined absolutely by death, finitude is transformed. Eternity is now evident, however still obscure. Now, in short, there is hope, one made manifest by and through the Resurrection.

With the change in time, from a despair of finitude to the hope of eternity, comes a change in how I accordingly experience that time. The metamorphosis at work is not merely conceptual or abstract, but attestable and experiential, as it overturns the entire tenor of one's being-in-the-world. As it is a *new* time, so too it incites a change in my bodily comportment. Merleau-Ponty often characterized our incarnate condition as if it solely involved visible surroundings. Falque does not make the same mistake. Instead, he emphasizes that the Resurrection, in having opened a horizon beyond the quotidian and visible, alters how we inhabit the world of the everyday. Accomplishing a revolution down to even the innermost depths of our being, it transforms the incarnate experience responsible for having given us initial access to the world. As Falque comments, the Incarnation and Resurrection each in its distinctive but corollary ways change what it means to be embodied. For one thing, the field of possibility is now greater. Everything I do under the sun takes on a broader significance, for it is done under the weight of an eternal glory, present ambiguously, yet fully still-to-come: "The 'theological incarnate'—that is, the Word made flesh—does not come simply to superimpose itself upon the phenomenological incarnate—that is, the flesh of the human; it decides to dwell in it and transform it."[5] The classic phenomenological problematic of the body with its accompanying notions of perception, time, and world, therefore provides a benchmark for testing the motto to which Falque will frequently recur in *Crossing the Rubicon*: "*The better one theologizes, the more one philosophizes.*"[6] What, we may ask, does such a statement mean for phenomenology and for our understanding of the body generally?

First, as he notes, to theologize better is to take seriously the idea that what is needed is not merely a theology that thinks phenomenologically (Henri de Lubac or Hans-Urs von Balthasar), but a phenomenology that, facing the problem of the body squarely, admits the legitimacy of what he calls "*the counterblow of theology on phenomenology,*" a move which, as he hastens to add, "has not only been unconsidered but has yet to be carried out."[7] At a minimum, traveling the path Falque has in sight will mean that instead of "dividing philosophy and theology up into two utterly separate worlds," we are called to do both, "seeking in ourselves a new mode of unity."[8] Contrary to the well-known criticisms associated with Dominique Janicaud and others, this approach is not a desertion of phenomenology, but one whose undertaking has a guiding ambition faithful to phenomenology's traditional emphasis on descriptive accuracy, to fidelity to the cause of describing what appears as it appears. In fact, as Falque often says, it is the one who insists on denying the rapport between theology and philosophy who is guilty of deserting the cause of phenomenology. In the end, to maintain any kind of facile division between them requires distorting the experiential fact that the body is as open to God as it is the world. Merleau-Ponty and others may have done well to locate the body in terms of its openness to the visible world, yet this does not mean there is nothing more to which the body stands open.

It therefore falls to phenomenology today to correct this omission. Ascribing to a dogmatic partition between theology and philosophy will not aid that effort. In fact, it reinforces the problem, by distorting the richness of the body's significance. As Falque observes, the methodological atheism of someone as Heidegger does not preserve phenomenological purity. Rather, it stipulates what will count as purity dogmatically. Without any justifying appeal to the things themselves, it decides what will be allowed to appear. No one can deny that it is correct to be cautious about allowing unfounded metaphysical extravagancies to intrude into phenomenology. But one can rightly agree with such a statement only as long as it is taken simply to mean that traditional metaphysical systems potentially distort our view of what otherwise would be experientially manifest. For at the same time, it is as necessary to also stress that, very often, this worry about metaphysical extravagance has been used by a phenomenology in name only to rationalize its decision to ignore what it knows it might be forced to admit *does* appear, were it to quit hiding behind pronouncements that amount to a false pretense of methodological neutrality. Why, indeed, think there is anything truly neutral about the rejection of God from phenomenology? The idea that methodological atheism is neutral is a dream, and the way it carves a gap between theology and philosophy is far from helpful.

Thus, Falque will propose an entirely different approach. Acknowledgment of the Resurrection, he says, not only in the mode of a possibility (here Jean-Luc Marion's account of the saturated phenomenon comes to mind), but as an attestable historical event with the power to experientially transform us and the world around us, shifts how we see and do philosophy. And no wonder. For a start, it changes how we ourselves personally occupy the world bodily. The change in attitude concerns how we experience time, and what in turn we choose to do with the time that we are given. Time still as before leads to death, for there is no escaping death, but in leading us there, time no longer grants death the last word. Death ceases to be the absolute it had been before. Falque himself is very careful not to understate the finitude of our being-in-the-world. And yet, there is nothing about acknowledging that finitude which means such finitude cannot be surpassed.

As Falque's work on the relationship between the body and finitude shows, it is the role of grace in the economy of the mortal body that points to the glorified one to come. Tracing the transformation from life in the natural body to one that hopes for the spiritual body to come, he articulates how the grace of God is the power at work within us. As Falque says in "Descent into the Abyss," the opening chapter to *The Wedding Feast of the Lamb*, it is the Holy Spirit that transforms our experience of the world by first transforming our bodily condition: "All the same, it has been the constant admission of weakness in Christianity that has only too rapidly led us to disregard the power of the Holy Spirit that is capable of bringing about our metamorphosis."[9] And as he says later in that same text, being-before-God involves a mode of incarnate existence not to be understood, with Nietzsche, as a form of weakness, but as one of power. Or rather, to use the Pauline terminology, it is a strength that finds itself in weakness:

> It should be evident, then, even to those who might have doubted it, that the true weakness of the Christian comes not from a renunciation of power (the power of the body, in particular); that is a mistranslation of a false idea of power that is mistakenly denounced by Nietzsche. Rather, it comes from entrusting power to another (the Holy Spirit in him) so that *his* power, even *his* energy, is fulfilled in us.[10]

How, though, is that power to be received, if we are not always already endowed with it? To answer, an inquiry analytic of the body will be necessary.

To begin with, we must admit that the Resurrection has changed the world, no matter whether I am willing to accept that it has. I did not initiate it, and I am just as powerless to negate it. It has happened, and its having happened is not something I can make unhappen. The most I can do, if I am so disposed, is to ignore the fact it has happened, or perhaps try to contest it is a fact by denying that it truly happened. If this is the attitude I adopt, one of indifference, incredulity, or ingratitude, then although the world has changed, I will not. I will experience the world as it was before Christ, namely as without hope. And hence, such an individual will remain as he always was, just as he found himself, as someone destined to live out his days beneath the shadow of death. Whoever confronts the event of the Resurrection yet refuses to be changed by it carries on as ever.

As for such a one, this is the one who does not repent. In the present context it is important to stress that repentance, as the original Greek in the New Testament itself tellingly suggests, is not simply a "change of mind"; for it is a change of mind regarding where I want to go, and what I am willing to give up in order to get there. In changing my mind, so too my actions change. Better said, it is a change of heart. And if the heart is the center of our being, that is because it determines not only where we are presently, for where we are is expansive, involving where also we want to be. As Jean-Louis Chrétien has said, "Je ne suis pas où je suis, je suis où je vais, je suis où je tends, je suis où j'aspire."[11] For better or for worse, we follow our hearts. "In repenting," as Falque therefore notes, "the conscience is *coram Deo*. Morality gives way to religion. In this leap—now from morality to religion—resides the entire problematic of the decision, precisely in the context of a philosophy of religious experience, which is not satisfied with a philosophy of religion alone."[12] The first exercise of spiritual power, thus, is when we exercise our natural ability to admit that there is a power above us, and that we cannot become what we are fully able to be without making room for that transcendent power to enter into us. Paradoxically, the first genuine act of power on our part is one of submission, for to honestly admit to our wrongs is to concede that they are simultaneously wrongs not against others only, but above all wrongs before God. Without such an admission, there can be no radical change. Thus, it is only by exposing our natural body to the authority of God that we make ready to receive the power God wishes to grant us, a grace that can transform our lives by God's acting through and with us. To submit to the Holy Spirit is to yield our bodies to it as well.

Faith, then, is not mere belief. It is synergistic fidelity, that is, loving obedience to the promptings of the Holy Spirit. As Falque will note correctly, there accordingly can be no cooperation with God when I remain turned against him. To repent before God, as he observes, is therefore something that "renders us not inoperative but capable of cooperating."[13] For as the next page over says, "this fulfillment in the Spirit is not uniquely given to us as a dispensation, but to give us the capacity to co-operate with it."[14] Far from involving a desire for the otherworldly brought on by wish fulfillment (Freud), or a faith rooted in bad faith (Sartre), or a self-loathing weakness (Nietzsche), Falque has in mind a hope that is attestable here in the now experientially, through and in the body of whoever yields to such power. This life in the Spirit (to speak as the Apostle Paul did) is not at all what it is caricatured to be by those who do not yet know anything about it for themselves. Contrary to common criticisms, the perception and action at work here is neither one of fantasy, mania, or fanaticism:

> I am not suggesting a return to the unbridled Prometheism of a Nietzsche or to the all-encompassing apologetics of some Romanticism. Rather, if the force comes from an Other and will be shared, I am not reduced to exposing myself to it but to participating in it: Christ promises on the day of his Ascension in the announcement of Pentecost: "you will receive *a Force* [*dunamin*] when the Holy Spirit comes to you."[15]

What Falque highlights, rather, is a power harnessing self-restraint, not unchanneled and aimless enthusiasm. If it is necessary to affirm what ordinarily is forgotten, that is, the "possible cooperation between humans and God,"[16] it is largely due to the history of modern thought, beginning with the creation of the university in the Middle Ages, having partitioned philosophy from theology. As Falque comments, "Only the history of philosophy and theology erected that wall. The twentieth century created the breach in it; the twenty-first century will have to find a passage through it."[17] And what, indeed, will provide the ferry through this passage besides the body, and the reflection that considers it?

Ultimately, if working out how Falque himself understands that passage demands an examination of his critical appropriation of Merleau-Ponty's own phenomenology of the body, it is necessary first to note that we owe part of the answer to the analyses of Michel Henry, which, emphasizing the self-impressional pathos of a flesh crushed against itself in self-feeling, were nonetheless always sure to emphasize that there was a component of heteronomy or transcendence involved in how we originally come into possession of ourselves: I am free to choose what I shall do with my bodily powers, but I never chose to choose them, and the limits of what I may choose are themselves in turn not a matter of my choosing. As Henry never tired of noting, that I am able to deploy my incarnate powers is not itself a power I was free to give to myself. I am invested with that power, and never starting from and by myself. I find myself already endued with such power prior to any decision on my own part intervening. Put into possession of these powers, I had nothing to do with finding myself so empowered. First of all, then, there is as Henry notes no such thing as a bodily power starting from itself. Even Henry who is the thinker of radical immanence *par excellence*, who always took the greatest care to accentuate how the immediacy of our incarnate self-experience was different than the mode by which things manifest themselves through intentional transcendence, the *I can* always already indicates a power beyond itself explaining how those powers, in not having originated from ourselves, cannot be explained with sole reference to the *I can*. Indeed, for Henry, the "transcendental illusion" of the *ego* is precisely its taking itself to be the origin of its own powers. That I *am able* to do anything whatsoever is, even for Henry, therefore ultimately conditioned from without. And if there is a realm of what lies beyond the capacity of my powers to have ever accomplished on their own, it is important to recognize that possessing any such power over them is something beyond the body's inherent capacities to have given itself.

A thought emerges from this realization naturally. No doubt it is tempting to see the fact that we are not the originators of our own bodily powers as implying a kind of limitation. That is something that until now we have highlighted. Here, however, Falque's account of the body intervenes, suggesting another way of interpreting this condition of limitedness. His way of viewing the matter can be summarized in a hypothesis, one reversing our ordinary tendency to associate limitation with weakness: instead of considering our being put into possession of our powers as a strict limitation, what if we see it as what potentially, in certain circumstances and under the right conditions, serves as a reservoir of power, as a surfeit of force exceeding what the body's ordinary capacities rendered us unable to perform? Hence, in the last analysis, could the fact of our being placed into possession of the *I can* be what broadens, rather than constrains, the thresholds of possibility? When interpreted as a matter of authority, no one denies that to be subject to a power beyond oneself is to suffer from a certain limitation. Anyone in that condition no longer is absolutely free. Ordinarily, it is with an understanding of power in this foregoing sense, as a phenomenon of authority and autonomy, that we identify such freedom with power itself: the more freedom the more power, and the more power the more freedom. Thus, to admit that our bodily powers are not from ourselves would seem to involve an imposition on our freedom and in turn our power. But why not consider the possibility that the customary correlation between freedom and power does not always hold? Might not the fact that we are so limited be what lays the basis for the expansion (rather than the constriction) of the body schema's field and depth of possibility? It is this limitation (taken in the sense that it is not up to us that we have the powers we do) that the ordinary field of possibilities is thereby fixed. But might not that limit, once determined, be exceeded, not by us, but by the very power first responsible for having given us the powers we have?

Admittedly, the suggestion requires that we countenance a paradox. Typically, we think, the one subject to any higher authority than himself is less powerful than the one who is unfettered. Autonomy's final power is its sovereignty to do as it wants. There may be something to that idea in some cases, particularly in the political and social contexts. But does the same hold true with the body? Far from it. Actually, there is reason to think that the autonomous body, which acts as if it is subject to nothing but what it decides for itself is worth pursuing, while assuring a measure of liberty from any fetters besides those legislated by itself, leads only to the most bitter of bondages: the one imposed by itself. Rather than cultivating the absolute freedom it had willed as its highest measure, the autonomous body, or better, the one who lives autonomously, ends up a slave.

Where the ancients spoke of the passions, we today, following the idiom of Nietzsche and Freud, speak of the drives. But whether one prefers the classical or the modern idiom, things are the same. Is the drunkard free? The sexually promiscuous? What about the drug user, or the pornography watcher? The libertine disregards the moral law. Indeed, he may reach a point where he rejects even the notion that there is any such law. And yet, while one is free to disregard moral constraints, one is not free to avoid the ugly and painful consequences inevitably attending having done so. There is a delusion at work here, because originally in the mind of the one who disregards these constraints was the hope that it is possible, contrary to what all experience teaches, not to reap what one chooses to sow. In this case, the illusion consists in thinking that the absolute freedom to pursue happiness via pleasure will lead to satisfaction. For as the desert mirage recedes as one draws near to it, so too the contentment one is seeking. Schopenhauer, for example, was to note that desire always returns after it has been sated, and so there is no deliverance in desire. Not only is it that desires can never be satisfied because they return. In fact, very often, once they have been indulged, they not only return, but they return more strongly than ever before. Far from tempering it, indulging only intensifies the craving. When, then, the body relies on its own powers to pursue carnal things, it ends up a prisoner to the passions. The exercise of its freedom to seek what desire desires leads, not to the liberation for which it yearned, but bondage.

Of course, this account of the passions invites a number of familiar objections. Let us address a first. In his assessment of Henry's phenomenology of life, Falque takes great pains to emphasize that the body is not immaterial or angelic, but material and organic. As he remarks, "Only without reading Tertullian or in reading him poorly, is it possible to think that the flesh of Christ is no more than an illustration of the lived body in its interiority or auto-affection."[18] The phenomenological tradition, he notes, arguably has lost the sense of the body as organic. But then what about Falque's invoking the Incarnation, does not doing so merely repeat the same tendency in Henry that Falque wishes to avoid? Is not to unpack the organic body in reference to the Incarnation to do so in a way that takes the body as *not* the organic, but instead as the "transcendent," the "metaphysical," the "trans-substantial," or even the "mystical"? Is not this simply to take on, without the least argument, but rather by dogmatic choice, the assertions of Christian theology?

This objection, however, misfires. As readers of Falque will know, the third work of his trilogy, *The Wedding Feast of the Lamb*, delves into the problem of the body, articulating what Falque calls the "spread body" (*corps épandu*). Explicating the manner in which the Resurrection changes everything demands an accounting of how it transforms finitude, a transformation which itself transforms the body. Hence, an account of the body is imperative. "As I explained earlier," Falque comments in the chapter "Return to the Organic," "[*The Wedding Feast of the Lamb*] was inspired by my sense of something lacking, or rather something left over, after my book on the *Metamorphosis of Finitude*: the topic of the 'living or biological body.'"[19] Neither the mathematized *res extensa* of science (Descartes) nor the flesh of lived experience (Husserl, Merleau-Ponty, and Henry), it is the organic and material body, the body of chaotic drives and passions. In our present state we are dust, whereas in the Resurrection we will have a glorified body—the body will be immortal. Falque's attention to the organic dimension of the spread body, thus, emphasizes the full arc of time by facing up to the corruptible nature of our current body. In facing the corruptible nature of the organic body, the eschatological horizon of the human condition itself comes thematically into view, for it is in facing this condition that it becomes possible to raise the notion of an immortality that might overcome the dissolution of our spread body destined for the grave. The possibility of a bodily immortality (and hence Resurrection) is already tacit, by transposition, in the event of death itself. Death is an inevitability, to be sure, yet there is no logical contradiction involved in thinking of it as reversible. And more, because the organic body is what is to be resurrected and glorified into a spiritual body, the eschatological promise of immortality accentuates, rather than neglects, our current organic condition. Anyone unfamiliar with Falque's work whom would insist that the spiritual body promised in the Resurrection will no longer be one with the brain, eye, ear, or tongue is confusing his own opinions about what he thinks the promise of immortality entails with what Falque actually thinks it is said to entail. Falque's view is not mere opinion or speculation; it is grounded in the Gospel accounts. For the forty days that Christ was risen before his Ascension, he ate as a man with an organic body, consuming fish and honeycomb. And did not Thomas touch the print of the nails in his side? The natural body we occupy in the time that leads to death, thus, serves here and now as the eschatological basis for the hope of the future glorified body, no less than Christ's own crucified body was the basis of his glorified body. There is nothing ephemeral about any of this. The hope of immortality (and the life of the Spirit that sustains it) is a matter of the blood and sinews of this, our mortal body. Hence, to criticize Falque's position of angelism is to miss the mark widely.

Indeed, if, as we have seen, the Christian conception of existence in the mortal body as an existence lived in light of the example of the Incarnation and the eschatological promise of the Resurrection cannot be justifiably said to deny the body's organic reality, there nevertheless is another, even similar, objection waiting to be addressed. May not it be objected that the Christian, by assuming the existence he does, thereby in some sense shreds ties with fellow humans? Is to assume the vocation of living in the Spirit to do so at the price of denying our bond, our commonality with others? The objection is not uncommon, but it is unjust. For nothing in fact could be any further from the case. As Falque himself says, "the Christian will not be satisfied with extracting himself from the sphere of common humanity."[20] The Christian does not deny the existence of the world, does not distrust the perceived world, does not ignore the reality concerning his organic condition, does not evade the death to which he by that fact is handed over to. What he denies is that this accounting of finitude is the whole story. We are finite, yes, and we must all face death undoubtedly. But the Resurrection opens a passage through death, having demonstrated that God is more powerful than it. As ever, the point is not one of insisting on empty hope or blind faith (it is seldom remarked that the events of sacred history are as well or better attested as those of ancient history that the skeptic does not dispute), but of submitting to an event which, once embraced, transforms the most intimate mode of our everyday being-in-the-world.

Inevitably, the question will be asked: are these statements regarding the Holy Spirit and the body philosophical or theological? But does it matter? In reading an ancient work as Justin Martyr's "Dialogue with Trypho," it is very evident, especially to the modern reader who is unaccustomed to the ancient context, that according to the understanding of everyone at the time of the events in question, whether unbelieving Greek, unpersuaded Jew, or early Christian, philosophy itself was agreed to be an inquiry into "divine things."[21] When those who disputed the Apostles or earliest Church Fathers did so, nobody thought to object to the kerygma on the grounds that the Christians who were proclaiming Christ Jesus were doing *theology*, not philosophy. When, for instance, Paul reasoned at Mars Hill with the Stoics and Epicureans, many mocked him, disagreeing with what he had to say, but no one thought it pertinent to discount what he had to say on the supposed rationale that Paul was violating some kind of *a priori* methodological purity essential to philosophy, having surreptitiously imported presuppositions said to belong to what was deemed theology. To the contrary, the division we think we know is in fact artificial; the academic consensus that today asserts we ought to be beholden to this intellectual division of labor simply ignores that this division was one unknown to the ancients. For not only Justin but also Polycarp, Clement of Alexandria, Irenaeus, and others, there simply was thinking. Philosophy for the ancients was not first a matter of ideas, but more so a matter of how to live. As such, from Plato on, philosophy commonly was characterized as an inquiry into "divine things." What Runar M. Thorsteinsson says of Seneca's Stoicism can be said of the other major Greek philosophical schools of the time: "In the ancient world, philosophy and theology were so closely connected that rarely was a philosophy without a theology and there rarely was a theology without a philosophy."[22] Every school had a master who exemplified its way of life. Christianity was no exception, for whom Jesus, while divine, was also the greatest of human moral sages. Drawing on Pierre Hadot's work, Thorsteinsson observes how, as we have observed, beginning with Justin Martyr in the second century, Christianity itself was treated as a philosophy. "In fact," he explains, "as Hadot convincingly points out, the very fact that Christianity, at least from the second century on, presented itself as a philosophy confirms that the ancients conceived of philosophy as a way of life."[23] To acknowledge philosophy is a way of life is accordingly to concede Christianity belongs to the philosophical context; it cannot be ignored by a thought that considers itself philosophical. With these ancient roots of philosophy in view, it becomes possible to see how a Christian phenomenology today should not be seen as a betrayal of phenomenological method, but rather as an attempt to accomplish its deepest ambitions. It desires a return to a true philosophy inspired by the ancient example, one whereby the disagreement of first importance concerns what the truth of the matter is, not what field of academic labor is responsible for seeking it.

As Falque's work on the body is a continuation of that ancient but forgotten pedigree, let us conclude with some remarks that it seems to me accord with his phenomenology's attempt to make evident the natural body's relation to the God who through grace strengthens it. The Spirit is invisible, but it is known, particularly through and by the activity done in the body. If the one who today lives on bread alone does so, it is not by necessity, but by choice. One is free to live by the power of one's own strength alone. But why do so, when that is to choose death? In the wake of the Resurrection, there is no need to continue living under the shadow of death. The Spirit that raised Jesus from the dead is the same power that gives all life its power, which is why it is more powerful than anything, death included. This life of the Spirit, however, must be accessed on God's terms, not our own. Before we can experience it, we must submit to its ways; before we may know its strength, we must admit the weakness owing to the limits of our own; before it exalts us, we must know humility; before we are made full, we must empty ourselves; before our lives can be saved, we must lose them. Through the Incarnation and Resurrection, God has taken the initiative. Still, to be transformed by the Spirit requires *us*, the decision of the *I can*: "For the kingdom of God is not in word, but in power" (1 Cor 4:20).

NOTES

1. Justin Martyr. "Fragments from the Last Writings of Justin," in *The Ante-Nicene Fathers: The Writings of the Fathers down to A.D. 325 Volume 1*, edited by A. Roberts and J. Donaldson. (Grand Rapids, MI: W.B. Eerdmans Publishing Co., 1950), 302.

2. Emmanuel Falque, *The Metamorphosis of Finitude: An Essay on Birth and Resurrection*, translated by George Hughes (New York: Fordham University Press, 2012), xx.

3. Emmanuel Falque, *Crossing the Rubicon: The Borderlands between Theology and Philosophy*, translated by Reuben Shank (New York: Fordham University Press, 2016), 22.

4. Falque, *Crossing the Rubicon*, 22.

5. Falque, *Crossing the Rubicon*, 98.

6. Falque, *Crossing the Rubicon*, 107.

7. Falque, *Crossing the Rubicon*, xx.

8. Falque, *Crossing the Rubicon*, 158.

9. Emmanuel Falque, *The Wedding Feast of the Lamb: Eros, the Body, and the Eucharist*, translated by George Hughes (New York: Fordham University Press, 2016), 9.

10. Falque, *The Wedding Feast of the Lamb*, 111.

11. Jean-Louis Chrétien, *Symbolique du corps: La tradition chrétienne du Cantinque des Cantiques* (Paris: PUF, 2005), 30.

12. Falque, *Crossing the Rubicon*, 108–09.

13. Falque, *Crossing the Rubicon*, 114.
14. Falque, *Crossing the Rubicon*, 115.
15. Falque, *Crossing the Rubicon*, 115.
16. Falque, *Crossing the Rubicon*, 114.
17. Falque, *Crossing the Rubicon*, 148.
18. Falque, *Crossing the Rubicon*, 150.
19. Falque, *The Wedding Feast of the Lamb*, 119. In §19 "In Flesh and Bones," Falque gives a fourfold distinction of the body: the physical body (Körper in the naturalistic sense of something extended), the biological body (*Leib* as the organic or spread body), the body of lived experience (*Leib*-körper in the proprioceptive sense of self-knowledge), and the corporal and spiritual flesh (*Leib* in the phenomenological sense of flesh).
20. Falque, *Crossing the Rubicon*, 77.
21. Justin Martyr, "Dialogue with Trypho," in *The Ante-Nicene Fathers: The Writings of the Fathers down to A.D. 325 Volume 1*, edited by A. Roberts and J. Donaldson (Grand Rapids, MI: W.B. Eerdmans Publishing Co., 1958), 194.
22. Runar M. Thorsteinsson. *Jesus as Philosopher: The Moral Sage in the Synoptic Gospels* (Oxford: Oxford University Press, 2018), 30.
23. Thorsteinsson, *Jesus as Philosopher*, 18.

Conclusion

To Die of Not Writing

Emmanuel Falque

As a conclusion to our work on "debates" and "confrontations," we are here reissuing one of the early texts (though here largely renewed and modified) by Emmanuel Falque on the sense of writing. The distinction at work between academic writing, writing in debate, and the conjoined practice of philosophy and theology is precisely what allows us to see the whole of his work ever still in progress. There is here the search for the unity of life and thought that the author has always claimed.

We do not write simply because institutions require it or to satisfy the demands of one's academic cursus, however legitimate these reasons are. Before or rather beyond such requirements, the act of writing is the site of transcribing oneself, a mode of being upon which the author in his very existence depends, as though to not write was to necessarily perish: "You ask me whether your verses are good," responds Rainer Maria Rilke in the first of his *Letters to a Young Poet*, which he addresses to Mr. Kappus. "You look outside yourself, and that above all else is something you should not do just now. Nobody can advise you and help you, nobody. There's only one way to proceed. Go inside yourself. Explore the reason that compels you to write; test whether it stretches its roots into the deepest part of your heart, admit to yourself whether you would have to die if the opportunity to write were withheld from you."[1] *Would you but die of not writing*? Such is the question, as essential for an author as it is for the reception of a text by a reader. Writing is first an "existential challenge" before it is a matter of intellectual stakes or a public profession.

Yes, we can think and produce within the university, and Martin Heidegger did not fail to rightly emphasize the point. But what remains to be said is to never draw solely from collectivized research (academics) or from an assembled community (ecclesiastics). To overly neglect the indispensable solitude of the act of writing is to at times verge toward losing oneself in the recognition that the trending phenomena will all too soon forget. "*All* alone" do we think and "*all* alone" do we write, alone not in the sense of closing oneself up in one's writing niche, but only to the extent that—here appealing to the universality of thinkers who have preceded us—we don't fail to *place ourselves in relation* in daring to take a position. Writing often suffers from saying nothing at all, not from the lack of good exposure, but from failing to *decide*. So we will distinguish two, or rather three types of writing, which, up until now, we have always wanted to practice simultaneously: academic writing, writing in debate, and writing at the crossroads.

First, *academic writing*. This is necessary, and constitutes the common ground among writers who don't content themselves in thinking from the vantage point of themselves alone, in the false pretension of absolute novelty. The act of appealing to our predecessors, throughout the entirety of a tradition both philosophical and theological, belongs to the *universitas* of the research community. Without tradition, there is no transmission, and it is the merit of academic work that we won't cease to recall. We confuse at times, even often, the legitimate ambition of popularization with the absence of conceptuality, thus reveling in the act of taking root from one's own vantage point alone. The university, with the requisites proper to it, has thus the merit of recalling that the standards of thought imposed on us also produce fruit for those who submit to their practice and heed to its demands.

However, we will not content ourselves with academic writing alone. For by merely interrogating the tradition, we often forget the necessity of positioning ourselves. The second type of writing comes to the fore so that we might position ourselves, not only in a set of historical debates, though strongly legitimate in their own right, but also before that which constitutes our contemporaneity. *Writing in debate*, the second mode of writing, arises so that we might *decide* in relation to the debates of our day. By living too far removed, as though supposing writing to be a purely atemporal act, we forget that no thought ever gives itself in the complete absence of presuppositions. And the preconception we have of the world is to interrogate it rather than reject it. Those who make up our time, as much in philosophy as in theology (even if at times, now as much as before, the debates of theology in fact take form *inside* of philosophy), are those with whom we should spend our time. To position oneself today, in our current time, is not to get caught up in polemics but simply to pose an act of affirmation and to dare to hold oneself to a decision. The medievals already practiced this in their famous disputes (*disputationes*) that didn't fail to renew an art of debate that we have at times forgotten. Every author must remember this too when they position themselves. The use of *respondeo* loses itself at times from the fault of not daring to participate. Let us then, starting now, take part: to not dispute is to renounce thinking. And the dispute today shall employ the means of our day, at the opposite risk of cloistering oneself in a past already elapsed.

The third type of writing, *writing at the crossroads*, maintains or holds together both the historicity of the first (*academic writing*) as well as our contemporaneity of the second (*writing in debate*). Our age so suffers from a division of disciplines—of philosophy and theology—which, while necessary for a time, has thus already passed its time. How we should get along though. There is no question here of denying the distinction of disciplines and schools. Philosophy and theology require neither the same procedures (problematic in philosophy and overly demonstrative in theology) nor the same points of departure (the "natural man" for philosophy and the "revealed God" for the theologian). But the encounter remains possible, and even necessary, in our time more than ever. By second-guessing ourselves on the threshold or taking a temperature check, we go without taking a leap and plunging into the deep. A conjoined practice of philosophy and theology thus drives us to horizons often unexplored wherein the author alone takes unique responsibility this time.

The great theological questions of yesterday are as much those of our own day—the motifs of the Incarnation, the sense of the redemption, the stakes of the resurrection, etc.—and yesterday's discourses must be reformulated in the framework of today's categories (on nature and the world, the soul-body and the flesh, creation and finitude, etc.). It is not at all the question here, though it goes without saying, of denying or rejecting that which constitutes and has constituted our historicity—on the contrary. The concepts of the past form and have formed that for which we still search today. To re-interrogate is neither to deny nor even to reject the strength or foundation of past formulations. It is only to realize a conjoined practice of philosophy *and* theology from which theology, and even philosophy, has always been renewed: Saint Augustine with a view to Platonism, Saint Thomas with Aristotelianism, and the contemporary philosophers of today with phenomenology, analytic philosophy, epistemology, as far as I can tell.

This *conjoined practice of philosophy and theology* thus fully engages "its author" and "the genre of its exposition." Since every word or speech act involves "publicity" to some degree—which is not enough of course to constitute the legitimacy of this act—its author assumes the risk of her personal decision. Its genre of exposition in that philosophy, in its difference with theology, requires a heuristic rather than didactic approach, from the order of research rather than the order of teaching, picking up from the first words that are not to remain identical to the last words. It is thus to behold each other "eye to eye" rather than to turn one's back, that the philosophers and the theologians will enrich each other. The best way to be oneself is to not flee from oneself, but to hold fast within the milieu and believe that an "I" and a "Thou" will be born of this shared community: "The *Thou* . . . appears and addresses him out of the mystery. . . . Spirit is not in the *I*, but between *I* and *Thou*. . . . Spirit is the word."[2]

NOTES

1. Rainer Maria Rilke, *Letters to a Young Poet*, translated by Mark Harman (Cambridge, MA: Harvard University Press, 2011), 30.

2. Martin Buber, *I and Thou*, translated by Ronald Gregor Smith (Edinburgh: T&T Clark, 1937), 39.

Bibliography

Adam, Charles and Paul Tannery, eds. *Œuvres de Descartes*, volume 9. Paris: Vrin—CNRS, 1898.
Alvis, Jason W. *The Inconspicuous God: Heidegger, French Phenomenology, and the Theological Turn*. Bloomington: Indiana University Press, 2018.
Aquinas, Thomas. *Summa theologiae*. London: Blackfriars, 1964–1976.
Aquinas, Thomas. *Summa contra Gentiles: On the Truth of the Catholic Faith*, book 3, *Providence*, Part I. Translated by Vernon J. Bourke. Garden City: Doubleday, 1956.
Aristotle, *The Complete Works of Aristotle: The Revised Oxford Translation*. Translated and edited by Jonathan Barnes. Princeton, NJ: Princeton University Press, 1984.
Asad, Talal. "Reading a Modern Classic: W.C. Smith's *The Meaning and End of Religion*." *History of Religions* 40 (2001): 205–22.
Augustine. *Confessions*. Translated by Henry Chadwick. Oxford: Oxford University Press, 1998.
Balthasar, Hans Urs von. *The Glory of the Lord: A Theological Aesthetics; Studies in Theological Style: Clerical Styles*. Edited by John Riches, translated by Andrew Louth, Francis McDonagh, and Brian McNeil. San Francisco: Ignatius Press, 1984.
Barnes, Timothy David. *Tertullian: A Historical and Literary Study*. Oxford: Clarendon, 1985.
Barsby, John. *Terence: The Woman of Andros, the Self-Tormentor, the Eunuch*. Cambridge: Harvard University Press, 2001.
Barth, Karl. *Evangelical Theology: An Introduction*. Translated by Grover Foley. Grand Rapids, MI: W.B. Eerdmans Publishing Co., 1979.
Barth, Karl. *Church Dogmatics II*. Edited by G. W. Bromley and T. F. Torrance, translated by G. T. Thompson and Harold Knight. Edinburgh: T&T Clark, 1957.
Baumgarten, Albert I., Jan Assmann, and Guy G. Stroumsa, eds. *Self, Soul, and Body in Religious Experience*. Leiden: Brill, 1998.
Beiser, Frederick C. *The Romantic Imperative: The Concept of Early German Romanticism*. Cambridge: Harvard University Press, 2003.
Bell, Catherine. *Ritual: Perspectives and Dimensions*. New York: Oxford University Press, 1997.
Bellantone, Andrea. *Métaphysique possible, philosophie de l'esprit et modernité*. Paris: Édition Hermann, 2012.
Belli, Manuel. *Al di là del limite. Filosofia e teologia nella proposta di Emmanuel Falque*. Milano: Glossa, 2015.
Benedict XVI. *Verbum Domini: Post-Synodal Apostolic Exhortation*. London: Catholic Truth Society, 2010.

Bettenson, Henry S. *Documents of the Christian Church*. Oxford: Oxford University Press, 1943.
Bianchi, Enzo. "La sacramentalità della Parola." In *Il vangelo celebrato*, edited by E. Bianchi and G. Boselli, 191–217. Milano: San Paolo, 2017.
Bianchi, Enzo. *Praying the Word. An Introduction to* Lectio Divina. Translated by J. W. Zona. Athens: Cistercian Publications, 1998.
Blanchette, Oliva. *Maurice Blondel: A Philosophical Life*. Grand Rapids, MI: W.B. Eerdmans Publishing Co., 2010.
Bloechl, Jeffrey. "Eschatology, Liturgy, and the Task of Thinking." In *From Theology to Theological Thinking*, edited by Jean-Yves Lacoste. Charlottesville: University of Virginia Press, 2014.
Blondel, Maurice. *Action: Essay on a Critique of Life and a Science of Practice*. Translated by Oliva Blanchette. Notre Dame: University of Notre Dame Press, 2004.
Blondel, Maurice. *The Idealist Illusion and Other Essays*. Translated by Fiachra Long. Boston: Kluwer Academic Publishers, 2000.
Blondel, Maurice. *Oeuvres Complètes, Tome II 1888-1913*. Edited by Claude Troisfontaines. Paris: Presses Universitaires de France, 1997.
Blondel, Maurice. *The Letter on Apologetics, and, History and Dogma*. Translated by Illtyd Trethowan and Alexander Dru. Grand Rapids, MI: W.B. Eerdmans Publishing Co., 1994.
Blondel, Maurice. *L'Action: L'action humaine et les conditions de son aboutissement*. Volume 2. Paris: Félix Alcan, 1937.
Blondel, Maurice. *L'Action: Le problème des secondes causes et le pur agir*. Volume 1. Paris: Félix Alcan, 1936.
Blondel, Maurice. *L'Être et les êtres*. Paris: Félix Alcan, 1935.
Blondel, Maurice. "Le quinzième centenaire de la mort de Saint Augustin (28 Août 430): L'unité originale et la vie permanente de sa doctrine philosophique." *Revue de Métaphysique et de Morale* 37:4 (1930): 423–69.
Blondel, Maurice. "Les ressources latentes de la doctrine augustinienne." *Revue Néo-Scholastique de Philosophie* 27 (1930): 261–75.
Blondel, Maurice. *La pensée: La genèse de la pensée et les paliers de son ascension spontanée*. Volume 1. Paris: Félix Alcan, 1934.
Blondel, Maurice. *La pensée: La responsabilité de la pensée et la possibilité de son achèvement*. Volume 2. Paris: Félix Alcan, 1934.
Blondel, Maurice. *Le procès de l'intelligence*. Paris: Bloud & Gay, 1922.
Blondel, Maurice and Emmanuel Tourpe. *"Mémoire" à Monsieur Bieil: discernement d'une vocation philosophique*. Paris: CERP, 1999.
Bloom, Harold. *The Western Canon: The Books and School of the Ages*. New York: Riverhead Books, 1995.
Boey, Koen. "Blondels Metaphysica van de Wil." *International Journal for Philosophy and Theology* 62:3 (2001): 317-38.
Bonaventure. *Collations on the Six Days*. Translated by Jose de Vinck, Works of Bonaventure 5. Quincy: Franciscan Press, 1995.
Bonaventure. *Opera Omnia*. Volume 5. Firenze: Quaracchi, 1891.
Boublil, Élodie and Christine Daigle, eds. *Nietzsche and Phenomenology: Power, Life, Subjectivity*. Bloomington: Indiana University Press, 2013.
Bouillard, Henri. *Blondel and Christianity*. Translated by James M. Somerville. Washington: Corpus Books, 1969.
Bourgine, Benoit. "Récension de Emmanuel Falque, Passer le Rubicon." *Revue théologique de Louvain* 46 (2015): 100–04.
Bourgine, Benoit. "Philosophie et théologie en process d'Alliance." *Revue des sciences religieuses* 102 (2014): 519–38.
Breton, Stanislas. *Du principe: L'organisation contemporaine du pensable*. Paris: Cerf, 2011.
Breton, Stanislas. "Réflexions sur la fonction méta." *Dialogue* 21:1 (1982): 45–56.
Brunier-Coulin, Claude, ed. *Une analytique du passage: Rencontres et confrontations avec Emmanuel Falque*. Paris: Editions Franciscaines, 2016.
Buber, Martin. *I and Thou*. Translated by Ronald Gregor Smith. Edinburgh: T&T Clark, 1937.

Bultmann, Rudolf. *Jesus Christus und die Mythologie: Das neue Testament im Licht der Bibelkritik*. Hamburg: Furche-Verlag, 1964.
Carrouges, Michel. *Les machines célibataires*. Paris: Arcanes, 1954.
Cavanaugh, William T. "'A Fire Strong Enough to Consume the House': The Wars of Religion and the Rise of the State." *Modern Theology* 11 (1995): 397–420.
Chalier, Catherine. *Les lettres de la Création. L'alphabet hébraïque*. Orbey: Arfuyen, 2006.
Chauvet, Louis-Marie. *Symbol and Sacrament: A Sacramental Reinterpretation of Christian Existence*. Translated by Patrick Madigan S.J. and Madeleine Beaumont. Collegeville: The Liturgical Press, 1995.
Chrétien, Jean-Louis. *Under the Gaze of the Bible*. Translated by John Marson Dunaway. New York: Fordham University Press, 2015.
Chrétien, Jean-Louis. *Symbolique du corps: La tradition chrétienne du Cantinque des Cantiques*. Paris: PUF, 2005.
Chrétien, Jean-Louis. *The Ark of Speech*. Translated by Andrew Brown. New York: Routledge, 2004.
Claudel, Paul. *The Essence of the Bible*. Translated by Wade Baskin. New York: Philosophical Library, 1957.
Clines, David. *Interested Parties: The Ideology of Writers and Readers of the Hebrew Bible*. Sheffield: Sheffield Academic Press, 1995.
Collingwood, Robin G. *An Essay on Metaphysics*. Oxford: Clarendon Press, 1940.
Conway, Michael A. "A Positive Phenomenology: The Structure of Maurice Blondel's Early Philosophy." *Heythrop Journal* 47:4 (2006): 579–600.
Corrigan, Kevin. *Evagrius and Gregory: Mind, Soul and Body in the 4th Century*. New York: Taylor & Francis, 2016.
Coutagne, Marie-Jeanne. *L'Action, une dialectique du salut*. Paris: Beauchesne, 1994.
Crisp, Oliver and Michael Rea, eds. *Analytic Theology: New Essays in the Philosophy of Theology*. Oxford: Oxford University Press, 2009.
Cuneo, Terence. *Ritualized Faith: Essays on the Philosophy of Liturgy*. Oxford: Oxford University Press, 2018.
Daly, Gabriel. *Transcendence and Immanence: A Study in Catholic Modernism and Integralism*. Oxford: Clarendon Press, 1980.
Davidson, Donald. *Essays on Actions and Events*. Oxford: Oxford University Press, 1980.
Davies, Eryl. *Biblical Criticism: A Guide for the Perplexed*. London: Bloomsbury, 2013.
Delbos, Victor. *Le problème moral dans la philosophie de Spinoza et dans l'histoire du spinozisme*. Paris: Félix Alcan, 1893.
Derrida, Jacques. "Faith and Knowledge: The Two Sources of 'Religion' at the Limits of Reason Alone." In *Acts of Religion*, edited by Gil Anidar, 40–101. London: Routledge, 2002.
Derrida, Jacques. *Writing and Difference*. Translated by Alan Bass. Chicago: University of Chicago Press, 1978.
Documents of the Second Vatican Council. http://www.vatican.va/archive/hist_councils/ii_vatican_council/index.htm.
Doherty, Cathal. *Maurice Blondel on the Supernatural in Human Action: Sacrament and Superstition*. Brill's Studies in Catholic Theology. Leiden: Brill, 2017.
Duméry, Henri. *Critique et religion, Problèmes et méthodes en philosophie de la religion*. Paris: SEDES, 1957.
Duns Scotus, J. "Prologue of the Ordinato." Translated by Peter L. P. Simpson. Unpublished manuscript, December 2012. http://www.aristotelophile.com/Books/Translations/Scotus%20Prologue.pdf.
Dupont, Christian. *Phenomenology in French Philosophy: Early Encounters*. Dordrecht: Springer, 2014.
Falque, Emmanuel. *Ça n'a rien à voir lire Freud en philosophe*. Paris: Cerf, 2018.
Falque, Emmanuel. *Crossing the Rubicon: The Borderlands of Philosophy and Theology*. Translated by Reuben Shank. New York: Fordham University Press, 2016.
Falque, Emmanuel. *Dieu, la chair, et l'autre, D'Irénée à Duns Scot*. Paris: PUF, 2008.

Falque, Emmanuel. "Evil and Finitude." In *Evil, Fallenness, and Finitude*, edited by Bruce Ellis Benson and B. Keith Putt, 77–96. Cham: Palgrave MacMillan, 2017.

Falque, Emmanuel. *God, the Flesh, and the Other: From Irenaeus to Duns Scotus*. Translated by William C. Hackett. Evanston, IL: Northwestern University Press, 2015.

Falque, Emmanuel. *Le livre de l'expérience. D'Anselme de Cantorbéry à Bernard de Clairvaux*. Paris: Cerf, 2017.

Falque, Emmanuel. "Limite théologique et finitude phénoménologique chez Thomas d'Aquin." *Revue des sciences philosophiques et théologiques* 92:3 (2008): 527–56.

Falque, Emmanuel. "Mal et Finitude: Dialogue Avec Ricœur et Lévinas." *Études Theologiques et Religieuses* 92:2 (2017): 413–31.

Falque, Emmanuel. *Nothing to It: Reading Freud as a Philosopher*. Translated by Robert Vallier and William L. Connelly. Leuven: Leuven University Press, 2020.

Falque, Emmanuel. *Parcours d'embûches: S'expliquer*. Paris: Editions Franciscaines, 2016.

Falque, Emmanuel. *Saint Bonaventure and the Entrance of God into Theology. Afterword: Saint Thomas Aquinas and the Entrance of God into Philosophy*. Translated by Brian Lapsa, revised by William C. Hackett. St Bonaventure: Saint Bonaventure University, Franciscan Institute Publications, 2018.

Falque, Emmanuel. *Saint Bonaventure et l'éntrée de Dieu en théologie*. Paris: VRIN, 2000.

Falque, Emmanuel. "The Collision of Phenomenology and Theology." In *Quiet Powers of the Possible: Interviews in Contemporary French Phenomenology*, edited by Tarek R. Dikka and W. Chris Hackett, 211-27. New York: Fordham University Press, 2016.

Falque, Emmanuel. "The Extra-Phenomenal." *Diakrisis Yearbook of Theology and Philosophy* 1:1 (2018): 9–28.

Falque, Emmanuel. *The Guide to Gethsemane: Anxiety, Suffering, Death*. Translated by George Hughes. New York: Fordham University Press, 2019.

Falque, Emmanuel. *The Loving Struggle: Phenomenological and Theological Debates*. Translated by Bradley B. Obishi and Lucas McCraken. London; New York: Rowman & Littlefield International, 2018.

Falque, Emmanuel. *The Metamorphosis of Finitude: An Essay on Birth and Resurrection*. Translated by George Hughes. New York: Fordham University Press, 2012.

Falque, Emmanuel. "Théologie et philosophie: nouvelles frontiers." *Études* 404:2 (2006): 201-10.

Falque, Emmanuel. *The Wedding Feast of the Lamb: Eros, the Body, and the Eucharist*. Translated by George Hughes. New York: Fordham University Press, 2016.

Falque, Emmanuel. "Toward an Ethics of the Spread Body." In *Somatic Desire: Recovering Corporeality in Contemporary Thought*, edited by S. Horton, S. Mendelsohn, C. Rojcewicz, and R. Kearney, 91–116. Lanham: Lexington Books, 2019.

Falque, Emmanuel. *Triduum philosophique: Le Passeur de Gethsémani, Métamorphose de la finitude, Les Noces de l'Agneau*. Paris: Les Édition du Cerf, 2015.

Farley, Matthew. "Introduction." *Crossing the Rubicon: The Borderlands of Philosophy and Theology*, translated by Reuben Shank, 1–13. New York: Fordham University Press, 2016.

Fish, Stanley. *Is There a Text in This Class? The Authority of Interpretive Communities*. Cambridge: Harvard University, 1980.

Fish, Stanley. "Literature in the Reader: Affective Stylistics." In *Reader-Response Criticism: From Formalism to Post-Structuralism*, edited by Jane P. Tompkins, 70–100. Baltimore: Johns Hopkins University Press, 1980.

Foucault, Michel. *The Order of Things: An Archaeology of the Human Sciences*. London: Routledge, 2006.

Freud, Sigmund. *The Standard Edition of the Complete Psychological Works of Sigmund Freud*. Translated by James Strachey. Volume XXII. London: The Hogarth Press and the Institute of Psycho-Analysis, 1986.

Gabellieri, Emmanuel. "Blondel S. Weil et la Panchristisme. Vers une 'métaxologie.'" In *Maurice Blondel et la quête du sens*, edited by Marie-Jeanne Coutagne. Paris: Beauchesne, 1998.

Gabellieri, Emmanuel. *Être et Don: Simone Weil et La Philosophie.* Bibliothèque Philosophique de Louvain 57. Louvain-la-Neuve: Editions de l'Institut, Supérieur de philosophie; Peeters, 2003.

Gabellieri, Emmanuel. "Entre 'vérité du monde' et 'vérité de Dieu,' l'homme tout court'?" In *Une Analytique Du Passage: Rencontres et Confrontations Avec Emmanuel Falque*, edited by Claude Brunier-Coulin, 191–218. Paris: Éditions Franciscaines, 2016.

Gabellieri, Emmanuel. *Etre et Don: Simone Weil et La Philosophie, Bibliothèque Philosophique de Louvain 57.* Louvain-la-Neuve: Editions de l'Institute, Supérieur de philosophie; Peeters, 2003.

Gabellieri, Emmanuel. *Le Phénomène de l'entre-Deux: Pour Une Métaxologie.* Paris: Hermann, 2019.

Gadamer, Hans-Georg. *Truth and Method.* Second revised edition. Translated by J. Weinsheimer and D. G. Marshall. London; New York: Continuum, 2004.

Gadamer, Hans-Georg. *Wahrheit und Methode, Gesammelte Werker I: Hermeneutic I.* Tübingen: Mohr-Siebeck, 1990.

Gilbert, Paul. "Ecriture phénoménologique et méthode patristique. Les frontières de la philosophie et de la théologie selon Emmanuel Falque." In *Une analytique du passage. Rencontres et confrontations avec Emmanuel Falque*, edited by Claude Brunier-Coulin, 365–87. Paris: Éditions Franciscaines, 2016.

Gilbert, Paul. "L'attenzione del pensiero. Emmanuel Falque, la filosofia, la teologia e la fenomenologia." In *Emmanuel Falque. Tra fenomenologia della finitezza e teologia dell'incarnazione*, edited by Carla Canullo and Paul Gilbert, 13–38. Firenze: Le Lettere 2014.

Gilson, Étienne. *L'Espirt de la philosophie médiévale.* Paris: VRIN, 1932.

Gilson, Étienne. *Introduction a l'étude de Saint Augustine.* Paris: VRIN, 1929.

Gire, Pierre. "Métaphysique, théologie et mystique chez Maître Eckhart." In *Penser la religion. Recherches en philosophie de la religion*, edited by Jean Greisch, 170–87. Paris: Beauchesne, 1991.

Gregory the Great, "Homily VII." In Book I of *The Homilies of Saint Gregory the Great on the Book of the Prophet Ezekiel.* Translated by Theodosia Tomkinson and Juliana Cownie. Etna: Center for Traditionalist Orthodox Studies, 1990.

Greisch, Jean. "Où passe le Rubicon? Un problème de géographie spirituelle." In *Une analytique de passage: Rencontres et confrontations avec Emmanuel Falque*, edited by Claude Brunier-Coulin, 315–40. Paris: Éditions Franciscaines, 2016.

Greisch, Jean. "Bulletin philosophie et christianisme." *Recherches de science religieuse* 102 (2014): 129–55.

Gschwandtner, Christina M. *Degrees of Givenness: On Saturation in Jean-Luc Marion.* Bloomington: Indiana University Press, 2014.

Gschwandtner, Christina M. *Postmodern Apologetics? Arguments for God in Contemporary Philosophy.* New York: Fordham University Press, 2013.

Guardini, Romano. *La Polarité: Essai d'une Philosophie du Concret Vivant.* Paris: Cerf, 2010.

Hadot, Pierre. *Exercices spirituels et philosophie antique.* Paris: Études augustiniennes, 1981.

Heidegger, Martin. *Being and Time.* Translated by Joan Stambaugh. Albany: State University of New York Press, 2010.

Heidegger, Martin. *Being and Time.* Translated by John Macquarrie and Edward S. Robinson. Oxford: Blackwell, 1967.

Heidegger, Martin. *Identity and Difference.* Translated by Joan Stambaugh. New York: Harper & Row, 1969.

Heidegger, Martin. *Kant and the Problem of Metaphysics.* Translated by Richard Taft. Bloomington: Indiana University Press, 1997.

Heidegger, Martin. *Phenomenological Interpretations of Aristotle.* Translated by Richard Rojcewicz. Bloomington: Indiana University Press, 2001.

Heidegger, Martin. "Phenomenology and Theology (1927)." In *Pathmarks*, edited and translated by William McNeil, 39–62. Cambridge: Cambridge University Press, 1998.

Heidegger, Martin. *Phenomenology of Religious Life.* Translated by Matthias Frisch and Jennifer Anna Gosetti-Ferencei. Bloomington: Indiana University Press, 2010.

Heidegger, Martin. *Sein und Zeit*. Tübingen: Niemeyer, 1993.
Henrici, Peter. *Hegel und Blondel: Eine Untersuchung Über Form Und Sinn Der Dialektic in Der "Phänomenologie Des Geistes" Und Der Erstern "Action."* Munich: Berchmanskolleg, 1958.
Henry, Michel. *Philosophy and Phenomenology of the Body*. Translated by Girard Etzkorn. The Hague: Martinus Nijhoff, 1975.
Henry, Michel. *The Essence of Manifestation*. Translated by Girard Etzkorn. The Hague: Martinus Nijhoff, 1973.
Hugh of Saint-Victor. "La parole de Dieu." In *Six opuscules spirituels*, Sources Chrétiennes, 155, translated by Roger Baron. Paris: Cerf, 1969.
Husserl, Edmund. *Analyses Concerning Passive and Active Synthesis: Lectures on Transcendental Logic*. Translated by Anthony J. Steinbock. Dordrecht: Kluwer Academic Publishers, 2001.
Husserl, Edmund. *Ideas Pertaining to a Pure Phenomenology and a Phenomenological Philosophy*. First Book. Translated by Fred Kersten. Dordrecht: Kluwer, 1983.
Husserl, Edmund. *Ideas Pertaining to a Pure Phenomenology and a Phenomenological Philosophy*. First Book. Translated by Fred Kersten. The Hague: Martinus Nijhoff, 1982.
Husserl, Edmund. "Universal Teleology." Translated by Marly Biemel. In *Husserl, Shorter Works*, edited by P. McCormick and F. Elliston. South Bend, IN: University of Notre Dame, 1981.
Husserl, Edmund. *Méditations cartésiennes*. Paris: Vrin, 1980.
Husserl, Edmund. *Experience and Judgment*. Translated by James Spencer Churchill and Karl Ameriks. Evanston, IL: Northwestern University Press, 1973.
Husserl, Edmund. *Cartesian Meditations: An Introduction to Phenomenology*. Translated by D. Cairns. The Hague: Nijhoff, 1960.
Husserl, Edmund. *Cartesianische Meditationen und pariser Vorträge* (*Husserliana I*). The Hague: Nijhoff, 1950.
Huysmans, Joris Karl. *Down There*. Translated by K. Wallis. Chicago: The Black Archer Press, 1935.
Illich, Ivan. *In the Vineyard of the Text. A Commentary to Hugh's* Didascalicon. Translated by V. Borremmans. Chicago: University of Chicago Press, 1993.
Jaer, A. de and A. Chapelle. "Le Noétique Et Le Pneumatique Chez Maurice Blondel. Un Essai De Définition." *Revue Philosophique de Louvain* 59 (1961): 609–30.
Janicaud, Dominique. *La Phénoménologie Eclatée*. Paris: Éditions de l'Éclat, 1998.
Janicaud, Dominique. *Le tournant théologique de la phénoménologie française*. Paris: Éditions de l'Éclat, 2001.
Janicaud, Dominique. *Phenomenology and the "Theological Turn": The French Debate*. Translated by Bernard G. Prusak. New York: Fordham University Press, 2000.
Janicaud, Dominique. *Phenomenology "Wide Open": After the French Debate*. New York: Fordham University Press, 2005.
Jauss, Hans. "Literary History as a Challenge to Literary Theory." In *Toward an Aesthetic of Reception*. Minneapolis: University of Minnesota, 1982.
John Paul II. *Fides et Ratio*. Encyclical Letter. http://www.vatican.va/content/john-paul-ii/en/encyclicals/documents/hf_jp-ii_enc_14091998_fides-et-ratio.html. September 14, 1998.
Justin Martyr. "Dialogue with Trypho." In *The Ante-Nicene Fathers: The Writings of the Fathers Down to A.D. 325. Volume 1*. Edited by A. Roberts and J. Donaldson. Grand Rapids, MI: W.B. Eerdmans Publishing Co., 1950.
Jung, Carl. *Contributions to Analytical Psychology*. Translated by H. G. and Cary F. Baynes. London: Kegan Paul, Trench, Trubner & Company, 1942.
Jung, Carl. *Mysterium Coniunctionis: An Inquiry into the Separation and Synthesis of Psychic Opposites in Alchemy*. Translated by G. Adler and R. F. C. Hull. Collected Works of C.G. Jung. Volume 14. Princeton, NJ: Princeton University Press, 2014.
Kearney, Richard. "Where I Speak From: A Short Intellectual Autobiography." In *Debating Otherness with Richard Kearney: Perspectives from South Africa*, edited by Daniël P. Veldsman and Yolande Steenkamp, 31–62. Cape Town: AOSIS, 2018.

Kierkegaard, Soren. *Kierkegaard's Writings: Either/Or*, Part II. Translated by Howard V. Hong and Edna H. Hong. Princeton, NJ: Princeton University Press, 1987.

Knepper, Timothy David. *The Ends of Philosophy of Religion: Terminus and Telos*. New York: Palgrave, 2013.

Knight, Taylor. "In a Mirror and an Enigma: Nicholas of Cusa's De Visione Dei and the Milieu of Vision." *Sophia* (2019): 1–25.

Koci, Martin. *Thinking Faith after Christianity: A Theological Reading of Jan Potačka's Phenomenological Philosophy*. Albany: SUNY Press, 2020.

Koyré, Alexandre. *From the Closed World to the Infinite Universe*. Baltimore: The Johns Hopkins Press, 1957.

Lacoste, Jean-Yves. *Dictionnaire critique de théologie*. Paris: PUF, 1988.

Lacoste, Jean-Yves. *Recherches sur la parole*. Leuven: Peeters, 2015.

Lalande, André and Société française de philosophie. *Vocabulaire de la Société Française de Philosophie*. Sixth edition. Paris: Presses universitaires de France, 1951.

Leclercq, Jean. *The Love of Learning and the Desire of God: A Study of Monastic Culture*. Translated by Catharine Mirashi. New York: Fordham University Press, 1982.

Leibnitz, Gottfried W. "Discourse on Metaphysics." In *Philosophical Essays*. Translated by Roger Ariew and Daniel Garber. Indianapolis: Hackett, 1989.

Levinas, Emmanuel. *Beyond the Verse: Talmudic Readings and Lectures*. Translated by Gary D. Mole. London: Athlone Press, 1994.

Levinas, Emmanuel. *Entre Nous: On-Thinking-of-the-Other*. Translated by M. B. Smith and B. Harshav. New York: Columbia University Press, 1988.

Levinas, Emmanuel. *Ethics and Infinity*. Pittsburgh: Duquesne University Press, 1985.

Levinas, Emmanuel. *Existence and Existents*. Translated by Alphonso Lingis. The Hague: Nijhoff, 1978.

Levinas, Emmanuel. *Le temps et l'autre*. Paris: PUF, 1989.

Levinas, Emmanuel. *Le temps et l'autre*. Paris: PUF, 1979.

Levinas, Emmanuel. *In the Time of the Nations*. Translated by M. B. Smith. Bloomington: Indiana University Press, 1994.

Levinas, Emmanuel. "Is Ontology Fundamental?" In *Entre Nous: On-Thinking-of-the-Other*. Translated by Michael B. Smith, 1–10. London: Continuum, 2006.

Levinas, Emmanuel. "*It Is Righteous to Be?*" *Interviews with Emmanuel Levinas*. Edited by J. Robbins. Stanford: Stanford University Press, 2002.

Levinas, Emmanuel. *Of God Who Comes to Mind*. Stanford: Stanford University Press, 1988.

Levinas, Emmanuel. *On Escape*. Translated by B. Bergo. Stanford: Stanford University Press, 2003.

Levinas, Emmanuel. *Otherwise than Being: Or Beyond Essence*. Translated by A. Lingis. Pittsburgh: Duquesne University Press, 1998.

Levinas, Emmanuel. "Reflections on the Philosophy of Hitlerism." *Critical Inquiry* 17:1 (1990): 62–71.

Levinas, Emmanuel. *Time and the Other*. Translated by R. A. Cohen. Pittsburgh: Duquesne University Press, 1987.

Levinas, Emmanuel. *Totality and Infinity: An Essay on Exteriority*. Translated by Alphonso Lingis. Pittsburgh: Duquesne University Press, 2013.

Levinas, Emmanuel. *Totality and Infinity: An Essay on Exteriority*. Translated by Alphonso Lingis. The Hague: M. Nijhoff Publishers, 1979.

Levinas, Emmanuel. "Transcendenz und Verstehen." In *Der Mensch in den modernen Wissenschaften*, edited by K. Michalski, 171–84. Stuttgart: Klett-Cotta, 1985.

Lewis, Thomas A. *Why Philosophy Matters for the Study of Religion & Vice Versa*. Oxford: Oxford University Press, 2016.

Libera, Alain de. *La Mystique rhénane, d'Albert le Grand à Maître Eckhart*. Paris: Édition du Seuil, 1994.

Lieb, Michael and Emma Mason, eds. *The Oxford Handbook of Reception History of the Bible*. New York: Oxford University Press, 2011.

Lossky, Vladimir. *Théologie négative et connaissance de Dieu chez Maître Eckhart*. Paris: Vrin, 1960.

Lloyd, Geoffrey E. R. *Polarity and Analogy: Two Types of Argumentation in Early Greek Thought*. Cambridge: Cambridge University Press, 1966.
Lubac, Henri de. *The Drama of Atheist Humanism*. San Francisco: Ignatius Press, 1995.
Mackinlay, Shane. "Phenomenality in the Middle: Marion, Romano, and the Hermeneutics of the Event." In *Givenness and God: Questions of Jean-Luc Marion*, edited by Ian Leask and Eoin Cassidy, 167–81. New York: Fordham University Press, 2005.
Maleuvre, Didier. *The Horizon: A History of Our Infinite Longing*. Berkeley: University of California Press, 2011.
Mandolini, Clara. "Blondel and the Philosophy of Life." *Analecta Husserliana: The Yearbook of Phenomenological Research* 53 (2009): 253–73.
Marion, Jean-Luc. *Réduction et donation*. Paris: PUF, 1989.
Marion, Jean-Luc. *Prolegomena to Charity*. Translated by Stephen E. Lewis. New York: Fordham University Press, 2002.
Meister Eckhart. *Die Lateinischen Werke*, Band 1,1. Hgg. Konrad Weiss, Stuttgart: Kohlhammer, 1965.
Merleau-Ponty, Maurice. "La nature ou le monde du silence." In *Maurice Merleau-Ponty, La nature ou le monde du silence*, edited by Emmanuel de Saint-Aubert, 44–53. Paris: Hemann, 2008.
Merleau-Ponty, Maurice. *Nature: Course Notes from the Collège De France*. Translated by Robert Vallier. Evantson: Northwestern University Press, 2003.
Merleau-Ponty, Maurice. *The Visible and the Invisible*. Translated by Alphonso Lingis. Evanston, IL: Northwestern University Press, 1968.
Merleau-Ponty, Maurice. *Signs*. Translated by R. McCleary. Evanston, IL: Northwestern University Press, 1964.
Merleau-Ponty, Maurice. *In Praise of Philosophy*. Translated by John Wild and James Edie. Evanston, IL: Northwestern University Press, 1963.
Nagel, Thomas. *The Last Word*. Oxford: Oxford University Press, 2001.
O'Leary, Joseph. "Phenomenology and Theology: Respecting the Boundaries." *Philosophy Today* 62:1 (2018):99-117.
O'Leary, Joseph. "Review of Passer le Rubicon: Philosophie et théologie. Essai sur les frontièrs." *Theological Studies* 64:2 (2013): 841-45.
Pascal. *Pensées*. Edited and translated by Roger Ariew. Indianapolis: Hackett, 2004.
Patočka, Jan. *An Introduction to Husserl's Phenomenology*. Chicago: Open Court, 1999.
Péguy, Charles. "Note conjointe sur M. Descartes." In *Œuvres en prose completes*, 1280. Paris: Pléiade, Gallimard, 1992.
Peruzzotti, Francesca. *Lo scritto e il suo lettore. In ascolto di Jean-Luc Marion, Martin Heidegger, Jean-Louis Chrétien*. Milano: Mimesis, 2015.
Peterson, Jordan. *Maps of Meaning: The Architecture of Belief*. London: Routledge, 1999.
Plantinga, Alvin. *Warranted Christian Belief*. Oxford: Oxford University Press, 2000.
Pontifical Biblical Commission. *The Interpretation of the Bible in the Church*, edited by J. L. Houlden. London: SCM Press, 1995.
Reagan, Charles. "Interview Avec Paul Ricœur." *Journal of French and Francophone Philosophy* 3:3 (1991): 155–72.
Reagan, Charles. *Paul Ricœur: His Life and His Work*. Chicago: University of Chicago Press, 1996.
Ricœur, Paul. *Critique and Conviction*. New York: Columbia University Press, 1998.
Ricœur, Paul. *La critique et la conviction*. Paris: Fayard, 1995.
Ricœur, Paul. *From Text to Action: Essays in Hermeneutics, II*. Translated by Kathleen Blamey and John B. Thompson. Evanston, IL: Northwestern University Press, 1991.
Ricœur, Paul. *From Text to Action: Essays in Hermeneutics, II*. Translated by Kathleen Blamey and John B. Thompson. London: Athlone Press, 1991.
Ricœur, Paul. *Oneself as Another*. Translated by K. Blamey. Chicago: University of Chicago Press, 1992.
Ricœur, Paul. *Soi-même comme un autre*. Paris: Seuil, 1990.
Ricœur, Paul. *Hermeneutics and the Human Sciences: Essays on Language, Action and Interpretation*. Edited by John B. Thompson. Cambridge: Cambridge University, 1981.

Ricœur, Paul. *The Conflict of Interpretations: Essays in Hermeneutics*. Edited by Don Ihde. Evanston, IL: Northwestern University Press, 1974.
Ricœur, Paul. *Freedom and Nature*. Translated by Erazim V. Kohák. Evanston, IL: Northwestern University Press, 1966.
Ricœur, Paul. *Philosophie de la volonté I: Le volontaire et l'involontaire*. Paris: Aubier, 1950.
Rilke, Rainer Maria. *Letters to a Young Poet*. Translated by Mark Harman. Cambridge: Harvard University Press, 2011.
Rivera, Joseph. "Introduction: Futures of the Theological Turn." *Philosophy Today* 62:1 (2018): 89-97.
Roberts, Tyler. *Encountering Religion: Responsibility and Criticism After Secularism*. New York: Columbia University Press, 2013.
Romano, Claude. *Event and Time*. Translated by Stephen E. Lewis. New York: Fordham University Press, 2014.
Rosenblatt, Louise. *The Reader, the Text, the Poem: The Transactional Theory of the Literary Work*. Carbondale: Southern Illinois University, 1978.
Sadler, Gregory. *Reason Fulfilled by Revelation: The 1930's Christian Philosophy Debates in France*. Translated by Gregory Sadler. Washington, DC: The Catholic University of America Press, 2011.
Saint-Aubert, Emmanuel de. "Rereading the Later Merleau-Ponty in the Light of His Unpublished Work." In *The Oxford Handbook of the History of Phenomenology*, edited by Dan Zahavi. Oxford: Oxford University Press, 2018.
Saint-Aubert, Emmanuel de, and M. Merleau-Ponty. *La Nature Ou Le Monde Du Silence*. Hermann Philosophie. Paris: Hermann, 2008.
Saint-Aubert, Emmanuel de. *Vers une ontologie indirecte: Sources et enjeux critiques de l'appel à l'ontologie chez Merleau-Ponty*. Paris: J. Vrin, 2006.
Saint Augustine. *Discours sur les Psaumes*, Volume 2. Paris: Cerf, 2007.
Sandberg, Anders and Nick Boström. *Whole Brain Emulation: A Roadmap*. Oxford: Oxford University, 2008.
Schilbrack, Kevin. *Philosophy and the Study of Religions: A Manifesto*. Malden: Wiley-Blackwell, 2014.
Schwartz, Regina M., ed. *Transcendence: Philosophy, Literature, and Theology Approach the Beyond*. New York: Routledge, 2004.
Sequeri, Pierangelo. "La struttura testimoniale delle scritture sacre: teologia del testo." In *La rivelazione attestata. La Bibbia tra Testo e Teologia*, edited by G. Angelini, 3–27. Milano: Glossa, 1998.
Serres, Michel. *Le système de Leibniz et ses modèles mathématiques: Etoiles, schémas, points*. Third edition. Épiméthée. Paris: Presses universitaires de France, 1990.
Smith, John H. "Religion and Early German Romanticism: The Finite and the Infinite." In *Brill's Companion to German Romantic Philosophy*, edited by Elizabeth Millán Brusslan and Judith Norman, 60–96. Leiden: Brill, 2018.
Smith, Wilfred Cantwell. *The Meaning and End of Religion: A New Approach to the Religious Traditions of Mankind*. Minneapolis: Fortress, 1963.
Spanneut, Michel. *Le Stoïcisme des Pères de l'Église*. Paris: Seuil, 1957.
Stein, Gertrude. *Everybody's Autobiography*. London: William Heinemann, 1937.
Thorsteinsson, Runar M. *Jesus as Philosopher: The Moral Sage in the Synoptic Gospels*. Oxford: Oxford University Press, 2018.
Tresmontant, Claude. *Introduction à La Métaphysique de Maurice Blondel*. Paris: Seuil, 1963.
Tresmontant, Claude. *La Métaphysique Du Christianisme et La Naissance de La Philosophie Chrétienne*. Paris: Seuil, 1961.
Vieillard-Baron, Jean-Louis. "Spiritualisme et spiritualité." *Laval théologique et philosophique* 69:1 (2013): 5.
Weil, Simone. *Gravity and Grace*. London; New York: Routledge, 2002.
Westphal, Merold. *Whose Community? Which Interpretation?: Philosophical Hermeneutics for the Church*. Grand Rapids, MI: Baker Academic, 2009.
Wimsatt, W. K., and M. C. Beardsley. "The Affective Fallacy." *The Sewanee Review* 57:1 (1949): 31–55.

Wittgenstein, Ludwig. *On Certainty*. Edited by G. E. M. Anscombe and Georg Henrik von Wright, translated by Denis Paul and G. E. M. Anscombe. New York: Harper and Row, 1972.

Woody, William C. "Embracing Finitude: Falque's Phenomenology of the Suffering 'God with Us.'" In *Evil, Fallenness, and Finitude*, edited by Bruce Ellis Benson and B. Keith Putt, 115–34. London: Palgrave MacMillan, 2017.

Wright, Tamra, Peter Hughes, and Alison Ainley. "The Paradox of Morality: An Interview with Emmanuel Levinas." In *The Provocation of Levinas: Rethinking the Other*, edited by R. Bernasconi and D. Wood, 168–80. London: Routledge, 1998.

Falque's Books

All entries are translated and published in English.[1]

The Metamorphosis of Finitude: An Essay on Birth and Resurrection. New York: Fordham University Press, 2012, 193 pages.
God, the Flesh, and the Other: From Irenaeus to Duns Scotus. Evanston, IL: Northwestern University Press, 2015, 376 pages.
Crossing the Rubicon: The Borderlands of Philosophy and Theology. New York: Fordham University Press, 2016, 195 pages.
The Wedding Feast of the Lamb: Eros, Body, and Eucharist. New York: Fordham University Press, 2016, 302 pages.
The Loving Struggle: Phenomenological and Theological Debates. London; New York: Rowman & Littlefield, 2018, 273 pages.
Saint Bonaventure and the Entrance of God into Theology. Afterword: Saint Thomas Aquinas and the Entrance of God into Philosophy. New York: Saint Bonaventure University, Franciscan Institute Publications, 2018, 262 pages.
The Guide to Gethsemane: Anxiety, Suffering, Death. New York: Fordham University Press, 2019, 159 pages.
Nothing to It: Reading Freud as a Philosopher. Leuven: Leuven University Press, 2020, 136 pages.
The Book of Experience: From Anselm of Canterbury to Bernard of Clairvaux. Notre Dame: Notre Dame University Press, 2020 (forthcoming).

NOTES

1. For the complete bibliography (and all books and papers in French, English, and others languages), see https://cvrecherche.icp.fr/cvrecherche/cv/pdf/cv_falque_emmanuel_fr.pdf.

Index

aesthetics, 19, 24n48, 96, 112
Aquinas, Thomas, ix, xviii, 6, 8, 16, 17–18, 19, 23n42, 23n46–24n47, 24n50, 150
Aristotle, 10, 22n24, 46, 165, 182
atheism, xxv, xxxv, 26, 28, 32, 57, 58, 107, 143, 166, 179, 192
Augustine of Dacia, 6
Augustine of Hippo, xviii, xxxiii, xxxvi, 10, 22n25, 91n49, 92n77, 145, 147n49, 205

Balthasar, Hans Urs von, 18, 19, 24n48, 176, 178, 191
Barth, Karl, 15–16, 19, 23n41, 23n43
being-in-the-world, xviii, xxii, xxiii–xxiv, 191, 193, 199
Blondel, Maurice, xxix, xxxiii, 18, 76, 81–88, 90n31, 163, 176, 178–183, 185n33–185n34
body, xiv, 4–6, 8–11, 21, 52, 56–58, 61n4, 80, 92n78, 109–116, 128, 132n21, 150–153, 156–161, 187–200, 201n19; the hermeneutics of, 93–94, 98–102, 105n37, 107, 108, 121–127, 130; and resurrection, xxxiv, xxxv, 155, 197; spread body, xxxi, 113–115
Bonaventure, 18, 22n20, 123–124, 131n9–131n10, 150, 152
Breton, Stanislas, x, 137, 182, 185n38
Bultmann, Rudolf, 15, 19, 45, 50n16, 143

Catholicism, xvii, xxii, 27, 37, 49, 61n12, 66, 94, 103n8, 122
Chrétien, Jean-Louis, x, xvii, 3–4, 10, 22n19, 54, 60n2, 125, 129, 131n13, 131n18, 154, 194, 200n11
christology, 124, 141, 167

Derrida, Jacques, 4, 10, 30, 40n7, 76, 89n4, 109, 165
Deleuze, Gilles, 4, 49, 119n31, 164, 165, 171, 175, 179
Descartes, René, xxxvi, 11, 15, 19, 28, 145, 156, 183, 197

Eckhart, xxxii, 135–137, 145, 150, 159
embodiment, xxxiv–xxxv, 34, 57, 109, 113, 115, 119n31, 125, 155, 158, 187
eternity, xxxv, 168, 177, 190–191
eucharist, 6, 7, 10, 58, 65, 95, 103n8, 122, 126, 127, 128, 129, 130

finitude, xiv, xx, xxiii, xxix, xxxii, xxxiv–xxxv, 11, 16–19, 57, 70, 113–117, 121, 124–125, 138–144, 151–161, 164–183, 191–193, 197–198
flesh, 4, 9–13, 76, 78–85, 103n8, 109, 111–116, 118n24, 124–127, 137, 139–140, 145, 151–152, 176, 190–191, 195, 197, 201n19
Foucault, Michel, 49, 103n13, 165, 171, 177

Index

Freud, Sigmund, ix, 12, 75–76, 80, 145, 194, 196

Gadamer, Hans-Georg, 3, 5, 30, 94, 97–102, 104n32, 143
Gilson, Étienne, xxxiii, 156, 160
Greisch, Jean, xxx, 93–95, 98, 100, 102, 165

Hadot, Pierre, 150, 153, 155, 199
Hegel, Georg Wilhelm Friedrich, xxi, 13, 145, 161, 166
Heidegger, Martin, ix, xvii, xix–xx, xxiii, 3, 10, 12, 13–15, 18, 45, 48, 68, 71n19, 88, 89n7, 90n30, 100–101, 103n13, 125, 132n20, 139, 143, 153, 154, 165–170, 175–180, 183, 192
Henry, Michel, xvii, xx, xxxiii, 75, 125, 152–161, 178, 195, 197
Hugh of Saint Victor, 9, 127
Husserl, Edmund, ix, xvii, xxiv, xxxvi, 11–12, 20, 26, 31, 42–43, 75–76, 77–79, 84–88, 137, 153–155, 159, 166, 180, 187, 190

the incarnation, xxx, 10, 19, 57, 61n15, 109, 112, 113, 114–115, 119n31, 141, 147n38, 167–168, 171, 191, 197–198, 205
the infinite, xxv, xxxiii, 20, 50n13, 77–78, 108, 114–116, 153, 166, 170, 175, 177–180, 182–183; the preemption of, xxi, 181

Janicaud, Dominique, xix–xxi, xxiv, xxxv, 43, 54, 78, 80, 82, 153–155, 180, 192
John Paul II, 61n12, 164, 165
Judaism, 3, 5–6, 66, 71n16, 95, 103n8, 103n10, 118n26

Kant, Immanuel, xxxv, 15, 26, 44
Kearney, Richard, 61n11
kenosis, 109, 113–114, 116, 118n26, 125
Kierkegaard, Søren, xviii, xxxvi, 13, 14–15, 34, 145, 152

Lacoste, Jean-Yves, xvii, xxiii, xxxviin5, 3–4, 165, 166
laïcité, xviii, 54, 65

Levinas, Emmanuel, xvii, xxx–xxxi, 3–9, 13, 41, 43–44, 50n13, 51, 53–54, 75–79, 82–83, 94–95, 107–117, 124, 129, 143, 152, 158, 160, 166, 175
liturgy, 4, 8, 19, 34–36, 42, 64–65, 68, 95, 103n10, 132n21
love, 15, 16, 35, 165, 168
Lubac, Henri de, 165, 166, 179, 181, 191

Marion, Jean-Luc, x, xvii, xx, xxvii, 3–4, 32, 44, 51, 52–54, 61n11, 75, 86, 125, 154–155, 175, 178, 192
Marx, Karl, ix
Merleau-Ponty, Maurice, xvii, xxii, 11–13, 43, 61n15, 75–79, 81, 83–85, 113, 143, 165, 167, 188–189, 190–192, 195
metaphysics, ix–x, xxxiii, 20–21, 149–161, 185n38
modernity, 11, 28, 29, 165, 177

Nicholas of Cusa, 143, 183
Nietzsche, Friedrich, x, 3, 13, 15, 76, 80, 181, 193–196

O'Leary, Joseph, xx, xxi
ontology, ix, 5, 78, 83–84, 88, 89n19, 107–108, 160

Paul, the Apostle, xviii, 3, 35, 47, 118n26, 193, 194, 199
Pascal, Blaise, xviii, xxxvi, 10–14, 20, 31, 33, 181
Plato, 189, 199, 205
postmodernism, 29, 58, 96, 184n25
prayer, 4, 19, 35, 42, 56, 65
protestantism, xxx–xxxi, 5–6, 8–9, 20, 66, 122; and hermeneutics, 94–96, 103n10

the resurrection, 14, 18, 19, 61n15, 64, 140–142, 152, 164, 167–168, 171, 172, 176, 179, 183, 190–193, 197–200, 205. *See also* body and resurrection
revelation, xix, xxii, 13, 64, 78, 109, 128–131, 132n21, 139, 155, 164, 171, 172, 176, 190
Ricœur, Paul, x, xvii, xxii, xxx, 15, 27, 33, 42, 44, 46, 48, 51–54, 93–98, 100–103, 103n13, 109, 122, 143, 169

scripture, xxxi, 5–8, 10, 46, 95–98, 121–130, 132n21, 140

secularization, 19, 29, 38–39, 55, 57–58, 107; and university, 69, 71n18. *See also* laicité

suffering, xiv, xxx–xxxiii, 4, 21, 107–117, 118n24, 138–140, 151, 152–153, 155–161, 190

Tertullian, 4, 37, 118n24, 150, 197

the theological turn, xiv, xvii, xx–xxi, xxiv, xxv–xxvii, xxxv, 3, 29, 43, 51, 53–54, 60n2, 75, 76, 153, 154

trinity, 11, 15–16, 30, 37, 140, 141, 144

Wittgenstein, Ludwig, 12, 47, 143

the world, xxxii, xxxviin22, 17, 21, 36, 77, 78, 80, 83, 87, 97, 114, 121, 124, 129, 136–142, 151–153, 159, 161, 164, 168, 177, 187, 188, 191, 198. *See also* being-in-the-world; the book of, 8, 127–128; life-world, x, xviii, xxii, xxv; trust in, xxvi, xxviii, 11–12, 16, 30, 43–44, 57–58, 142, 147n41; without God, 166, 169–172

About the Contributors

Jason W. Alvis is a docent and project leader of the "Revenge of the Sacred" project supported by the Austrian Science Fund (FWF P-31919) at the Institute for Philosophy, the University of Vienna. He is the author of *The Inconspicuous God: Heidegger, French Phenomenology, and the Theological Turn* (2018), and *Marion and Derrida on the Gift and Desire: Debating the Generosity of Things* (2016).

Barnabas Aspray is junior research fellow at Pembroke College, Oxford. Born in England, and raised in both England and Ecuador, he worked for a number of years as a software engineer at the BBC before abandoning that career to pursue philosophical and theological studies. He completed his PhD at the University of Cambridge in 2019, writing on the early Paul Ricœur's concept of finitude and its relation to transcendence.

Bruce Ellis Benson is professorial fellow at the University of Vienna and senior research fellow at the Logos Institute, University of St Andrews. He has taught and engaged in research at Loyola Marymount University, Wheaton College, the KU Leuven, and Union Theological Seminary. He is the author or editor of thirteen books, including *The Improvisation of Musical Dialogue: A Phenomenology of Music* (2003), and the award-winning *Pious Nietzsche: Decadence and Dionysian Faith* (2008), and *The New Phenomenology*, with J. Aaron Simmons (2013). His most recent edited books include *Evil, Fallenness, Finitude* (2017). He is the author of more than 100 articles and book chapters. He serves as the executive director of the Society for Continental Philosophy and Theology and Philosophy of Religion editor for *Syndicate Journal*.

Lorenza Bottacin Cantoni is post-doc research fellow in philosophy, University of Padova, Italy. She is the Italian translator of Falque's *Passer le Rubicon* (*Passare il Rubicone. Alle frontiere della filosofia e della teologia*, 2017). She was a visiting scholar at the Boston College and recently spent a semester as assistant professor at Tohoku University in Sendai, Japan. She is the author of the volume *Metafore per l'altro. Levinas e la generosità della parola tra sofferenza e significazione* (2020) and she is currently writing a book on Kafka, Blanchot, and Levinas.

Carla Canullo is professor at the University of Macerata in Italy. She focuses on the French philosophy, phenomenology, and hermeneutics. She has recently also extensively dealt with the philosophy of religion and interreligious dialogue, ethics and human rights, and the ethos of Europe as a translated political and cultural identity. She is the author of numerous books, including *Il chiasmo della traduzione. Metafora e verità* (2017).

Jakub Čapek is associate professor of philosophy at the Faculty of Arts, Charles University, Prague. His areas of specialization cover twentieth-century German and French philosophy, especially phenomenology and hermeneutics; philosophy of action; philosophy of perception; and questions of personal identity. He published a monograph on Merleau-Ponty and also co-edited the volume *Pragmatic Perspectives in Phenomenology* (2017).

William L. Connelly is currently a doctoral student in philosophy at the Institut Catholique de Paris. His research is focused on developing a doctrine of inspiration based upon the later work of Maurice Blondel. He serves as a secretary of the International Network in Philosophy of Religion and is an associate editor of the INPR Journal *Crossing*.

Steven DeLay is an independent scholar living and working in Winston-Salem, North Carolina. An Old Member of Christ Church, University of Oxford, he is the author of *Before God: Exercises in Subjectivity* (Rowman & Littlefield, 2019) and *Phenomenology in France: A Philosophical and Theological Introduction* (2019).

Victor Emma-Adamah is a PhD candidate in philosophy of religion at the Faculty of Divinity, University of Cambridge. He works at the intersection of modern French philosophy and its theological and phenomenological traditions. His current research is a philosophical ressourcement of nineteenth- and twentieth-century French Spiritualism (with emphasis on the works of Maine de Biran, Félix Ravaisson, Maurice Blondel, Henri Bergson, and Louis Lavelle). He also works on the notions of soul and body in the materialist and vitalist traditions of early modern philosophy in the interactions between Western philosophy and African thought.

Emmanuel Falque is professor of philosophy at the Institut Catholique de Paris, honorary chair and founding member of the International Network in Philosophy of Religion, and the author of numerous monographs, including *Nothing to It: Reading Freud as a Philosopher* (2020) and *Loving Struggle: Phenomenological and Theological Debates* (Rowman & Littlefield, 2018). He is an expert in medieval philosophy and phenomenology. His recent research focuses on the relationship between philosophy and theology, finitude, and the phenomenology of the body.

Tamsin Jones is associate professor of religion at Trinity College (CT), where she teaches courses in the history of Christian thought, gender, and religion, and the philosophy of religion. She is the author of *A Genealogy of Marion's Philosophy of Religion: Apparent Darkness* (2011), as well as articles in the *Journal of Religion*, the *Journal of Theology and Sexuality*, *Political Theology*, and *Modern Theology*. She is currently working on the concept of religious experience as it is discussed in continental philosophy and against the backdrop of trauma theory.

Richard Kearney is the Charles Seeling Professor in Philosophy at Boston College. He is the author of numerous book (including two novels and a collection of poetry) and the editor of many others, including *The Art of Anatheism*, co-edited with M. Clemente (Rowman & Littlefield, 2018). Currently, he is the director of the Guestbook Project *Hosting the Stranger: Between Hostility and Hospitality*.

Katerina Koci is a post-doctoral researcher at the Protestant Theological Faculty, Charles University, Prague. She defended her PhD at KU Leuven in 2017. In 2018, she was awarded the Jan Patočka Junior Visiting Fellowships at the Institute of Human Sciences in Vienna. Her research interests include feminist theology, philosophical and textual hermeneutics, and art (especially literature) as a medium of religious experience. Currently, she works on sacrifice at the intersection of philosophy, gender, and biblical studies.

Martin Koci is a post-doctoral researcher at the Institute for Philosophy at the University of Vienna. His research focuses on the theological turns in contemporary continental philosophy and theology in a postmodern context. He specializes in the French phenomenology, its Anglo-American reception, and the work of the Czech phenomenologist Jan Patočka. He is the author of *Thinking Faith after Christianity: A Theological Reading of Jan Patočka's Phenomenological Philosophy* (2020).

Francesca Peruzzotti studied both philosophy and theology in Milan and obtained a PhD in philosophy in Modena (Fondazione Collegio san Carlo) in cotutelle with Institut Catholique de Paris, with a thesis concerning the question of time and eschatology in Jean-Luc Marion and Hans Urs von Balthasar. She is now adjunct professor of theology at the Università Cattolica del Sacro Cuore in Milan. Her field of research concerns the intertwining of theology and philosophy, phenomenology, in particular the theory of the text, sacramentality, and eschatology. She is the author of *Lo scritto e il suo lettore. In ascolto di Jean-Louis Chrétien, Jean-Luc Marion e Martin Heidegger* (2015) and many other essays.

Andrew Sackin-Poll is a doctoral candidate in the French Department of the University of Cambridge, and a member of Trinity Hall of the same university. He has translated works by Jean-Louis Chrétien, Emmanuel Falque, Michel Henry, and François Laruelle. He is currently working on his first book project called *Le Grammaire de l'âme* to be published in the coming year.

William C. Woody, S.J., is a Jesuit Scholastic of the United States East Province of the Society of Jesus. Currently studying at Boston College in preparation for priestly ordination, he previously taught in the philosophy departments of the College of the Holy Cross (Worcester, Massachusetts) and Saint Peter's University (Jersey City, New Jersey). His research interests focus primarily on continental philosophy of religion, specifically phenomenology of religious experience and prayer, sacramental and liturgical theology, and contemporary considerations of forgiveness and reconciliation.

www.ingramcontent.com/pod-product-compliance
Lightning Source LLC
Chambersburg PA
CBHW022011300426
44117CB00005B/128